THE NEW COUPLE

the NEW Couple

WHY the OLD RULES don't work and what does

Maurice Taylor and Seana McGee

HarperSanFrancisco
A Division of HarperCollins*Publishers*

PERMISSIONS

For reasons of confidentiality, we have changed the names, circumstances, and other identifying information of individuals mentioned in this book, unless otherwise noted. In some instances, we have also created composite interviews from narratives that were similar. In all cases, the stories faithfully reflect the ideas, attitudes, and experiences of the people we met and worked with in our private practice, workshops, and presentations.

Grateful acknowledgment is made to Barbara De Angelis, Ph.D., for permission to use an adaptation of the Emotional Map and Duplication Technique from her book *How to Make Love All the Time* (Rawson Associates, 1987; Dell Books, 1988; Dell Publishing, 1991), in the Peace Process, which appears in Chapter 6.

Grateful acknowledgment is also made for permission to reprint material copyrighted by the following authors and publishers:

"Nunna Yer Beeswax" from *The Huge Book of Hell* by Matt Groening. Copyright © 1997 by Matt Groening. All Rights Reserved. Reprinted by permission of Penguin Books USA, NY.

"I Make You Angry" from *Life in Hell*® by Matt Groening. Copyright © 1997 by Matt Groening. All Rights Reserved. Reprinted by permission of Acme Features Syndicate.

Permissions are continued on page 347.

HarperCollins books may be purchased for educational, business, or sales promotional use. For information please write: Special Markets Department, HarperCollins Publishers Inc., 10 East 53rd Street, New York, NY 10022.

HarperCollins Web site: http://www.harpercollins.com

HarperCollins®, 📖®, and HarperSanFrancisco™ are trademarks of HarperCollins Publishers Inc.

Designed by Lindgren/Fuller Design

FIRST EDITION

Library of Congress Cataloging-in-Publication Data
Taylor, Maurice
The new couple : why the old rules don't work and what does / Maurice Taylor and Seana McGee.—1st ed.
    p. cm.
Includes bibliographical references and index.
ISBN 0–06–251633–7 (cloth)
ISBN 0–06–251634–5 (pbk.)
    1. Man-woman relationships. 2. Couples. 3. Marriage. 4. Love. I. McGee, Seana, 1954– . II. Title.
HQ 801.T3 2000
306.7—dc21   99–054291

00 01 02 03 04 ❖/RRD(H) 10 9 8 7 6 5 4 3 2 1

contents

acknowledgments

While a couple possesses an enormous, often untapped, potential to accomplish amazing feats, every twosome needs community. Likewise, all coauthors need tons of support, a lesson we learned progressively over this book's seven years of gestation. While we anticipated many long hours sequestered together at the computer, we never imagined the hundreds of big and invisible relationships that would spring from the fulfillment of this important aspect of our joint mission in life, which *The New Couple* has come to represent. We are deeply indebted to the following individuals for their love, support, encouragement, and belief in us, without which this project would have never come into being.

First and foremost, we wish to extend our heartfelt thanks to our agent and very dear friend, Lois de la Haba, for the deep commitment and masterful guidance that she has shown us over the past five years and at every stage of this project's development.

In Singapore, we thank our brother and partner on the path, Santha Kumar, for opening his heart and handing us the keys to Southeast Asia; to Naresh Mahtani, Esq., who gave us the rock we stood on; to Chomil Kamal and the Government of Singapore for embracing and promoting our vision of healthier couples and, hence, healthier families everywhere; to Robert Kiyosaki and Money and You for early inspiration; to Vijayan Nambiar for community support; to Y.C. Lim, M.D., for his open-minded psychiatric approach; and to Harold Robers, Ph.D., for expert and compassionate professional consultation and steadfast belief in us and our message.

Stateside, we offer our heartfelt thanks to Barbara Nichols, the first to see the potential of our concept; Zul Azhar, our agent's assistant extraordinaire, who meets challenge with serenity; Laura de la Haba, who has been a champion from the get-go; and Brenda Segel and her department at HarperCollins for belief in the book's international appeal. Our respect and gratitude also go to our tireless team at HarperSanFrancisco, including Stephen Hanselman, John Loudon, Liz Perle, Margery Buchanan, Meg Lenihan, Terri Leonard, and Susan Walker Naythons. Special thanks to Renee Sedliar for her enthusiastic and witty support and Kathy Reigstad for superb, indeed intuitive, copy-editing. We are grateful to the art department for their ingenious cover and lovely book design, and we appreciate the commitment of Diane Gedymin and the very warm welcome and vision of Mark Chimsky and Karen Bouris during the early stages of the project. Alan Kubler, Ph.D., enhanced our efforts by an excellent technical read of the manuscript, author Susan Page was invaluable in the development of our proposal, and librarian Marisa Bowen provided research excellence. To Sondra Gatewood at Acme Features Syndicate, we extend thanks for sharing our vision and for gracious overtime.

We offer special acknowledgment to Michael Kahn, Ph.D., our clinical director at the Integral Counseling Center, who was a major influence on our psychotherapeutic approach. We would also like to applaud our therapist and healer friends for fine work in keeping us inspired and unstuck, in particular Geoff Brandenburg for his wisdom, brilliance, and heart, and Harriet Jasik Sage, LCSW, Betty Baca Tanner, Pamala Oslie, Barbara Reiner, MFT, the Hoffman family, and especially Raz and Liza Ingrasci and Volker and Jeanette Krohn.

To our other friends, family, and support people throughout the world, we send gratitude and love, in particular: Rob for being the brother who was there every inch of the way; sister Melissa and brother Tom for their unflagging encouragement and love; niece Jessie for her intelligent "postmodern" perspective and editorial acumen; and nephews David for his marketing savvy and Leo for his just being. Seana also thanks her family members Janet, Jude, Vanessa, Larry, and Mike, and Maurice thanks the Bakalians, the Dierks, Barbara, and Betty, all of whom helped us better know who we really are in the inimitable way only family members can. Our heartfelt appreciation also goes to Aunt Saundra and "Tut" for proving that one need not be young to embrace what's new; Lee Glickstein and the members of "Bonnie's Circle" for weekly drafts of heaven; and Timothy Dwight (from his elevated perch),

Antony di Pinto, Steve Roth and Bob Zinkhan, Jeffrey Mendelsohn, John Driscoll and Chanthanom Ounkeo, Manny Mansback, M.F.T., Fred Schwobel, Karen and John Leland, Bill Grimason and Claire Costantini, Erica Valentine and Michael Mittleman, Kimberly and Carla Sharman, Joseph Greco, Bjorn Turmann, Gloria Craig and Christian Van Stolk, Mary Kocy and John Rusk, Richard Robbins, David Scherer, Meeuwis Van Rijswijk, Ronen and Zohar Wohlfarth, and Akiko Iijima for loving us all the way. We also wish to acknowledge our past loves, who have also been integral to the evolution of our work and our hearts.

We offer deep gratitude to the many young people we've counseled in the United States and overseas for leading us so poignantly to their parents, the very couples who inspired our specialization. We are equally grateful to all our other Taylor McGee Human Relations and Couple Consultancy clients and workshop participants—those both in and out of couples—for possessing the courage and self-love to insist that intimate relationship go beyond where it's been shackled for so long.

Finally, Seana would like to acknowledge her parents, Bob and Bobbie McGee, for being the grand spirits they were and for helping her open sacred doors to herself. And Maurice would like to extend deep gratitude to his parents, Joan and Jim, in heaven and Bali, respectively, for teaching him, in their very different ways, how to be with another truly and for aspiring to bring education—and human beings along with it—to their next level.

introduction

In our day, a truly successful relationship seems well-nigh miraculous, especially to those of us who fear that we're condemned to remain forever rudderless when it comes to long-term love. Yet human beings don't yearn for anything that isn't possible. As a very wise person once said, miracles don't really exist; they're simply phenomena ruled by laws of nature that our scientists have yet to discover. Well over a decade ago, when we started teaching, training, and counseling couples as a team—which was also just about the moment we met—we were already convinced that such natural laws must also exist for love, that there must be a way for *everybody* to have emotionally and sexually deep connections that last. And we embarked on a singular quest to find those laws, hoping to introduce sanity to love.

To tell the truth, our resolve wasn't only work-related; it wasn't *only* for our clients that we began our search for the most cutting-edge information and the most effective, enduring-results-producing techniques (though serving couples was, and still is, our joint mission in life). We were also, quite frankly, mad about each other, which made us bound and determined to do everything in our power not to let the gift of our own precious love fade away. Our commitment to the healer-heal-thyself ethic—which says that if one talks the talk, one had better walk the walk—also became immediately relevant: no sooner did we two therapists (ourselves veterans of several failed relationships) fall in love with each other than we had huge problems with each other! Thus, inspired both by professional research and ethics and by the passion between us, we became adamant about figuring out this thing called *committed monogamous relationship* and discovering the laws that govern it.

Our research was underpinned by our eclectic theoretical orientation—a hybrid of humanistic, depth, self, and transpersonal psychologies, systems theory, and the recovery model—and based on our separate and mutual clinical experiences working with couples, parents, and single persons in community counseling centers, schools, and hospitals in the United States and in private practice in Asia, as well as on our own relationship. In fact, over the first two years together, we dated, broke up twice, got engaged, then married. Along the way, we sampled a variety of couple counselors, relationship experts, and workshops. In short, as though it were a carburetor from yesteryear, we repeatedly took our own relationship apart into a million pieces and meticulously put it back together again. While the value of the techniques and processes we sampled—their power to crack open our hearts, blow our minds, and set our spirits free *as individuals*—was unquestionable, and though many of these approaches deepened our intimacy *as a couple* as well, none offered the cogent relationship tenets we were seeking.

As fate would have it, we moved to Singapore soon after our marriage, where, in addition to the seminars and lectures we conducted for the government and private organizations, we co-counseled and trained couples, and we practiced psychotherapy with singles. Our clients, members of both the international and local communities, hailed from every corner of the globe—in fact, fifty-five world cultures in all. This unusual international experience gave us a broad clinical base from which to draw our data.

THE TRANCE OF TRADITION

> The first decade of marriage,
> we're husband and wife.
> The second ten years, we're best friends.
> The third, brother and sister.
> And the fourth decade—*two sisters*.
> EASTERN EUROPEAN FOLKLORE

In seeking our answers, we kept observing the same problem. To our great relief, however, that problem didn't indicate that the modern scourges of love—namely, the fifty-percent divorce rate, "trial" marriages, serial monogamy, and the fact that scores of would-be partners are remaining "scared single"—are proof that the moral fabric of society is unraveling or that we, as a species, are devolving, as some might fear. In fact, it suggested just the opposite.

And what's the problem we encountered? Irrespective of the specifics that brought people to our office, talks, and workshops, the vast majority of those we worked with were, on some level, struggling with a familiar but invisible foe: the traditional model of marriage. This status-quo arrangement still held seductive sway over even the most contemporary among them, coupled or not. In fact, tradition was draped around everyone's lives and loves like an iron curtain, causing inestimable confusion, anxiety, blame, heartbreak, and failure.

While any couple with children knows only too well how intensely socioeconomic factors can pressure us into traditional roles, what's not so well recognized is the power of our own psychology to do the same thing. The fact is the old template has been burned into our psyches for far too long to be shaken with firm resolve alone. Furthermore, no matter how enlightened we may be or how vehemently we swear to "do relationships" differently from our parents, our "inner traditional" gets us nearly every time. (Rather than using the word *traditionalist,* which suggests *deliberate* adherence to ways of the past, we refer to someone unconsciously locked in the past as a *traditional*.) Inherited erroneous and outdated tapes about how to run our partnerships do a thorough job of placating, guilt-tripping, or otherwise setting us up for failure. These include the idea that successful partnering (and parenting) should be a matter of instinct, and that intellectual prescriptions and platitudes—such as "Do something nice for each other every day," "Try harder," "Be positive," "Never go to bed angry," and "Treat your spouse as you would a stranger"—can build (and mend massive fissures in) trust.

When we're unconsciously clutched by convention, we end up in the either-or situation that futurist Barbara Marx Hubbard warns us about in *Conscious Evolution,* sacrificing our *co-creativity* for *procreativity.* For although the traditional way promises safety, belonging, continuity, and everything comfortable and known—the very archetype of home—its shadow looms long. Unjust expectations, faulty assumptions, unnegotiated roles and responsibilities—not to mention the destructive myths of the male provider and the good wife and mother—creep up on all of us unawares. Like a drum we can't help marching to, tradition mesmerizes, cunningly persuading partners that the old rules really do work to bring about happiness and healthy longevity in love. That's why we call this phenomenon the "trance of tradition."

HIGHER-ORDER NEEDS

We're convinced that the real problem, far from devolution, is that while human beings have actually *evolved* as a species—*and as love partners*—the inherited model of marriage and relationship has remained largely unchanged. That model ignores not only our unquestionable needs to learn to love ourselves and to find and fulfill our true life's work, but also the need for authentic, ongoing emotional connection with another.

Recognition of these "higher-order" needs for self-love, mission in life, and emotional intimacy is revolutionary for couples. It beautifully responds, once and for all, to the modern relationship koan, "Do I have to give up me to be loved by you?" The answer is no. *We can't love each other unless we're working on loving ourselves; and we can't truly love ourselves unless we're both realizing our own personal dreams.* Honoring higher-order needs offers an essential hedge for today's partners, many of whom see the potential loss of personal identity and dreams as the biggest challenge in committing to another person—a challenge greater even than the typical fears of abandonment, divorce, abuse, and failure.

When we exalt the trinity of self-love, mission in life, and emotional intimacy in our own relationships, we are, perhaps for the first time, synthesizing in a practical way our *individual* prerequisites for happiness with those of *relationship*. This is couple potential in its rawest form: rather than threatening our individuality, a committed relationship can actually enhance it—even launch it—and reveal to us our own true power and the full range of our gifts.

As we all know, the traditional model was never meant to marry our higher individual and couple needs. Rather, it was designed to accommodate our "lower-order" needs—namely, the needs for food, shelter, physical safety, and a sense of belonging to our tribe. For example, some of us, on looking back, might realize that we formed certain early relationships in large part as a response to peer pressure or out of a fear of not "belonging" in a couple. Still, many of today's partners are well above the survival level of existence and are already actively engaged in meeting higher-order needs: the enhancement of self-esteem has long been a part-time job for many, and finding our life's purpose has been a sincere objective. Nevertheless, this task of obeying individual-oriented higher-order needs becomes exceedingly difficult *once we're mated with another*. And though so many of us yearn to transcend the war between the sexes in order to come together in a new and authentic way, and are willing to work hard in our relationships to achieve emotional intimacy, these goals, too, elude us.

The villain, again, is that incredibly powerful (yet largely unarticulated) old paradigm, probably internalized when we watched our parents struggle in their own marriages. The traditional model keeps us in a kind of limbo—one foot stuck in the past, the other mired in an unsure present. The old way not only fails to make love of self, mission in life, and emotional intimacy explicit; it actually functions as their major saboteur.

Since no one sat us down as a group and told us the good news about our own advancement, too many of us have been left to believe that we can "get by" as individuals and partners with unaddressed low self-love and unfulfilling work, and "manage" in our relationships with withering (or nonexistent) emotional intimacy. And we innocent victims of evolution end up, consciously or unconsciously, trying to cram ourselves and our partners into an old shoe that doesn't fit—the traditional model of marriage—even though it's been obsolete for generations.

Our research led us to conclude that partners who fail to enshrine as part of the symbolic marriage contract the development of self-love, mission in life, and true emotional intimacy can expect to pay in the currency of their own psychological and spiritual well-being—and risk becoming another depressing statistic.

Naturally, this isn't the first era in which couples have felt the emergence of more evolved needs. People in our parents', grandparents', and even ancient forebears' times had the dubious pleasure of these urges as well; it's just that they didn't acknowledge them and couldn't address them. The difference now, forty years after psychologist Abraham Maslow laid out the model for self-actualization, is that we've hit a kind of critical mass: when the influence of tradition marginalizes our higher-order needs these days, partners typically become self-destructive or relationships dead-end. Clearly, for more people than ever before, addressing the higher-order needs is no longer optional. Thus we define the traditional model of love as *any relationship ideal that doesn't honor the higher-order needs for self-love, mission in life, and true emotional intimacy.*

A NEW MODEL OF LOVE

It was clear to us that the laws we were seeking would have to be part of an overall vision—a sparkling new model of love that not only honored these more sophisticated requirements for relationship, but also boldly replaced the traditional. After all, though it's been oft repeated that relationship is a journey, not a destination, it's neither fair nor viable to ask lovers today to head out for parts unknown using a map—or a model—that's fifty-plus years old. Above all, this replacement would have to be strong enough to keep us all from defaulting back into the trance of tradition.

As the larger picture came into focus, the exact dimensions of this model—what would later become the laws—vividly revealed themselves in the negative: in other words, we noticed certain facets of relationship the neglect of which consistently got couples (our own included) into trouble. Conversely, we also noticed that a respect for these facets—each of which was integrally connected to one of the higher-order needs—seemed to help keep couples healthy. Though ignoring one facet alone was often enough to do a couple in (and respecting one alone was never enough to save them), partners were usually tripped up by a cluster of them.

Though they wore many faces, these standard couple conundrums always boiled down to some variation of the following:

1. Lack of a passionate initial connection
2. Unwillingness or inability to prioritize the health of the relationship
3. Inability to deal with emotions
4. Inability to listen from the heart
5. Entrenched unfairness
6. Inability to make peace and restore broken trust
7. Seemingly irreconcilable points of conflict
8. Undiscovered or unmanifested life purpose for one or both partners
9. Emotional or financial dependencies
10. Unwillingness to embrace healing and education for the relationship

THE TEN NEW LAWS OF LOVE

To our delight, we realized that each of these problems was linked to a binding principle. In those principles lay the essence of what we sought—the natural laws of love. And since none had been specifically articulated in previous generations, we called them the Ten "New" Laws of Love. They follow:

1. *Chemistry,* the first New Law of Love, refers to those indescribably special energies we feel with our true beloved. Composed of great sexual and friendship connections, chemistry provides the juice and synergy that all partners need to get through the rapids of relationship.

2. The second New Law of Love is *priority.* It represents our commitment to keep our chemistry alive by doing the "work of relationship" and by weeding out unhealthy preoccupations.

3. *Emotional integrity,* the third New Law of Love, involves our commitment to establish our couple—that composite of all aspects of our relationship—as an "emotional safe zone." It asks us to take responsibility for the full deck of our emotions and to examine—and endeavor to heal—any emotional blind spots, buttons, or issues that cause either one of us strife.

4. The fourth New Law of Love, *deep listening,* involves hearing each other straight from the heart. It represents our willingness to learn how to listen to our partner's words with respect and to the feelings underneath with compassion.

5. *Equality,* the fifth New Law of Love, is about self-respect and fairness. Though differences exist between all partners, this law asks us to be open to discussion when either one of us feels that an imbalance is hurting us or unjust, and to do something about the situation if necessary.

6. The sixth New Law of Love is *peacemaking.* It involves our commitment to keep the peace and restore trust every time it's broken. This law entails having explicit bottom lines, acknowledging the nuclear power of anger, and knowing how to manage it.

7. *Self-love,* the seventh New Law of Love, asks that we work toward valuing, validating, and accepting ourselves no matter what—and that we clear up any unfinished emotional business from childhood that's being played out in our relationship.

8. The eighth New Law of Love, *mission in life,* represents our commitment to discover and fulfill our life purpose—our ultimate and exalted adult job—and to make sure that our partner does too.

9. *Walking,* the ninth New Law of Love, involves our resolve to work to clear up any emotional and financial dependencies that keep us from feeling autonomous and free within the relationship (and thereby keep us from enjoying true interdependence). Being *willing* and *able* to "walk" if need be is the best guarantee that a couple will stay *truly* together.

10. The tenth and final New Law of Love, *transformational education,* represents our commitment to go outside the couple to learn and heal if ever we get stuck on any of the first nine laws.

Ever since our discovery of these Ten New Laws of Love, we've been using them—and the associated processes and tools described in this book—as our own comprehensive diagnostic, educational, and healing system in a variety of settings. They flesh out what we call the New Couple model of relationship and have aided the many couples—and singles focused on relationship issues—that we've worked with for more than a combined twenty years in setting out on the path to success in love. More often than not, the tenets have transformed tenuous bonds into strong, loving, and creative alliances and provided a hopeful ideal toward which we can all strive.

Now, in published form, these laws can serve as an introduction to the emerging worlds of couple health and couple potential and provide the basis of a lexicon—a new language of love—to describe partnership that thrives. Couples can use these laws as a checklist to determine what is and isn't working in their current relationship, while singles can use them to conduct "autopsies" on past relationships and to troubleshoot present and future relationships. The laws have been proved to work for partners of all stripes—whether living apart, together or married, straight or gay, lesbian or bisexual, with children or without; and they're already in use by organizations and practitioners around the world. It pleases us to honor any partners who embrace this system with the designation "New Couple."

As for our own couple, the laws plainly function as a sacred scaffolding, stabilizing and enriching our relationship just as they do that of the couples we serve. Having befriended our fair share of dragons—which, of course, we expected—we can't imagine where we'd be without these laws to fall back on. To their credit, we're still very much each other's absolute best friend, and our life continues to be an exciting reflection of both our individual and our joint dreams made manifest. Because these laws have repeatedly proved their effectiveness over the years—serving as a hologram of couple health for ourselves, our clients, our workshop participants, and our lecture and radio audiences—we were inspired to write this book.

We begin our presentation with two reader quizzes (found immediately after this Introduction). The first allows partners to test their New Couple quotient; the second allows singles to test their New Couple *potential*. The rest of the book's formatting is straightforward, with one law presented per chapter. Although each law builds on the next, they're interdependent—functioning as a net, rather than a ladder—which means that they need to be applied concurrently. The only exceptions are chemistry (the first New Law of Love), which is a prerequisite to the following nine, and transformational education (the last New Law of Love), which is the fail-safe mechanism for the whole system.

Each chapter features an introduction to the law itself, a discussion of the law's history in romantic relationship and its influence—or lack thereof—on traditional couples past and present, and a concluding section illustrating the transformational impact of the law on New Couples today. Additionally, chapters include easy-reference "keys" to each law and thought-provoking questions to add an experiential dimension and help readers identify any traditional hangovers that they've inherited from their family. At the back of the book is a glossary titled "The New Language of Love," which offers simple definitions of *The New Couple*'s most essential terms and concepts. That's followed by a reference list that includes books we recommend for further reading as well as sources we consulted in doing research for this book; it also provides page numbers for quotes used in text.

CODEPENDENCE AND THE STAGES OF RELATIONSHIP

Two dynamics of committed monogamous relationship that pertain to every law—and will be mentioned throughout the book—are the ought-to-be-famous developmental stages of relationship and the in-some-quarters-misunderstood-and-unpopular notion of codependence.

While relationships always represent an intense learning curve, most of us eventually realize that the grandest lesson is not how to love another person (though that's grand indeed), but how to love ourselves. In fact, *The New Couple* assumes that, save for an avatar here and there, every human being on earth, aware of it or not, is hard at work on this project. The nitty-gritty of raising our self-love requires that we reverse two unhealthy tendencies: the first, to place others' needs before our own; and the second, to seek acceptance from others before we accept ourselves. These particular forms of emotional dependence fall under the unglamorous rubric of *codependence*.

The newly enamored among us might feel at cross-purposes with the goal of self-love, believing that the objective in true partnership is for us to become less "selfish." But as Chapter 7 teaches, this is a misguided understanding of both self-love and selfishness. Just as flight attendants instruct us to place the oxygen mask over our own face before we assist our dependents, we must pay proper attention to you-know-who before we can be of any real good to anyone else. True and healthy love of oneself is the bedrock of authentic emotional intimacy, which is why it's earned the distinction of being both a higher-order need and a New Law of Love. Despite its primacy, recovering self-love isn't the dismal prospect it might seem to some. Since our naturally high self-love is diminished with early caregivers, and therefore our low self-love is actually *learned* in childhood, it can be *un*learned in adulthood with our intimates. Happily, committed romantic relationship is a great vehicle for this endeavor—*so long as our beloved other is of the same philosophy and is dedicated to the same goal.*

The second dynamic has to do with the progression of relationship. Love's journey isn't static; it's a *process* that consists of three distinct and absolutely predictable stages. Couples either progress through these or, like so many of our ill-prepared traditional foremothers and -fathers, get stuck somewhere in the middle. *The New Couple* calls these stages of love "intoxication," "the power struggle," and "co-creativity."

The intoxication stage, which lasts roughly two weeks to two years, is a high and memorable time for most partners. These are our days of wine and roses, when the mere prospect of seeing the face or hearing the voice of our beloved is capable of producing a thrill. For many of us, this is the only time we let ourselves lapse into a fantasy of being in and feeling unconditional and perfect love. The ultimate anesthetic, this first stage of romantic love has the power, at least temporarily, to blot out the pain of our insecurities and imperfections—hence its bittersweet name.

Nevertheless, the intoxication stage of relationship ends; and it's *supposed* to end, as night replaces day, though few of us accept this fact. Instead, we confuse what's really an ephemeral state with true love and blame ourselves or our partner for its dissolution. That's why it's impossible to overemphasize the need for couples to expect the passing of this period, to prepare for the onset of the second stage, *and to be assured that much greater things are in store.*

Traditionally, the second stage of relationship—power struggle—has gotten a bad rap, characterized as either a war zone or an occupied territory. It's been so confounding for so long that this period of partnership has come to be seen as synonymous with romantic commitment itself. And yet, of course, it isn't. The power struggle is just a phase—something we all go through, like adolescence and "the terrible twos." The problem in previous generations was that most couples didn't have the luxury of the education or tools to "resolve" this touchy phase of relationship. That meant it went on—as it still does for many of us—till death or divorce.

On its surface, the power struggle is just that—the point in a relationship when, no matter how much each of us would like to deny it, those dreaded conflicts start to emerge. Unfortunately but predictably, the euphoria of oneness and complete acceptance erodes, we "get used to" each other, and dissatisfaction seeps into a crucible that might once have seemed impenetrable. Often, to the embarrassment of both of us, we regress into two pouty, competitive children, each one evidencing unfair or simply unbearable behaviors and putting forth, openly or surreptitiously, our unconscious, irrational agendas of "Me first," "I want, I want," "Leave me alone," or "Please don't leave me at all." If our tiffs are noisy, we're most likely headed for firefights; if the disagreements are quiet enough that they can be ignored, freezeouts lie ahead.

Either way, Beloved has become Beloved Enemy. No longer our precious salve, our partner now seems the salt in our wounds. Though to the unenlightened among us, this second stage may seem like a dirty trick, this isn't the case. For whether we know it or not, the power struggle has surprisingly little to do with our mate. Rather, it's predominantly a flash-back, a further act within the incomplete drama of our younger years, which has found in our adult relationships a second stage upon which to enact itself. Once we recognize and learn from this fact, the power struggle can become the most healing and empowering period in our adult lives, enriching our significant relationships.

Certainly, the passage of time alone never transports any of us out of the middle stage of relationship. Still, this stage can be brought to a con-clusive and beneficial end. In fact, the bulk of *The New Couple* is dedicated to teaching partners how to do this—how to move on, as soon as pos-sible, to wondrous co-creativity. The way out is always *through,* which in this case means committing to the Ten New Laws of Love—that is, to the "work of relationship." New Couples are specifically asked to learn a basic relationship skill set and undertake two ongoing processes. The skills are these: *emotional literacy,* which includes emotional awareness and fluency; *deep listening; anger management; conflict resolution;* and *negotiation.* The processes are *individuation,* which involves becoming emotional peers with the members of our family-of-origin, and *resolving transference,* a kind of ghost-busting, which entails interrupting our unconscious tendency to try to work out with our partners unresolved early relationships with our primary caregivers.

Together, the New Couple skills and processes are the nuts and bolts of this book. A sure formula for keeping our precious chemistry alive, they also help us avoid creating relationships that either replicate tradi-tional marriages or are knee-jerk reactions to them. And while becoming a New Couple isn't an overnight affair, the skills and processes required can be easily and successfully learned over time. Furthermore, they don't require a perfect performance, just a genuine commitment. *Apollo 11,* the spacecraft that made the first successful lunar landing, was on course *only three percent of the time*—and it made it safely both ways!

The work of relationship is never entirely over: all couples are works in progress. Still, it gets much easier—and soon the "wow of relation-ship," which we experience when our initial chemistries actually endure, is on its way. And, as those of us who commit to the Ten New Laws of Love notice, the power struggle *does* yield to co-creativity—which, inci-dentally, is not a mythic state. Almost imperceptibly, as day replaces night, and sometimes even before we expect it, interdependence becomes reflexive and a greater peace prevails between us—yet never at the price of passion. Emotional intimacy becomes our way of life together, our ability to love and honor ourselves expands, and our individual missions are firmly on the march.

If we've chosen parenthood, one of the major benefits of our intention to cross into this last stretch of the relationship journey is the trickle-down effect that co-creativity has on our children. Although it's still not adequately recognized, *functional couples make functional parents.* The most powerful parenting technique we can use—and the most positive gift we can offer our children—is the role model of genuine partnership—a union in which each partner not only loves and respects but also openly champions the other.

As we move out of the power struggle and tap the potential of our couple, our mutual focus shifts away from problems and avoidances in our relationship and turns toward further exciting adventures and greater purpose. (If ever the world needed every partner's solid and heartfelt contribution, it's now!) No matter the glitches and backslides, when we commit to pole-vaulting out of the power struggle with the help of the Ten New Laws of Love, a soft landing in co-creativity is just ahead. As we create a life we love with the love of our life, we're able finally to celebrate both our priceless individuality *and* a stellar connection.

We wish you joy and success in the creation of *your* New Couple!

Seana McGee and Maurice Taylor
Summer 1999
West Marin County, California

What's Your New Couple Quotient?
A Quiz for Couples

Each partner takes this quiz separately. Check the *yes* or *no* box for each of the following questions. (If you're currently working on the issue addressed by a particular question—whether in a class or program, in therapy, or in a support group—check *yes* for that question.)

YES   NO

☐ ☐   1. Do you routinely share your most important thoughts and feelings with your partner?

☐ ☐   2. Do your two bodies seem to love each other independent of your minds?

☐ ☐   3. Do you tell your partner your greatest secrets and your greatest shame?

☐ ☐   4. Are you managing your work hours so that they're not a problem in your relationship?

☐ ☐   5. Are you managing your use of food so that it's not a problem in your relationship?

☐ ☐   6. Are you managing any use of addictive substances and compulsive behaviors so that they're not a problem in your relationship?

☐ ☐   7. Are your relationships with friends, ex-partners, and colleagues sufficiently straightforward that they present no problems in your relationship?

☐ ☐   8. Are your relationships with family members sufficiently straightforward that they present no problems in your relationship?

☐ ☐   9. Do you regularly level with each other about how you feel toward each other?

☐ ☐   10. Do you let your partner know when you're feeling guilty or overly responsible about anything, particularly the relationship?

☐ ☐   11. Do you let your partner know when you're feeling self-blaming or ashamed about anything, particularly the relationship?

YES NO

☐ ☐ 12. Are you able to label appreciation, gratitude, admiration, and love at the moment you experience them?

☐ ☐ 13. Are you able to label fear, sadness, and anger at the moment you experience them?

☐ ☐ 14. Are you able to tell your partner these same feelings in such a way that he or she can hear and accept them?

☐ ☐ 15. Do you feel heard by your partner well enough that you're confident he or she could accurately represent you to a third party?

☐ ☐ 16. When your partner talks to you about matters that are important to him or her, are you especially attentive?

☐ ☐ 17. Do you and your partner carve out special time at least once a week to share what's really going on for you?

☐ ☐ 18. Do you both feel that the way money is earned and managed in your relationship is fair?

☐ ☐ 19. When you think of all the day-to-day duties and responsibilities of your life together—including those relating to finances, the household, your social life, relationships with parents and extended family members, childcare and education, and maintenance of car and yard—do you feel that they're divided fairly between the two of you?

☐ ☐ 20. Have you openly discussed with your partner how any differences in gender, age, race, ethnicity, income, and financial status make you feel?

☐ ☐ 21. Have you openly discussed with your partner how any differences in talent, career, educational status, and advantages of upbringing make you feel?

☐ ☐ 22. Do you two consistently, either on your own or with facilitation, resolve conflicts until all resentment is dissolved?

☐ ☐ 23. Are you able to tell your partner when you're feeling angry, irritated, frustrated, or resentful without being aggressive, disrespectful, or frightening?

☐ ☐ 24. Are you able to tell your partner when you're feeling angry, irritated, frustrated, or resentful without shutting him or her out?

YES NO

☐ ☐ 25. Have you clearly expressed to your partner that violence, verbal abuse, and sexual betrayals are unacceptable to you?

☐ ☐ 26. Have you clearly expressed to your partner that substance abuse and other self-destructive behaviors are unacceptable to you?

☐ ☐ 27. Are you two able to effectively negotiate and make deals to handle areas of conflict?

☐ ☐ 28. Are you aware that the most confounding issues with your partner relate to the most confounding issues with your parents, siblings, and others you grew up with?

☐ ☐ 29. Are you able to stick up for yourself with your partner?

☐ ☐ 30. Are you able to stick up for yourself with your friends and colleagues?

☐ ☐ 31. Are you able to stick up for yourself with your family members?

☐ ☐ 32. Are you aware of, *and working on,* your areas of low self-esteem?

☐ ☐ 33. Do you trust and follow your intuition?

☐ ☐ 34. Are you doing work that's deeply fulfilling and contributes to the greater good?

☐ ☐ 35. Are you supporting your mate to do work that's deeply fulfilling and contributes to the greater good?

☐ ☐ 36. Do you feel that you have the inner strength to leave your partner if your baseline conditions for relationship are violated or ignored *and* outside help has been refused or has failed?

☐ ☐ 37. Are you as an individual able to support yourself financially in a lifestyle that's acceptable to you?

☐ ☐ 38. Do you consider yourself emotionally independent?

☐ ☐ 39. Are you willing to pursue whatever educational and healing options are necessary to keep unresolved issues and conflicts from damaging your relationship?

☐ ☐ 40. Are you willing to pursue whatever educational and healing options are necessary to raise your self-esteem, if low self-esteem threatens your relationship?

HOW TO CALCULATE YOUR
NEW COUPLE QUOTIENT

Partners total their *yes* responses separately, then combine them for a New Couple total.

Your New Couple Quotient

- If your quotient ranges between 80 and 69, congratulations! You're a stellar New Couple—and a wonderful role model for others. This book will teach you how to deal with glitches, safeguard your success, and give you a language to describe what you're already doing so well.
- If your quotient ranges between 68 and 57, congratulations! You two are well on your way to becoming a New Couple. This book will teach you how to get all the way home and actualize the New Couple model of relationship, give you a language to describe that model, and help you safeguard your success.
- If your quotient ranges between 56 and 45, you definitely take your relationship seriously. This book will teach you how to slough off those cobwebs of tradition and actualize the New Couple model of relationship, give you a language to describe that model, and help you safeguard your success.
- If your quotient ranges between 44 and 33, you're valiantly battling the trance of tradition. This book will teach you how to break the trance and actualize the New Couple model of relationship, give you a language to describe that model, and help you safeguard your success.
- If your quotient ranges between 32 and 21, you're succumbing to the trance of tradition, although you're fighting back from time to time. This book will be your welcome wake-up call. It will teach you how to break the trance and actualize the New Couple model of relationship, give you a language to describe that model, and help you safeguard your success.
- If your quotient ranges between 20 and 0, you're firmly under the spell of the trance of tradition. Let your quotient jolt you into a life of much greater love and happiness. This book will teach you how to break the trance and actualize the New Couple model of relationship, give you a language to describe that model, and help you safeguard your success.

What to Do with Your New Couple Quotient

If you answered *no* to questions . . .

- 1, 2, or 3, pay special attention to *chemistry,* the first New Law of Love
- 4, 5, 6, 7, or 8, pay special attention to *priority,* the second New Law of Love
- 9, 10, 11, 12, 13, or 14, pay special attention to *emotional integrity,* the third New Law of Love
- 15, 16, or 17, pay special attention to *deep listening,* the fourth New Law of Love
- 18, 19, 20, or 21, pay special attention to *equality,* the fifth New Law of Love
- 22, 23, 24, 25, 26, or 27, pay special attention to *peacemaking,* the sixth New Law of Love
- 28, 29, 30, 31, 32, or 33, pay special attention to *self-love,* the seventh New Law of Love
- 34 or 35, pay special attention to *mission in life,* the eighth New Law of Love
- 36, 37, or 38, pay special attention to *walking,* the ninth New Law of Love
- 39 or 40, pay special attention to *transformational education,* the tenth New Law of Love

What's Your *Potential* New Couple Quotient?
A Quiz for Singles

Singles, check the *yes* or *no* box for each of the following questions, responding with a future partner in mind. (If you're currently working on the issue addressed by a particular question—whether in a class or program, in therapy, or in a support group—check *yes* for that question.)

YES NO

☐ ☐ 1. Is it essential to you that a partner function as your best friend and that you be able to share your most important thoughts and feelings with him or her?

☐ ☐ 2. Is it essential to you that you have true sexual chemistry with a partner?

☐ ☐ 3. Is it essential to you that a partner be emotionally trustworthy and that you be able to tell him or her your greatest secrets and your greatest shame?

☐ ☐ 4. Do you feel able to manage your work hours so that they wouldn't be a problem in a relationship?

☐ ☐ 5. Do you feel able to manage your use of food so that it wouldn't be a problem in a relationship?

☐ ☐ 6. Do you feel able to manage any use of addictive substances and compulsive behaviors so that they wouldn't be a problem in a relationship?

☐ ☐ 7. Are your relationships with friends, ex-partners, and colleagues sufficiently straightforward that they would present no problems in a relationship?

☐ ☐ 8. Are your relationships with family members sufficiently straightforward that they would present no problems in a relationship?

☐ ☐ 9. Is it essential to you that you be able to regularly level with a partner about how you feel toward each other?

☐ ☐ 10. Is it essential to you that you be able to regularly let a partner know when you're feeling guilty or overly responsible about anything, particularly the relationship?

YES NO

☐ ☐ 11. Is it essential to you that you be able to let a partner know when you're feeling self-blaming or ashamed about anything, particularly the relationship?

☐ ☐ 12. Are you able to label appreciation, gratitude, admiration, and love at the moment you experience them?

☐ ☐ 13. Are you able to label fear, sadness, and anger at the moment you experience them?

☐ ☐ 14. Would you be able to express these same feelings to a partner in such a way that he or she could hear and accept them?

☐ ☐ 15. Is it essential to you that a partner be able to listen to you from his or her heart for the life of your relationship?

☐ ☐ 16. Do you feel able to sustain your ability to listen to a partner from your heart over the life of your relationship?

☐ ☐ 17. Is it a priority to you that you and a partner have quality time together on a regular basis?

☐ ☐ 18. Is it essential to you that the way money is earned and managed in a relationship be completely fair?

☐ ☐ 19. Is it essential to you that all the day-to-day duties and responsibilities of your life together—including those relating to finances, the household, your social life, relationships with parents and extended family members, childcare and education, and maintenance of car and yard—be divided fairly between you and a partner?

☐ ☐ 20. Is it essential to you that you be able to discuss with a partner your feelings about differences in gender, age, race, ethnicity, income, and financial status?

☐ ☐ 21. Is it essential to you that you be able to discuss with a partner your feelings about differences in talent, career, educational status, and advantages of upbringing?

☐ ☐ 22. Is it essential to you that you and a partner be able to consistently, either on your own or with facilitation, resolve conflicts until all resentment is dissolved?

☐ ☐ 23. Is it essential to you that you be able to tell a partner when you're feeling angry, irritated, frustrated, or resentful without being aggressive, disrespectful, or frightening?

☐ ☐ 24. Is it essential to you that you be able to tell a partner when you're feeling angry, irritated, frustrated, or resentful without shutting him or her out?

YES NO

☐ ☐ 25. Would you be able to clearly express to a partner that violence, verbal abuse, and sexual betrayals are unacceptable to you?

☐ ☐ 26. Would you be able to clearly express to a partner that substance abuse or other self-destructive behaviors are unacceptable to you?

☐ ☐ 27. Would you be able to effectively negotiate and make deals to handle areas of conflict with a partner?

☐ ☐ 28. Are you aware that the most confounding issues with partners relate to the most confounding issues with your parents, siblings, and others you grew up with?

☐ ☐ 29. Would you be able to stick up for yourself with a partner?

☐ ☐ 30. Are you able to stick up for yourself with your friends, colleagues, and housemates?

☐ ☐ 31. Are you able to stick up for yourself with your family members?

☐ ☐ 32. Are you aware of, *and working on,* your areas of low self-esteem?

☐ ☐ 33. Do you trust and follow your intuition?

☐ ☐ 34. Are you doing work that's deeply fulfilling and contributes to the greater good?

☐ ☐ 35. Would you support a partner in doing work that's deeply fulfilling to him or her and that contributes to the greater good?

☐ ☐ 36. Do you feel that you would have the inner strength to leave a partner if your baseline conditions for relationship were violated or ignored *and* outside help had been refused or had failed?

☐ ☐ 37. Are you as an individual able to support yourself financially in a lifestyle that's acceptable to you?

☐ ☐ 38. Do you consider yourself emotionally independent?

☐ ☐ 39. Are you willing to pursue whatever educational and healing options are necessary to keep unresolved issues and conflicts from damaging a relationship?

☐ ☐ 40. Are you willing to pursue whatever educational and healing options are necessary to raise your self-esteem, if low self-esteem threatens a relationship?

HOW TO CALCULATE YOUR
POTENTIAL NEW COUPLE QUOTIENT

Total your *yes* responses to get your *potential* New Couple quotient.

Your *Potential* New Couple Quotient

- If your quotient ranges between 40 and 35, congratulations! You have fifty percent of what it takes to be a stellar New Couple. This book will teach you how to turn your wonderful vision into a new model of relationship with another person and give you a language to describe that model.
- If your quotient ranges between 34 and 29, congratulations! You're not far from your full New Couple potential. This book will teach you how to take it all the way, help you actualize this new model of relationship with another person, and give you a language to describe it.
- If your quotient ranges between 28 and 23, you've thought very seriously about healthy relationship. This book will teach you how to slough off remaining cobwebs of tradition, help you actualize this new model of relationship with another person, and give you a language to describe it.
- If your quotient ranges between 22 and 17, you're valiantly battling the trance of tradition. This book will teach you how to break the trance, help you actualize this new model of relationship with another person, and give you a language to describe it.
- If your quotient ranges between 16 and 11, you're succumbing to the trance of tradition, though you're fighting back from time to time. This book will be your welcome wake-up call. It will teach you how to break the trance, help you actualize this new model of relationship with another person, and give you a language to describe it.
- If your quotient ranges between 10 and 0, you're firmly under the spell of the trance of tradition. Let your quotient serve to jolt you into a life of much greater happiness and self-love. This book will teach you how to break the trance once and for all, help you actualize this new model of relationship with another person, and give you a language to describe it.

What to Do with Your *Potential* New Couple Quotient

If you answered *no* to questions . . .

- 1, 2, or 3, pay special attention to *chemistry,* the first New Law of Love
- 4, 5, 6, 7, or 8, pay special attention to *priority,* the second New Law of Love
- 9, 10, 11, 12, 13, or 14, pay special attention to *emotional integrity,* the third New Law of Love
- 15, 16, or 17, pay special attention to *deep listening,* the fourth New Law of Love
- 18, 19, 20, or 21, pay special attention to *equality,* the fifth New Law of Love
- 22, 23, 24, 25, 26, or 27, pay special attention to *peacemaking,* the sixth New Law of Love
- 28, 29, 30, 31, 32, or 33, pay special attention to *self-love,* the seventh New Law of Love
- 34 or 35, pay special attention to *mission in life,* the eighth New Law of Love
- 36, 37, or 38, pay special attention to *walking,* the ninth New Law of Love
- 39 or 40, pay special attention to *transformational education,* the tenth New Law of Love.

Whatever your quotient, this book can be an invaluable resource in helping you select a partner and create and sustain a New Couple. We recommend that you give this quiz to any partner you're thinking about getting serious with. Share your results with him or her, and ask if he or she is willing to do the same with you. Then you can both use the above guide to identify areas that need attention and the book itself to prevent those areas from becoming threats to your new relationship.

1. CHEMISTRY
the first new law of love

TOM AND MELISSA

Tom: I had an idea that Melissa and I were on the same journey. She even had a name for it—The Africa Ride. I fell in love with her sitting in a big tent in the desert—talking, talking, talking. That was part of the ride. Each long conversation was a journey in itself, leading me to new places where I was thrilled to be and where I wouldn't have gone without her.

Melissa: We were on location in Morocco. It was mid-afternoon and Tom was driving us through the desert in a tiny white Saab. He put his hand up to the windshield, the long dark fingers spreading protectively across the glass. Without knowing exactly why, I put my hand up too and touched the glass. In that moment, in that tiny tin car heading into the bright orange sun toward a place I'd never been, I looked at him and felt a complete sense of warmth and comfort. I knew we were home.

ERICA AND MICHAEL

Erica: I knew Michael was *the* one during the six-hour return trip from Napa where we'd spent our first weekend together. Throughout the entire drive it felt as though I were surrounded by a golden, loving orb of warmth. When I looked at him, I experienced the subtle presence of not only my father and mother, but all the good parts of my past relationships as well. That's when I knew that this relationship was what in Hebrew is called *besheret*—meant to be.

Michael: Erica's skin is so incredible, it's enough simply to touch her to be infused with pure love. And it was this gentle touch, this precise feeling that I had searched for all my life. I remember one day in particular. I just opened my eyes and saw, lying next to me, my own morning sun. In that moment, I knew that with this special person, my world was in balance and everything set in its rightful place.

JOHN AND CHANTHANOM

John: We were sitting on a beach in Corpus Christi. When Chanthanom and I touched, I had a tingling feeling, as if I were putting my hand into warm water, or into a glove that fit superbly. I had a sense of an inevitability without having consciousness that it was inevitable, that things were happening.

Chanthanom: John came round one night to my brother's house for dinner. At some point during the meal, I looked up into his face. I caught the sweetness in his eyes, his special smile—and I just knew that this was the love of my life.

STEVE AND BOB

Steve: I threw a party to celebrate Bob's forty-fourth birthday, inviting his closest friends. After dinner, as we all sang Happy Birthday, I walked toward him carrying the cake, candles ablaze, holding it before him. In that very instant when he blew out his candles, I felt something shift deep inside me: It was my heart, opening wide. In that snapshot moment, I realized, This isn't someone I just admire. This Bob is my life partner. And, from then on, he would be *my* Bob.

Bob: I was giving an art show at my house when he arrived. Though it wasn't the truth of my heart, I found myself greeting him politely, like any other guest. Suddenly, I realized what I'd done and that's when our relationship hit a fulcrum and tilted. There'd be no turning back: I knew that from that moment on it would be inadmissible to hurt this person in any way. Where there was one, there now were two. Beyond all doubt, this relationship was my future.

Quotes from actual couples using their true names

When two people "click"—when something meshes, there's an instantaneous fit, and sparks fly—it's called *chemistry*. This nonscientific use of the term is nearly slang though it captures the essence of many of our culture's favorite descriptions of love: the attraction of opposites, the recognition of soulmates, love at first sight, even the sense of a long-overdue homecoming. There's no doubt that chemistry is a naturally occurring wonder, an undeniable, powerful force between human beings, and one that continually intrigues and seduces us with its romantic promise. Yet it remains a bona fide mystery to science—one that biologists and psychologists have worked hard to crack.

Some researchers theorize that romantic chemistry is a complex biochemical interaction involving either little-understood pheromones or subtle physical scents. Others call it the result of interpersonal attraction based on personality profiles and physical typologies. Yet another camp insists that chemistry derives from an unconscious template—a crazy quilt of our early caregivers' "good" and "bad" characteristics—which functions like a mate-selection software program pre-set to sound off attraction bells. Still others are convinced that chemistry signals the ultimate deal—a special contract between two evolving souls to be fulfilled if they so choose.

The first Law of Love, the Law of Chemistry, argues with none of the above. Its intention is merely to legitimate this amazing phenomenon: to raise the profile of chemistry, elevating it from slang by revealing and validating its true dignity, and then to establish it as a prerequisite for the healthy selection of a mate. This law urges us to insist that genuine chemistry be present in any relationship to which we commit, and to be certain that we're capable of detecting it.

Though chemistry and the intoxication stage of relationship are often confused, the two are clearly distinct. The latter is ephemeral—just a phase—characterized by a high that's the result of the excitement of a new connection. Chemistry, on the other hand—though it may or may not be experienced as a high—is a soulful, energetic resonance between two people *that need never dissipate*. This durability is precisely what lends chemistry the solidity to function as the cornerstone of the Ten New Laws of Love—and the key that unlocks the next nine. This characteristic, in addition to the fact that chemistry is the only law that can't be taught, learned, or otherwise acquired, is why we begin our book with the Law of Chemistry.

Couples can use this first law to more deeply understand what does and doesn't work in their existing relationship. As we noted in the Introduction, chemistry is the foundation of rapport; all the other principles of partnership are layered on top of it. This doesn't mean that chemistry never wavers in a healthy relationship. It's predictable—almost inevitable, even—that the chemical magic will weaken as the power struggle intensifies. Luckily, there's an antidote to such chemical entropy—namely, a couple's commitment to the nine other New Laws of Love. These have been designed precisely to help keep chemistry alive, especially as couples work their way through the power struggle and move into co-creativity.

It's important to note that the antidote found in the New Laws of Love works only if there's something to revive. We can't skip the chemistry altogether, nor should we downplay its importance. It's not the end of the world if our chemistry is a tad bit run down—even a *lot* run down—*but we must have reveled in it once upon a time*. Though we like to think that love conquers all, and that good communication or a crackerjack couple counselor can fix all relationships, this simply isn't so. Even the most conscientious application of the nine other New Laws of Love can't make up for a serious deficit in the chemistry department.

If you're single, this first New Law of Love promises immeasurable benefits in the mate-selection game. We invite you to use the presence or absence of chemistry as a yardstick when interviewing potentials. This can dramatically refine your search, saving you a lot of time, effort, and awkwardness. Checking someone out for chemistry is also a great chance to practice a high grade of self-love: if you accept the challenge to be as honest as possible in the assessment process, you'll spare yourself some heartache down the road. Given the importance of chemistry, your definitive personal ad (whether in print or etched in your heart) could read, "Seeking a one-in-a-million other who is willing to commit to the Ten New Laws of Love *and with whom I have chemistry—New Couple style*."

CHEMISTRY, NO DOUBT

Though the jury may be way out on chemistry's root cause, there are no doubters regarding its existence. Chemistry is especially apparent blown up on the big screen. Like Bogie and Bacall, co-stars whose chemistry can melt celluloid—and the audience along with it. The absence of co-star chemistry makes a similarly strong impression—usually a major flop. The film illusion of love fails when two acting paramours don't "have it."

Viewers end up squirming in their seats, chalking the failure up to bad casting and—yes, we're all quick to recognize it—a lack of chemistry. The fact is even Academy Award winners can't *enact* chemistry if, on some level, something special isn't cooking between them.

Similarly, famous pairings in literature and history, such as Heathcliff and Catherine from *Wuthering Heights,* Antony and Cleopatra from Shakespeare, and even Abelard and Heloise from the twelfth century, become classics largely because of the complex chemistry revealed between the lovers. And it's our intense fascination with these characters that confirms our belief in the exquisite Law of Chemistry.

As in art, so in life: although it often takes time to recognize true chemistry, it cannot be faked. Nor can it be cultivated, created, or otherwise willed into being. Though it's a hard lesson, sometimes we need to find out for ourselves that we can't force a spark.

Consider the case of Hector and Melanie. Both long-term loners, these two had never met, though they belonged to the same loose circle of friends—friends who, by the way, were convinced that they'd adore each other. When they were finally introduced, knowing of their friends' hopes for them, they were disappointed and embarrassed to discover that something was missing. Optimists at heart, they got together a few times over the next several weeks, but that elusive something was *still* missing. They didn't want to disappoint their well-meaning matchmakers, but there was no bluffing it: they left each other cold.

Wherever it comes from—the vast cosmos or tiny molecular connections—chemistry is a gift. It's the exception, not the rule. And brutal as it may seem, two people either have it or they don't.

NEW COUPLE CHEMISTRY: HAVING IT ALL— GREAT SEX *AND* BEST FRIENDSHIP

> With words spread
> softly as the golden fall around our feet,
> we arrange to one leaf;
> and speak the emergency of our two hearts'
> beat, pressed between green velvet walls.
>
> GLORIA VERNON CRAIG,
> *Collected Poems, 1995–2000*

New Couple chemistry has a definition all its own. First of all, lest there be any confusion on this point, it definitely does include great sex. But it goes way beyond a special sexual connection. Two people jell all over the place: their bodies, their personalities, their minds, their hearts, their energies. Bottom line: they're each other's greatest companion by far, in and out of bed, and they acknowledge that both aspects of the relationship are equally important.

This unique form of commingling is more than energetic; it's *synergetic*. And it endows a partnership with a combined level of energy—and therefore potential—that far exceeds what each partner would be capable of alone.

It can't be denied that energy attracts, as Shanti and Martin, two forty-something businesspeople, demonstrate. They speak of having "noticed each other's energy" from across the conference hall in Denver, where they met. Like long-lost friends, they spent the night "catching up," and, to their amazement, discovered that they shared a vision: to found a community for unwanted infants. It took two weeks for these two to make it into bed, and another week to get out. Today, two-and-a-half years later, this unstoppable husband-and-wife team have braved their share of subcontinental heat and dust (and he a bout of dengue fever) and are busy interviewing surrogate mothers and scouting construction sites from their new center in Bangalore, India.

New Couple chemistry isn't only inherently creative, it's also both empowering and deeply healing. Unlike the thunderbolt experience of Shanti and Martin, the initial meeting of Winnie and Brad was characterized by a feeling that Winnie described as a "warm, silken bath." Brad was sweet and easygoing—"like an oversized lap dog," she said—but sometimes maddeningly absentminded and stuck in his career as a local civil servant. Her personality, on the other hand, was like that of an "overbred racehorse," according to Brad. Extremely high-strung, she was known as a compulsive achiever—even among her ambitious colleagues at the commodities brokerage where she worked. Over the years, their opposite effects on each other proved transformative. Winnie worked weekends to qualify as a Shiatsu massage therapist, building a thriving practice. "It really grounded me to launch my mission in life," she said. Brad stepped out as a consultant and pulled together a community water conservation project that mushroomed county-wide. "I feel more powerful as a person," he confided, "much more like who I really am."

Sexual Chemistry: Nectar of the Gods

When I am with you, we stay up all night.
When you're not here, I can't go to sleep.
Praise God for these two insomnias!
And the difference between them.

JELALUDDIN RUMI,
QUATRAIN 36, *Open Secret*

Some say that sexual chemistry defies description. Yet poet Jelaluddin Rumi, quoted above, has no trouble capturing the ecstasy most of us mortals associate with the delights of the flesh—this despite the fact that, unlike the sex act itself (which drives the perpetuation of the human species), sexual chemistry is a matter of the sublime. It's the real thing, the genuine article, the raw connection. Definitely one of those you've-got-to-be-there experiences. When chemistry blesses lovers, time, thought—even the physical form—can seem to cease to exist. Indeed, true lovers often have the impression that their bodies love each other, quite apart from their minds (and possibly even their hearts).

But buyer beware: relationships afire with sexual chemistry alone are often fraught with drama. Furthermore, because rampaging sexual chemistry can annihilate discernment, the newly initiated can easily get burned. The greatest risk is seen during the early intoxication stage of a relationship, when an intense carnal connection can render new sex partners blind to the reality of the personality they're in bed with.

"She's my soulmate," Bart exulted on day fourteen of his tryst with Annaleis. Though twenty years and two graduate degrees separated them, Bart was convinced that the younger woman, a dancer, was the perfect foil for "this overeducated professional," as he liked to call himself. "And she wants me all the time," he went on—unlike Maggie, his high school sweetheart (and wife): "After twenty-five years, *she* thinks I'm the wallpaper." On day thirty-five, Bart awoke to a three-part revelation: other than the details of the night before, he and Annaleis had nothing to talk about; his object of desire had no out-of-bed potential at all; and for Annaleis, he was (ouch!) just a fling.

Bart has a lot of company. Indeed, it's a worn-out truth in our day that sexual chemistry can impair judgment. It can also be the basis for serial monogamy, a pattern of hopping out of one relationship and into another. The exiting occurs predictably, during that crucial passage out of the intoxication stage into the power struggle, when sexual chemistry starts to fade. We once overheard two twenty-year-old guys, members of a rock band, deliberating over precisely this subject in an outdoor café. "I usually pick girls for sexual reasons," one revealed to his cohort. "But when that intensity starts to mellow, there'd better be something else there." His youthful wisdom was spot on: sexual chemistry alone can't sustain any relationship. What's more, it can be the stuff of a certain type of sexual addiction, as is discussed in the next chapter.

Though these shadow sides of sexual chemistry can be long and dark, what can deceive can also inspire. The great trickster named sexual chemistry moves some humans to their highest creative expression. For others of us, sex with chemistry might be the closest thing to a religious experience we'll ever know. And if we desire a long and healthy relationship in the third millennium, delicious sex remains—in tandem with best-friendship chemistry—plainly sine qua non.

Best-Friendship Chemistry: The Elixir of Stimulation and Safety

Best-friendship chemistry is rare. But when it occurs, it's uncanny; in fact, it can blow us away. A rapport that's mutually energizing, it makes us feel part of an amazing reciprocal flow. As Martin and Shanti learned, the recognition of this energetic connection between oneself and another can feel like an unexpected reunion. Both partners are struck with a deep sense of familiarity, of déjà vu; it's as though somehow each already knows (and is known by) the other. As Rumi crooned:

> The minute I heard my first love story
> I started looking for you, not knowing
> how blind that was.
> Lovers don't finally meet somewhere.
> They're in each other all along.
>
> QUATRAIN 1246, *Open Secret*

The blessing of best-friendship chemistry allows two people to deeply "get"—that is, easily and naturally understand, and feel understood by—the other. It makes them curious about and respectful of each other's feelings and opinions. In the presence of best-friendship chemistry, two people share a genuine mutual admiration, and they speak of it openly and frequently. The best-friend brand of chemistry motivates a couple to stick up for and give one another the benefit of the doubt. Even if they risk all in so doing, the truth will come out between them, because they know that their connection depends on it. Best-friendship chemistry leads lovers to be excited by each other's dreams of the future and to laugh at the same things. Best friends also completely delight in each other's company and conversation, which makes them try to include each other in their activities, though they do just fine apart.

After five years together, Kent and Ramone can still turn tedium—even a trip to the recycling center!—into a major adventure. When two people resonate at the same frequency, it doesn't matter what they do. It's fun, or it feels good, simply because they're together. Best-friendship chemistry is certainly the most bonding and fulfilling of all interpersonal experiences. In fact, being close this way is what we all crave most.

So does that mean that only partners who have similar personalities can experience best-friendship chemistry? Isn't it true that *opposites* attract? Unfortunately, there's no hard-and-fast formula for calculating the potential affinity of two personalities. Best-friendship chemistry is a question of partners' energies complementing each other. On the one hand, that chemistry can express itself in similar personalities, like Dwight and Isabelle, a couple who met in acting school and often keep each other in stitches for hours doing impersonations. On the other hand, it can show up between so-called opposites. Ellie, for example, is an extrovert. Morris, a contemplative, is her best audience. "How can I stay angry when she's so funny?" he complained with a grin. Ellie leaped to praise him: "Morris lets me be down. He's the only one I feel really free to be myself with."

While what makes for such harmony seems inscrutable at first glance, there's actually some method to the magic. Our counseling of couples with best-friendship chemistry has exposed a fascinating parallel. In case after case, partners with even radically dissimilar family histories reveal, over time, a strikingly similar depth of emotional and psychological hurt. Take Rex and Angela. Great friends in the epic sense, if you saw these spouses of fifteen years conversing over lunch, their level of excitement and intensity would make you think they'd just met.

Not that the two former math majors have always been strangers to volatility. In fact, their frequent arguments were one of the things that brought them to our office for couple therapy. "You just can't help it; your family is so screwed up," was her favorite way to zing him when she was angry. With this he could hardly argue: alcoholic father, criminal brother, chronically supine mother—thus began Rex's personal docket. Her family, in contrast, looked like modern-day Cleavers: stable, clean-cut huggers fluent in the language of "I love you." Finally, to Rex's surprise, three months into couple work Angela broke through the family mystique: "I always felt so suffocated," she cried. "My father was a volcano, about to erupt; my mother's eyes were always welling with tears. Now I understand: they suppressed everything—*everything!* And I ended up thinking *I* was the crazy one." Rex felt a rush of compassion. He took Angela's hand. "To think how many times I've envied your family situation; it looked so good. Could our suffering really have been so similar?"

Rex and Angela are a beautiful example of a couple whose family backgrounds—the externals—are poles apart, yet whose wounding is revealed, with some scratching of the surface, to be commensurate. This is true for many couples—even among those whose styles of emotional expression and levels of functioning in the world appear as different as night and day. (The extreme form of this interpersonal dynamic is the unhealthy "chemistry" found between the addict and the co-addict, which we'll discuss further in the next chapter.)

Whether or not two partners are aware of this parallel-wounding dynamic, a matching emotional landscape can set the stage for powerful empathy and bonding. This empathic connection, as important as the sexual component, is the primary building block of emotional intimacy. (Remember, along with self-love and mission in life, emotional intimacy is one of the three higher-order needs that underpin all Ten New Laws of Love.)

Still, best-friendship chemistry and best friendship itself are two different things. The latter takes time to develop, while best-friendship chemistry, as we have seen, can be experienced instantaneously. This is not to say that two individuals become best friends right off the bat; rather, they feel immediately, in their heart and gut, the potential of best friendship.

An Invitation to Reflect on the Law of Chemistry

We offer readers several opportunities in each chapter to interact with the material we're presenting. Each time you see the heading "An Invitation to Reflect on . . . ," you'll find several questions that prompt you to think about (and discuss) a particular aspect of one New Law of Love. Unless the heading specifies otherwise, the questions are intended for both couples and singles. If you're in a couple, respond to the questions individually; then discuss your answers with your partner. If you're single, respond with your last major relationship in mind.

- How would you describe the kind of chemistry you enjoyed when you first fell in love? Was it best-friendship, sexual, or New Couple chemistry (that is, an amalgam of both)?
- Where are your various chemistry levels today? (If you find that they've diminished, this isn't catastrophic. The remaining nine New Laws of Love are designed to reignite them.)
- How do these current levels affect your self-love? Your emotional intimacy?

EMOTIONAL TRUSTWORTHINESS

Clicking with someone isn't *solely* a matter of being stimulated. New Couples must be able to function as confidants as well—guardians of each other's inner secrets. The cultivation of emotional intimacy demands this role, actually *depends* on it. In other words, both individuals must not only be turned on by the other's personality, they must also see the other as an *emotional safe zone*. When two people click, they know in their heart of hearts that the other would never lie to them or intentionally hurt them. They're free to be their authentic selves with each other, and this safety encourages even greater authenticity. In fact, if there's anyone to whom they could reveal all their warts and weirdnesses, their deepest, darkest secrets—not to mention their dreams and general magnificence—it's their beloved other. And he or she feels the same trust in return.

This quality is called *emotional trustworthiness,* and although it's not a chemistry in and of itself, it's an essential element of best-friendship chemistry. At its best, it's an active type of support—one that involves validating, even defending, each other's emotions, thoughts, intuition, and personal rights. Because emotional trustworthiness is the basis of emotional intimacy, it needs to be obvious to some degree when two people first meet each other.

Christian sensed it from the outset: "I knew right away that Beatrice was different, solid," he confided to his best male friend. "She wasn't a flake." Christian's observation reflected a self-loving concern on his part. After all, Beatrice was destined to be his future very best friend in the entire world.

Some people are naturally emotionally trustworthy; others just appear to be. In fact, accurately determining whether a woman we're getting to know really is a "good person" or our new colleague really is a "nice guy" can be an education in itself. Most of us have at least the latent ability to become emotionally trustworthy. But, like any ability, it needs to be developed. Upcoming New Laws of Love, including emotional integrity, deep listening, peacemaking, priority, self-love, walking, and transformational education, will provide all the support we need to develop this all-important quality.

An Invitation to Reflect on the Law of Chemistry

- Did you consider your partner emotionally trustworthy when you first met, or did the two of you have to work at it?
- Do you consider your mate emotionally trustworthy today?
- How does your current level of emotional trustworthiness affect your self-love? Your emotional intimacy?

ESSENTIAL COMPATIBILITIES— MORE *IS* BETTER

Certainly, it's clear by now why strong and natural best friendship *and* sexual rapport constitute the basics of New Couple chemistry. But for more and more of us pondering the selection of a mate, the requirements will be a hair stiffer than the bare minimum. Some people see shared dreams, passions, and life goals as equally fundamental to a successful partnership. Others insist that the beloved be of similar intellectual or spiritual bent or possess a simpatico worldview (be it political, religious, or cultural). Still others find creative and artistic kinship to be an essential element in a long-term prospect; and there are those who demand that recreational, avocational, or lifestyle tastes be in harmony.

While each of these could actually be considered a kind of chemistry in its own right (depending on the intensity of the energy), they're all, at a minimum, important forms of compatibility. The New Couple model calls them *essential compatibilities.* Unlike attributes, which are characteristics a person possesses—for example, looks, status, money, and education— essential compatibilities involve an orientation to life that can be shared. Neither attributes nor essential compatibilities need be judged in isolation, however; they're an integral part of sexual and best-friendship chemistries.

For Matthew and Jerene, the love of design is almost as important as good sex. Everything about their life—from the cottage they've renovated to the small graphic design firm they co-own—revolves around their shared aesthetic sensibility. "It's as though we were hatched in the same box of paints," Matthew said.

Of course, intellectual compatibility can be every bit as exciting as artistic. Charles and Virginia's discussions about literature and politics kept them up late, even years into their marriage. "Every once in a while, usually late at night, we would hit a vein," Virginia explained. "Then, well, it was two very sleepy campers the next day." "I've always loved the way that woman's mind works," Charles added. "Just when I think I can predict what she's going to say, she bursts out with an offbeat but absolutely original opinion about, say, the constitutionality of the latest Supreme Court decision. The woman's a genius—and it turns me on." This isn't just intellectual compatibility; it's intellectual *chemistry.* Virginia and Charles not only respect each other's thinking, their alchemy of ideas actually creates new thought. And the op-ed page of their local newspaper, to which they occasionally contribute, reaps the benefit.

The following spiritually compatible couple must have known intuitively where to find each other. Beryl and Howard, both divorced and in their late forties, met in an adult-ed class on science and spirituality at their neighborhood church. It was over chai, on the night of their third session, that each realized someone special had shown up. "Of course, I thought he was a fox," Beryl said. "But my attraction to him had just as much to do with our shared passion, our common beliefs about the nature of the universe." Both have been convinced since that day that a shared spiritual philosophy would be vital to any successful relationship they engaged in. Mohammed and Liza each knew before they fell in love that a prospective mate would need to share their religious devotion to Islam. They were both thrilled when they first agreed to set money aside on a weekly basis for a pilgrimage to Mecca in Saudi Arabia; they planned to go once their children were in school.

Because whether or not to procreate is one of the most monumental decisions in adult life, compatibility on this point needs to be established well in advance of marriage if at all possible. Lena very much wanted to have children of her own. Still, she married Ned, a man twenty-five years her senior who had three grown kids and no desire to have more. It took the woman years to be able to talk about it: "I was unable to assert *before* getting married that I absolutely wanted kids, at least one child," Lena admitted. "I guess I really abandoned myself."

Arnold handled the issue much better: he broke his relationship with Evie off as soon as she revealed to him the depth of her misgivings about having children. They were on a backpacking trip in the Trinity Alps. "There's too much of the world—and of myself—that I have yet to discover," Evie said with tears in her eyes. It was a tender moment, a moment of genuine intimacy, but for him it was decisive. "I knew she might eventually have come around, but it was too risky," he said. "My own mother was ambivalent about having kids, and as good a job as she did raising us, I'm determined that my children will have a mother who wants them as much as I do."

It's up to each individual to judge whether we could be fulfilled spending our life with a partner with whom we don't share essential compatibilities. While the same compatibilities aren't essential for everybody—*our* New Couple might be able to thrive without sharing a particular passion or an interest in philosophy, religion, or intellectual or artistic pursuits—the abundance of matchmaking services and the length of personal classifieds in alternative weeklies suggest that people "in the market" for mates are pretty picky about getting what they do want and weeding out what they don't. Wish-lists specifying essential compatibilities and attributes range from the salutary—New Couple compatibilities such as those listed above—to the harmlessly superficial to the seriously dysfunctional, such as a request for a Sugar Daddy or Mommy, a well-endowed partner willing to play personal choirboy, or a mail-order bride to act as a maid, mother, or worse.

New Couple chemistry is sometimes the only long-term elixir needed to launch a healthy relationship, however, as this next couple demonstrates. Vera and Tatsuo had nothing in common except English as a second language. Born and raised in Germany and Japan, Vera was an investment banker; Tatsuo, a Japanese musician. The couple obsessed over different hobbies, read different literature, ate different foods, and worshiped different gods. But when they came together, their raw New Couple chemistry could have melted diamonds. They so trusted each other that over the first six months of their relationship, they divulged the entire unabridged stories of their lives. It helped that they smiled at the same things and that their lovemaking was more powerful than anything either of them had previously known.

Tatsuo and Vera's marriage vows, which the couple co-wrote, were impressive—particularly the clause in which they committed "to acknowledge and resolve all conflict through to resolution." He especially would be asked to push the envelope over the years, because such an agreement would require that he break with his culture and bring third parties into matters traditionally reserved for the family.

The couple's devotion to the health of their relationship, as is often the case, proved fertile ground for the flowering of latent essential compatibilities. In no time, this fledgling New Couple was delighting in an array of passions new to them both, including mountain biking and parenting an adorable Newfoundland puppy.

COAST TO COAST CHEMISTRY

New Couple chemistry is a delicious hybrid of best friendship, wonderful sex, and as many compatibilities as two people can handle. Not that all this is evident upon first impression, of course. Throughout the full year during which we surreptitiously spied each other here and there on campus, for example, we appreciated the other as particularly sexy, but that's where the interest ended. Seana, Maurice surmised, was the ultimate eastern-seaboard yuppie. Indeed, she was born and bred in Boston, spoke French fluently, and had trained in journalism in both Paris and New York. Maurice, though, thought she was a snob. To Seana, Maurice was the ultimate laid-back Californian. Backpacking in the Andean and Alaskan wilderness piqued his early passion. Though with his degree in political philosophy and his trenchant perception she knew she had met her intellectual match, Maurice was also born five and a half years too late to match her chronologically. Seana thought he was a hippie.

Despite these early misgivings, the chemistry between us became abundantly clear during our first lengthy conversation as we sunned together on a redwood deck at a graduate school retreat. Maurice remembers: "Six months before that day, I was running on a beach searching my soul, but not thinking at all about my love life. I was granted an emotional preview, actually a revelation, of my future partner. She would not only be consummately sexy, but also someone with whom I would co-create, co-adventure, and cuddle. We would enjoy a parity of our personal powers; in other words, she wouldn't give herself away, no matter how hard I might push—and, boy, can I push! Months later, during that luminous talk in the sun, I realized that Seana—beautiful, loving, brilliant, and with chutzpah to spare—was literally the woman of my dream."

For her part, Seana recalls: "As I looked into Maurice's golden-green eyes in the late-afternoon sun, my fate suddenly dawned on me. *Oh, my God,* I thought; *I'm going to marry this young guy.* But the realization came as a shock to me. First of all, I was thoroughly enjoying being on my own and had no desire to get involved with anyone. Second, he didn't at all fit the vague picture of who I thought I'd eventually want to end up with—an older, more established, urbane type. Instead, here was this gorgeous, emotionally honest younger man with a mind like a laser. And it was undeniable: he was absolutely *it*—my partner in mind, body, and spirit."

Modern couples can't thrive without being aware of precious energies such as these and insisting on a partner with whom they feel them. True chemistry is more than pragmatic. It's our first hedge against the obstacles that are fated to accompany the challenging power-struggle stage of our relationship, when unhealed or denied wounds from childhood make their reappearance. When finally we find that unique individual—that someone with whom we have the most profound New Couple chemistry—we generally also discover that he or she is the person most adept at bumping into, and then royally pushing, our biggest buttons. And as we'll explain later, it *has* to be this way. Our beloved is a perfectly designed composite of some of the most cherished and unappreciated traits of our parent figures—or else there would be no chemistry! Chemistry is the cosmic joke, the golden carrot that inspires us to clear the field of our own unconscious, pull its weeds, and stay motivated to become fully creative as individuals—and co-creative as couples.

An Invitation to Reflect on the Law of Chemistry

- Did you share essential compatibilities when you first met?
- Do you share them today?
- How do shared and unshared essential compatibilities affect your self-love? Your emotional intimacy?
- If either one of you has developed new interests since you met, do you share these with each other?
- How do these new interests affect your self-love? Your emotional intimacy?

An Invitation for Singles to Reflect on the Law of Chemistry

Jot down the names of all your past significant romantic partners. Focusing on one at a time, answer the following:

- Did you two ever have chemistry? If so, was it the best-friendship or sexual variety, or did you enjoy New Couple chemistry (an amalgam of both)?
- If you had best-friendship chemistry, how did this make you feel? How did it affect your self-love? Your emotional intimacy?
- If your best-friendship chemistry faded, what caused this to happen? Was the fading due to a lack of sexual chemistry, of emotional trustworthiness, or of essential compatibilities? Did the onset of the power struggle cause your best-friendship chemistry to fade?
- If you lacked best-friendship chemistry, how did this make you feel? What prompted you to settle without it? How did that lack affect your self-love? Your emotional intimacy?
- If you had sexual chemistry, how did this make you feel? How did it affect your self-love? Your emotional intimacy?

- If your sexual chemistry faded, what caused this to happen? Was the fading due to a lack of best-friendship chemistry or of emotional trustworthiness? Did the onset of the power struggle cause your sexual chemistry to fade?
- If you lacked sexual chemistry, how did this make you feel? What prompted you to settle without it? How did that lack affect your self-love? Your emotional intimacy?
- If you had New Couple chemistry, what happened to the relationship? Can you remember when either one of the vital chemistries started to fade? What caused this to happen? Was the fading due to a lack of emotional trustworthiness or of essential compatibilities? Did the onset of the power struggle cause your New Couple chemistry to fade?
- Did you consider this person emotionally trustworthy? How did that trustworthiness make you feel? How did it affect your self-love? Your emotional intimacy?
- Did you share essential compatibilities? Name these. How did that sharing make you feel? How did it affect your self-love? Your emotional intimacy?
- Jot down areas of compatibility you consider essential to a relationship to which you'd commit for the long-term.
- Imagine yourself with a partner with whom you share New Couple chemistry and essential compatibilities. How does this make you feel? What kind of life can you envision together? If such a person is difficult to imagine, why is this so? What are your beliefs about what's possible in a relationship?
- Imagine yourself with a partner with whom you lack New Couple chemistry and essential compatibilities. How does this make you feel? What kind of life can you envision together? If you think you're capable of settling for this, what would cause you to do so?
- Ask yourself honestly if you're willing to wait until you meet someone with whom you share New Couple chemistry and essential compatibilities.

CHEMISTRY PAST AND
THE TRADITIONAL COUPLE

The colloquial use of the word *chemistry* to describe a special rapport between intimates has long enjoyed a slightly racy connotation. In its day, the chemical reaction between Clark Gable and Vivien Leigh in *Gone with the Wind* was considered almost X-rated. Society was obviously still reacting to its conservative Victorian roots when that movie was first released. Yet whatever the reading of such romantic, swashbuckling films was on the obscenity scale, their popularity was telling: like the romantic poetry, fiction, and drama of preceding centuries, it evidenced a strong historical human desire for chemistry-infused relationships.

High Magic, Low Magic

Unfortunately, the pressures of material survival and, in American culture at least, the legacy of Puritanism, effectively barred the masses from having for themselves the kind of sexy liaisons—that is, real chemistry—enjoyed by their fictive heroes. Never fear: romantic fantasy galloped in to the rescue. This widespread form of escapism rescued all manner of captives—not only those suffering in soulless unions but also those simply suffering. One client, Gwen, mentioned her grandmother Guinevere, after whom she'd been named. "My girlfriend's nanas played canasta; mine was into romance," she said. "Once I walked into her room and caught her nervously shoving something under her pillow. After she died, I found a collection of weird Victorian novellas. Poor thing. She had to put up with my grandfather—now *there* was a Romeo! Once he gave her a new frying pan for their anniversary."

This "cure" of romantic fantasy is ages old: countless women—and probably more men than have been generally acknowledged—have used it to soothe their woes, including the pain of no connection (or only a withered connection) with their spouse. In the distant past, this kind of fantasy occurred strictly in the head; it was the preferred stuff of daydreams. Later, romantic dreamers became consumers who coveted pulp fiction; and today, of course, television soap operas are the staple du jour, along with the impersonal intimacy of connections that require a modem and a mouse. It's sad to ponder the loneliness of those generations of traditional spouses who never tasted true chemistry and instead comforted themselves with make-believe.

Even today, romantic fantasy remains a trap that precludes real relationship and therefore real chemistry and connection. Twenty-four years old and desperately alone, Tina has watched the movie *Titanic* more than two dozen times. A self-described true romantic, proudly "addicted" to Danielle Steel, she's papered the walls of her studio apartment with images of Leonardo DiCaprio. "Beautiful people in outrageous situations—that's what I love," she asserted. "Especially those endings; I can always count on the heroes to melt together in sheer ecstasy. I believe that this kind of romance exists—even for me."

Late one night, Tina tuned in as we discussed New Couple chemistry on the radio. Her call to our office the next day was breathless: "What you two were describing, I want that so badly I can taste it." But her own story was far from romantic. Her dragons, somewhat shy at first, appeared one by one. The first was her terror of being abandoned. This had already happened once: when Tina was two, her mother had left the family and not returned until Tina was in high school. The second dragon was equally brutal: the belief that she didn't deserve a loving mate. It was powerful too, for Tina had never let herself have a boyfriend for more than a month. Reaching a critical turning point during our conversations, she realized for the first time that this predicament was directly linked to the disappearance of her mother twenty-two years earlier. She also learned that her preoccupation with the perfect man was an unhealthy obsession—pure fantasy—and that it had precluded her from experiencing real love in her life.

Like the news and entertainment media, which have vulgarized sexual chemistry by treating it with steamy sensationalism, romantic fantasy has also trivialized the concept of couple chemistry over the decades, undermining it as a serious consideration in creating stable relationships. Still, all has not been lost. On some level, the low magic of fantasy heralded the burgeoning of the higher-order need for emotional intimacy. And many people can still cut through the muddle and hype to define chemistry much as the New Couple model does—that is, a strong fusion of both sexual *and* personality attractions.

Traditional Mate Selection

Thanks to the advent of love marriages, partner-picking in Western culture has been based on love for a number of generations, and in Eastern cultures such choices are ever more common. Ostensibly, this great leap forward for Eros freed us from following the often heavy edicts of family, society, culture, and survival needs; finally, we could follow the dictates of our hearts.

But has choosing for love historically meant the same thing as choosing according to chemistry? Ideally, yes. The highest form of "getting along" has always been recognized as a special kinship of both body and personality—and that's the definition of chemistry—although it hasn't traditionally been specified as a formal criterion for mate selection. And the friendship component of chemistry certainly hasn't been ignored. In her tips for a happy marriage, Abigail Van Buren, AKA "Dear Abby," says that friendship is at the heart of all good relationships. That's certainly true of the marriage Larry's parents enjoyed—a marriage that he saw as one in a hundred million. "God knows they had their fights," he said, a tear moistening his eye, "but those two jitterbugged right up until the end." For most people, however, the old lower-order needs—needs for safely belonging to the tribe and keeping a roof overhead—have long skewed the trajectory of Cupid's arrow. They've often compromised love's selections and kept the reality of an absolute-love marriage at bay.

Obviously, individuals did, in times past, gravitate toward those with whom they had New Couple chemistry and compatibilities. Alicia and Ted, who had already celebrated their golden wedding anniversary, were residents of a posh retirement community in the Arizona desert. They clearly adored being together—and made no secret of their hot sex life. "They were notorious," said a former neighbor, obviously still irritated. "Can you imagine making such noise at their age? I was sure they did it for attention. It was disgraceful!" While most couples of previous generations probably possessed (at least initially) some kind of friendship-based or sexual compatibility, surely the gods smiled down on couples like Ted and Alicia who found both. And they did exist. Still, it was unlikely that more than a handful were able to preserve their singular gift. For without relationship skills and emotional healing, the power struggle could easily render their chemistry inert.

Caught Without Chemistry

Those who ended up marrying partners with whom they didn't get on famously were, for one reason or another—reasons that included family, cultural, or religious pressures (sometimes exacerbated by emotional wounding)—focused on lower-order needs. In the case of Tony and Luisa, a combination of such reasons forced a marriage that, on a chemistry level, was never meant to be. "We were childhood sweethearts," said the sixty-year-old Luisa, who had her first individual counseling session following her husband's death from cirrhosis of the liver, "but we grew apart. When, during the Korean War, Tony called me to say that he'd been drafted, we decided to spend one evening together, for old times' sake. We were still good friends, just not really passionate about each other. I don't know if it was because I felt sorry for him, but we ended up being intimate for the first time. I guess it was just one of those hormonal things."

Luisa realized that she was pregnant soon after that encounter. "I'm strongly Catholic now, but back then I thought about getting an abortion. My mother would have punished herself until she died if I'd refused to marry him—and sent me back to Puerto Rico. I can't imagine what Tony's father would have done to him. He was from the Old Country—in Italy." When the shotgun wedding took place, Luisa was eight months pregnant and Tony reeling from his experiences in battle. "It was like that in those days," Luisa pointed out. "Anyway, he was a good man. And God has given me beautiful grandchildren I can take care of now."

In the fifties, the value of true relational chemistry was little appreciated. Tony's and Luisa's families and cultural upbringing, like those of so many others, didn't allow for the mistakes of the inexperienced. And the times couldn't wait for Tony and Luisa to discover who, for each of them, would have been the one who had it all.

Settling

Today, though it's less likely that those of us who tend toward the traditional will be caught by unwanted pregnancy or other circumstances that might obligate us to uphold the family honor, we still settle in astonishingly high numbers; in other words, we commit to partners with whom we don't vibrate on all the requisite planes. What is it that compels us to

do this—to shortchange ourselves in the single most important relationship of our adult lives?

Usually, the more frightened we are about our emotional and material security (not to mention physical survival), the less able we are to
think about our higher-order need for intimacy—the kind of deep intimacy that chemistry affords. If children are on the agenda for the future,
as they often are, people sometimes settle as a panicked response, wanting
to start this endeavor before it's too late; women, especially, are frightened by the ticking of their biological clocks.

Fear of ending up alone is another incentive for settling; we might
harbor deep-seated worries that we can't take care of ourselves, or believe
that we have no value unless we're welded to another person. Even discovering our unique identity as individuals can daunt us, in which case
marriage might appear the perfect place to hide. Sometimes we dare not
stick to our standards—or even set them in the first place—out of sheer
cynicism; we simply despair of ever finding a truly kindred spirit and
persuade ourselves that the idea is undiluted fantasy. Such a dim view of
committed monogamous relationship probably results from witnessing
the failure of our role models' relationships, not to mention our own
unhealed heartbreaks.

Any combination of these factors—in addition to, or aggravated by,
the family, cultural, and religious pressures mentioned earlier, and by the
social stigma associated with singledom—can convince us to commit
without chemistry. If you consider yourself at risk for settling for any of
the above reasons, or if you worry that you settled in committing to your
current relationship, Chapter 10 ("Transformational Education") will
direct you to the assistance you need.

Regardless of the specifics that contribute to settling, this symptom of
low self-love is always tragic. The tragedy lies in the inestimable loss not
only of our own happiness but also that of the children who issue from a
chemistry-challenged union. It's hard enough to preserve chemistry once
we discover a person with whom we really have it. Without these vital
juices, however, a relationship can't help but desiccate. The real fantasy is
not that our true mate exists, but that true love can be sustained without a
new model of relationship and a commitment to work at it.

When we do settle, however, it's not for nothing. We usually insist
on certain essential compatibilities, attributes, or both. Still, we can no

more build a relationship with these alone than we can construct a castle out of sand. But those of us who, overly conscious of security or veneer, try to make it without the super-glue of New Couple chemistry are in for a Sisyphean task, as Arthur and Marlo's story illustrates.

These two were running scared—and facing all three of the biggest challenges to chemistry: they were anxious to start a family, they were ashamed at still being single, and Arthur held firmly the belief that their tepid connection was as good as it could get. Anyway, they both reasoned, the essentials were there; they were compatible with regard to religion and the desire for children.

Marlo's conservative adulthood was a reaction to her rebellious adolescence, itself a response to her father's untimely death by his own hand when she was eleven. This prodigal daughter adopted her faith's tenet that a woman's highest calling is motherhood. Like a number of only children, she was set on a big family—at least three children of her own. The only problem was her biological clock, which (now that she was thirty-two years old) was ticking more loudly than ever. As lovely as Marlo was, her intense desire to get married and pregnant proved too much for most men she met.

Then Arthur showed up at choir practice—and her dream of a big, happy family finally took form. The middle child of seven, this fireman had had almost no one-on-one time with his parents—save for his mother's intense scoldings. Thus, like his fiancée, Arthur's bitter early circumstances made him intent on creating a stable family. This feature, together with their shared faith, made it easy for them to seal the deal.

Still, Arthur and Marlo were no match for each other, in terms of either personality or passion. Conversations were monosyllabic, and though each found the other exceptionally attractive, their caresses left them flat. Arthur knew it: "You can't have everything," he readily admitted to his minister before the marriage. "But she'll be a good mother to our children—and, unlike Mom, she's not a screamer," he added with a shudder. For her part, Marlo presented a blithe facade to family and friends. But her diary knew the truth, and she prayed to God that come their wedding night, Arthur would become the warm, romantic husband she wished and hoped he could be.

Marlo and Arthur capitulated because they were too afraid to hold out. Unresolved childhood hurts muzzled the voice of their intuition, which (attributes and essential compatibilities notwithstanding) surely urged them to wait, to choose higher. As is true for many traditionals in our day, the unconscious desire to meet lower-order needs for security and belonging—and the possibility of experiencing, through our offspring, the childhood we've always yearned for—can keep us from imagining a relationship possessing the magnetic pull prescribed by the first New Law of Love.

Either Lovers or Friends, But Never Both

Tradition started the war between the sexes, but *we're* the ones keeping it going today. Too many of the more traditional among us still see lovers and best friends as two different animals—and marriage as a lifetime in a lockup. Barry, a snowmobile salesman, loved to joke about this dilemma with his friends: "Women—you can't live with them, and you can't live without them," he'd chant. But his conclusion that committed relationship was something akin to best enemyship was deadly serious. Also true of many traditionals, he framed chemistry entirely in terms of sex. Not that his fiancée, Alice, a waitress, didn't enter the relationship with her own prejudices: "Mother said a girl has to have the upper hand," she'd expound to her girlfriends. "You should always pick a man who loves you more than you love him—otherwise, you might end up in a back alley flat broke." Though in bed Alice and Barry created a veritable bonfire, their odds for success as spouses weren't high.

In fact, for this groom, the bachelor party was historic; it represented the end of an era. "Last night was my final bit of fun with the boys," Barry announced (between artful sniffles) in his wedding speech. "As of tonight," he continued, "a lifetime of hell. Only kidding, honey," he added, dramatically leaning over to kiss his new bride. Though her girlfriend was furious, Alice defended her husband. "Oh, all guys are like that," she explained on the way to the powder room. "Anyway, he'll get his. I've just charged five hundred dollars to our new joint credit-card account."

This lively couple actually had heaps of essential compatibilities. When they first met as ski instructors at Lake Tahoe, their passion for black-diamond runs paled only in comparison to their nocturnal carnality. Barry and Alice also loved hang-gliding, bungee-jumping, and gourmet dining. Though they were friends superficially, enjoying these many shared interests, they were incapable of best-friendship chemistry because their biases about the opposite sex precluded emotional trust. Clearly, Alice had been indoctrinated by her mother (who'd married a string of rich alcoholics) to see men as a necessary evil. And perhaps Barry's mistrust of women stemmed from his father, whose own "old-fashioned" mother used to slap his dad's face. Or perhaps it came from his mother, whom he'd watched take endless flak from his father before she took it out on her son.

Sexism, man-hating, and misogyny aren't just curses passed down through tradition. As Barry and Alice illustrate, these predispositions are *inevitable* by-products of emotional wounding. We'd never fault Barry and Alice for holding the erroneous notion that they can't have it all with the same person—that is, a life-mate as an intimate friend—because they came by the notion honestly. And while their transformation into a New Couple would require a profound healing journey for both, in their own families at least they'd be serving a grand purpose: ending generations of gender warfare.

An Invitation to Reflect on the Law of Chemistry as It Pertains to Your Parents

- Did your parents have New Couple chemistry? How did this affect their self-love? Their emotional intimacy? How did this make you feel?
- How did they preserve, or lose, whatever chemistries they had?
- Did your parents consider each other emotionally trustworthy? How did this affect their self-love? Their emotional intimacy? How did this make you feel?
- What essential compatibilities did your parents share? How did this affect your parents' self-love? Their emotional intimacy? How did this make you feel?
- How would your childhood have been different had your parents subscribed to the Law of Chemistry? How would your own couple be different (or, if you're single, how would past relationships have been different)?

CHEMISTRY AND THE NEW COUPLE

The New Couple is definitely the choosy couple. Whether they realize they're doing it or not, in trolling for lifelong partners they're looking beyond attributes to energies; indeed, they're looking for a lover-as-best-friend. Self-inquiry has taught them a lot, not just about themselves but also about what they require in a mate: they've learned from deep rapport with *self* that they must insist on deep rapport with *another*—and nothing less. Because they've reached that realization, New Couples are willing to make the necessary investment in time. And because they've elevated their own intuition to the status of primary guiding force—at least equal to the intellect—they're great at detecting chemistry. It's that gut reaction they're waiting for, that moment of recognition that tells them without a doubt, *This is the one with whom I'm going to spend the rest of my life.*

Staying Singularly Busy: Two Interpretations

Using the chemistry yardstick to find someone who's got the right measurements can test one's mettle. There were times when Nanette got exasperated and confused. "Maybe I'm suffering from severe perfectionism—or delusions about the existence of a heavenly half," she mused. Boris also tried to get his head around the long wait: "It seemed that the fussier I was, the lonelier I was setting myself up to be." In the end, though, each held fast. The wait was to Nanette's credit, for she exemplified healthy pickiness. Boris, though, was another story: representing the opposite end of the spectrum, he thought he was exercising discernment but in reality was simply scared single.

Instinctively, Nanette knew that the worst thing for her self-esteem was to remain idle. So, "in the meantime" (as she thought of it), she threw herself into the discovery of her mission in life and came up with a winner. Over an eight-year period, she dreamed up and implemented a successful multidisciplinary program to help homeless families get back on their feet. Now Nanette is busy writing a book on the subject. "But I'm dangerously distracted," she said, beaming at François, the divorced minister she met last year. "And boy, do we have chemistry—and everything else! Good thing I didn't cut back on my specifications!" Yet the

brand-new couple is realistic too. Their third getaway together took them
to a weekend workshop for couples. "We're learning to resolve conflict
before it resolves our chemistry," François said with a laugh.

During his run-up to relationship, Boris, like Nanette, built himself
a wonderfully rich life. He crafted custom guitars and then traveled the
world to deliver his masterpieces in person. "You don't have to play guitar to be picky," the notoriously fussy single used to say with a wink.
But after five years, his friends were starting to give him grief—and he
wondered himself if something wasn't amiss. "I was super-attracted to
this singer I met in Europe last year," he said in his first counseling meeting. "We had espresso in a busy café. It felt as if we were the only people
in all of Florence. Graciella was so beautiful, and obviously interested in
following up—but I ducked out. I'd convinced myself it was just a summer adventure."

It didn't take long for the artisan to see that his problem was fear of
intimacy, a common symptom of deficit self-love. Boris wasn't waiting
for the woman with whom he'd "have it all"; on the contrary, he was
using the standard of true chemistry as an excuse to avoid relationship
altogether. The underlying issues were complex. The twenty-seven-year-
old had already had his heart shattered once—in college, at the hands of
a visiting professor. The affair had caused a scandal to which the adminis-
tration had responded decisively: he had been sent to the school shrink;
she had been sent back to South America.

Overinvolvement with his reclusive and moody younger sister also
weighed heavy on his psyche. Boris had taken care of her since their
childhood, their parents having been emotionally and often physically
absent, and she'd moved into his flat as soon as she finished high school.
Though he loved her deeply, it wasn't appropriate for him to have been
put in the position of parenting her. Naturally, the experience had
drained him over the years, and had predisposed him to feel responsible
for her—which he *still* did. Therapy helped Boris see that meeting the
woman of his dreams represented a huge unconscious threat. Maybe she'd
hurt and embarrass him like his first love, or turn into a burden like the
sister he loved. And who would take care of his sister if his focus moved
elsewhere? Fortunately, once he'd understood that his suspiciously over-
the-top standards were really masking fears, Boris was determined not to
let chemistry pass him by again.

Confused by Chemistry

Seeking someone with whom we have New Couple chemistry is typically a process of experimentation. While this is healthy and necessary, when either sexual or best-friendship chemistry runs unusually high, we can be blinded into believing that we've got both. Sometimes, as in Cassandra's case, discernment can fly out the window, leaving us at serious risk.

After dating Tyrone for two months, Cassandra was smitten—or so, in her lustful state, she thought. "We were born to be together," the twenty-three-year-old graduate student who'd recently received her one-year chip from Narcotics Anonymous said with a sigh. "Tyrone says he's been waiting his whole life to meet me!" Cassandra couldn't talk enough about her new boyfriend, a semi-professional baseball player. Nor could she stop exclaiming over their carnal encounters. "He barely has to touch me," she enthused. "It's as though my entire life disappears."

Things were just as heated up outside this couple's bedroom as they were in it. In fact, within days Tyrone was chasing Cassandra around her place, gripping her wrists and hurling accusations at her. "You're checking out other guys," he'd scream. But like many of us who are capable of losing our senses to sex, Cassandra was caught in the seductive cycle of violence and passionate reconciliation. "It's so cool when we make up," she rationalized. "Tyrone and I always end up back in bed, and then we fly for hours."

One night her girlfriend Isadora dropped in—and witnessed such a horrible scene that she telephoned Cassandra the next day to voice her concern. "That guy is dangerous," Isadora warned. "I don't know how you can put up with him—immobilizing you like that and then refusing to leave your house when you tell him to. You should call the police!"

Cassandra was taken aback; she'd had no idea Tyrone was breaking the law. And until she heard her friend's wise words, she'd always assumed that it was *she* who was driving *him* nuts. Cassandra broke the relationship off with Tyrone and entered counseling. There she came to understand that the intensity of her sexual bond with him affected her like a drug, inducing both highs and lows. That bond not only inured her to the abuse, but also blinded her to her need for other vital connections, such as best-friendship chemistry, essential compatibilities, and (above all) emotional trustworthiness.

Confounded by Friendship

While some of us might find ourselves blinded by chemistry of the sexual variety, others accept relationship without this crucial criterion. This can occur, in part, because the friendship connection is so strong. Usually, though, it's more complicated than that, as Lynne shows us. When she first met Rorey, they spent six hours chatting like two girlfriends. "We had absolutely everything in common; within moments, we could have finished each other's sentences," she recalled fondly. "With my history of going for bad boys, Rorey was a real step up, and I decided to grab him." Actually, she'd known several Roreys in high school. They were always available with a shoulder to cry on when her latest hot guy cheated on her. But when it came to a date, the answer was invariably no. "I'd hate to wreck our friendship," she'd explain, glancing up from under her thick lashes.

Now twenty-six, Lynne was intent on breaking this pattern. Lynne's spiritual orientation included the belief that she could create her own reality with her thoughts. So although Rorey in no way embodied her physical type, she tried to dismiss her disappointment when their first kisses had the feeling of cotton wool. "I know with time I can get into it," she insisted to herself. Secretly, however, she wished that he were gay so she wouldn't have to reject him sexually. They made love, but Lynne always fantasized throughout—about former boyfriends with whom she'd had sexual chemistry and even, eventually, about any stray guys who'd recently caught her fancy.

Lynne hit bottom when she nearly consummated some intense petting with a man she worked with. She couldn't deal with the self-hate that this incident engendered, but she was afraid to let Rorey in on the truth. "I was convinced it would devastate him," she commented later. Soon, however, Lynne would barely let Rorey touch her—and she beat herself up over this too. Lynne felt guilty that she couldn't overcome her aversion to such a great guy, and she considered herself a miserable failure, essentially because she was unable to fabricate sexual chemistry out of thin air.

Finally, Lynne sought therapy to get at the root of what she thought was possibly sexual dysfunction on her part. When her counselor asked whether she'd ever had sexual chemistry before, Lainey replied in the affirmative. "But they were jerks," she said with emphasis. The truth was that Lynne was blinded by her best-friendship chemistry with Rorey—

which rendered her unrealistic with regard to her need for genuine sexual rapport. Additionally, she was overcompensating for her past self-destructive choices—choices that had never been properly analyzed.

Once Lynne understood the roots of her relationship with Rorey, she could master her first lesson in New Couple chemistry—namely, that you can't talk yourself into it. An exceptional sexual connection is a gift; it can't be created through visualization or developed over time *if the initial resonance isn't there.* "Well, I guess it's back to the drawing board," Lynne said, sighing heavily. "Dating does get on my nerves, but at least now I know what I'm looking for, and it's got to be there right up front." The breakup with Rorey was tough, but it freed each of them to fall in love with two special others who thrilled them as both pals *and* lovers.

Out of Touch with Chemistry

While for some of us the big lesson about chemistry is that we must insist on both kinds in order to have a relationship that really sings, there are cases in which the all-telling thrill is present but, for complex reasons, is hard to detect. Partners who find themselves in such a predicament often realize that their current relationship isn't the first one missing special pizzazz. Often, chemistry has eluded them with all their previous lovers as well. In Wilhelm's scenario, a lifetime of dull sex finally alerted him to a chemistry problem.

A civil servant working at an embassy in the Middle East, Wilhelm got on swimmingly with his colleague and new romantic interest, Bettina. "Right," she agreed in the couple's first counseling session together, adding, "everywhere except in bed. He's just going through the motions," Bettina said, her voice cracking. "Sure, we both achieve orgasm, but I don't know. Who's ever heard of seeing stars unilaterally?" The thirty-year-old woman knew that she didn't turn her boyfriend on. And no number of heartfelt protestations on Wilhelm's part could sway Bettina from this conviction. "Maybe there's something off, *really* off, with me," the thirty-two-year-old man suggested shyly.

Soon it was revealed that Wilhelm had never experienced genuine sexual chemistry with anyone. "Barely a couple notches up from masturbation" was how he summed up making love with a partner. And further exploration showed that his experience with solo sex wasn't altogether fulfilling either. Wilhelm discovered that his inability to enjoy exciting sex with the woman he loved was a symptom of a deeper problem: a sexually inappropriate relationship he'd had with an older female cousin while he was growing up. Wilhelm's memory of this relationship, and his realization of its importance, shocked him. It also took a load off his mind. "I can't believe it; I almost completely forgot what Jill used to put me up to as a kid. It really was humiliating." Bettina felt great compassion for her beloved, and the new information gave her hope for their future together—"Though I'd like to give that woman a phone call to remember," she added.

Wilhelm was referred to several sex-abuse specialists before he found one with whom he felt really compatible. Then he worked alone, and sometimes with Bettina, to heal the past and learn how to be with another person safely and sensually in the present. But Wilhelm is still frustrated. "I wish there'd been someone who could've told me about this stuff earlier. I've been blaming myself for so long—and missing out big time with my sweetheart. Just think: I might even have lost her!"

We were pleased to be able to shed light on this problem for Wilhelm and Bettina (and for the numerous other couples we've seen who've struggled with this issue). To our dismay, however, an untold number of partners and individuals alike continue to suffer unsatisfactory sex lives—and even sexual proclivities that worry and upset them—because of undiagnosed but highly treatable sexual abuse in their past. Though Wilhelm was lucky enough to recall the hurtful incidents from his youth, a large percentage of those with such problems find that the wounding events are beyond conscious recall. This leaves the symptoms alone to bear witness. Until the trauma is resolved, those symptoms linger on, wreaking havoc in their intimate lives and blocking the ecstatic experience of deep emotional and sexual connection with even the most trustworthy, attractive mates.

Just as sexual chemistry can, for some of us, defy detection, so too can we lack that gut-level knowing that this other person is the one, *even though he or she actually is.* Lars had been dating Minnie for nearly two years but blamed himself for what he thought was the terrible truth: "I love her, but I'm not *in love* with her," he stated flatly in his initial individual session. "I don't know if I've ever really loved anybody, come to think of it." And yet the couple had terrific sexual chemistry. "I'm really into her," he said. "She's special that way." It was the thirty-three-year-old cell-phone

technician's first time in counseling—he'd agreed to go at Minnie's prodding—but the issue wasn't chemistry. Throughout the last eight months,
he'd been waking them both up in the middle of the night, hollering.
Minnie would lovingly nudge him awake, then hold him until he fell
back to sleep. "She's a wonderful person," he said fondly, "a real angel."
The nightmare was always the same: Lars was ten years old, being chased
out of his childhood home and into the snow, barefoot, by an unseen foe.

As months passed and his personal work deepened, Lars began moving through some old, pent-up fears. Most of them were associated with
the brutal late-night treatment meted out to him over the years by several of his mother's many boyfriends. Lars was grateful when his nightmares ceased. And then something unexpected happened. "Minnie
walked up to me in a mall where we'd set a rendezvous," he reported. "I
looked at her as though for the very first time. My eyes filled with tears. I
said to myself, *I'm crazy about this woman!*"

As Lars deepened his relationship with himself, his bond with
Minnie intensified. Eventually they were both able to bask in the New
Couple chemistry that was their birthright. If you doubt your capacity
to enjoy chemistry with anyone, perhaps unfinished business from the
past is clogging your lines. In that case, immerse yourself in the Law of
Transformational Education. With a bit of diving, you—like Lars and
Wilhelm—might find the special energies that are there for your love,
swirling right under the surface.

When we start out as two highly selective individuals, take the time for
market research, and choose by design, not default, we're practicing the
fine art of intentional mate selection; and, whether we realize it or not,
we're also taking the first step toward becoming a New Couple. Committing to each other based on a recognition of chemistries, compatibilities,
and emotional trustworthiness guarantees that we'll have everything we
need to be absolute and lifelong best friends, not to mention co-adventur-
ers, possible co-parents, and who knows what else. For New Couple
chemistry is creative, healing, and transformational. Still, whether we wait
for the deluxe package or nab the next person who comes down the pike,
each one of our loves functions as a powerful teacher (though sometimes
the lesson is about what we *don't* want in a partner or how we need to
love ourselves more).

But don't we all deserve to spend our lives with someone with whom we can disarm our sexual weapons—our games and tricks and wiles—once and for all, putting them on the table? And don't we all deserve to climb into bed every night with a special soul who really lights our sexual fire? That's why it's wise to remember that if we get tangled up with a person with whom we're short on chemistry, the seat's taken; there'll be no spot for the real beloved when he or she comes along.

So, whether it's already happened or is yet to be, what do we do once we've made the great connection? First, we must overcome the widespread belief that chemistry inevitably dies—and that there's nothing we can do to stop the demise. For while the high of intoxication does end, and the power struggle will ensue, the good news is that *chemistry itself need never diminish*. Ensuring chemistry's continued presence is what the remaining New Laws of Love are all about. In fact, all ten laws are interdependent, because while we need a bold model of relationship (such as the Ten New Laws of Love) to preserve our chemistry, only chemistry can inspire us to carry out what those laws propose. Chemistry is the force that empowers us to navigate, in good faith, the perils of the power struggle—and ultimately to cruise into co-creativity. Clearly, every ounce of our couple's chemistry is indispensable. And when together we commit to the whole nine yards—that is, the last nine New Laws of Love—we can transform our organic chemistry into couple alchemy and our relationship into gold.

The Key to Chemistry

Insisting on a partner with whom you share *both* sexual passion *and* best friendship is the key to the first New Law of Love.
This means finding a partner who . . .
- Ignites fires of passion
- Is emotionally trustworthy
- Shares any essential compatibilities that are necessary to you

2. PRIORITY
the second new law of love

JULIET: O Romeo, Romeo! wherefore art thou Romeo?
    Deny thy father and refuse thy name;
    Or, if thou wilt not, be but sworn my love,
    And I'll no longer be a Capulet.
ROMEO *{aside}:* Shall I hear more, or shall I speak at this?
JULIET: 'Tis but thy name that is my enemy.
    Thou art thyself, though not a Montague.
    What's Montague? It is nor hand, nor foot,
    Nor arm, nor face, nor any other part
    Belonging to a man. O, be some other name!
    What's in a name? That which we call a rose
    By any other name would smell as sweet.
    So Romeo would, were he not Romeo called,
    Retain that dear perfection which he owes
    Without that title. Romeo, doff thy name;
    And for thy name, which is no part of thee,
    Take all myself.
        WILLIAM SHAKESPEARE, *Romeo and Juliet*

Now that we understand the basics of New Couple chemistry, we have the raw materials necessary to create the relationship we all so want. Our next task is to embrace the idea that good chemistry need never be lost. Our commitment to the next nine New Laws of Love can put us on the path to a lifetime of true togetherness.

The first stepping-stone is the Law of Priority, which is designed to ensure that these special energies don't evaporate during the day-to-day march of our lives. As we've seen, sooner or later even the most perfect new partnership is pulled by developmental tides beyond intoxication and into the power-struggle stage of relationship. Though our love may be deep and strong, disappointments, disillusionments, and discomfort are sure to crop up, either subtly or otherwise. When this happens, most of us respond as if instinctively. Without knowing it ourselves, we start to emotionally withdraw from—and tune out—our beloved other and focus in on something or someone else. These preoccupations seem, for a time, to help. They afford us relief from the pain of our lack of connection and the anxiety caused by problems piling up.

But it can only undermine our love if we follow that unconscious urge to withdraw. This book guides us in defying that urge in order to maintain our chemistry and a balanced focus on our relationship. Not that it ever could or should revert to the all-consuming entity that our relationship was during the intoxication stage. Instead, it ought to develop into a strong, loving crucible in which all the other elements of a joyful life can be forged—a place where self-love and mission in life can be nurtured and draughts of emotional intimacy regularly imbibed.

Who or what might be the symbolic illicit lover that steals the thunder from a precious partnership? Anything—a substance, a behavior, an activity, another person—is a potential culprit. The first challenges to the primacy of love relationships are usually jobs, the people with whom we grew up (that is, our family-of-origin), and favored diversions. Eventually, any of these can crowd out the couple. Of course, other, more visible bedevilments can also snap the connection: these include imbalanced, codependent relationships with people outside the couple, as well as alcohol, drugs, or any other addiction, compulsion, obsession, or psychological problem that rules one or both partners. It's a fact—and a tragically common occurrence—that even the most divinely ordained relationships wilt not only in the presence of such notorious chemistry killers as contempt, violence, and sexual betrayal, but also when exposed to the harshness of behaviors that hurt the individual self. When it comes to the need to make the health of the couple a priority, never has it been more appropriate to say, "Two's company, and three—whether that third is a person, a behavior, an interest, an activity, or a substance—is a crowd."

COMMITMENT WITH A CAPITAL C: THE WORK OF RELATIONSHIP

The Law of Priority asks us to go beyond the reranking of what might be our habitual ordering of things; it even demands more than simply committing to our partner in one of the standard senses—that is, consenting to monogamy, cohabitation, or marriage. More significantly—and this is the revolutionary bit—it requires that we agree upon a new model of relationship, that we become what's described in these pages as a New Couple. Together we vow to apply, to the best of our abilities, the Ten New Laws of Love—to do, in short, *the work of relationship*. This assumes that whatever one of us considers "a couple issue" will be honored as such by the other. Obviously, for any couple, this represents a serious commitment. And once the commitment is made, it takes time (as does any work-in-progress) to unfold.

It's been said that the crisis of our era is one of time. Nevertheless, maintaining the dynamism of our duo can never happen if we don't carve out substantial chunks of this precious commodity for ourselves. This means scheduling quality time for the relationship the way we schedule any other high-priority appointment—that is, using a Day-Timer or Palm Pilot to make dates for romance, heavy talks, general silliness, and the other special activities suggested throughout this book.

An Invitation to Reflect on the Law of Priority

As you approach the exercises in this chapter, remember that the presence or absence of New Couple chemistry profoundly affects a couple's experience with each law.
- Do you make time together a priority? If so, how?
- How does your time together—or lack thereof—make you feel? How does it affect your self-love? Your emotional intimacy?

Usually the deprioritization of a relationship comes about innocently. After two years of cohabitation, Dane and Helena found themselves retreating nightly to separate corners of their duplex. He could talk of nothing but his brutal new boss; she, having lost her father just before she met Dane, was preoccupied with the problems of her widowed mother. Their mutual retreat wasn't a result of animosity; rather, it was a polite attempt to spare each other their woes. Regardless of the kindness of their intentions, the consequence was more and more time spent apart. Helena and Dane hadn't realized that in avoiding airing their stress, they would end up avoiding each other as well. Unhappy with the result, the couple decided to experiment for one week with an after-work walk and talk—twenty minutes allotted to clear away the residue from the day and put the subjects of boss and mother behind them for the evening. It worked. Helena and Dane found not only relief from their worries but also an unexpected intimacy.

Still, some of us are genuinely put off by the notion that *work* is involved in keeping love alive—even if it's work of the growth variety, whose returns are sweet and often immediate. As we noted earlier, all a couple needs for success is chemistry and a willingness to apply the New Laws of Love. But that was too much for Joe, one unhappily employed husband we met with. He put it to us point-blank: "A fifty-hour week is as much hassle as I can handle. If this marriage can't run by itself, I must have picked the wrong person."

This was Joe's version of romantic fantasy, and initially we couldn't convince him otherwise. He rejected the idea that marriage, like any worthwhile collaboration, hits glitches and needs tune-ups, in-services, and training sessions. With his mind shut tight, he spurned any education—not to mention the New Laws of Love—and dropped out of counseling after one session. Months later, to our surprise, Joe came back. He'd had a crisis at work and nearly been fired, and he'd taken out his frustrations on his partner, unfairly blaming her. When she walked out, he walked in, ready to fight for his marriage. It took a crisis of major proportions for Joe to see the wisdom of doing "the work." "I'd never have believed that our relationship could go to a new level," he remarked after two months. "In fact, I didn't even know we were stuck." Perhaps most surprising to him was the cavalcade of new insights he gained about himself and his family-of-origin. As Joe found out, for any of us to get unstuck—much less dance—we've got to be willing to perceive and handle relationship a new way. We've got to do whatever it takes to keep our chemistry alive—*both* of us.

SYNERGY: A ROYAL PAYBACK

Doing the work of relationship doesn't just conserve chemistry, it also potentiates synergy. As systems theorists tell us, the combined potential of a high-functioning dyad is far greater than the simple sum of its two individual parts. But the incredible energy source within a relationship can be tapped only when we make the health of our couple a top priority. The performing arts have long proved the power of the well-tuned team to create masterpieces. Witness the dance wizardry of Fred Astaire and Ginger Rogers and the musical-theater magic of Rodgers and Hammerstein or the Gershwin brothers; consider the legendary alchemy of pop geniuses John Lennon and Paul McCartney, who still have the world humming Beatles tunes many decades after they were hits.

Sally and Howard are superb examples of synergy. These two Gulf War vets could hardly believe the dynamism they wielded as a twosome. When their paths first crossed, long after their tours of duty had ended, Sally and Howard found each other in similar boats: both were disgruntled in dead-end jobs, and both had demons to nurse from the past. Despite the unseaworthiness of these boats, the couple's mutual commitment to building a healthy relationship was able to turn their lives around. The strength of their emotional bond enabled them to deeply support each other and begin picking up the pieces after their shattering experiences in the war, reassembling them into an awesome whole. Within three years, Sally and Howard had co-founded a documentary film production company. When we last saw these courageous two, they were planning to adopt a refugee baby.

It's high time that *all* of us become conscious of—and exploit—the amazing potential of the romantic union. Then we can, like Howard and Sally, use it to launch a joint entrepreneurial endeavor, or (more typically) rely on its power as we support each other's individual mission. Whatever our project—be it career, family, avocation, or creative venture—it has a greater chance of succeeding if it's grounded on the bedrock of a prioritized relationship. There's a lot of excitement and adventure ahead for those who provide that grounding, because the synergy of the New Couple is packed with surprises. Failing to capitalize on this readily available and renewable resource is not only a waste, it's a shame. Those who forfeit love's synergy never know what they could have had, done, or been!

INDIVIDUATION:
GROWING INTO TRUE ADULTHOOD

It might come as a surprise to many that scores of wonderful relationships fall apart every day because, to one degree or another, mates haven't yet emotionally "left the nest." The process of really and truly growing up, of becoming psychological adults vis-à-vis the people we grew up with, is called *individuation*. And although the concept is well known in psychological circles, it has somehow escaped mass consciousness. Individuation isn't about running away from, rebelling against, or cutting ourselves off from our families, as a term such as "leaving the nest" might imply. Unless we've worked through lingering familial problems therapeutically, these are nonsolutions that drain both the individual and the couple.

We can consider ourselves individuated from our family-of-origin—a term that encompasses not only parents, but also siblings and extended family members—when we're no longer driven by the need for their approval or ruled by the fear of disappointing, hurting, or angering them. Individuation represents a shift from familial authority to inner authority. It allows us, as equal and healthy adults, to *choose* whether to accept the guidance and advice of those we grew up with, rather than living under their dominion.

Individuation, like all personal development, is a process. *We don't just jump out of a cab and find ourselves psychological adults.* It's a perennial undertaking—and for some of us it's a real ordeal, because our family-of-origin is the most powerful emotional system we'll ever be part of. The trance of tradition is in full force when it comes to individuation: outmoded and unconscious notions of loyalty—products of long family traditions—hypnotize us. Often they demand that even as adults we say yes (when we mean no) to family requests and go along with expectations reflexively. In short, they ask us to subordinate our personal power.

It simply doesn't occur to some of us that we can negotiate as adult peers with family members. Perhaps we believe, albeit misguidedly, that the benefits of a high level of involvement with parent figures—be the involvement financial or otherwise—outweigh whatever damage that involvement might do to our couple relationship. Whatever the reason, we perpetuate our roles as eldest child, bad boy, dutiful daughter, rescuing sister, baby of the family, responsible grandson, or attentive nephew and end up double-bound—torn between family and spouse—and stuck in an emotional web of guilt, responsibility, and obligation. Unindividuated relationship thus mimics classic codependence, though it's specific to family members.

No matter how you slice it, *individuation is about setting clear and healthy boundaries with our families.* It requires, first, that we become conscious when we're feeling burdened, disempowered, or disrespected by family members or are acting out of guilt, obligation, or fear. It then demands that we formulate a clear understanding about what we really want from and with family members. Finally, it asks us to lovingly assert our wishes, putting our new understanding into practice.

Cathy silently struggled with the expectations of her wealthy great-uncle. With the support of her husband, she finally succeeded in putting her foot down, halting the onslaught of his "subtle" warnings that time was short for delivery of the nieces and nephews he was so eager to hold (and to pass his fortune on to). And he didn't write her out of his will—something she couldn't have foreseen with any certainty, given his broad hints about heirs.

Benjamin and his wife finally had to move out of his grandmother's neighborhood because the old woman was unable to resist telling his wife how to raise their two children. Though they still miss her blueberry pies, the new sense of space—of being captains of their own ship—has proved to be a source of bonding.

Illuminating and untying unconscious entanglements with parents, siblings, and other family members allows us to emerge simultaneously into adulthood *and* selfhood. It sets the stage for a new kind of exchange with our family-of-origin—ideally, an exchange in which we enjoy equal status as peers. We're able to look parents in the eye and welcome the wisdom of their years. They, in turn, can appreciate and possibly benefit from the insights and innovations of our times. Most important, as Judit and Jacob learned in due time, cutting the psychic apron strings allows for—indeed, is a prerequisite for—true partnership within the couple.

Coming to Terms with Our Parents

When Judit and Jacob met that hot summer on a kibbutz, Jacob's father had just left his mother for a junior doctor on staff at his teaching hospital. But that didn't stop the twenty-three-year-olds from having the summer of their lives and falling deeply in love. Never had either imagined it possible to be so passionate with someone who felt so much like an old friend. "To me," Jacob marveled, "it felt as though we were almost the same person." By day, between chores, they'd compose poetry in secret. By night, they'd hit the backroads, heading straight for the Dead Sea. There, under a canopy of stars, the young lovers would picnic—and recite their fresh creations. "It always seemed like the daylight would never end," Judit recalled. "Just getting through dinner was torture. And our lovemaking—oh, my God!" The pair went straight back to Detroit after their stint on the kibbutz, marrying posthaste.

Though they delighted in their married state, all was not bliss. Jacob felt, as they settled into their new apartment, as though his parents' divorce had been lying in wait; it knocked the wind right out of him, he said. But even this crisis only seemed to deepen their emotional trust— at least initially. Too soon, however, their sweet newlywed life turned sour: in fact, it began turning around his mother, Suzannah.

"I was the one who invited her to move into the neighborhood," Judit offered. "She was so broken-down and needy. At the time, it just seemed like the right thing to do." Jacob began medical school soon after Suzannah's move. Judit, who had been looking for a job as a nurse, ended up caring for her mother-in-law instead. "It was like a ritual," said the young woman. "Every night, Suzannah would come for dinner. She was actually very kind and maternal," Judit conceded. "*She* wasn't the problem. The problem was Jacob; he just wasn't there anymore. He barely noticed me, even in bed. At first I assumed it was school, but it wasn't. It was her. No matter how much he did for his mother, he always felt guilty that he wasn't doing more."

From their lengthy conversations at the kibbutz and her many conversations with Suzannah, Judit realized that Jacob's preoccupation with his mother's well-being hadn't begun with her divorce. He'd unconsciously taken on this "job" long ago, as a little boy. Judit and Jacob were ripe for a New Couple makeover and an introduction to the second New Law of Love.

Wallace and Lulu tangled with individuation much sooner in their relationship than Judit and Jacob did. The issue first came up during the early part of the intoxication stage of their relationship, on the occasion of his first invitation to dinner at Lulu's parents' house. Wallace was particularly eager to meet the father to whom his new girlfriend seemed so close. While Wallace found him to be jovial and welcoming, some of the older man's nonverbal communication with Lulu struck him as odd. Several times during and after the elaborate dinner prepared in his honor, Wallace noticed that Lulu and her father shared long gazes he could only describe as romantic. On the drive home, Wallace pulled no punches: "What's up with the way you and your father look at each other?" he asked. "It's almost as though you two were going out or something," he explained, loosening the knot on his tie. Lulu looked confused. "What I have with Daddy is special," she responded. "You couldn't be jealous, could you?" she asked, laughing incredulously.

As Wallace pursued the issue in a coaching session for couples, the complexity of Lulu's family dynamic began to emerge. As he'd suspected, the flavor of his new partner's relationship with her father *was* subtly romantic. "Come to think of it, Dad looks at me the same way Grandma looks at him," Lulu said thoughtfully, realizing that on her father's side of the family, the style of loving across genders bordered on the romantic. "It's true," Lulu conceded with a sigh, visibly relieved to have this dysfunction revealed. "I've felt very strange about my father's attention since I was a child. It's as though I were somehow responsible for him or he needed something from me." Wallace was grateful that he'd decided to make an issue of what he'd seen that night. And he admired Lulu's courage. He knew that many partners in similar families would be loathe to look at the patterns on the familial underbelly, perhaps not realizing that doing so would allow them to resuscitate their chemistry. Wallace said later, "My honesty really paid off. It gave Lulu permission to reveal how she felt, and I can't help but feel prized."

Wallace teaches us that when it comes to matters of individuation, a mate's powers of observation are invaluable. (There's no telling, though, whether spousal feedback will stir us like a refreshing breeze or jolt us like a knock on the head.) Mates are often far more objective about our family-of-origin than we are. As we like to tell the couples we work with, fish are the last ones to know they're swimming in water, much less that the water might be polluted! Just as fish in a tainted tank might assume that water everywhere is purple, we might assume that families everywhere function just like ours—that, for instance, everyone yells at each other or barges in on each other in the bathroom, that all fathers drink a six-pack after work, or that, like Hannah, all married women make an obligatory phone call a day to parents.

Though the meddlesome in-law is a well-known marriage cliché, Hannah was unaware that she dragged precisely this kind of bugaboo from her family-of-origin into her couple. The intense involvement she'd had with her parents up through her adult life continued uninterrupted right into the intoxication stage of her relationship with Yves. Predictably, this issue became the main ingredient of their power struggle, which lasted for years—through the birth of their children and beyond. Eventually, after affairs on both sides had all but drained their trust, they even sank to enlisting their kids directly in their conflict by speaking disparagingly to them about each other.

Although they first approached us for help in "uncoupling," fate smiled down on these two, largely because the "crimes" each had committed against their marriage were similar enough to place them on an almost level playing field. Hannah stated her goal earnestly: "We want to stop hurting each other and spare the kids—to break up, you know, *amicably*." Yves's first words, however, were far less mature. "I *hate* her parents," he stated bluntly. "Hannah can't make the slightest decision without consulting them. From the very beginning, she'd spend hours of our *romantic* weekends with them on the phone." Yves didn't hide the irony as he uttered the word *romantic*. Hannah looked affronted. "But they were devastated when I moved out of the house," she said defensively. "I was the baby, their whole focus in life. Yves just doesn't understand them."

We could see that Yves had shared the nuptial bed with his in-laws long enough. Hannah's partner, relegated to third place after her parents, felt deeply betrayed by her continued allegiance to her family-of-origin. And yet Hannah didn't see things that way. Like so many mates in her position, she thought that the problem lay with Yves; she blamed him for being unwilling to indulge her parents. She was totally blind to her principal problem—the fact that she was the unwitting victim of a stupendous guilt trip by both her parents, who alternately badgered and begged her to give them "a reason to live." They knew no different either, of course, since their own parents' "love" had ruled their lives. Still, in her completely unindividuated state, Hannah was unable to feel the injustice of their expectations and set healthy limits. She continued to

play the outdated role of dutiful daughter, and it seemed that she'd protect her parents to the bitter end.

It's because her own situation was so familiar to Hannah that she
couldn't see how her relationship with her parents was hurting her—and
her relationship with Yves. (Another case of purple water!) And yet the
hurt was there: Hannah's lack of boundaries with her parents collapsed
her marriage—or nearly did. But Hannah came through in the crunch.
When her parents, having heard about the couple's first session and
their intention to divorce, commended her decision to "leave that man,"
Hannah finally reached the boiling point. A lifetime of suppressed but
healthy anger found its first true expression: "I'm a married adult
woman," she announced to them with as much compassion as she could
muster. "I love you and I'll always honor you as my parents, but Yves is
my husband."

With these daring words, Hannah committed her first conscious act
of individuation from her parents. Yves was floored. She went through
with the breakup all right—she divorced her parents! With this first
boundary firmly in place, she and Yves were then free to take the next
step: together, they designed and scripted a special ceremony and
renewed their vows to each other. They embarked on the process of healing their bruised union and got down to the exciting business of creating
the shared life that they'd always envisioned.

While many men and women fail to complete the individuation
process, Hannah's case is an example of *extreme* parental domination.
According to the model presented by Dr. Patricia Love in her book *The
Emotional Incest Syndrome,* Hannah is a textbook example of the "chosen
child"—and as such, a victim of what Love calls "emotional incest."
Nonsexual in nature (at least in Hannah's case), this incestuous dynamic
is characterized by emotional rather than physical invasiveness.

"He Ain't Heavy, He's My Brother"

Equally important is restructuring and balancing our relationships with
our siblings. Sometimes "sibs" help us with this endeavor; sometimes
they sabotage us. Usually, though, it's a mix. And there's no question
that shucking certain roles—a much-cherished role as big sis or kid
brother, for example—can involve labor pangs and downright fear.

Hank ought to know. He openly admitted loving his younger brother Chico more than himself. "I've always been there for him," he told us during his first couple session with his girlfriend, Eleanor. "And thank God for that, because our parents never were." But Eleanor's initial sympathy had run its course long before they came to us. "He calls you at four in the morning, owes you thousands of dollars, and now wants you to cosign a personal loan," she responded with exasperation. "What about the down payment for our house?"

Ever the baby of the family, Chico still had Hank seduced. "I'm just waiting for the big deal," Hank quoted him as saying frequently, with a promise for everyone in his voice. Chico always had a scheme for getting rich quick—along with a criminal record for forgery and fraud. Despite Chico's troubles with the law, he could always sell an idea to Hank, who played the stable, solvent straight man to his brother's con.

Hank realized for the first time, as he talked to us about his situation, that what he'd seen as taking care of his younger brother was actually allowing himself to be exploited by a man unwilling to grow up and take responsibility for his own life. Hank went home, called his "little bro," and said no. During the six months after he put the beneficent-brother role to rest, he didn't hear a word from Chico. And yet his guilt persisted. "I just wish I could shake this feeling that I've let him down," he told us.

Though Hank readily saw the irrationality of his self-condemnation, the feelings of guilt and the anxiety about being rejected lingered. They're feelings that must be faced by anyone who embraces the process of individuation—faced and ridden out. Ironically, these very feelings—guilt, anxiety, and a sadness akin to grief—are often signals that growth vis-à-vis brothers, sisters, parents, extended family members, and even old friends is taking place. "I guess there was no other solution," Hank sadly told us during our last session. "I know I wasn't helping either one of us before—and it wasn't fair to Eleanor."

Even when becoming peers with brothers and sisters takes a less dramatic form, it can still feel like a big deal. Julie, for example, planned to tell her older sister that she and her husband wanted to hold the Kwanza celebration at her house this year. When she picked up the phone, however, her hand was shaking. Eric, another candidate for individuation, decided that for the health of his love life he had to confront his older brother. With much trepidation, he set an ultimatum: "If you don't stop teasing me about my past girlfriends, I won't visit you with Ann anymore."

Initiating Individuation

Whether individuation involves separating from parents or from siblings and other family members, it's a rite of passage parents probably weren't designed to initiate. Unless our parents came from another planet—someplace where they were taught how to psychologically nudge their offspring out of the nest—the work is up to us. Leaping into adulthood *with* our parents' consent is the ultimate act of maturity. *Without that consent,* acknowledging and addressing individuation issues can be the toughest task of our adult life. In fact, at times it may seem that individuation couldn't possibly have been intended to be accomplished in a single lifetime. Still, we must break the spell of our role as child and begin to grow ourselves up—whatever it takes. One of the processes at the heart of the New Couple model, individuation is an integral dimension of the work of relationship. And the importance of supporting each other to this end can't be overstated. If individuation problems have already caused acrimony in your couple, it's critical that you address and heal them. Fortunately, the skills you'll be learning as we discuss the next eight New Laws of Love will provide all the help you'll need. With those skills, you'll find that flying the coop of your family-of-origin, essential to the process of prioritizing your relationship, is empowering and bond-strengthening. Though it's a daunting task, you could be in for a surprise: individuation can ultimately prove liberating for everyone—even those from whom you've separated.

Though it's been a long haul, in our couple we've helped each other become aware of unhealthy patterns in a wide variety of outside relationships. Today we enjoy an incredibly loving and supportive community of family and friends, many old and many new. The powerful process of individuation has resulted in tremendous personal empowerment and has helped us maintain the sweetness of our bond.

An Invitation to Reflect on the Law of Priority

- Are you performing family roles that burden, disempower, or disrespect you? If so, with whom, and what roles?
- What might motivate you to do this?
- How does playing old roles make you feel? How does it affect your self-love? Your emotional intimacy?

Pointers for Achieving Individuation from Family-of-Origin

Individuation means setting clear and healthy boundaries with all members of your family, for the health of your relationship. As we saw earlier, it demands a commitment to . . .

- Become conscious when you're feeling burdened, disempowered, or disrespected by family members or are acting out of guilt, obligation, or fear
- Formulate a clear understanding about what you really want from and with family members
- Lovingly assert your wishes, putting your new understanding into practice

ADDICTIONS AND COMPULSIONS: THE PRICE OF PAYING HOMAGE TO THE GOD OF AVOIDANCE

When one or both partners suffer from any addiction or compulsion, the beloved other always ends up playing second fiddle. Everything in the addict's (or compulsive's) life is subordinated to the continuance of the addiction (or compulsion) of choice.

Addictions and compulsions are defined as repeated behaviors that cause harm to one or more of the core areas of adult life—namely, health, livelihood, *and primary relationships.* Addicts and those suffering from compulsivity may or may not be aware of either the behaviors or the harm they cause. But even when they *are* aware, all their attempts at control fail. This out-of-control quality—a blending of powerlessness and self-destructiveness—is the essence of addiction. *It's despair made manifest.* Eventually, both addiction and compulsion render life unmanageable. In intimate relationships, they function like black holes, ruthlessly inhaling chemistry and vaporizing trust.

It's helpful to separate addictions into two major types, *substance* and *process.* Substance addictions involve something consumable, such as alcohol, drugs, or food. Process addictions, on the other hand, involve activities rather than substances; the major process addictions are work, sex, and gambling. Although it's possible to ruin our lives and relationships overdoing *anything,* including working out, spending, earning, watching television, using the computer, playing video games, caregiving, and being absorbed in activity in general, these are usually considered compulsions—lesser beasts—rather than true process addictions. Again, the litmus test for all these is self-destructiveness—that is, a negative impact on health, livelihood, and/or primary relationships—in combination with a lack of control. Whatever name we give the above behaviors, all have the potential to destroy a love relationship.

Ask Robin. Her boyfriend, Leo, was fascinated by every aspect of his computer system: games, business applications, the latest hardware. His newest obsession, however, eclipsed all the rest: "I love to surf the Net," Leo confessed. "I can get lost for hours, browsing through the world's data banks, chatting with hundreds of people, or just seeing what's new." Robin knew this only too well.

"Yes, he gets so lost I can never find him anymore," she replied with daggers. "Sometimes he doesn't call me for days. In fact, he was up all night twice last week. Frankly, I can't see how he can function at work— except that he goes on-line there too." What it came down to was this: Leo was mainlining on-line. It took some work for him to admit that his "hobby" wasn't just a passion—it was a compulsion. And because of it, his life was becoming truly unmanageable. Robin, proving her intelligence and self-love, used the support of a therapeutic session to deliver the bottom line to her beau: "You're already married, Leo—to the monitor. I adore you, but I have to put you on notice: this town isn't big enough for both AOL and me."

When we stay in a relationship with a nonrecovering addict, an untreated mentally ill person, or a criminal—neglecting our own wishes and needs—we fall into the classification of *codependents* or *enablers*. We literally *enable* our partner to continue the process of self-destruction, simply by our willingness to maintain a relationship despite his or her behavior. Surprisingly, our denial about the seriousness of the problem can be even more vehement than that of the so-called sick person. Both denials are often fatal to love and always inimical to recovery. Our "support" prevents addicts from hitting bottom—that point at which, finally, the addiction or compulsion causes more problems or pain than it helps avoid. Hitting bottom is a necessary first step in any genuine recovery process.

Sheila, a gifted professional speaker, had been blacking out on alcohol throughout her ten-year relationship with Ernest. Her history included two detoxes, revolving-door attendance at AA, and even several intoxicated appearances on stage. She had become persona non grata to half her friends and family members. In fact, the only person who'd hung in with her for the duration was Ernest. But even his limit had been reached.

"I've blamed myself long enough," he told us, resignation in his voice. "I'm not putting myself between Sheila and her death wish anymore. If she dies, I'll just have to live with the guilt." It wasn't until Sheila, registering a blood-alcohol level of point-two percent, hit a pedestrian with his company car and caused Ernest to lose his job and hit his own rock bottom that he was able to admit *his* addiction—to Sheila.

"It's weird, but it really is *my* problem: I'm a soft touch for those good-looking crash-and-burn types . . . no pun intended." Ernest decided that he'd had enough "excitement" and committed to three Al-Anon meetings per week. (Al-Anon involves support groups for those in relationship with addicts.) "Sheila is staying at her sister's for a month, and I'm keeping the focus on me," he said. "It's taken me so long to really understand what you meant when you said I needed to learn to take care of myself."

Ernest now runs on the beach every day with his gorgeous Bernese mountain dog, and his life is on a steady upward trend. "Sheila has earned her six-month chip at AA," he announced to us with an increasingly typical detachment. "But far more important," he said with a wink, "is my *own* chip—from Al-Anon."

Truth be told, we're *all* compulsive about certain things, a little nuts about others. It's only a matter of degree. People with addictions can be warm, loving, generous, and charming. More often than not—some addiction experts say there's a definite correlation—addictive personalities are highly creative and often spiritually inclined. But like the temporary high of a chemical substance, their condition—as long as they're still out of recovery—renders them incapable of sustaining chemistry of any sort, even if they're otherwise doing the work of relationship. This is because their primary relationship is to the substance or process that holds them in its grip.

In terms of priority, nothing threatens a couple like the inferno of untreated addiction, mental illness, criminality, and codependence. The drama these disorders engender is pervasive in couples and lies at the heart of much of our work with them. Unless both parties commit to a professional or Twelve-Step group recovery program, couples born in addiction are doomed. Even though some of us might be able to stop "using" without this kind of help, we typically fall into the "white knuckling" syndrome when we do so (a brittle, anxious state known also as "dry drunkenness"); alternatively, we may transfer to another addiction or simply self-destruct in a different way. The good news is that we've worked with many couples in recovery who've succeeded. In time, many of them have transformed themselves and their relationship, reemerging into some of our most stellar New Couples.

An Invitation to Reflect on the Law of Priority

- Are you concerned about your use of any particular substance or that any particular behavior is out of control?
- If so, how does this make you feel? And how does this use of substance or this behavior affect your self-love? Your emotional intimacy?

Sex and Love Addictions

The newest kids on the recovery block—addictions to sex and love— assume many faces. Though the more far-out forms—embellished with all sorts of other kinks—have been amply hyped on television talk shows, the unsensational, often subtle (yet inevitably unraveling) effects of these addictions on true love aren't discussed nearly enough. In fact, many couples routinely tolerate, ignore, or dismiss as inconsequential the manifestations of these disorders.

There's a lot of misinformation and mythology surrounding both sex and love addictions. The first category, sex addiction, for example, isn't the exclusive domain of the clichéd "sex maniac" or "nympho"—the one who seems to want to "do it" all the time with anything that walks—as many might think. Sex addiction covers a wide range of behaviors and preoccupations of a sexual nature. Some sex addictions are deviant, such as the behavior of pedophiles and your garden-variety flasher in a rain-coat; some are not, such as the desire to have oral sex four times a day. Some sex addictions are acted out, such as that of the man who actually *has* oral sex four times a day, every day; and some are not, such as that of the woman who merely fantasizes about sexual acts in the boardroom with her assistant. In his groundbreaking book *Out of the Shadows: Understanding Sexual Addiction,* Dr. Patrick Carnes characterizes sex addiction as fixation on sexual thoughts or compulsive repetition of sexual behaviors. Like all addictions, sex addictions are out of control, whether the sufferer admits it or not. Partners thus afflicted aren't bad people; rather, they're symptomatic and need treatment. Almost invariably, they themselves were victimized as children in ways that their present idiosyncrasies echo, although the memories might not be accessible to them.

The second category, love addiction, is a two-headed beast. One aspect hooks people on romance; the other, on relationship. Hardly the realm of the hopeless romantic, there's nothing sweet or cute about all-consuming preoccupations that preclude real feeling. A typical romance addict compulsively seeks that ecstatic, sentimental moment—be it the candle-lit dinner or dancing in the moonlight. While this might seem merely corny—not the stuff of true disorder—romance addiction is no Camelot: as you'll see, it's an emotional disorder with real costs.

Romance addicts' first cousins, those who get high on a relationship, commonly feed on the thrill of the intoxication stage of coupledom and fly from person to person in this quest. One well-known form of this malaise is serial monogamy. Is it the same as codependence? Not at all. Relationship addicts are into the newness of the next intimate encounter. Codependents are addicted to a certain style of relating whereby their own essential needs are subordinated. Some overlap exists, however, in that both relationship addicts and codependents obsess over other people to distract themselves from their own problems.

Pablo and Ted, four years a couple, were committed to a monoga-mous union. It was a well-thought-out decision, one that went beyond their healthy fear of contracting HIV and the desire to consecrate their strong feelings for each other. This couple was enlightened to the fact that sex outside the relationship would destroy their emotional intimacy and trust—qualities that were precious to them. But despite their close-ness, Ted and Pablo wrestled with the nature of their commitment. Ted, it turned out, was still close to a number of his ex-lovers. He was a mover and shaker in the hospitality industry, and his highly social post made it easy for him to entertain his former partners—which he did regularly.

Pablo said that it hadn't bothered him at first. Gradually, though, it had begun to eat away at him. "I don't know why I feel jealous," he said in the couple's first session. "I know Ted isn't sleeping with these guys, but something just doesn't feel right." Pablo insisted that his partner was "different" when he came home from one of his soirees, but it was hard for him to hold on to that conviction when it seemed so petty. "I guess it's just me," he concluded ruefully.

Ted, for his part, was fed up. "Oh, come on!" he erupted. "They're just *friends*. It would be different if we lived in New York, where all *your* exes live." But these two were seriously committed to working the nitty-gritty, and by hour's end Ted came clean. "An elegant meal, the hushed voices, the furtive flashing of eyes—doesn't everyone find that irresistible? Come to think of it," he turned suddenly to his lover, "I'd absolutely *kill* you if I thought you were up to such fun with someone else! I wouldn't care how *over* your relationship was!"

Thus did this New Couple begin their journey. It was a shock for Ted to learn that he was under the spell of a classic romance addiction, although once he understood it, he was convinced that it applied more to his mother than to himself. Since he placed his relationship with Pablo in unreserved first place in his life, Ted was willing to join a group for gay romance addicts. With some help from us, the two also successfully drafted agreements they could both live comfortably with for social encounters.

Luckily for them, this couple in recovery had what is called a "high bottom"; in other words, fundamental trust was still intact when they took remedial action. Pablo's unhappiness with his mate's habit was enough to catalyze the process of recovery. As is often the case in addiction-ridden relationships, the codependent had to make the first move. And he did. By respecting his own feelings of discomfort and possessing the wisdom to seek professional help, he achieved damage control and ultimately turned the tide of this couple's future.

In this case (but typically as well), the confrontation of an addiction—which, remember, for couples is a crisis of priority—resulted in greater closeness than the couple had ever known before. Specifically, what sprang up for Pablo and Ted was a new interest in their childhoods; together, they delved into their pasts as both sought to understand the forces that had made them what they were as men and lovers.

Though confronting addiction is necessary for recovery, sex and love addictions are particularly susceptible to the "I know, but . . ." syndrome, in which the codependent partner "knows" (but doesn't *know*) that his or her partner is acting out a sex or love addiction. The partner with the addiction might, say, be in the habit of renting sexy videos or taking long lunches with his secretary; she might have "a thing" about flirting with the guys at the tennis courts or going clubbing with "the girls," leaving her husband at home with the kids. And the codependent partner plays dumb, first fostering and then accepting the pretense that all is as it should be. Yet even if not a word is said about these "minor enjoyments," they're not without consequence. They put hairline cracks in the most precious part of our intimate relationship: emotional trust. The sooner we can all be honest about such issues, the better.

So why do we intimates lie to ourselves? Why do we ignore or pardon behaviors by our partners that, on a deep level, really hurt us? How could we let "minor indiscretions," actions that might be symptoms of compulsivity around sex and love, slide—until it's too late? Maybe it's because we're all still treading the wake of the sexual revolution. It's become almost a matter of political correctness to be "cool" about the subject of sex. In an attempt not to appear petty, puritanical, uptight, controlling, or jealous, we allow a benign tolerance to take hold; we minimize how we feel about these "little" issues, even when they devastate us.

Furthermore, and perhaps this is the more generic explanation, even the slightest inkling of the existence of an addiction or compulsion (of any sort) bodes ill for a relationship. If it's our modus operandi to sweep things under the carpet generally, we'll surely deadbolt in the cellar of our unconscious every harbinger of something as heavy as an addiction. And yet addictions are even *more* likely to spell curtains for the relationship when the acting-out persons—both the addict and the codependent—refuse to admit that there's a problem and commit to recovery.

Confronting addiction is always frightening, especially for the addict. As whistleblowers, we must meet our partner's initial paralysis and denial in the face of an addiction with the greatest compassion and patience. But warn we must: unaddressed sex and love addictions cannot be ignored with impunity. The sense of betrayal always builds up within the codependent, becoming a peril of even greater magnitude—one that threatens to drain the lifeblood of our partnership.

Sometimes even the most egregious behaviors continue unchallenged and unabated under the nose of an insecure spouse. Enrique's secret burst with his briefcase. While walking on a city street with his wife, Jennifer, he was jostled by a fellow pedestrian. The briefcase opened with an ominous click and dumped the contents at their feet: a cache of pornographic magazines and videos. In her ignorance about the nature of addiction—and of the misogyny that underpins the "appreciation" of degrading images of women—Jennifer blamed herself. "I'm not sexually appealing anymore" was her conclusion. Finally, at her sister's prodding, she agreed to see their parish priest for help. An enlightened clergyman, schooled in counseling and addiction theory, he drew Enrique out from the shadows.

This addict's life had truly become unmanageable: the patronage of adult bookstores and sex clubs, the unsafe sex in brothels, and the debts the couple owed as a result—Jennifer finally saw and understood all these. When the downward spiral of addiction was finally interrupted by unintended disclosure, Enrique experienced a wave of crushing shame—and then, to his astonishment, tremendous relief. He followed up with a regimen of daily Sex and Love Addicts Anonymous (SLAA) meetings and entered weekly psychotherapy.

"Sure, I'm stunned by his sex addiction, the woman-hating, and all the lies," Jennifer said in session. "But I'm more horrified by what it says about me. How could I have been so unaware?" Jennifer had a chance to explore her blindness in a weekly group she joined for spouses of sex addicts. There it became crystal clear to her that as the daughter of two alcoholic parents, she was virtually set up to fall for and then play the benighted codependent to an addict of one stripe or another.

This inspiring couple needed to be apart before they could come together again as healthy individuals. They spent their solo sabbaticals continuing to immerse themselves in personal work, including, for each, separate attendance at weeklong healing intensives. They knew what was ahead—no less than from-the-ground-up rebuilding of trust that had been reduced to smithereens.

THE SHADOW SIDE OF WORK

You do not need to leave your room.
Remain sitting at your table and listen.
Do not even listen, simply wait.
Do not even wait, be quite still and solitary.
The world will freely offer itself to you to be unmasked.
It has no choice, it will roll in ecstasy at your feet.

FRANZ KAFKA, *The Great Wall of China:*
Stories and Reflections

While for almost any couple the need to earn a living is inescapable—and pursuit of a mission in life is always a worthy goal—work can conceal a double edge. If prioritized over the relationship, our worldly business can take on the proportions of an addiction or compulsion. Workaholism is defined by Dr. Christian Komor, stress expert and author of *The Power of Being,* as compulsively doing what we think we should do instead of what we choose to do. Along with all its derivatives, including type-A behavior, hurry sickness, perfectionism, and compulsive activity, this syndrome has become a massive problem in our society today. A whole movement has sprung up in response, and many formerly high-powered professionals and executives now subscribe to the so-called voluntary simplicity lifestyle. They're managing their mania by opting for jobs that offer less stress and more free time in exchange for lower salaries, and they're embracing the resulting scaled-down spending. Though these solutions are available, workaholism can be exceedingly tricky for couples.

Considered an "upgraded" process addiction, that is, less deleterious than sex or gambling addictions, workaholism can—and often does—generate societal kudos; big business, politics, the arts, and entrepreneurship thrive on it. Indeed, success in some professions and organizations demands a workaholic commitment. Yet the twenty-four-hour beeper, seventy-percent travel schedule, sixty-hour work week, and nightly entertainment of clients spell emotional and physical disaster. There's a difference between working hard and letting work rule your life.

While we can fault the dog-eat-dog world for such craziness, we individuals share the blame. The fact is we could place some of these players on a chartered cruise to nowhere for three days—cell-phone batteries dead and Internet down—and they'd be pulling nails out of the teak decking with their teeth. Is this urgency about activity out of control? Self-destructive? You bet. But it serves a purpose: for many of us who live this imbalanced lifestyle, it's a grand avoidance. Like any addiction, it functions as an escape from our personal demons and from intimacy. As an issue of priority, it quite simply annihilates love.

Jaime and Gita had no problem identifying their issue as one of priority. On special assignment for his newspaper syndicate, Jaime had been working seventy hours a week for the past year. There was no doubt in Gita's mind which mattered more to him—his work or their relationship. She was at the end of her rope—and her hope. "I've tried everything! I know he's a workaholic, and I know what that means about me: I'm the enabler of a news hound!" she groaned in our first session. "I've tried everything—being nice, being mean, protesting on behalf of the kids. Nothing worked. It wasn't until I hit bottom—I told him I was ready to leave if he didn't come with me to your office—that he took me seriously."

Though both claimed to be at a total loss as to what to do, Gita had already found her solution: to leave the relationship unless Jaime was willing to commit to "work the issue" in counseling. Still, even though she had no other recourse, she thought that the condition she demanded was too extreme. Gita didn't realize that this "tough-love" stance was inescapable if the relationship was to survive. Later, this tendency to feel guilty when she asserted her needs emerged as one of Gita's patterns.

And Jaime, despite the brilliant managerial skills he wielded at the office, claimed that it had never occurred to him to negotiate his way out of his dilemma at home. "There's nothing I can do about it," he told us, looking dazed and confused. "At the end of the day, the project has to succeed; three hundred people are counting on me for their jobs. Gita complains about my working Saturdays, but if I were *really* doing my job right I'd be there one hundred hours a week." As Jaime saw it, if he didn't martyr himself for his company, all his subordinates and their families would starve. This was *his* pattern: getting bogged down in black-and-white thinking—the result of an inability to conceptualize moderate solutions—and believing that the relationship would take care of itself.

With the support of Workaholics Anonymous, this courageous couple metamorphosed from a traditional couple, ruled by their personal demons and antiquated expectations of each other, to a New Couple whose relationship would form the scaffolding of a far more rewarding life for both. "I'm glad that Gita had the guts to hold her ground," Jaime admitted the last time we saw him. "After all, who from the deathbed ever regretted not spending more time at the office?"

The Third Wheel: Codependence with Persons Outside the Couple

Family entanglements and partner-to-partner codependence aren't the only unhealthy relationships that can disrupt the integrity of a couple. Unbalanced relationships with friends, bosses, colleagues, housemates, neighbors, and even strangers can, and often do, have the same hurtful effects.

Caroline didn't enjoy the company of Alice, a moody co-worker, but because Alice was new in town and "all by herself," she ate lunch with her every day and drove her home every night. Caroline's husband, Paul, who heard about these encounters every night over dinner and often joined the women for lunch, got fed up the second time she asked Alice to join them for a weekend at their favorite lake. He leveled with her, explaining his concern, and that was enough to pull Caroline out of her unconscious caregiving. "I don't know what I was thinking," his wife commented. "Of *course* Paul was unhappy with Alice around. Sometimes I wondered myself if I was going overboard, but I was so afraid of getting the silent treatment at work if I cooled things down. That didn't happen, though: Alice has already found somebody new to lean on."

An Invitation to Reflect on the Law of Priority

- Are you concerned that some aspect of your behavior could indicate addiction to work, gambling, sex, romance or relationship, or compulsive use of television, computer, or anything else?
- If so, how does this make you feel? And how do these behaviors affect your self-love? Your emotional intimacy?
- Are you involved in any relationships outside the family that are nonreciprocal, draining, stressfully preoccupying, or otherwise codependent?

• If so, how does this make you feel? And how do these
  relationships affect your self-love? Your emotional intimacy?

PRIORITY PAST AND
THE TRADITIONAL COUPLE

> ...One day, reaching out to each other,
> they found a barrier they could not penetrate,
> and recoiling from the coldness of the stone,
> each retreated from the stranger on the other side.
> For when love dies, it is not in a moment of angry battle,
> not when fiery bodies lose their heat.
> It lies panting, exhausted
> expiring at the bottom of a wall it could not scale.
>
> ANONYMOUS, *The Wall*

Putting the couple on the back burner has traditionally been seen as both
a necessity and a virtue. For our great-grandparents, grandparents, and
parents, material well-being, procreation, and childrearing were undeni-
ably the first orders of business. Sacrificing oneself for one's children, taking care of one's parents, and providing the best possible life one could
for those near and dear were cultural norms, and those norms may well
have suited the times.

Nonetheless, their effect on the intimacy and health of couples was
debilitating, because the values underlying the norms forced partners to
subordinate their own nascent higher-order needs—for self-love, mission
in life, and (most relevant to the Law of Priority) true emotional intimacy. Furthermore, traditionals of yesteryear had no formula, no solid
model such as the Ten New Laws of Love, to assist them in maintaining
their chemistry.

The result? Even though in their hearts most traditional spouses
deeply cared for each other, their love life was devalued, fading as quickly
as a sweet dream—and was replaced by just about everything else. To
make matters worse, relationship work simply wasn't done, the subject of
love wasn't studied, and there were no relationship experts. As a subject
of assessment or improvement, love just didn't exist.

The Child-Centered Family:
Borrowing from the Past

"The children must come first" was the credo of yesterday, when any couple who took a holiday without the children caused raised eyebrows at the least and was judged to be negligent at the worst. And so, in many quarters, it still goes. The traditional belief in the superiority of the child-centered over the couple-centered family is one of the gravest misconceptions we come across as marriage and family counselors.

At a survival level, as parents we're responsible for sheltering, clothing, and nourishing our offspring. While most parents see the limited time with our children as precious—all we have is a single go-round lasting twenty or so years—neglect is ever rampant. Even when material support is ample, many kids today still aren't getting enough quality family and one-on-one time (especially with fathers, despite the increasing presence of "new dads").

Be that as it may, couple-centeredness doesn't mean child neglect. At issue here is many couples' tendency to throw the spouse out with the baby's bathwater. In a hundred and one subtle and unnecessary ways, we're still deprioritizing couple intimacy "for the sake of the children," and that spells danger.

Failure to take care of one's own partnership inevitably results in unmet emotional needs. The unconscious struggle over emotional issues was frequently the stuff of our parents' marriages, as it continues to be today. When the profound need for emotional intimacy languished in earlier generations, traditional spouses had no choice but to connect closely with something or someone other than the spouse—work, family-of-origin, friends, or (most typically) children.

Substituting intimacy with offspring for intimacy with spouse is a subtle phenomenon—one that's almost always beyond parental ken. Yet we must learn to recognize it, because using our children for our unmet couple needs is unfair and hurtful to everyone. It forces kids to play spousal roles and even sometimes to parent their parents. We can see examples of this problem all around us: we might find ourselves recruiting our child to side with us in an argument against our spouse, or adopting our child as a best friend and confidante, as (however unwittingly) Mary did.

Mary thought that the "incredible tightness" she enjoyed with her eldest daughter was the hallmark of first-rate parenting. "Amanda tells me absolutely everything—about her friends, boys, school, you name it," she informed us with pride. "I know it's special because the other mothers tell me their thirteen-year-old daughters seem allergic to them. Maybe it's because I'm so open with her about *my* life," she theorized. "My daughter is just so mature. I can even talk to her about my husband (well, my *second* husband)—that's her stepfather. I'm serious: her advice is super." Mary said she'd had this kind of close communication with her husband when they were first married, but it had died what she called a "natural death." It saddened her to have lost it, but, as she said, "At least I have Amanda."

Mary's kind of sharing with her daughter is inappropriate—a classic example of poor parental boundaries. While heartfelt intimacy is healthy and even necessary between adult intimates, and while some children may seem open to it with their parents (apparently enjoying the deep emotional self-disclosure of a caregiver), in reality it overburdens them. It causes them to grow up too fast, because they end up feeling responsible for the parent's emotional welfare. In addition, the partner (whether consciously or not) sees the overinvolvement with the children as a betrayal, a supplanting of the healthy prioritization of the couple.

Giving too much "power" to a child is also a result of unhealthily delegated couple needs. For example, some parents routinely allow their children to interrupt conversations or always sleep with them at night. (Even if this second is a conscious decision to subscribe to the "family bed" parenting practice, both partners would do well to honestly ask themselves if following this fashion isn't perhaps also a symptom of waning chemistry.) Others never lock the bedroom door or take time away together. Still others are almost obsessively conscientious in their desire to be available to their children—generally in an effort to avoid their partners or themselves.

In the long term, the price of using children to address adult needs is always the emotional connection of the couple, not to mention their sex lives. Some people willingly pay that price, claiming that they'd do anything to help their children. And yet we all know that kids learn more from what parents do—and *are*—than from what they *say*. A commitment to paying needed attention to the couple is one of the greatest gifts parents can give their kids: for when the king and queen are sitting squarely on their thrones, children are free to be children, safe in the knowledge that all's well in the kingdom.

The Lopsided Priority: Relationship Work as Women's Work

It could be argued that prioritization of the relationship isn't a new idea at all, that even traditional couples practiced it. Well, sort of. Running the relationship was considered the domain of the "better half" (if considered at all), since it was generally believed that women were "better at that sort of thing"—an arrangement that freed the male to win the bread and tend to worldly matters. This perspective, which we call the *lopsided priority,* was questionable at best.

What were women tending to anyway, when they ran the relationship? Social life? Church groups and PTA? Their husband's physical health? Real relationship health—namely, intimacy, communication, and trust—couldn't have been handled alone by even the most zealous wife, even had it not been terra incognita. Couple health never was and never will be a unilateral affair.

That's true even for a "happy" couple such as Mirkka and Rikard. Everybody knew theirs to be the warmest hearth in the neighborhood; Mirkka's cocoa, loving ear, and twenty-four-hour mirth were its most beloved staples. And the PR flowed perennially: "Your father and I love each other so much," Mirkka cooed to her brood of four. "And he's so proud of you!" Who wouldn't assume her marriage to be the picture of mutually positive regard? Who could have guessed that for years this flawless performance had effectively camouflaged her husband's real state, which was as sulky and taciturn as hers was gay? Rikard's invisibility when guests were around was the best this man offered. He was glued to the television set the rest of the time, and his family tiptoed around him. None of the kids wanted to risk "upsetting Dad," lest they unleash the quiet rage that caused his face to contort and redden, his burly body to tremble. Mirkka, however, seemed not to notice.

Once the children were grown and gone, Mirkka was hit hard with an unfamiliar feeling of emptiness. She was able to persuade Rikard to join her at our consulting room for a couple "tune-up." There, to our growing discomfort, she spoke effusively about their life together—protesting too much, it seemed—while he uttered not a word. The imbalance of their energies seemed to tilt the room on its side. Finally, Mirkka's glee ran its course. In its absence, her underlying desperation and loneliness were clearly visible. *Still* nothing from Rikard—no words, no emotion.

Though this may well have been the first time that Mirkka had ever parted the veil of artifice to give vent to her true feelings (in facial expression and demeanor if not words), we guessed that it might also be the last. Mirkka's day in court had proved a painful washout. Too proud to admit the failure of her marriage and too afraid to leave Rikard, she typified the lopsided tradition with her plan for "saving the marriage." Squaring her shoulders and shaking hands firmly as she left us, she revealed the future: with the grim determination of a martyr, Mirkka would grin and bear it.

As this traditional couple illustrates, when one member (generally the woman) counts on the centrality of the relationship and the other doesn't, the so-called committed one suffers tremendously. The imbalance shoves the woman into the vulnerable "pursuer" role while the man plays the safe "distancer." She's automatically in the one-down position. This diminishes her self-esteem, and the resulting inequality dashes any possibility for true emotional intimacy. Sadly, for Mirkka and countless others, the "wife's work" entails espousing the party line and pretending to the world that all is well.

A year after Rikard and Mirkka left our office, Rikard called. He was newly recovering from a triple-bypass operation and wanted to come in with his wife. The ensuing session unfolded in a manner markedly different from the last. "I don't know quite what to say, but I've had things the wrong way around," he began. "I love this woman, and I want to make it right." With this declaration, Rikard and Mirkka commenced the journey back to one another. They dealt not only with their youngest years in their families-of-origin but also with their own imbalanced history together. As they traversed the many peaks and troughs, Mirkka finally got good and angry—and learned to express that emotion consciously.

Rikard, speaking literally, made an observation that the rest of us can benefit from metaphorically. "They had to cut me up to wise me up," he said at one session's close. "But I guess that's what it took to see the light." Mirkka smiled and touched his arm with affection. Exercising her newfound assertiveness and a budding sense of humor, she quipped, "Honey, help! I think I'm hearing things."

Today this commendable pair are leaders in the Marriage Encounter program at their church, and they're proof positive that you don't have to be a new couple to be a New Couple.

Truly, the traditional setup turns the principle of priority on its side. And as must be clear to you now, the traditional lopsided priority mimics the dynamic of the codependent to the addict—and it did so long before the syndrome had a name. Some of the traditional women today who are relationship-addicted are very likely the daughters, granddaughters, and great-granddaughters of earlier undiagnosed codependents whether these older relatives were male or female.

In many families and across many cultures, women's chronic neglect of self—a kind of martyrdom—has been intentionally role-modeled and elevated to a virtue. Motivated by fears of being alone and discovering their true identity, traditional women over the centuries have been unable to imagine life without the cover of their husbands. And this sad syndrome persists today, as even financially solvent career women fall anew into the trap of lopsided prioritization (or struggle to extricate themselves from it). Panic and desperation—simultaneously causes and by-products of lopsided prioritization—are a heartbreakingly low-grade fuel upon which to run a marriage. Still, run it they do, at great cost. In Mirkka's case, the cost was plunging into a romantic fantasy about her husband's reciprocity of commitment. The ghost partner—the traditional husband—ultimately fares no better. Now, as then, he ends up feeling guilty, suffocated, or imprisoned.

Occasionally, though not often, the lopsidedness of prioritization tips the other way: the husband is the one devoted to keeping the relationship going. Such a husband is typically the father of children whose mother is sick, emotionally disturbed, or addicted. In the role of ersatz relationship monitor, he's charged with the pragmatics of managing the household as well as seeing to the health of all its relationships; in short, his job is keeping the family together.

Jack was such a dad. His wife, Elaine, given to alternate spells of depression so severe she couldn't get out of bed and elation so potent she couldn't get into it, had been diagnosed with bipolar disorder. Both the mania and the depression could last weeks at a time and were often punctuated by hospitalizations. The periods of relative stability that followed were welcome to the family, but confusing. "Will Mummy be all better after this?" the children would wonder. Throughout all this, Jack maintained his job, ran the household, and saw to the material and emotional needs of their three girls. He was coping, but just barely.

The tragedy of mental illness notwithstanding, Jack and Elaine were no different than many other couples of their generation: their marriage was also in deep trouble. Since their courting days twenty-five years earlier, long before Elaine's deterioration, his patience with his wife had been self-destructive. Her instability had been obvious way back when they were dating, and friends and family had been concerned. He'd brushed them off with a laugh. "I've got my own little Zelda," he'd brag, referring to writer F. Scott Fitzgerald's artistic but disturbed wife. A classic Mr. Nice Guy, Jack had fallen in love with someone who could never be there for him. Later, he unwittingly acted the codependent to the vicissitudes of Elaine's escalating manic depression.

The family situation was worst when Elaine refused her medication. Her reluctance for pharmaceuticals was understandable; the pills made her tired and emotionally flat. Nevertheless, skipping her dosage—which she did frequently—precipitated two-week manic binges. The whole family was then thrown into a devastating cycle of hospitalization, stabilization, and reunion—a cycle that wouldn't have been necessary had she taken her meds.

Even in the dismal situation of spousal mental illness, steps can be taken to prioritize the couple relationship and ensure its greater health. Had Jack availed himself of professional counseling years earlier, he would have realized that the ball was in his court. He could have learned how to honor his own limits and state his bottom line to Elaine: that if she refused to care for herself, he'd be forced to take the children and leave. Such an ultimatum would have spared all of them innumerable traumatic episodes.

Standard for their times, though, Jack and Elaine sought no psychotherapy until their children started having problems at school. Then they brought them to our office for "fixing." As is often the case, these kids were merely carrying the symptoms of their parents' dysfunctional marriage. When Jack and Elaine figured out that they'd have to spend more time on our couch than their kids would, they balked. In the end, however, they had the wisdom to consent to our outside help. Today these two will tell anyone who cares to ask that in couples where one member suffers from mental illness, ongoing high-quality emotional support is a lifestyle—and lifelong—decision; it's also a supreme mark of self-love. True priority demands that both parties have equal and primary commitment to the health of the couple. Here, as with all Ten New Laws of Love, mutuality is paramount.

The Two-Sided Nonpriority: Relationship Work as Irrelevant

Professional singers Dashell and Danielle, both divorced, met at an audition. They fell for each other's voices and, before long, into each other's beds. As a couple, they made a splash. Soon they were the darlings of every gathering, be it with the family or in the biz. They moved out of the intoxication stage of their relationship—and a glorious intoxication it was—and into the power struggle seemingly without strife. These two simply never fought. They hardly even complained. Each sailed smoothly and imperceptibly into his and her respective obsession.

When their marriage was one year old, Danielle landed a role in a new musical. The passion she'd once felt for her handsome husband now blazed for the roar of the crowd. Dashell had no such good fortune. In fact, just after her lucky break, he got his: six fractures in the left femur. Though this halted Dashell's career, a new drama soon opened for him: a string of dalliances with the physical therapists and nurses who were part of his "rehabilitation." He convinced himself that he was proud of his wife ("not a jealous bone in my body") and that thanks to her new love affair with the spotlight, she wouldn't be bothered by his brief affairs.

Ten years into their duet, we met this couple, on the advice of Danielle's psychiatrist. Danielle had happened upon a photograph of Dashell with one of his paramours in an industry rag. Even though the couple hadn't had a meaningful conversation in years and crisis signs were posted all around, Danielle reacted to the photo (and all it implied) with shock. Several life-threatening binges on drugs and alcohol later, it was clear that Dashell had finally succeeded in gaining his famous wife's attention.

When this fast-moving, cosmopolitan couple got down to the work of their relationship, their fascination for psycho-spiritual growth seemed unbounded. Deep and ultimately rewarding truths emerged from their individual sessions. Danielle quickly saw that while she'd worked hard for her success and could feel good about that, she'd made it more important than her relationship with Dashell. Once she'd left him in the dust professionally, she was embarrassed, despite herself, by his flagging career. All attempts to try to "help" him—offering unrequested (and unwelcome) advice, for example—proved futile and humiliating.

In *his* individual sessions, Dashell talked about his history of cheating on his first wife. Danielle had known about it, he said, but they'd never really cleared it up. "How could Danielle ever have trusted me?" he wondered. "*Did* she ever—even at first? And how could I have made her the laughingstock of the entertainment community?" He finally realized that he was in the grips of an unconscious vendetta. "She had the audacity to outshine me!" he joked self-deprecatingly.

Such brave and brutal emotional honesty was music to everyone's ears. Danielle and Dashell did successfully overhaul their marriage. Although it didn't happen overnight, they eventually got their priorities straight.

An Invitation to Reflect on the Law of Priority as It Pertains to Your Parents

- Did your parents make time together a priority? If so, how? How did this affect their self-love? Their emotional intimacy? How did this make you feel?
- Did your parents perform family roles that burdened, disempowered, or disrespected them? If so, with whom, and what roles? What might have motivated them to do this? How did this affect their self-love? Their emotional intimacy? How did this make you feel?
- Did either of your parents abuse—or was either one addicted to—any particular substance? How did this affect their self-love? Their emotional intimacy? How did this make you feel?
- Did either of your parents struggle with overwork, gambling, sexual compulsivity, or other such excesses? How did this

affect their self-love? Their emotional intimacy? How did this
make you feel?

- Was either of your parents involved in any relationship
  outside the family that was nonreciprocal, draining, stressfully
  preoccupying, or otherwise codependent? How did this affect
  their self-love? Their emotional intimacy? How did this make
  you feel?

- How would your childhood have been different had your
  parents subscribed to the Law of Priority? How would your
  own couple be different (or, if you're single, how would past
  relationships have been different)?

PRIORITY AND THE NEW COUPLE

New Couples know that keeping chemistry healthy and vibrant means
prioritizing their relationship. They block out time together and pay
attention to matters of individuation—taking an honest look at family
ties and roles and evaluating how these might be influencing their couple.
Equally important, these lovers are on the watch for outside relationships
with friends and colleagues that might verge into codependence. They
watch their attitude toward work, not to mention their use of alcohol,
drugs, food, television, the computer, and anything else that might
threaten to control them and eat away at their intimacy. Finally, those
committed to a more evolved kind of relating agree to do the work of
relationship with the help of a new model of love.

Like all couples who have sipped from the spring of true chemistry,
Patrick, forty-one, and Evie, forty-three, were acutely aware and dis-
tressed when the beauty and magic started to wane. He headed up adver-
tising for a pharmaceutical-industry publication, and she lectured and
wrote about gourmet food. It was the second marriage for both, with
three teenage children between them.

Patrick respected the power of good individual psychotherapy; he'd
been in and out of therapy since the point in his first marriage when he'd
realized that his relationship with his wife was bereft of sexual chemistry.
Evie was a former chef; she too had found counseling indispensable. It
had helped her overcome the panic attacks she'd suffered before exams at

the culinary academy. "But my therapist told me I'm cured," she'd jest at moments of anxiety.

Despite their devotion to their respective missions in life and the bolstering of their self-love that years together had accomplished, this couple had some lessons ahead on how to fulfill the third higher-order need: the need for long-term emotional intimacy. "It was so different in the beginning," Patrick lamented. "We were both over the moon, and I'd tell anyone who'd listen all about Evie." Evie sounded wistful as well. "I was hoping we were exceptional, praying that this wouldn't happen to us," she confessed. While it was obvious that these two were somewhat confused about the distinction between chemistry and the intoxication stage (on some level believing that if they had the first, the power struggle would never occur), they also had an issue with prioritization.

Very understandably too. For with two demanding jobs and kids applying to college, it was easy for Patrick and Evie to avoid the whole issue of what to do about the loss of their electricity. "I suppose we were convinced that with two decades of individual work between us, we wouldn't need to have our relationship supervised as well," Patrick said only half-jokingly. "Of course, private time together would have helped." His partner reached inside before she added, "I guess a part of me has been afraid that even with Patrick, whom I love like no one else, it would be childish to think that chemistry could last."

After some months of couple therapy, Patrick and Evie renewed their commitment to intimacy. With two of their three kids now off at school, the couple began to relish the time they had to chat, "as we did in the beginning." Weekends were reserved for cooking up storms in the kitchen and for long walks on the beach—in short, for restoring their emotional intimacy. To their utter amazement, they got a new lease on their love life. "I guess I really had been indoctrinated," Evie commented, "expecting good sex to go by the wayside."

In fact, the joy of this revival inspired Evie and Patrick to take their sex life a step further: they researched tantric sexual practices and within seven months both became adept at multiple orgasm. "I never thought this would be possible," Patrick said enthusiastically. "It's not like the intoxication stage again, because we trust each other so much more now. And our lovemaking—well, it's so beautiful it brings the universe to her knees." These two are a testament to the central teaching of the second

New Law of Love: that is, if the *presence* of chemistry in a relationship isn't an act of will, its *maintenance* surely is—and first of all, we must prioritize it.

The New Mixed Marriage

As we all know, people who would be attracted to the New Couple model don't always end up together; sometimes a potential New Couple partner is married to a traditional. Whether the partners are formally hitched or not, we call such unions "new mixed marriages." There are two kinds of such marriages. The first starts out with two traditionals; then, somewhere down the road, one partner gets hooked on the subject of higher-order needs (whether it's referred to as such or by other names) and the other partner doesn't. The second, like the marriage of Bobby and Cherie, profiled below, is "premixed."

All mixed marriages of this latest kind have the potential to become New Couples. However, it usually takes special circumstances (read: *crises*) to catalyze a person into a genuine interest in self-love, mission in life, and emotional intimacy. Triggering events often include death of a loved one, illness, heartbreak, or a perceived failure. Though it may be difficult to see at the time, these losses contain the potential not only to launch us onto a path of self-discovery, but to hatch a New Couple as well.

"I realize now that being in a relationship with Bobby was like driving a car with the emergency brake on," Cherie said. She readily admitted that she'd entered this mixed marriage "with both eyes open"; at the time the choice had seemed wise. After all, Cherie had chosen Bobby based on a whole *stack* of good reasons—not only best-friendship and sexual chemistry but also prodigious recreational and musical compatibilities. "We lived for mountain-climbing and rock 'n' roll," she boasted in her first session. "Together we bagged the baddest peaks and were in the front row for every major band that came through town. I knew he was against the counseling that I was in," Cherie said, becoming more serious. "But in every other way, Bobby was the greatest—and the sexiest—man on earth."

To their mutual dismay, this adventuresome duo was locked in the power struggle within a year of marriage—and Bobby's "brakes" had turned hydraulic. His reluctance to look under his own surface translated into a refusal to do the work of relationship. "He'd rather lead an expedition up a mile-high sheer granite wall with no toeholds than talk about us," Cherie said. Resolute at the beginning, Cherie planned to "love him into changing." But such classic rescue techniques never work. They're simply the codependent solution to an imbalanced—actually, a lopsided prioritization of the—relationship. They often (as in this instance) border on romantic fantasy, and they always speak of low self-love on the part of both partners.

Bobby did eventually release his brakes and begin to prioritize his relationship, but it took a shattering tragedy to change him—a tragedy that could have left him bitter and even more shut down. It occurred during a climb he led in the Karakoram Range in Pakistan. A series of pitons ripped out, and two of his dearest climbing buddies tumbled a thousand feet to their death. Worse still, Bobby was the one who'd laid the protection that gave way. Thus began one traditional husband's climb down into himself—and into the heart of his relationship. As he later confessed to the members of his bereavement group, "To me, climbing down has always been scarier anyway."

Priority Perfect

Theoretically speaking, exemplary Annabella and Fritz had little to learn from us about the Law of Priority. In practice, too, they'd done amazingly well. Their eight-year relationship was still brimming with vitality and affection. Not surprising, really: it was the centerpiece of their lives.

These loving people had labored long and hard to keep their relationship prominent. Kids, career, and their families-of-origin had been breathing down their necks from the start. Nevertheless—and we don't know if it was by the grace of their intellect or of their intuition—they just seemed naturally to know what was important. For one thing, they understood about the time it takes to maintain a healthy relationship. They routinely checked into local hotels and left their kids with Fritz's parents. This was their way of "running away from the circus" and "reconnecting."

Professionally, this twosome was also in great shape. Academics both, and ambitious to boot, Fritz and Annabella had managed to successfully support each other in identifying and fulfilling their missions in life.

This process included three grueling graduate programs between them, and an exciting transcontinental move that benefited both their careers. As parents, however, they were feeling the pressure to subordinate their needs as a couple to those of their two toddler boys. This balancing act, along with the hope of acquiring more effective parenting skills, was what initially brought them to us.

The concept of individuation wasn't foreign to either Fritz or Annabella, though the term was new. While each had dealt effectively with individuation in their young adulthood, residual family-of-origin issues weighed particularly heavily on the couple at this point in their lives. The problem was Annabella's stepfather, who'd raised her from babyhood. He was a practicing alcoholic, though he'd long ceased to be a destabilizing force in his daughter's life. Annabella had made sure of that by attending Adult Children of Alcoholics meetings, where she'd learned (and still had to be reminded) to stop feeling responsible for her stepfather's illness and to set limits with him regarding his bellicose drunken behavior. When Fritz entered the family, however, the man's animosity had found a new target. The problem was that Annabella had trouble seeing it.

"I know he's trying to be nice to me, at least for Annabella's sake," Fritz told us. "But when I'm with him, I still have the uncanny feeling that I have a bull's-eye tattooed on my forehead." Annabella laughed nervously. "I know he can be awful," she admitted, "especially after he's had a couple. But Fritz is so much stronger than Dad. He can take it."

As can be expected periodically with even the most recovery-conscious individuals, Annabella was suffering a relapse into her long-standing codependence with her stepfather—this time, at Fritz's expense. It didn't take long, however, for her to see how unfair it was to expect her husband to tolerate disrespect from anyone—including the man who'd brought her up. And Fritz needed to learn how to validate his own right to be respected—no exceptions.

With some facilitation, this couple worked out the solution they needed: they structured future visits with the stepfather for mornings, before he started drinking, so that when he visited with his grandsons he'd be on his best behavior. The process of Annabella's finally recognizing the problem that her stepfather presented to her husband, empathizing with his distress, and then solving it jointly with Fritz proved intimate and bonding. What was even more crucial to the relationship was the dramatic demonstration of her commitment to make Fritz's emotional welfare a real priority. Because Fritz and Annabella were truly a New Couple, Annabella did what we all must do for the essential trust of the relationship: she weighed in on the side of her spouse.

Committing to the second New Law of Love and prioritizing our relationship isn't an act of heresy; nor, even if we have children, is it selfish. As the New Couples presented in these pages demonstrate, investing time and energy in preserving our God-given chemistry amid the circus of our lives benefits not just our primary relationship, but also us as individuals, our children, our extended family, and even society at large. We begin by being honest about the wide variety of diversions and dysfunctions that might ail us—from enmeshment with our family-of-origin or children to any unaddressed addictions or compulsions. Since this second New Law of Love represents a fundamental commitment to do the work of relationship, it serves as the backbone of the eight that follow.

The Key to Priority

Prioritizing your relationship to keep chemistry alive is the key to the second New Law of Love.

This means committing to . . .

- The Ten New Laws of Love, which embody the "work of relationship"
- The process of individuation from your family-of-origin—that is, becoming the emotional peer of parents, siblings, and other extended family members
- Managing work hours, outside codependent relationships, compulsive behaviors, and the use of food and addictive substances

3. EMOTIONAL INTEGRITY
the third new law of love

Emotions rule: it's now an established fact. Indeed, in his best-seller *Emotional Intelligence,* Dr. Daniel Goleman (writing from a brain-science perspective) concludes that high "EQ"—our emotional quotient—vies with high IQ as the heart and soul of our success and fulfillment. If one of today's hottest cartoons is any indication, being savvy about our couple's emotional life is even *fashionable.* The characters in Matt Groening's excruciatingly honest relationship strip, *Life in Hell,* are rife with guilt, anger, and angst—and everyone seems to love it.

The New Couple takes emotional intelligence to the next level—to that of integrity. This third New Law of Love concerns itself with responsibility and wholeness *with regard to our emotions.* It asks us, as partners, to take full responsibility for the whole range of our emotional being. That means we commit to learning how to deal with the rocket fuel—variously named anger, sadness, fear, guilt, shame, joy, and love—that courses through our bodies, our lives, and especially our intimate relationships. Equally important, we both agree to examine, on an ongoing basis, the feelings that underlie our behaviors.

This law acknowledges a dangerously neglected fact of committed monogamous life: that the greatest extremes of emotion we're likely to experience in adulthood will come about not only in the crucible of our relationship, but as a result of our being together—especially during the power struggle, the second stage of our couple journey. And the Law of Emotional Integrity provides us with a solution to this problem: real preparedness for the stormy weather that's sure to come. It helps keep affective explosions—and implosions—from destroying a couple's chemistry, and (as a result) functions as a long overdue cornerstone of couple trust.

Specifically, the third New Law of Love invites us to commit to being *emotionally honest* with ourselves and each other, and to acquire two essential emotional skills: *emotional literacy* and *emotional management.* Let's look at these elements more closely:

- *Emotional literacy* involves both *awareness* (that is, knowing what we're feeling) and *fluency* (that is, being able to speak to each other in the true language of the heart). This aspect of emotional integrity must be addressed first (in life as well as on paper), because without it, neither emotional honesty nor emotional management is possible, no matter how good our intentions.

- *Emotional honesty* means being willing to acknowledge emotional issues and the entire range of our feelings—be they good, bad, or ugly—to ourselves and to our beloved other. Both literacy and honesty must be in place before emotional management can kick in.
- *Emotional management* requires the willingness and ability to deal with excessive negative feelings proactively, in a healing and creative way.

When a couple commits to the full curriculum—literacy, honesty, and management—they're on the road to emotional mastery in the most modern sense of the term. What's more, they're paving the way to achieving the higher-order needs for love of self and emotional intimacy—and perhaps sparing themselves their own version of Groening's life in hell. (Unfortunately, this curriculum is incomprehensible to those who are unskilled as emotional listeners. That's why deep listening is the subject of the next chapter!)

Cyril and Janna caught themselves early on in their power struggle. With chemistry to die for, they were surprised after one year of marriage to find that their repertoire of emotional maneuvers was inadequate to deal with the daily curveballs their relationship hurled at them.

"I wouldn't let on about my resentments because I was sure they'd hurt Janna," said the twenty-five-year-old accountancy intern at the launch of his emotional education, "and I couldn't understand why she would get so sad." Cyril's wife shook her head vigorously. "See?" she interjected. "He always mistook my silence for sadness. Actually, I was *mad*." Cyril continued: "Anyway, it would go on like this for days until the dam burst, and then we'd end up drowning each other in a flood of pent-up emotion."

Janna and Cyril were relieved to learn that a new commitment and the skills of emotional literacy and management could transform the way they handled the difficult emotions. Instead of continuing their catch-as-catch-can approach, which was starting to erode their friendship, this couple learned that emotions can be both expressed and tamed in a healthy way. Their reward for this effort was an environment where their favorite emotion, love, could thrive.

THE EMOTIONAL SAFE ZONE

Emotional integrity is momentous for coupledom, because it exposes an issue that's plagued relationships since people first cohabitated in caves: emotional safety. Whereas love, honor, respect, and the unacceptability of violence have long been the standards of a good marriage, baseline emotional safety has yet to be officially acknowledged as an ideal. An emotionally safe relationship is one in which the healthy expression of each partner's full range of feelings is not only encouraged, but is held to be essential to the longevity of love. A simple but powerful matter of respect, this kind of safety necessitates a commitment from both partners to work hard to not misuse or mismanage emotions. In everyday terms, it means an agreement that any form of shaming, manipulation, or scaring of the other is unacceptable—and that both partners will do whatever it takes to recognize and weed out such bedevilments.

An Invitation to Reflect on the Law of Emotional Integrity

As you approach the exercises in this chapter, remember that the presence or absence of New Couple chemistry profoundly affects a couple's experience with each law.

- Is your relationship an emotional safe zone? If yes, what makes it so? If no, what keeps it from being safe?
- How does the presence (or lack) of an emotional safe zone make you feel? How does it affect your self-love? Your emotional intimacy?

This law doesn't ask for perfection, recognizing that the willingness to stumble and fall eventually produces the most graceful stride. But it does ask partners to take responsibility for adequate preparation. Like a storm-preparedness protocol, emotional integrity allows us to rest assured that we're ready for most meteorological irregularities.

Literally "energy in motion," e-motions *are* like the weather. They come and they go, apparently as they please. And whether their waves of energy thrash as forcefully as a gale or undulate as softly as a summer breeze, emotions are a force to contend with—even for married couple counselors! The key to emotional safety is know-how in the form of literacy, honesty, and management. Neither blithe dismissal nor muscling into submission can ever take care of strong feelings. We can no more will our feelings away than shout down the sun. Nor, despite the most valiant efforts, can we tidily stuff them away somewhere. It's a law of physics that energy of any sort can be neither created nor destroyed; it merely changes form. So out will our feelings come, in one form or another. And it's best to be ready.

As indestructible—and damaging—as they may be, feelings have no IQ. Whether welcome or dreaded, rational or apparently irrational, feelings just *are;* there are no smart or stupid ones. For this reason, it's illogical—and an example of garden-variety emotional invalidation—to accuse our beloved of being "dumb" to feel whatever way he or she happens to feel.

Likewise, the affective realm possesses no inherent morality; in other words, there are no good or bad, right or wrong feelings, either. In fact, to say to our lover, "You shouldn't be feeling that way," is not only emotionally invalidating, it's as nonsensical as judging the rain. Still, like other potentially destructive forms of energy, emotions do present ethical considerations, and for that reason they demand some serious responsibility-taking in any couple relationship.

So how should that responsibility be delegated within the couple? Well, ultimately each partner is responsible individually; everyone has a unique emotional weather system for which he or she is solely responsible. But, you may ask, can't a lover *make* you feel certain ways? Actually, no. He or she might become adept at predicting your reactions and moods, and intentionally push your "buttons" in order to either delight or abuse you. At the end of the day, however, your emotional wiring is your own business—and it's up to you to safeguard it.

EMOTIONAL TRAUMA: THE GREATEST CHALLENGE TO EMOTIONAL INTEGRITY

You'd think that with all the EQ hoopla in the media these days, lovers would have already jumped onto the emotional-intelligence bandwagon and covered half the distance to emotional integrity. Not so. Certainly, the distance is vast: only a handful of today's adults are schooled to know the difference between a feeling and a thought. Add to that the fact that fifty percent of all marriages are failing, in large part due to lack of emotional skills, and we'd surely conclude that lovemates ought to be keen to learn. Still, despite the stats and shelf upon shelf of self-help books designed to bring couples up to emotional snuff, relatively few of us have actually achieved such mastery. The situation is so dire that, in some circles, even the ability to call a feeling by its real name isn't a given. We're all familiar with the not-so-funny example of one spouse roaring at the other, "What do you mean I'm angry?!" a cliché that's still terribly apropos.

So why do so many of us still have a serious deficit when it comes to emotional smarts? Is it a simple lack of interest, or do we give up too easily? While some of us seem not to care about our emotional fitness, many others are serious about it. Nevertheless, we all have problems getting our hearts and heads around emotions. Even some of the most psychologically sophisticated couples, and those who gladly devour all the EQ information they can get their hands on, are unable to cultivate emotionally satisfying relationships. It would seem that both aware partners and those operating in the dark have no recourse but to "deal with" their emotions by numbing their feelings, acting them out in a hundred-thousand different ways, or denying them straight up.

Buttons and Lows

A compassionate stance is needed here. The affective domain *is* daunting, feelings *are* confounding—and the reason goes way beyond shyness, pride, character defects, personal communication styles, and gender. As Swiss psychologist Alice Miller so powerfully articulates in her highly acclaimed *The Drama of the Gifted Child*, the real issue goes much deeper: most of us, whether we're avid about or disinterested in the subject of emotion, have trouble dealing effectively with our feelings because of a specific kind of emotional wounding called *trauma*. Usually unidentified, and therefore unhealed, emotional trauma makes dealing with all strong and negative feelings either off-putting or overwhelming for a large share of the population. Along with Miller, many psychologists believe that some kind of emotional trauma (whether major or minor) is at the root of all our neuroses, obsessions, addictions, codependencies, and irksome personality patterns. As if that weren't bad enough, trauma also keeps bumping us into a fight-or-flight mindset: whenever it rears its ugly head, we fear that we're at risk for not being able to meet our lower-order needs (even though we might have, for example, material abundance, a partner, and family and friends who care about us).

While most people accept the idea that everybody's got buttons—highly emotionally charged hurts from childhood waiting to be triggered—it's not so widely known that many of these hurts were actually *traumatic*. In other words, the initial damaging incident wasn't just hurtful to the developing personality, it was shocking. The young self sought emotional protection by going into a daze—that is, psychologically leaving the scene. (This reaction, technically known as *dissociation*, typically looks to the bystander like no reaction at all.) Years or even decades later, when an incident reminiscent of the initial trauma occurs with a partner (or parent or friend), the button gets pushed. The adult self is likely to go back at that moment into some level of shock, repeating the initial daze response. This reaction is often followed by confusion, general upset, even inexplicable rage. The important point for couples is that this sort of innocent replay creates tremendous strife—*and it happens all the time.*

Take this commonplace but frustrating scenario in the elevator of Sally and Harry's condo. She criticized his clothes. He reacted: at first a bit stunned and embarrassed, then perplexed and finally annoyed, he fumed to himself, stepped out the elevator door, and shot away from his partner into the garage. Though Sally's remarks, like all judgments, were unacceptable (a form of inappropriately expressed anger, as we'll see later in the chapter), Harry's reaction was also unacceptable—overblown, given the prompt. So why did these otherwise intelligent people behave so seemingly irrationally?

First Sally, since she "started it." As a child, she was intensely embarrassed by the strange hats her mother insisted on wearing. Thus Harry's outfit—which on this day (as per his custom) was a bit loud—triggered a mild traumatic response in her, occasioning the initial comment. Harry, for his part, was heckled as a ten-year-old by the neighborhood schoolkids about his parochial-school uniform. Though he didn't consciously remember how he felt about that as a child, the heckling informed his reaction to Sally. In fact, unbeknownst to both of them, her unsolicited feedback triggered another traumatic response— this time in Harry.

Once all this background came out over the course of several sessions of couple therapy, a breakthrough in Sally and Harry's emotional communication was imminent. Sally said, "If we hadn't gotten the full story, *both* stories, I'm sure we'd have continued to replay this silly but awful drama." Harry agreed, adding, "I'd have given her the silent treatment till kingdom come. And to think that I had no idea why I'd get so ticked off." Sally jumped back in: "It almost broke my heart when he talked about walking down the street as a kid, all alone, in his little white shirt with the emblem and bow tie, being harassed by those bullies. I can see why he likes to dress differently now." Harry was touched: "And I can relate to her story. My father used to get really loud at hockey games. I couldn't stand it."

Whereas for some mates, the trauma theory might seem a little heavy, even implausible, Sally and Harry discovered the magic of learning the truth about each other's big buttons: sharing intimate personal histories not only explains seemingly irrational and unfair behavior, but also creates empathy. In the process, it can open up two hearts like nothing else.

Oversensitivity and Overreactivity

Like many people, Harry mistakenly charged himself with the emotional crime of oversensitivity. A close relative of overreactivity, this is a common but hurtful misnomer for what's actually the symptom of unhealed trauma. The terms *oversensitivity* and *overreactivity,* though often used synonymously, are subtly different. The former judges one's *feelings* to be inappropriate, while the latter focuses on one's *actions*.

Responses that we categorize as oversensitive or overreactive only *seem* inappropriate or irrational, however. While in their current context they're excessive, they're dependable measures of the severity of the original emotional injury; in other words, they show us the size and shape of the first hurt. They're supremely logical, therefore; and as Harry and Sally learned, they merit the utmost compassion.

An Invitation to Reflect on
the Law of Emotional Integrity

- What are your emotional buttons and your areas of
  oversensitivity or overreactivity? (These may be the same.) Do
  you criticize—or even condemn—yourself for these? If so, why?
- How does it make you feel to learn that these are the result of
  childhood emotional trauma? Are you now able to feel (or
  imagine feeling) compassion for yourself about your emotional
  buttons and areas of oversensitivity or overreactivity?
- How do your buttons and areas of oversensitivity or
  overreactivity affect your self-love? Your emotional intimacy?
- Can you list your partner's buttons and areas of oversensitivity
  or overreactivity? Do you criticize—or even condemn—him
  or her for these? If so, why?
- How does it make you feel to learn that your partner's buttons
  and areas of oversensitivity or overreactivity are the result of
  childhood emotional trauma? Are you able to feel (or imagine
  feeling) compassion for him or her about these?

The majority of couples have yet to find out that traumatic emotional
wounding is universal: we all suffer from it to some degree. Children are
far more fragile than many of us want to believe, and this fragility results
in many more traumatized adults than we can imagine. And contrary to
popular belief, trauma need not be the result of dramatic, newsworthy
events. In addition to "small" incidents such as Harry's, subtle conditions
that occur over time—like growing up with a mildly depressed father or
overworked and impatient mother—often get internalized as normal.
These can have as traumatic an impact as terrifying episodes, and they
produce similar symptoms. As hard as this may be for many of us to
swallow, seemingly idyllic childhoods can be imperceptibly traumatic.
This fact cannot be overstated.

Monya and Pete were amazed to discover that it was buried trauma in
her "happy" childhood that caused Monya's "overreaction" to her live-in
boyfriend's habits and got them in trouble. "It's incredible, but I know it's
true," the twenty-eight-year-old kindergarten teacher said during one of

her first couple sessions. "I do freak out when Pete leaves his boots in the hall. Now I realize it's because of all those years of being worried outsiders would see my parents' messy house." Her voice dropped to a whisper as she continued: "I died a thousand deaths every time the doorbell rang."

The couple learned three surprising bits of information that day: First, that Monya's anger was only the tip of her notorious tidiness button; on a much deeper level, she was afraid of reexperiencing (with her contemporary neighbors) the intense shame she'd felt as a child. Second, that what seemed like minor slings and arrows from her childhood were actually traumatic, capable of piercing the fine fabric of her adult love. And third, that most emotional trauma can be healed. Indeed, we need simply recognize each button as it's pushed, and recall how it was created, to declare the battle half-won.

When it comes to emotions, information is power, and for couples, general knowledge about emotional trauma can mean insight, freedom, and forgiveness. The concept of emotional trauma goes a long way toward explaining why so many of us have such difficulty getting our emotional houses in order. It accounts for why seemingly simple emotional tasks— such as saying "I love you" or controlling our anger—can be problematic, and why what should come naturally—such as being aware of emotions—doesn't. It also explains why talking honestly about the less pleasant feelings is a huge hurdle; high-end hurts raise the bar of emotional management impossibly high. Furthermore, understanding trauma demystifies the discouragement surrounding emotional issues among even highly motivated partners and exonerates those of us for whom emotion has become a four-letter word.

Since emotional integrity depends on emotional literacy, emotional honesty, and emotional management, it follows that this mainly unknown foe—emotional trauma—would cause it to go up in smoke. Tragically, until we all get the heads-up, as Harry and Sally did, innumerable lovers will continue to allow unrecognized childhood hurts to make the whole subject of emotions a big turnoff.

This news about the impact of early wounding isn't meant to provide fodder for yet another round of parent-bashing. On the contrary, it gives everyone a long-deserved break. First of all, it's the rare father or mother who intentionally traumatizes his or her children. Second, what parent (or great-great-grandparent, for that matter) wasn't once little? We can't pass on what wasn't done to us. As Bob Hoffman, a pioneer of emotional healing education, often said, "Everyone is guilty, and no one is to blame."

A commitment by any couple to be aware of unhealed emotional trauma holds great promise—and most likely much relief as well. Like nothing else, it can open the secret door to compassion. Such awareness contextualizes both our own and our partner's actions and reactions, revealing the deep logic beneath many of the skirmishes and mayhem of the power struggle. Perhaps the best news is that when we learn the sad stories that created our partner's buttons, it's far harder to push them! Once we all set off on the road to recovery from whatever unfinished pain we're harboring in our hearts, the emotional health of our unions will thrive. Encountering and communicating particular feelings will cease to be so threatening, and emotional integrity will become an attainable ideal.

An Invitation to Reflect on the Law of Emotional Integrity

- Are you aware of—or do you suspect—any childhood emotional trauma in your life? If yes, what is it? How does it affect your life? Your self-love? Your emotional intimacy?
- How do feel about exploring the possibility of childhood emotional trauma?
- Have you ever healed—or are you in the process of healing—any childhood emotional trauma? If yes, how? How has it affected—or how is it currently affecting—your self-love? Your emotional intimacy?
- Are you aware of—or do you suspect—any childhood emotional trauma in your partner's life? If yes, what is it? How does it affect your self-love? Your emotional intimacy?

EMOTIONAL LITERACY: HEART TALK

Expression is taken to the level of high art when people, especially love partners, become emotionally literate. Emotional literacy entails both awareness and fluency, as we noted earlier. When we're emotionally *aware,* we're able not only to know what we're feeling, but also to differentiate feelings from thoughts. When we're emotionally *fluent,* we're able to talk about the whole spectrum of our feelings.

Emotional Awareness

Feelings are sometimes difficult to discover—and often even more difficult to acknowledge. Yet hidden in your deepest feelings is your highest truth.
NEALE DONALD WALSCH, *Conversations with God, book 1*

Emotional awareness is the innate, but often stymied, ability to identify whatever feelings are true for us at any given moment. We can't afford to overlook this ability, or let it atrophy, because when we're out of touch with our feelings, we're out of touch with our deep desires and our higher-order needs. Fear, for instance, cues us when our personal safety, be it psychological or physical, is at risk; this protective function is a vital aspect of self-love. Excitement and passion, even envy, help point us in the direction of our true work, our mission in life. And the ability to feel compassion is inseparable from authentic friendship, a pillar of emotional intimacy.

It's often said that there are only two feelings, love and fear, and that all others are simply derivatives. While this may well be so, we all need to be familiar with the common short list: joy, relief, anger, sadness, shock, guilt, shame, jealousy, fear, and love. With the exception of special forms of guilt, shame, and anger, these are all generally healthy—that is, they serve to preserve and affirm life.

The so-called shadow emotions—namely, toxic types of guilt and shame, as well as the contempt cluster, which includes hatred, scorn, disdain, and contempt—are neither natural nor healthy, because they're based on false and hurtful assumptions about ourselves and others. Capable of exercising tremendous power over our existence, these ugly emotions are also the cause of untold couple jeopardy. Toxic guilt and toxic shame are both twisted forms of fear, the sad by-products of a distorted sense of who we really are. The contempt cluster, on the other hand, results from anger impacted—that is, unexpressed—over a long period of time. Not surprisingly, our unhealthy emotions almost always stem from our childhood days and those notorious emotional traumas. (The shadow emotions will be further discussed later in the chapter.)

Though we all know how powerfully emotions can hit us, sometimes when we're in highly charged situations—situations in which we'd expect to be brimming with, even overwhelmed by, emotion—we "numb out," unaware of any feelings at all.

Take Roman and Leela, for example. Whenever Roman yells at Leela, she shuts down. Does that mean she's completely devoid of feeling at such times? Not at all. It's physically impossible to have zero emotional response when something even mildly scary is happening to us. What's happening is that Leela is going into a low-level state of shock, a defense she developed in childhood to insulate herself from the harshness of her parents' arguments. And while numbing out now serves nicely to shield her from Roman's decibels, it also cuts her off from her own healthy fear and anger. If she and her partner don't interrupt their half-frozen dance of anger, the hole in Leela's emotional awareness could grow. And the numbness has been plenty destructive already; it's neutralized their chemistry and damaged their emotional trust.

Whether we know it or not, whenever two people communicate, emotion is not only present, it drives the interaction. This is every bit as true in low-charged situations as it is in the dangerous electricity of Roman and Leela's relationship. Still, incredible as it seems, scores of us—including many who are romantically involved—don't know this. We just haven't been taught. Though emotional literacy programs are increasing in public education, they offer too little, too late, for most of us.

Uninformed lovers—that's the majority of us—are left to believe that, besides animalistic urges and certain extreme emotional states, *thinking* is what motivates us. But this simply isn't true: thinking merely implements the dictates of our emotions. When we don't comprehend the primacy and omnipresence of emotions in all human affairs, we end up undervaluing emotional awareness—and seriously endangering our love lives. Being in the dark about our feelings is like being nuclear-powered without knowing it.

Even the super-rational corporate world recognizes the power of emotion and takes steps to minimize emotional risk and maximize emotional well-being for employees. Management has long improved efficiency—and the bottom line—by bringing in organizational-development consultants to work on the interpersonal relationships of staff members. And—surprise!—that work is all about feelings. Facilitators might, for example, focus on helping execs make at least some of their unconscious feelings conscious and then teach them how to communicate these feelings without offending. In fact, it's an organizational-development maxim that once the "personal stuff" is worked out, business matters take care of themselves. Unlike too many couples, the white-collar wizards are wise to the need for emotional awareness. And they're willing to put bucks behind the education.

IDENTIFYING BLIND SPOTS

Obviously, being emotionally aware isn't an all-or-nothing proposition; none of us is completely out of touch with all of our feelings. Rather, this first step toward emotional literacy comes in infinite shades of gray. After all, most of us chose our partners based on a rather sublime emotion— namely love. This demonstrates at least a *pinch* of emotional awareness. Clearly, it's not *gross* emotional blindness that's at issue here; it's selective blind spots—a lack of awareness with regard to specific emotions. (The term *blind spot* can also describe an inability to see issues that affect the couple and a lack of insight about what underlies them.)

Everyone has specific emotions that are problematic. These are, as you might guess, largely the fallout of unaddressed childhood emotional trauma. Surprisingly, the expunging of troubling emotions through blind spots plays no favorites: even those feelings assumed to be easiest for couples—namely, appreciation and love—are sometimes relegated to the periphery of consciousness, as are the more expected sadness, fear, guilt, shame, jealousy, and anger.

Though blind spots plague everyone, for couples in particular they can be devastating. Herman insisted he was "just being gentlemanly" when he offered her a second helping of tiramisu, but Maxine saw something else. Painfully more aware of her partner's feelings than he was, she read contempt in the churlish arch of his lip. Maxine hit the table with her fist in exasperation. "First he's contemptuous," she cried, "then he denies it." But Herman was genuinely unconscious of the scorn that fueled his gesture. Until they got help, he didn't recognize how much Maxine's weight issues irritated him: the constant fretting over her body image, the fad diets, and her long-standing refusal to do anything substantive about it. So, like many mates who are out of touch with their anger, Herman ended up expressing it indirectly by taunting her. This fermentation of disclaimed irritation into anger and then, over time, into the unhealthy emotion of contempt is fairly standard. It was certainly common in this man's experience: taunting was how Herman's own father transmitted unresolved, impacted anger to his mother.

Untended emotional blind spots can mean calamity for intimate relationships. Imagine the condition of Maxine and Herman's friendship—and of their sex life—given Herman's anemic emotional awareness. Though Herman truly didn't know what he was communicating, a lack of awareness is never an excuse for emotional dishonesty or mismanagement. But Herman wouldn't have been able to erect these two other pillars of emotional integrity (as he eventually did) had he not first learned how to identify what he was feeling. For emotions not only rule, they also rule *out* a lot of the good stuff of life unless we're aware of them.

NAMING FEELINGS

A cardinal task of emotional awareness is distinguishing emotions from thoughts. They're two entirely different animals. Thoughts include opinions, ideas, beliefs, judgments, and fantasies, to name just a few; and they're centered in the head. Emotions, many of which we've named in this chapter, are centered in the body. When they're experienced, they're accompanied by a specific group of physical reactions. Fear might begin as a tightening of our chest or stomach area, for example, and crescendo into shaking or trembling. Thoughts, on the other hand, don't themselves trigger physical reactions. However, they commonly trigger emotions, which then produce physical reactions. Imagine, for example, that you're trapped alone in a room with a bear. The *idea* of being trapped with a bear might provoke the *feeling* of anxiety (a form of fear), which in turn might cause your pulse to race.

Language contributes to our tendency to confuse feelings with thoughts—and to our emotional illiteracy. Say, for instance, that a husband tells his wife, "I feel that you were wrong to do that." This *appears* to be an expression of feeling. That's only because he used the word *feel,* however. The statement would have been more accurate if the man had said, "It's my opinion that you were wrong to do that." Though most opinions, like judgments and ideas, involve underlying emotions, they're part of the *thought* family and constitute activity of the intellect. Our feelings, on the other hand, are kinesthetic and constitute activity of the heart. Because we can't be truly intimate until we can share our feelings, any couple who mistakes a product of the intellect for a message from the heart is destined for discontent.

Emotional awareness also asks us to assign feelings their correct names. For some of us, this isn't the cakewalk it appears to be. Again, until very recently, this subject matter hasn't been taught in schools. Hence terms such as "bad," "tired," "upset," "bored," and "depressed" have passed for feelings. Not emotions themselves, they're actually a kind of code—face-saving substitutes for the real thing. (Remember, emotional directness has long evoked allergic reactions!)

"Bad" almost always means "sad" or "guilty." "Tired" can be either a bodily or emotional state (or a combination of both); as an emotional state, it's usually a reaction to anxiety or stress, which are members of the fear family. The word "upset" is often used to describe an admixture of anxiety, disappointment, and frustration. "Bored," which we all recognize as a teen favorite, is widely used by adults as well. It connotes denied or numbed feelings—generally a stew of anger, sadness, and fear. Used casually, "depressed" usually means "sad." Depression itself isn't a feeling; rather, it's a serious emotional condition that develops when we numb our emotions—particularly anger—over a long period of time.

An Invitation to Reflect on the Law of Emotional Integrity

- Are you able to be aware of all the emotions you feel at any given moment?
- Which emotions are easiest to recognize?
- Which are difficult—in other words, what are your emotional blind spots? (Remember, emotional blind spots aren't limited to negative emotions.)
- How does your level of emotional awareness affect your self-love? Your emotional intimacy?

UNHEALTHY EMOTIONS: TOXIC GUILT AND SHAME

Guilt and shame, interlopers in all love relationships, aren't generally recognized as having healthy and toxic varieties. Since we can't be expected to identify, or be aware of, feelings we've never heard about, these tricky emotions wreak considerable havoc in our lives.

Let's look at the healthy/toxic distinction. *Healthy* guilt lets us know when we've hurt our beloved by, for instance, breaking a promise. Though uncomfortable, this feeling has positive consequences: it discourages a repeat performance and teaches us to be more trustworthy in general. *Toxic* guilt, on the other hand, grows out of low self-love. It involves an unfair accusation—a guilt-trip we place on ourselves—that persuades us we're responsible for someone else's feelings. For example, we feel guilty when we say no, so we say yes—and then live to regret it.

Therese was invited on a date by a guy to whom she wasn't really attracted. When she declined, she felt sorry for him; she felt compassion for the loss and possible embarrassment her response caused him. "But I was so *relieved*," she later exclaimed. "Two years ago, I would have felt so guilty—so responsible for his heartache—that I'd have gone out with him anyway. What a nightmare I used to create for myself. Thank goodness I've shifted out of the idea that I'm going to destroy any man I turn down. As though he didn't have the self-esteem to get over it. Now *that's* an insult!"

Therese has magnificently recovered from a textbook case of toxic guilt. This unhealthy feeling, the signature symptom of codependence, *always* has negative consequences: it holds us accountable for the emotional status of others and coerces us into rescuing them. When we succumb to it, we give ourselves away, damage our self-love, and patronize the person we intended to help.

Shame is another two-faced emotion that couples must be able to both identify and nail. *Healthy* shame is reflected in a reasonable, self-protective concern about maintaining the high regard of others. *Toxic* shame, which author John Bradshaw has written about brilliantly in *Healing the Shame That Binds You,* is, like toxic guilt, a key characteristic of codependence and low self-love. It results in the unreasonable fear of being suddenly exposed to others as unlovable, inadequate, and rejectable—*even though these beliefs about ourselves are lies.*

The first kind of shame honors us as social animals; it keeps us from behaving in ways that risk ostracism, which few of us have the ego strength to tolerate. It would be self-destructive, for instance, to make love in one's front yard in plain view of the neighbors. Luckily, healthy shame wouldn't allow it. The second toxic kind of shame doesn't proscribe certain behaviors; rather, it vilifies the individual from within. Healthy shame calls our *action* wrong or bad; toxic shame condemns *us* as wrong or bad.

Kevin lied to his girlfriend about owing money to his ex. When Clara confronted him, he was flooded with both kinds of shame at once. Such "shame seizures" are common occurrences. The smaller part of his shame was healthy; its consequences were positive, because they reinforced Kevin's concern about maintaining Clara's trust. But the larger, more paralyzing feeling was definitely toxic: it horrified Kevin into believing that his girlfriend "now knew the ugly truth" about him—that he was worthless and unlovable. And to be seen by his beloved as the despicable person *he feared he was* felt absolutely excruciating.

Toxic shame is an epidemic problem for our culture in general and for lovemates in particular. In fact, many of us are so concerned about what others think of us that that concern becomes a motivating force in our lives and intimate interactions. As Kevin's example illustrates, toxic shame is based on self-rejection, a by-product of a distorted self-image.

Juanita used to sneak down into the basement in the middle of the night to dye her prematurely graying hair. It was toxic shame that drove her to that extreme, convincing her that her husband wouldn't love an aging wife—though she was only thirty-one years old. The truth was Juanita was unable to accept herself.

The same sort of fear—fear of being seen as inadequate and subsequently abandoned—precluded Warrick from admitting that he was lost while driving the car with his girlfriend, and it ignited a monstrous fight when she urged him to stop for directions. Toxic shame can also keep mates from disclosing important personal information to each other. For two weeks, Jed got up at five, dressed, and pretended he was going to a job from which he'd been laid off. He simply couldn't face his wife.

THE BLOCKING POWER OF TOXIC EMOTIONS

As we've seen, emotional awareness requires that we name all our feelings, including the toxic varieties. However, for each one of us, certain feelings are more difficult to identify than others. Though this condition may seem to be the result of simple embarrassment, there's more to it than that. Stereotypically, women have trouble getting in touch with their anger; men, with their sadness and fear. The reason we struggle with these healthy feelings is that unhealthy emotions overshadow them. The notorious toxic guilt and toxic shame have the singular ability to eclipse beautiful and natural anger, sadness, fear—even love and appreciation—creating emotional blind spots for partners of both sexes. Needless to say, these truly ugly emotions are the affective legacy of unresolved childhood trauma.

Whereas both unwholesome shame and unwholesome guilt block women's awareness of their anger, it's mainly toxic shame that blocks men's awareness of their sadness and fear. When these feelings are expressed in childhood, boys are often humiliated and girls are warned that they're making themselves unlovable. That's how toxic guilt and toxic shame, and their accompanying terror of abandonment, are seeded.

As the seeds sprout, these unhealthy emotions choke out the healthy ones. In women, the ability to get mad or say no is suffocated. As Marthe commented, "I was always supposed to be nice—even when my older brother took my candy and then made fun of me! By junior high, the only person I could get mad at was myself."

The gender conditioning of men is also pretty harsh. It quashes the healthy and necessary expression of sadness and fear. As a result, instead of being able to shed a tear or say "I'm scared" as appropriate, guys shut down lest they experience toxic shame. They panic at the thought that these unmanly feelings might expose them as incompetent or inadequate. In both sexes, the direct and natural expression of gender-proscribed emotions activates the same gut-level fear of being disapproved of—and ultimately abandoned. Here there's no gender gap; we're all afraid of the same thing.

What's the bottom-line consequence of toxic emotions for emotional awareness? One of our clients said it best. This frustrated man exclaimed to his wife, upon discovering the intensity of his own toxic shame, "How can you expect me to name a feeling I've been embarrassed into believing I don't have?" Fortunately, with the evolution of childrearing practices and the emotional liberation of both men and women, toxic guilt and toxic shame have loosened their grip somewhat; nowadays, women generally have easier access to their anger, and men are more likely to be in touch with their sadness and fear.

Sometimes, uncannily, the emotional blind spot of one partner shows up as an emotional excess in the other. It's as if the sighted partner is trying to supply what the blind partner can't. The energy of the banished emotions, which are stored under high pressure deep in the unconscious, does what all energy does: looks for a way to be released, making its way from one partner to the other. Lilly and Julius experienced this strange form of emotional lending when, after they'd lived together for barely three months, her cousin moved to town. "You're going to *love* Don," was all that Lilly said to her new beau about this relation. During their first evening out together, however, Don tossed back four screwdrivers. He then proceeded to recount a string of what must have been the most embarrassing moments of Lilly's adolescence. Though she looked a bit uncomfortable, she never made a peep.

Later, Julius was irate. "How could you have let him trash you like that?" he demanded. To Julius's surprise, Lilly stuck up for her relative. "You don't know what Don's lived through. His father gambled their family into the gutter. He means well. Anyway, it doesn't really bother me." Now her boyfriend was furious. "I don't care if he was raised by Attila the Hun. He has no respect for you." But Lilly would hear none of it. And as she continued to defend and deny, Julius grew ever more enraged.

"It's wild," Julius said after the couple had addressed the issue in couple counseling. "As soon as Lilly got at her true feelings—the hurt, the disappointment, especially the anger, although that took awhile—I calmed right down." Lilly eventually realized that what had blocked her awareness of her healthy feelings about Don's mistreatment was toxic guilt, an inappropriate sense of responsibility for her cousin.

The sort of unconscious emotional lending that Lilly and Julius experienced isn't limited to anger. When Pierre's father died, Pierre's stiff upper lip amazed everyone—as did his wife's grief, which was inordinate. "I didn't realize how unfair all that macho stuff was to Penelope," Pierre remarked months later. "She had to express the grief for both of us." It took scaling a wall of toxic shame for Pierre to healthily mourn. Penelope, who had since stopped crying, was grateful. "But I'm also impressed," she said of her sweetheart. "Pierre's much more of a man to me now that I can see his emotional depth."

Awareness has to be the first step in the process of gaining emotional literacy, because—as we've seen—we can't be literate about feelings we neither recognize nor acknowledge. With emotional education on the increase, the biggest obstacle modern couples face in their quest for aware-ness is unhealed trauma and the emotional blind spots it causes. Healing that trauma is part and parcel of "getting in touch." Once we're able to recognize and label what's going on in our hearts, sharing this important data with each other is just a sentence away.

An Invitation to Reflect on the Law of Emotional Integrity

- Are you able to tell the difference between healthy and toxic guilt? When might you feel healthy guilt? Toxic guilt? How do these emotions affect your self-love? Your emotional intimacy?
- Are you able to tell the difference between healthy and toxic shame? When might you feel healthy shame? Toxic shame? How do these emotions affect your self-love? Your emotional intimacy?

Emotional Fluency

Emotional fluency, the second component of literacy, involves our ability to speak the language of emotions in the most straightforward way pos-sible. This is best accomplished by using the I-statement, a formula in which the words "I feel" are followed by whichever emotion is appropri-ate. (For example, "*I feel* embarrassed when you interrupt me.") Despite the fact that this old communication workhorse remains the cutting edge for couple communication, it's stunningly underemployed.

Although to the uninitiated the formula of the I-statement might appear contrived, even silly, the I-statement is a lifesaver for couples, and its development rates as a coup of genius. Like neurotransmitters for the heart, I-statements enable communicators to travel safely over highly charged material and open new pathways to each other. When properly used, I-statements effectively keep the poetry and drama of human inter-course from becoming volatile or destructive.

Still, the effect of these special messengers is far from flattening; they don't induce boredom. In fact, though few couples realize it, the real cause of boredom in relationships is the withholding of emotional truth, not the absence of volatility. Conversely, the sure cure for couple doldrums is a bold session of truth-telling. Because I-statements are designed to facilitate this level of dialogue, they have the power to bring forth lots of passion.

True emotional intimacy is the province of the emotionally fluent— namely, those well versed in the use of I-statements. Romance would be short-lived indeed if we lovers couldn't identify our warm feelings—and articulate to each other those three crucial little words: "I love you." Still, important as affection is, it represents but one stripe of the rich rainbow of emotions we need to express, I-statement style, in order to enjoy this delicious, nonsexual form of intimacy. Technicolor communication is serious business for couples, and the short list of emotions just won't do.

The full monte includes six families of both healthy and unhealthy emotions (each with several members) that you'll eventually want to be part of your repertoire of expression. These groupings are (1) shock, surprise, and confusion; (2) anger, rage, resentment, frustration, annoyance, irritation, and impatience, as well as the contempt cluster—that is, hatred, scorn, disdain, and contempt; (3) sadness, grief, disappointment, hurt, and despair; (4) fear, anxiety, worry, insecurity, panic, and jealousy, as well as toxic guilt and toxic shame; (5) healthy guilt and healthy shame, and embarrassment; and (6) love, joy, admiration, appreciation, gratitude, relief, empathy, and compassion. Don't let the length of this inventory daunt you. It's likely that these terms are already embedded in your vocabulary. Attaining fluency is mainly a matter of slipping them into I-statements.

Chart of Emotions: The Six Families

1. Shock, surprise, and confusion
2. Anger, rage, resentment, frustration, annoyance, irritation, impatience, and the contempt cluster (hatred, scorn, disdain, contempt)
3. Sadness, grief, disappointment, hurt, and despair
4. Fear, anxiety, worry, insecurity, panic, jealousy, and toxic guilt and toxic shame
5. Healthy guilt and shame, and embarrassment
6. Love, joy, admiration, appreciation, gratitude, relief, empathy, and compassion

Though no one would argue that communicating the warm, fuzzy emotions strengthens any union, many lovemates have difficulty believing that communication of the so-called negative feelings (the ones featured in groupings one through five) could ever prove bonding—even if they're presented as I-statements. This aversion to expressing the pricklier sorts of feelings is understandable, given how little exposure most of us have had to the appropriate form of such expression. When Paolo dared say, "I'm disappointed you didn't get along with my mother," it wasn't the easiest communication Lizabetha had ever received. Still, using an I-statement was the gentlest way Paolo could begin the honest conversation these two needed to have—far better than, say, "You really let me down when you didn't click with my mother."

And another example: "I feel guilty about deceiving you, and I'm afraid you'll never trust me again"—that's how Akiko announced to her new lover what she called a mini-betrayal. Having earlier promised this lover, Michio, that she wouldn't see her ex again, the young woman not only had lunch with him, but ended up crying with him at the table. Michio matched Akiko's perfect form when he responded, "I feel jealous that you met with your old boyfriend. You know he still has the hots for you. And I'm shocked that you broke your promise." Their emotionally literate communication—using I-statements, of course—bodes well for the establishment of real trust.

Conventional couple wisdom has always cajoled partners to openly appreciate and praise each other as much as possible. (Naturally, the vehicle of choice for this special communication would be, as always, good old I-statements.) Though we know that such communication greases the wheels of long-term love, we still tend to understate the positive. Fortunately, Bruno has no such inhibition. When his wife, Giselle, applied to medical school for the second time, the forty-year-old carpenter's simple words, "I'm so proud of you," found their way straight to this weary applicant's heart. For her part, June felt genuinely cared for when, after she'd argued with her sister-in-law, her husband patiently heard out her side of the story. And it meant much more to him than a simple thanks when she said, "I feel so grateful. You've really tried to understand me."

FURTHER EFFECTS OF UNHEALED TRAUMA

Imparting emotional truth to your partner via I-statements is just another skill—normally a no-brainer once you both commit to actually doing it. One thing can make it difficult, however—what by now you might recognize as the great saboteur of emotional expressiveness: unhealed trauma. In the same way that an early shock to the system can deport certain feelings from awareness, it can also make articulating them problematic.

Cicily was only too aware of her shifting moods. Indeed, she religiously entrusted the full story of her emotions to her daily journal. But when it came to saying, "I'm frustrated with you," to her husband, Tilson, she was tongue-tied. "I've never thought it odd that I couldn't talk to him about that," the fifty-year-old bookkeeper remarked to her priest. "There are just certain things you don't say out loud." Eventually, Cicily was able to trace a portion of this self-imposed silence to a single backyard incident. She recalled that at five she'd watched her uncle severely punish her older brother for screaming, "I hate you!" When she saw that unexpected connection, it ignited her courage to speak her emotional truth to her mate directly, clearly, and healthily—using I-statements. While we might assume that anger typically figures as the hard-to-say and hence sometimes silent emotion (as was the case with Cicily), trauma can choke back our open expression of *any* feeling.

BACK TO THE BASICS

So what's the bottom line on fluency? The I-statement. We just can't say it enough. I-statements are to couples what basic chord-forms are to jazz artists: we've got to be able to play them competently to join a band—or make music with our beloved. Of course, we wouldn't *limit* our dialogue to I-statements—any more than a virtuoso would endlessly replay the underlying chords of a song. Quality communication between intimates has to be an improvisational blend of powerful emotional notes and the simple talk, the incidental music of everyday life. When the melody of our relationship comes around, and it's time for the emotional bottom line, we can jump in to enrich the sound with an I-statement. We can deftly spice up the muted tones and, when conflict threatens to separate us, cool down the sharps. With a little experimentation, any couple can use this handy trick of speech to get close enough for jazz.

The crowning skill of emotional literacy, I-statements serve a large-scale purpose as well: they function as an essential alternative to the rash of unconscious communications that rain down on—and eventually soak—long-term love. (The upcoming section on emotional management will go into detail on this subject.)

> ### Pointers for Becoming Emotionally Literate
>
> Emotional literacy involves both awareness and fluency. It requires a commitment to . . .
> - Consult the Chart of Emotions if you need help naming what you're feeling
> - Practice using I-statements to tell your feelings to your partner

EMOTIONAL HONESTY

The concept of emotional honesty, the second dimension of emotional integrity, is a little confusing for some couples. Often it's equated with the generic brand of honesty—the Honesty with a capital H that made George Washington and Abe Lincoln famous. But no, this isn't about divulging trysts and offshore bank accounts (though lying about such details clearly won't a happy household make). Rather, emotional honesty is about our willingness to acknowledge our true feelings—*all* of them—as well as emotional blind spots and issues that affect our partnership. It's honesty in its next incarnation—similar, yet more refined.

If this seems a bit over the top, don't worry. Being *willing* to do something isn't the same as *doing* it. It would be crazy to point out every single feeling as it strikes us. This special kind of honesty asks only that we acknowledge emotional states and situations if they become problematic for either partner.

Given that restriction, emotional honesty isn't a directive to deliver blow-by-blow reports to each other on every erotic dream or feeling of attraction to another that registers. Nor is it, as Will was soon to find out, a license to abuse our partner with abrasive opinions (which aren't feelings anyway, but thoughts!).

Will was under the misconception that, in the name of emotional honesty, he was obligated to say absolutely everything that occurred to him. One day, while they were still dating, he told his new friend Terrance that he thought Terrance needed surgical hair implants since he was balding prematurely. Where's the emotional honesty in *that* statement? It's an opinion about Terrance's looks, not a revelation of Will's feelings—at least not on the surface. "I guess I was being pretty passive-aggressive," Will admitted after Terrance called him on it. "He'd kept me waiting thirty minutes." So Will's unsolicited critique was emotional after all, but not honest. It was anger, communicated in a dangerously indirect fashion—masked as personal truth.

Will's stab at emotional honesty was a far cry from the frankness involved in this third New Law of Love (though with Terrance's help he was eventually able to figure out his feelings). Emotional honesty is never a blunt statement of opinion. Rather, it's a straightforward commitment to be as *emotionally real* with each other as we possibly can. That's it.

Because it's hard to be real when we're not conscious of our feelings, emotional honesty includes a commitment to become conscious (if we're not) and then tell the truth about what we feel. Even so, honesty would be impossible if we can't listen to each other nondefensively and with an open heart. Thus the art of deep listening will be taught in the next chapter.

Emotional honesty is very different from emotional awareness and emotional fluency: whereas awareness entails *knowing* what we feel, and fluency entails knowing how to *speak* what we feel, honesty is the willingness to speak what we feel *to our mates—and face whatever blind spots or issues threaten the trust between us*. This is as real as it gets. As you can see, each element of emotional integrity is a prerequisite for the next: we can't honestly speak up if we don't know what's up or how to get it across in an acceptable way.

Honesty in Action: Clay Feet

Julia couldn't figure out why she'd get so irritable every time Richard went out to his art studio to work on a canvas. "If anyone had asked me," she later said, "I'd have insisted I was his biggest creative support. But," she went on, "I realized that whenever I knew he was planning to paint, I'd start trying to find things we had to do together." First it was plants that needed repotting, then shopping for his parents' anniversary, even cleaning out the garage. "One Sunday," Julia remembered, "when I was sure he was intending to finish a painting, I prepared his favorite meal. I had to admit to Richard what I realized as I stirred the simmering spaghetti sauce: I was jealous of the time he spent in the studio—I felt abandoned!"

It took several months for Julia to reach that realization, to become aware of the anxiety that made her want to control her husband's behavior. Because she was naturally inclined toward emotional honesty, she was then willing to go to the next level and trace her feelings to their roots. In that process she made a profound discovery: concealed beneath the agitation, jealousy, and feelings of abandonment, a fledgling artist foundered within *her,* one who was yearning to be acknowledged. "Richard was already so accomplished," she remarked. "I dared not even think of myself in the same vein. But without tooting my own horn, I *did* win prizes for my sculptures at art shows in high school."

Though on an unconscious level it seemed to Julia that Richard was the neglectful one, she now saw that it was *she* who was neglecting *herself.* What saved the day for this couple wasn't just Julia's awareness of her feelings or her ability to link feeling with words; it was her honesty. If she hadn't had the guts to dig more deeply, she wouldn't have found the jealousy. More important, she might never have uncovered the creativity inside her. And her honesty wasn't limited to feelings; she made a point of revealing her insights to Richard as well. This resulted in an exciting new dimension in their relationship. "I feel so touched that Julia let me in on this," Richard said. "It makes total sense—that whiny behavior, well, that just wasn't her." He was only too happy to use his wholesale discount at the art-supply store to get Julia started on her first project: a representation in clay of her artist within.

Blind Spots and Emotional Safety

A mutual commitment to emotional honesty is a giant step toward creating an emotionally safe relationship—especially when we pledge to explore those blind spots. As we've said, practically every thought, word, and deed that transpires between us is driven by emotion. We're in effect bombarding each other with emotional messages and subjecting each other to emotion-driven behavior all the time.

Any emotional benightedness either partner suffers from is a setback for the relationship. Whether it's general resentment and anxiety or disappointment at our mate's reluctance to go to our high school reunion, feelings that we disown end up coming out anyway—by default and willy-nilly. That's why a commitment to illuminate as many blind spots as we can identify is essential not only to the emotional safety of our union but also to our precious chemistry. If we can get those squirrelly feelings and issues into our sights and talk about them, we can catch—and defuse—them before they build up to the level of implosion or explosion.

But busting blind spots is much more than an excellent measure of prevention for couples. In waking ourselves up to our deeper emotional truths, we simultaneously raise our level of self-love. While this dual process helps reveal those areas where we need to heal, it also points toward the direction of our greatest bliss.

Though they alternated the role, it was Kitty, a forty-two-year-old attorney, who functioned as the canary in the coal mine during one particular incident. "Balancing the monthly budget used to be so stressful," she began. "Hud just couldn't sit still. It seemed that every five minutes he'd be up—to get snacks, go to bathroom, let in the cat." Hud cut in: "Then, late one night, she lost it and just screamed at me, 'What's *wrong* with you?' We had it out then, and I had to tell her the truth: I just couldn't handle her making twice as much money as me. Every time we did the budget, it was like rubbing my nose in it."

Hud's blind spot was toxic shame; an unhealthy part of him just couldn't shake the self-invalidating idea that Kitty was worth more because she earned more. His courage under fire produced a breakthrough for both of them, however: Hud became determined to vanquish that hectoring inner voice, and Kitty's irritation was replaced with compassion.

Love's Hall of Mirrors

Would that we could sit atop mountains, suss out our blind spots, and become completely emotionally honest on our own—before we entered relationships. We'd be spared a lot of work, not to mention the sometimes disconcerting experience of having our partners see our blind spots first. All alone, however, such enlightenment is almost impossible to achieve, and attempting it could even encourage a state of self-delusion. The semi-solo route—reading self-help books, attending workshops, and going through therapy—is *more* viable; indeed, one can face many facets of oneself in this way. Still, no matter how we slice it, *the fast track to emotional honesty is always committed relationship*. For when it comes to scoping out blind spots, mates are endowed with night vision.

Like the best friends they are, Kitty and Hud helped each other toward vital growth. He trusted her enough to let her serve as a reality check, a faithful mirror of his emotional blind spots. Who knows how long it would have taken him to spot and annihilate that inner critic on his own? Likewise in *your* couple, if you commit to emotional honesty— and allow the loving scrutiny of your amour to penetrate your darkest corners—you too will be enlightened. Over time, you'll feel your way into who you really are. Such is the agony and ecstasy of long-term togetherness and emotional honesty.

Obstacles to Emotional Honesty

At times all of us in partnerships have trouble being emotionally honest; we're unwilling to acknowledge our true feelings about certain issues— even when our silence threatens the trust between us. When we're aware of the truth but refuse to utter it, or are defensive or dishonest, it's not because we're scoundrels or pathological liars. Our deceit is yet another complicated side effect of unhealed early trauma. Childhood trauma not only creates a host of buttons and blind spots, as we've seen, but it also makes emotional honesty exceedingly difficult. In fact, revealing specific feelings (or facing certain issues) can feel to the unhealed part of a person like a risk to dignity, security, or some other precious commodity—even life. In Victoria's case, the perceived risk touched her marriage.

This thirty-year-old boutique manager said that she didn't mind spending every summer vacation in Vancouver, visiting husband Josh's parents. "It used to make me angry, but now I'm used to it," she stated flatly. The truth of the matter was that it was now going on year four of the same-old same-old, and she wasn't happy. In fact, Victoria was angry, disappointed, and hurt; mainly, though, she was afraid. Her own parents had never been taught how to state their feelings and needs, nor did they know how to negotiate for a win-win. When she was four, her parents had had a row in which her mother was particularly adamant about an issue. "And Dad just walked out," she said in tears. "No wonder I couldn't tell Josh the truth about my feelings. Part of me was convinced I'd end

up in a huge confrontation, recreate the most painful scene of my childhood, and then lose my husband!"

For Ed, it was an issue of traumatic shame that kept the truth caught
in his throat. No matter how many times Ginger suggested couple counseling, he angrily declined to go. "I couldn't admit that we had a problem until she mentioned the D-word," he said in their last session of six
months of therapy together. "In my family, letting an outsider in on your
problems was like submitting yourself to a public undressing. It would
never happen." Both his parents had held the institution of marriage in
such high esteem that they'd been preparing him for the job since he was
a toddler. "I was trained to be a 'fine husband,' settle down, and make
them proud. The only thing worse than marital problems would have
been divorce." Ed was under the influence of an old trauma: the indirect
threat that if he wasn't successful as a family man, he'd lose his parents'
approval. This resulted in generalized toxic shame about his marriage.
Even calling a marriage counselor on the phone was like announcing to
his parents that he was a failure.

Sexual Jealousy: The Ultimate Dishonesty

Sexual jealousy has a long-standing reputation as the shadow side of love.
And because it's shameful in our society to be needy or insecure, sexual
jealousy is shrouded in toxic shame. Hence jealousy is particularly hard
for us to be honest about. Complex and powerful, it's perhaps unparalleled in its capacity to destroy trust and intimacy.

Perhaps because it's such a hot subject, sexual jealousy is often misunderstood. Though it's commonly associated with humiliation, revenge,
and withdrawal, these are but the jagged edges of the emotion expressed
indirectly; they're not jealousy itself. Like Beauty's Beast, sexual jealousy
gets banished from consciousness and then gets really ugly.

Sexual jealousy is different from the nonsexual, competitive variety
that Julia, the budding sculptor we met earlier, suffered with her
renowned painter husband. Hers was based strictly on toxic shame, a fear
of being exposed as inferior. Sexual jealousy, by contrast, is a bitter cock-
tail of both toxic shame and abandonment panic, which has its roots
in abandonment trauma. The fear of being assessed as less desirable or lovable than somebody else—and then dumped for it—surely makes sexual

jealousy the most dangerous emotion we risk feeling when we allow ourselves to fall in love.

Like all emotions, this heavyweight is universal. We've all got the potential to feel sexually jealous, even if we haven't had occasion to experience jealousy with awareness or have trouble owning up to it. Many of us who feel powerless over our beloved's opinion of us respond with rage. This affords us a temporary (though false) restoration of power and dignity. Others of us respond by denying any feelings of jealousy to ourselves, to our mates, or both. We can end up either withdrawing into a haze of fantasy, intoxicants, or other escapes, on the one hand, or seeking revenge on the other.

Debbie, a systems analyst for a large international firm, wore her sexual insecurities uncomfortably on her sleeve. Every time the dreaded feeling of jealousy arose, she'd bravely divulge it to her house-builder boyfriend. For his part, Marty sincerely believed that he didn't have a proverbial jealous bone in his body. "It's just not what's real for me. Maybe it's because my mom loved me too much," he joked. Debbie shook her head. "I can't imagine you really being *into* another woman," she responded in exasperation. "But you don't have to be *interested* in someone else for me to feel threatened. Even a twinkle in your eye when you talk to a cute shopkeeper makes me feel like a toad." Still, Marty remained incredulous.

When Debbie got a new mentor at work, her career began to take off under his tutelage. At least once a month she flew off to another city to co-lead a training with him. One night, as Debbie packed for such a trip, Marty asked in an exaggeratedly offhand manner about the hotel arrangements. Now it was Debbie's turn to be incredulous: "He has a daughter my age—and anyhow, I'm not attracted to him in the least." Marty assured her that he'd just wanted to know how "those corporate travel things work." Weeks later, as he was thumbing through a recent copy of her company's newsletter, he gasped in astonishment. Pointing to a group photo, he said, "Don't tell me that fat dude standing next to you is your boss?"

"Busted!" Debbie exclaimed, relieved that he was at last showing himself to be "vaguely human." To her shock, however, Marty went into a rage. An army of epithets about her new boss flew out of his mouth, culminating in an accusation of corporate greed and the destruction of the planet. Debbie just listened; she didn't have a clue what to say. When he finally cooled down, he looked more hurt than angry. "Okay, I feel intimidated by the guy—so string me up," he said, in a conciliatory tone. "He's an MBA worth megabucks; I'm a carpenter. I can't imagine him not being attracted to you, and I'm fed up with the two of you traveling together." Marty had finally gotten honest about his feelings. That accomplishment represented a watershed for Debbie, who could now feel for her lover a greater degree of trust. Her own load was also lightened; later, when she ran into him chatting with an attractive woman at their gym, she felt less threatened, since she now knew he'd been there too.

Marty's toxic shame precluded him from even imagining that he was capable of knowing jealousy firsthand. His initial experience with the feeling, back when he first wondered about the hotel arrangements, was easy enough for him to deny, but the denial couldn't last. When circumstances conspired to reveal his emotional blind spot, the truth spurted out of Marty like a geyser. Like all feelings, jealousy must obey the law of emotional physics: feelings will out. In this case the pressure was relieved by a bit of emotional lending. When Marty stifled the feeling that was so antithetical to him, Debbie was forced by the restrained pressure into double duty.

The power of expressing sexual jealousy (or any other difficult feeling) out loud to the other is often dramatic, as this couple illustrates. Being honest about jealousy up front can keep our relationship from going either numb or ballistic. Sometimes, however, being aware of and honest about our feelings of sexual jealousy isn't enough to diminish their intensity; in these instances, more serious interventions are in order. Emotional management, the subject we'll discuss in the next section of this chapter, can guide you here.

Emotional honesty is one of *the* places where the rubber hits the road in intimate partnerships. Lovers who are game to routinely acknowledge to each other their emotional bottom line deserve commendation. But those who take it one step further, being willing to submit to the emotional audit that emotional honesty demands, are truly brave. In allowing their mate to hold a loving mirror up to any blind spot, button, behavior, or issue *strictly because he or she believes it's hurting their friendship,* they shift their relationship into warp drive. These New Couples reveal an important secret of long-term love—namely, that boring, dead relationships often got that way through emotional *dis*honesty, and that making each other privy to our full emotional truth is the surest ticket to growth, contentment, and passion.

An Invitation to Reflect on the Law of Emotional Integrity

- Which areas in your life do you find it difficult to be emotionally honest about with your partner? (Remember, emotional honesty concerns itself with how we *feel* about things and personal issues. It's not about confessing that, say, we forgot to put the clothes in the dryer.) What are these areas of difficulty?

- Is your relationship an emotional safe zone where you feel comfortable being emotionally honest? If not, how does this make you feel? If yes, and you still find it difficult to be emotionally honest, why? How does this make you feel? How does this affect your self-love? Your emotional intimacy?

- Are you aware of—or has your partner pointed out—any issues that might be blind spots for you? Are you aware of any childhood emotional trauma, toxic shame, or unhealthy guilt associated with these? How do your blind spots affect your self-love? Your emotional intimacy?

- Are you honest with yourself and your mate about any sexual jealousy you might experience? Do you criticize—or even condemn—yourself for this? Now that you know that sexual jealousy is caused by early emotional trauma, are you able to feel (or imagine feeling) compassion for yourself? For your partner?

EMOTIONAL MANAGEMENT

The final component of emotional integrity, emotional management is the ability to deal with our negative feelings by expressing them responsibly; this includes a willingness to recognize when we're unable to do that. The mismanagement of feelings occurs when our biggest buttons are pushed or blind spots exposed. Undoubtedly, the resultant irresponsible handling of anger, fear, grief, jealousy, and toxic shame and toxic guilt figures front and center in the anatomy of most failed relationships. Over the centuries it's also contributed to the bad reputation that's come to characterize all the so-called negative emotions.

The reason negative emotions have gotten such bad press is that when we don't consciously manage them, we end up acting them out (or, as we'll explain below, acting them "in"). Thus emotional management hinges on one absolutely crucial skill: *our ability to distinguish between acting feelings out and expressing them in a healthy way.* Our commitment to learn this vital distinction, and to then refrain from acting out, is at the heart of emotional management.

Successful emotional management depends on emotional literacy and emotional honesty, because we can't deal responsibly with a negative feeling if we're unaware of it, can't articulate it, aren't willing to tell the truth about it, or (as is often the case with toxic guilt and toxic shame) haven't heard of it.

Since the only way we can properly manage our anger, grief, fear, jealousy, and toxic emotions *with our partner* is through responsible expression, the only way to communicate about these issues is through I-statements. (Of course, as individuals, we can work to resolve our negative feelings through emotional catharsis as well—through crying, for example, or the kind of anger-release work done in the safety of a therapist's office.) Every other means of communicating negative feelings to our beloved—whether it's body language, facial expression, verbalization, deliberate silence, physical behaviors, or even sighing—is, quite simply, a different variety of acting out.

Consider these examples: Nellie acted out her anger at Owen when she slammed the car door. Quinn acted out his grief over his lost cat when he spent the whole weekend locked in the cellar eating ice cream, watching the old black-and-white television, and ignoring his wife. Tally acted out her anxiety when she nagged Buzz to check the gas range twice before he left the house. Glen acted out his toxic guilt when he looked sheepish and apologized to his girlfriend after she stood him up.

Though the styles in which we can act out our emotions are as limitless as human creativity, they're all hurtful. The reason is simple: acting out always involves a victim. And that unlucky victim will be you, your mate, or (if you have kids) your little ones. As unbearably humdrum as it may seem to ask lovers to stick to such a rigid protocol for informing each other about hard-to-share feelings, only I-statements are honest, effective, and humane.

Acting Out and Acting In

Lots of acting out occurs because we're emotionally illiterate. Like our parents and our parents' parents before them, we innocently conduct our emotional lives according to what we learned in our families. Yet even some of us who've successfully gotten in touch with our feelings, who know about I-statements and are capable of being emotionally frank, still act out occasionally or even frequently.

Why do we persist in acting out? Unaddressed trauma is again the culprit, raising its ignominious head. More often than not, unilluminated blind spots, unhealed buttons, and unresolved issues compel the emotionally unskilled and the skilled alike to act out. The situation becomes exponentially more complicated the longer it continues unaddressed, because by their very acting out, traumatized intimates unwittingly retraumatize each other—and traumatize their children. A terrible couple and family ordeal is inevitable when negative emotions seep, slip, or otherwise emerge without our conscious control.

ANGER: ACTING IT OUT

For couples, anger seems to be the greatest emotional challenge. Like a noble warrior's sword, in its healthy form anger performs a mighty function: it lets us know when our rights are being violated, helps us uphold our self-esteem, and keeps us safe. But in order to receive its gifts, partners must be trained to wield it.

The first task in that training is to own anger, that is, to admit it when we are feeling it. If we fail at that task, anger can turn into a veritable monster. If we refuse to allow anger into our awareness, or sequester it uncommunicated, over time it goes bad. If denied its true expression, it has no choice but to deform itself into rage, hatred, or contempt, and in that state it's usually displaced onto a target or issue more acceptable to our unconscious. Think of the road-rager who acts out on the freeway, for example. He isn't principally angry at the driver who cut him off (though even he might not know who he *is* angry at). When anger is deformed into rage, hatred, or contempt *within a couple,* the violence that results—be it verbal, physical, or emotional—can go one of two ways: either we act out our feelings against ourselves, or we act them out against our partner—either of which can permanently damage trust.

The personal-development movement of the past thirty years has railed against the suppression of feelings—and rightfully so. But in the process, some emotionally intelligent partners have wrongly concluded that *any* expression is better than *no* expression. Hence even the egregious acting out of anger has sometimes been rationalized as healthy.

Bennet was proud of himself as he talked of an encounter with his wife, Irene. " 'That's it!' I said to myself. 'I've had it!' And I ripped Irene's head off." His eyes gleamed as he continued: "It felt so good, really thera-peutic, to get it all out." Well, that may be, but Bennet's victory over stuffed rage was Irene's victimization. Overly zealous, perhaps, in his assertiveness self-training, Bennet hadn't been schooled in the golden rule of anger expression: *There's no justification for abuse.* Period. Many methods exist to help us release our pent-up anger nonabusively—from writing a no-holds-barred anger letter that we never mail to screaming in a train tunnel, as Liza Minnelli did in *Cabaret.* (See Chapter 6, "Peace-making," for a full introduction to anger-management and conflict-resolution techniques.) All forms of acting out—not to mention tolerating the acting out of a partner—are unacceptable. They run the risk of trau-matizing (or retraumatizing) someone—usually a loved one—and they always hurt the actor him- or herself.

Acted-out anger has long been known to come in two basic varieties: aggressive-aggressive and passive-aggressive. Even today, Freud's clunky jargon provides the best description of the great anger divide, because both types need to be seen as aggression (though passive aggression, being less direct, is sneakier and harder to substantiate). Aggressive-aggressive behavior includes verbal abuse, coercion, threats, throwing and breaking things, and physical violence. Passive-aggressive behavior, on the other hand, includes victim talk, patronization, sarcasm, teasing, denial, withdrawal, and innumerable forms of sabotage. In his unforget-table play *Who's Afraid of Virginia Woolf?* (acted on-screen by real-life couple Richard Burton and Elizabeth Taylor), Edward Albee displays just about every conceivable permutation of both kinds of acted-out anger.

Ray, a production supervisor in a factory (and normally ultra-organized), had a habit of "forgetting" logistical details—but only when they pertained to his wife, Violette. But Violette wasn't perfect either: the consensus among Ray, Violette, family, and friends was that she had a problem with anger—specifically, containing it. "Maybe I scare him with my occasional outbursts, but he's flat-out driving me bonkers!" Violette said defensively during their first couple session. "He's so irresponsible!" And it was true. Ray's absentmindedness *was* irresponsible—but not in the little-boy way it seemed. Rather, he was irresponsible in the communication of his anger to Violette. Unknown to both of them, he was furious: "She bites my head off," he said, visibly embarrassed, "and I don't know why I let her get away with it." But Ray got his unconscious revenge. The last straw for Violette—the episode that brought them in to counseling—was his causing her to miss a plane by forgetting to call her a cab. This is vintage passive-aggressive acting out.

ANGER: ACTING IT IN

Counseling revealed that Ray's behavior with his wife represented only a fraction of his problem with anger. The worst part wasn't how he acted it *out;* it was how he acted it *in*—against himself. It was routine for this man to exercise and work to exhaustion, for example, even depriving himself of adequate sleep.

Like acting out, acting in is the result of our inability to express anger, fear, or sadness directly; the difference is that instead of turning these feelings against our partner, we turn them against ourselves. While we're all familiar with the phenomenon of "beating ourselves up," most of us haven't been taught that self-abusive behaviors, as well as toxic self-talk, is a response to unhealthy guilt and shame. Eventually this kind of emotional mismanagement can lead to compulsions and addictions, as it did in Ray's case.

Violette and Ray were deeply relieved to learn about the traps they were in and the steps they could take to get out. Both committed to pay serious attention to how they were feeling in the moment—in advance of acting in or out. They also agreed to put their feelings plainly to each other in the shape of I-statements.

Despite the adage about opposites attracting, it may seem peculiar that these two found each other—he with his penchant for forgetting, she with her button about irresponsibility. Such lifelong matchups between the two forms of aggression aren't unusual, however. We like to think that the magnetism between passive-aggressives and aggressive-aggressives points up an urge toward health and balance, an attempt to rectify an outmoded style of coping. Unfortunately, simple proximity can't accomplish such a feat. Bringing about a true neutralization of these equally dysfunctional extremes of expression takes a conscious commitment to literacy, honesty, and management.

INCITING ANGER: YOU-STATEMENTS

Besides versing themselves in the intricacies of passive-aggressive and aggressive-aggressive behaviors, another way modern couples can clean up their anger act is by editing their verbal communication. The weeding out of the you-statement can work miracles of peace and harmony. This evil stepsibling to the healthy I-statement was exposed in all its destructiveness by parenting expert Thomas Gordon. While he proscribed the use of you-statements as abusive to any child at any speed, the list below shows how harmful they can be to lovers too. In fact, you-statements, which have a distinctly authoritarian tone, account for nearly all the verbal acting out of anger between partners.

Lynette was stinging from a recent humiliation by her husband's best friend, Joel. Chet made no attempt to protect her, nor did he acknowledge the incident later. When she tried to bring it up, he dismissed it as trivial. Lynette was beside herself with feelings of betrayal and sadness but had no idea how to express her concern to him directly. Then, when Chet announced his intention to take Joel for a ride in his new car, she lost it. Here are some examples of the you-statements she might have launched at him, adapted from Gordon's *What Every Parent Should Know* and sorted according to different categories of verbal abuse:

- *Sarcastic:* I suppose you want to take Joel out to dinner now?
- *Threatening:* You'll be sorry if you go out with Joel.
- *Shaming:* Are you going running to Joel again?
- *Ordering:* You call Joel this minute and tell him you're not coming.
- *Warning:* If you see Joel, he'll probably insult you too.
- *Interrogating:* What were you thinking when you told Joel you'd pick him up?

- *Moralizing or preaching:* You shouldn't fraternize with a person like that, even if he is your best childhood buddy.
- *Advising:* You'd better stay away from that guy.
- *Evaluating:* Clearly you don't know any better than to go to out with him again.
- *Psychoanalyzing:* You're obviously continuing in your childish pattern of not being able to say no.
- *Teaching:* You need to learn how to stand up for me with your friend.
- *Guilt-tripping:* If you pick him up after what he did to me, I'm never going to be able to hold my head up again around your friends.
- *Blaming:* You're trying to humiliate me by going to see him.

Although it may seem anticlimactic, the only healthy and respectful way Lynette could have communicated her anger to Chet is via the simple I-statement: *I'm angry and hurt that you're going out with your friend after he insulted me.* Though prosaic, this communication is clean and fair—a good prelude to psychologically mature dialogue between the partners.

ACTING OUT FEAR

While most love partners are all too familiar with the faces of anger acted out or acted in, fear slips by us with little fanfare. Despite its low profile, the fear family—including anxiety, stress, panic, and terror—can seriously destabilize a relationship if acted out.

Even though Carol knew that John was very attached to their cat, it was impossible for her not to feel accused of being irresponsible after the twenty-eighth time he'd reminded her not to let Miou-Miou out as they were leaving for the day. Walter's example was more extreme: he scared his whole family by insisting on keeping what seemed like an arsenal of semiautomatic weapons in the cellar "just in case."

This sort of interaction occurs in epidemic proportions in couples today. "She's just neurotic" or "He's such a control freak" are typical of the ways we minimize, rationalize, and often dismiss these manifestations of fear. The truth is these behaviors—and an infinite number of others—belong on our ever-growing list of symptoms of unresolved trauma.

Our client Emmanuel was lucky, however. He discovered before it was too late for his new relationship that it's not necessary to live with free-floating fears; they're substantially healable. To his neighbors, who'd joke that they could set their clocks by his weekday comings and goings, Emmanuel seemed the very model of efficiency. But he knew that being an organizational monster wasn't all it was cracked up to be.

When Daisy, whom he married after many years as a bachelor, moved in, his stopwatch hit the fan. "I just don't know what gets into Emmanuel," she confided to her best friend. "When we were unpacking boxes last week, he got a saucer caught in one of my oversized café-au-lait cups. He struggled with it for a moment, his face bright red. Then he suddenly pitched the cup to the floor and shattered it."

Prior to this frightening scene, neither Daisy nor Emmanuel had any idea that the micromanagement of his life was a response to constant low-grade anxiety. Like substance abusers who stop using without structured support, those of us who suffer from untreated trauma and don't know it often resort to white-knuckle types of behavior like Emmanuel's; this gives us the impression that we have a modicum of control. Then, when something goes awry—we're blocked, or told no, or (like Emmanuel) presented with a frustrating situation—we blow.

"Yes, I do get annoyed, but inside I feel so off-center," Emmanuel told his counselor during his first solo session, arranged in the aftermath of the cup incident. "Now with Daisy in my life, things seem much more unpredictable," he continued. "It's not fair to her; this isn't the man she married, a nervous wreck."

Emmanuel soon got to the bottom of his extreme efficiency: those years in rough boarding schools, where he was scapegoated for being shy and brainy—attributes that still spell *nerd*—had engendered their share of fear and rage. Since he had thus far been unable to express those feelings directly, he and Daisy did some couple work to learn emotional literacy and management techniques. They're now working on communicating about their feelings with each other without damaging trust.

The Management Alternative

As we've seen, emotions are wildcards; they're not what we'd call *controllable*. Still, we have a great alternative to acting them out: managing them. Once we learn the simple but priceless distinction between healthy and destructive communication of feelings—in other words, between management and acting out (or in)—we're well on the way toward the goal of emotional integrity. When we then actually practice using I-statements, we come closer still. But the real points are scored when, like Emmanuel, Daisy, Ray, and Violette, we recognize that all our irritating, out-of-control, and unloving communications, be they expressed in word or in deed, are more than just blind spots, buttons, and unresolved issues. They're the consequences of serious early hurts, and as such they deserve a lot of patience and require a lot of hard work. Such hurts don't heal by themselves.

For most of the feelings people typically act out, including mild anger, the basics of this chapter—emotional literacy, emotional honesty, and emotional management—should be adequate to help a couple uphold its emotional integrity. If, however, you experience a surfeit of anger (which happens to all of us more frequently than we wish), there's much more help available. Chapter 6, "Peacemaking," will teach you and your partner exactly what to do.

An Invitation to Reflect on the Law of Emotional Integrity

- Which emotions are easiest for you to manage? Which are most difficult? In other words, which feelings might you tend to act out—in behaviors or you-statements—instead of expressing them responsibly in I-statements? Which feelings might you tend to act in—in self-abusive behaviors or toxic self-talk? How does any acting out—or acting in—you do make you feel? How does it affect your self-love? Your emotional intimacy?

- When you're sad, disappointed, or frightened, do you ever act these feelings out as impatience, anger, or rage? How does this acting out make you feel? How does it affect your self-love? Your emotional intimacy?

- In which areas do you have a tendency to attempt to control people or situations? What are the feelings underneath these tendencies? How does this acting out make you feel? How does it affect your self-love? Your emotional intimacy?

--- ------

EMOTIONAL INTEGRITY PAST
AND THE TRADITIONAL COUPLE

Social convention has always taught spouses to conduct themselves with integrity. *Love, honor, respect,* and *cherish* were catchwords of the traditional marriage, and they're still unquestionably fitting ideals for committed relationship today.

The problem, then as now, has always lain in the achievement. How could spouses be expected to live up to these ideals when their emotions—the highly potent fuel of everyday interactions and behaviors (indeed, of their very existence)—remained largely unknown, unexplored, and unmanaged? As we know, many couples fell short. Not knowing what went wrong, they couldn't help but incriminate themselves—or their beloved other.

The need for an understanding of a concept such as emotional integrity, with its sanity-preserving components of literacy, honesty, and management, was paramount during the reign of the traditional, as it still is. For if the old-fashioned vow to love, honor, respect, and cherish one's spouse was the *what,* then the new-fashioned law, the Law of Emotional Integrity, is the *how*.

The idea of emotional integrity is relatively modern. This means that only those members of past generations who were born exceptionally emotionally intelligent, recognizing literacy as a gift and touting its virtues, paid conscious attention to becoming emotionally aware, emotionally fluent, or emotionally honest. When anger got dangerous, its management of necessity became a focus, but all the subtle forms of aggressive-aggressive and passive-aggressive acting out were (out of ignorance) ignored.

Instead of worrying about emotional integrity, lovemates of the past were preoccupied with emotional permission—that is, with what they were and were not allowed to express. In this domain, the unspoken rules were exceedingly strict. For life partners specifically, the socially acceptable emotions were limited to a grand total of one: *love.* So acceptable, in fact, was the romantic variety of love that, as we know, this special song of the heart was awarded its own holiday and angel-designate.

As vital and healthy as the so-called negative emotions are, they weren't so lucky: the less visible they were, the better. The culture ascribed virtue, and survival value, to the control of these less popular emotions, especially when partners were under pressure. Social prohibitions knocked down anger, sadness, fear, and jealousy; then toxic guilt and toxic shame—which have always existed but weren't labeled until recently—finished them off. With that dual blow, partners were effectively barred from expressing all the more problematic feelings.

But as we know, emotional energy requires an outlet. Where there was no permission for spouses to feel and express their emotions in a natural fashion, they had to communicate indirectly, venting their feelings against themselves and each other, or denying them altogether. Unfortunately, this restrictive approach often quashed the celebrated feeling of love too.

In addition to restricting what people could do with the feelings they had, tradition dictated who could experience which emotions. Feelings were traditionally distributed along gender lines. This societal assignment of certain emotions to each sex represents one of the colossal injustices of Western civilization. What was the breakdown of emotions? Let's look at men first.

In many cultures, both East and West, men have historically been given free rein to experience anger and, on certain occasions, joy. However, as we mentioned earlier, the expression of the "feminine" emotions of fear, sadness, and love has been seen as (toxically) shameful. The Wailing Wall in Jerusalem, where male religious elders still publicly grieve, represents an exception. More typically, when a male disclosed his softer emotions to anyone—even his wife—it felt like a confession.

Our forefathers would have seen commitment to a marital principle such as emotional integrity as requiring that they abandon masks they'd spent a lifetime constructing—masks that they believed were the ticket to acceptance and belonging. The traditional male thus labored under a facade that precluded most intimacy with his lifemate. How many died when their hearts, brittle from lack of use, gave way to fatal attacks?

Over the course of history, women have suffered their own version of emotional oppression. Though they've long enjoyed the pleasure of showing love openly, and the mixed privilege of expressing fear and sadness (if not tainted by toxic shame), anger, the emotion linked to power, has been another story. Seen as aggressive and therefore unladylike, this healthy feeling has been weighed down by societal disapproval, often crushed right out of awareness. So too the unhealthy versions of guilt and shame.

Under such severe pressure, women's anger (obeying the laws of energy) would necessarily show up dysfunctionally in themselves and their intimate relationships. When combined with the residue of unresolved emotional trauma, displaced anger was responsible for the harsh wifely stereotypes of doormat, shrew, and hysteric. In the first, the compliant, passive-aggressive doormat type who denied all anger, that emotion could lead her to become a victim of spousal abuse and neglect. Her combative, aggressive-aggressive sister, the shrew, felt like a victim too, but because she was wont to get enraged, she was often rejected as scary and unlovable. The overly emotional, hysterical wife, who existed in a chronic state of panic, was often considered crazy; she sometimes ended up institutionalized. Each of these tragic personality types was denied an appropriate outlet for her healthy anger—and was terrified that she'd be abandoned should the anger surface.

Michael, a retired nightclub owner, and Monica, his librarian wife, came to counseling after thirty exhausting years of emotional mismanagement. At six-plus feet, the man towered over his petite spouse. Sadly, this was only the most visible sign of the domination, for theirs was the prototypical marriage of an aggressive-aggressive with a passive-aggressive.

Most rows at their house would begin and end with Michael's bellow: "I can't find my keys! Where are my keys?" Then came the accusations: "You used them last to drive to the market!" The impact of his voice often made Monica freeze: "Oh, dear," she'd say, both her voice and her hand trembling, "we'll find them." Then she'd buy time: "Where did you see them last? I'm sorry I took the car." Apologizing for his rage was also standard for this beleaguered wife.

Michael's big button—whether over the loss of keys or over anything else his wife was involved with—was the traumatic legacy of his own early years. His father, himself a victim of childhood abuse, used to turn his pent-up anger into violence against Michael and his mother. But perhaps worse than the physical mistreatment was how this man would shame the small boy for his every mistake and tender feeling. His mother, like Monica, stood by unable to respond. By the time Michael was five, toxic shame had already formed a tight seal around his little-boy heart and all the tears it contained.

Thus did Michael learn how to express his so-called bad moods— just like his father, by hurling you-statements that blame, command, and threaten. As to physical acting out, his resolution never to raise a hand—even in threat—to either his daughter or his wife had been honored.

Aware of a difference in their response types, Michael was mystified by Monica's obsequiousness. Having no way to know the cause—namely, her own unacknowledged early hurts—he misconstrued it as good-naturedness. And though he marveled at her seeming lack of moods, he was unable to stop steamrolling her. "Her sheepish, guilty ways infuriated me all the more," he admitted in a couple session, clearly perplexed. (In the face of his adolescent daughter's outbursts, however, his role reversed and he found himself backpedaling like Monica.)

His wife, too, bore all the symptoms of a difficult welcome to this world: her freeze response and trembling both spoke volumes about her own childhood experience with antiquated disciplinary methods; her distorted "global" sense of responsibility and knee-jerk "I'm sorry's" belied severe toxic guilt; and the fact that she stayed in this emotionally unsafe relationship for three decades before seeking help was a sign of abandonment trauma. Her father's unpredictability—exceptionally loving one minute, out of control the next—confused and terrorized her. Her mother's seeming lack of protective instincts conditioned Monica by age five to believe in the acceptability of being made to cower by a rageaholic intimate. Finally, she insisted that she felt no anger toward her husband—clearly Monica's biggest emotional blind spot.

These two were meant to find each other, as they learned in a touching series of couple sessions. Though a lifetime of acting their angers in and out had taken a heavy toll, there was a unifying similarity in the somber hues of the emotional landscapes that were revealed as husband and wife gradually peeled the onions of their individual pasts. Michael shed his first adult tear hearing Monica's story, the details of which he'd never known, and a deep mutual empathy was born. The simple precepts of emotional integrity—namely, literacy, honesty, and management—made sense to this couple. Slowly both contacted, then responsibly and honestly shared, their more difficult feelings.

Overcoming his acting out, especially the habitual use of you-statements, remains an ongoing challenge for Michael. Monica, on the other hand, struggles with her acting in—the constant self-blame and repression of her healthy anger. She's also learning to set limits, or leave the room as necessary, when Michael gets out of hand. It was her idea to use the safety of every session to read him her list of that week's grievances. He's yet to walk out during this exercise. In taking responsibility for their own buttons, blind spots, and uncomfortable issues, this traditional couple, like a caterpillar transforming into its more glorious self, is becoming a New Couple.

An Invitation to Reflect on the Law of Emotional Integrity as It Pertains to Your Parents

- Was your parents' relationship an emotional safe zone? If yes, what made it so? If not, what kept it from being safe? How did this affect your parents' self-love? Their emotional intimacy? How did this make you feel?
- What were your parents' emotional buttons and areas of oversensitivity or overreactivity? (These may be the same.) How did these affect your parents' self-love? Their emotional intimacy? Did they criticize—or even condemn—themselves for these? If so, why? How did this make you feel?
- How does it make you feel to learn that these are the result of childhood emotional trauma? Are you able to now feel (or imagine feeling) compassion for them about their buttons and areas of oversensitivity or overreactivity?
- Are you aware of—or do you suspect—any childhood emotional trauma in your parents' lives? How did it affect your parents' self-love? Their emotional intimacy? How did this make you feel?
- How would they have felt about exploring the possibility of childhood emotional trauma?
- Have they ever healed any childhood emotional trauma? If yes, how? How did this healing affect their self-love? Their emotional intimacy? How did this make you feel?
- Did your parents suffer from toxic guilt or toxic shame? How did this make you feel?
- Were your parents able to be emotionally honest? How did this make you feel?
- Were there any issues of sexual jealousy in your parents' relationship? How did this make you feel?

- Which emotions did your parents have the most difficulty managing? How did any acting out they might have done make you feel? How did it affect the health of their relationship?
- How would your childhood have been different had your parents subscribed to the Law of Emotional Integrity? How would your own couple be different (or, if you're single, how would past relationships have been different)?

EMOTIONAL INTEGRITY AND THE NEW COUPLE

When Alexis and Hans met five years ago at a yoga retreat, they were both recovering from divorce and both raising a school-aged child alone. She a loan officer, he a management consultant, each had made the rounds of the personal-development workshop circuit. They'd faced down innumerable dragons, were working to individuate from their families-of-origin, and together had studied their parents' marriages to undo any unwanted influence on their own. The couple was also serious about the emotional integrity of their relationship. They spoke the language of emotions and, knowing that ongoing blind spots and buttons seem to define our humanity, were committed to get to the bottom of any issue that affected either one of them. And today's issue affected them both.

"I'm so frustrated," Hans said as he opened the session. "Every time we go to the pool at our club, Alexis accuses me of looking around and 'getting off' on other women. She's becoming a regular eye-traffic controller!" Alexis didn't miss a beat. "I know, I know. Look, I'm embarrassing myself! It's just that ever since I had Adele, I'm overly sensitive. My body refuses to go back to the way it used to be. It's painful to be with Hans around skinny women in bikinis. This jealousy thing is new for me, and it's the pits." She turned on him suddenly: "Still, you *are* constantly scanning the environment. I'm afraid you're looking for some titillation!" Hans quietly countered his wife: "I really resent when you psychoanalyze me. You have no idea what's going on inside my head."

Though her postpregnancy shape had pushed Alexis over the edge, she'd been self-conscious about her body since she was twelve years old and made her first poolside appearance in a two-piece. According to her, that scene when her father and brother erupted in gales of laughter about her "baby fat" would be forever imprinted on her mind; it also left a scar of toxic shame that was newly sensitive to the touch. "I guess, on some level, it felt like that old pool situation again," she figured aloud. "And Hans's roving eyes proved one more time that my body was ridiculous."

Alexis's emotional honesty—her willingness to analyze her button to its source and admit to her toxic shame—opened Hans's heart and inspired him to tell his own story. "We were at a seaside family reunion. I was eight," he began. "When he saw me in a bathing suit, my favorite uncle shook his head in pity. 'Well, my son,' he said—and I'll never forget it—'you do have your mother's genes; in fact, you're shaped just like a girl.' It totaled me." And then to Alexis: "Haven't you noticed that I always wear a towel?"

Alexis's eyes brimmed with tears of compassion. Still, Hans knew that it was his turn to face an uncomfortable issue. "I don't know why I look around when I'm in public," he conceded. "And sure, if I see a beautiful woman, I don't exactly look away," he continued. "But that's not really what I'm looking for. It's just a nervous habit." It took some time for Hans to understand his public behavior; then it became clear: "My older sister did give me a hard time. She was mocking, actually really dominating," he remembered. "I suppose darting my eyes around was just my way of refusing to make eye contact with her." With that insight, he addressed Alexis: "I'm sorry. I hate to think that my weirdness has caused you so much pain. After all, you're not my sister—thank God!"

Thus did Alexis and Hans build a bridge of empathy over the painful parts of their past. Determined to keep any other invisible—but still open—wounds from wreaking havoc in their life together, they vowed not only to each take an inventory and warn the other about what they found, but also to do whatever they needed to heal. Though Hans would need to be vigilant about that blind area—and interrupt his unconscious "scanning"—he no longer felt as controlled by Alexis. For her part, Alexis's button got a break, and she understood the mislabeled oversensitivity over which she'd long beaten herself up. And now she knew that her husband's pattern was an old form of self-protection, not a hunt for someone sexier than she.

. . .

Emotional integrity is about loving, honoring, respecting, encouraging, and validating the full spectrum of our healthy feelings—and those of our beloved other. As revolutionary as it may seem, when we commit to the third New Law of Love, we're doing much more than taking responsibility for the power of our own affective world. We are, perhaps for the very first time in the history of romantic relationship, addressing the ideal of emotional safety. Though it's a fact few have been educated to know, all love partners are sitting atop mysterious reservoirs of unexpressed emotions, some of which date back to our earliest days. These murky emotional waters are destined to be brought to the surface when, during the power struggle especially, we inadvertently—yet inevitably—bump into each other's biggest emotional blind spots and buttons.

A New Couple's sincere and mutual effort to become literate, honest, and adept at managing emotions not only lays the groundwork for peace, an emotional safe zone, and a new kind of sanity between lovemates, it also creates ongoing opportunities for essential purification. For no matter how wild an emotion may be, a known feeling is always easier to tame than an exiled feeling—and a conscientious effort to get in touch with each one of our feelings is worth its weight in gold. Mastering basic emotional management skills, as well as the deceptively simple I-statement, is fundamental to maintaining the emotional integrity of our relationship. And because, as we'll see in Chapter 6, these skills are also the first steps in the resolution of conflict, we might never know how many El Niños even a little such competency has kept safely offshore.

Though it may be a stretch, and will certainly require deep trust in ourselves and our beloved, the willingness to dig out those old buried feelings and face them—even those we'd rather hide from ourselves and everyone else—can transform our lives. And as partners in New Couples frequently notice, the more comfortable we get with our own emotional privates, the more willing we are to allow our beloved a regular peek. (Sometimes, when called for, we might even permit a stranger—in the form of a therapist—to look as well.) And what a relief! Because once we know how to appropriately listen, the simple act of telling each other our emotional truth is the principal way we can clear up those awful, self-punishing feelings of toxic guilt and toxic shame that riddle us all.

The only way, then, is up. With a commitment to this third New Law of Love, we'll find that we naturally continue to inspire each other to ever greater heights of awareness, expression, and honesty. Over time, when early hurts are positively identified and empathized with, we might even experience some miraculous healings. Our self-love will shoot up, and we'll experience more space for feelings of fun in our emotionally safe relationship. Then who knows? Together, we may well be able to create our own relationship strip—only we'll name it *Life in Love.*

The Key to Emotional Integrity

Examining and healing emotional blind spots, buttons, and issues that cause *either* partner strife and establishing an emotional safe zone is the key to the third New Law of Love.

This means learning the skills that enable you to take full responsibility for your emotions—specifically, to . . .

- Become emotionally literate—that is, aware and fluent
- Become emotionally honest
- Manage all feelings, including those that are extreme

4. DEEP LISTENING
the fourth new law of love

When I ask you to listen to me and you start giving
me advice,
you have not done what I asked.
When I ask you to listen to me
and you begin to tell me why I shouldn't feel that way,
you are trampling on my feelings.
When I ask you to listen to me
and you feel you have to do something to solve my
problem,
you have failed me, strange as it may seem.
Listen! All I asked was that you listen!
Not talk or do—just hear me.
I can do for myself;
I'm not helpless—maybe discouraged and
faltering—but not helpless.
For when you accept as a simple fact that I do feel
what I feel,
no matter how irrational,
then I can quit trying to convince you
and get about this business of understanding what's
behind this irrational feeling.
When that is clear, the answers are obvious and I
don't need advice.
Irrational feelings make sense when we understand
what's behind them.

Perhaps that's why contemplation works, sometimes,
    for some people—
because the Divine is mute,
It does not give advice or try to fix things.
It just listens and lets you work it out for yourself.
So please, listen and just hear me.
And if you want to talk, wait a minute for your turn,
    and I'll listen.
Maybe if we both sit and listen to each other,
we will be able to solve even greater problems than
    our own—
perhaps we will even hear the mute voice of the Divine.

ANONYMOUS

Perhaps the divine human design—one mouth, two ears—was intended specifically for couples, a subtle indication of the correct ratio of talking to listening. It's divine indeed when partners can listen to each other twice as much as we talk. If we choose, we can shift the more passive part of interpersonal relating into an even higher gear—and learn to *deeply* listen. For while listening is still the greatest gift of love, *deep* listening is the gift that makes love last.

> *If, as Freud says, dreams are the royal road to the unconscious, deep listening is the royal road to intimacy.*

A GRATEFUL PARTNER

Together with emotional integrity, deep listening—that is, listening from the heart—is the essence of emotional support. It's different from the everyday sort of listening in that it offers no advice or judgment, nor does it attempt to fix anything. The silence it entails opens a delicious space, one that invites our beloved to go really deep, to contact and express the purest forms of his or her feelings, whatever they may be. The fourth New Law of Love asks us to listen not just for the story, but for the *feelings* our partner is having *about the story*. Deep listening functions, then, as the receptive end of emotional integrity, enabling the listener to field for the speaker the very feelings that emotional integrity helped both partners get in touch with, express, and be honest about. The most exalted form of deep listening empowers us to cull from our partners even their so-called negative feelings *about us*. For when done responsibly, such truth-telling is the surest way to keep lovers from drifting apart.

This modern age, with its virtual aural overload, seems to be all about transmission, not reception. Everyone, including romantic partners, is being turned into a listening target. Assaultive sound bites, coming from all directions and at high volume, are shortening our attention span, causing information indigestion, and numbing lovers emotionally. To keep ourselves from going nuts, we've all had to go a little deaf.

A CRISIS OF LISTENING

You'd think that in this modern-day Babel, we'd treasure the simple refuge of each other, eagerly seek the oasis of quiet that our relationship can provide. But this is often not the case. Instead, many of us go home and look for serenity in our audio-enhanced computer gadgetry and televisions. "Quiet" evenings with each other are spent watching videos in surround-sound or otherwise "recovering from the day." Unfortunately, however, when we're plugged in to entertainment, we're typically tuned out from each other.

Undoubtedly, recent information technology has created its own unique stresses, contributing to greater societal depersonalization than ever before. Still, the romantic estrangement many of us experience in our era is nothing new. Though far more expensive, the high-tech toys of today function much as the silent newspaper did in our parents' generation: besides helping everyone unwind, these gizmos also serve in part to cloak the emotional alienation that spreads subtly and gradually over lovemates—even partners who started out mad about each other. Clearly, whether we know it or not, what couples need now is (as the old song suggests) love, sweet love, in the form of being listened to—truly, madly, and deeply—every day.

Like emotional awareness, deep listening is a natural human ability that should come easily to each of us. So why does it continue to be such a bear for couples? After all, lovers rarely start out unable to listen to each other. During the intoxication stage of relationship, many of us are overwhelmed by the sense that no one ever has—or ever could—hear us as well as this newly beloved. To both partners' frustration, however, the pillow-talk days go fleetingly by. Without a commitment to both emotional integrity and deep listening, the thrill of truly *hearing* our partner inevitably gets lost as our simpatico feelings for each other become diluted by less fun, more complex feelings. Eventually, the ability to listen to each other at all starts slipping, as Kiryn and Donald discovered.

They had just turned the lights out when Donald broached a difficult subject: "I'm worried that Sarah isn't getting along with the other kids at school. She seems to hover around Mrs. Ellis in the recess yard when all the other kids are skipping rope." Kiryn, his wife of eight years, sighed. "I suppose it's the result of my being overprotective," she answered. "Why is it that I'm always the one blamed for our children's problems?" "That's not what I said," Donald countered. Now *he* was annoyed. "All I said was that I'm worried about her. I haven't drawn any conclusions— nor am I blaming anyone."

As with many couples untrained in the art of deep listening, consensual reality had begun to elude Kiryn and Donald more and more over time. Though his timing was definitely off, Donald *did* use an I-statement to tell his spouse his concern. Nevertheless, Kiryn was unable to hear him. All she heard was blame; in fact, she ended up accusing him of accusing her! Frustrated by the downward trend in their communication, they signed up for a weekend retreat for couples sponsored by their church. As the weekend progressed, the causes of the schoolyard-discussion breakdown in communication (and perhaps hundreds of conversations preceding it) became clear.

They realized that, without warning, they'd made their inexorable passage into the power-struggle stage of relationship; in fact, they'd been shipwrecked there for years. And as can be expected of this phase, Donald and Kiryn were subjected to the wildest emotional extremes and tightest shutdown of feelings in their adult lives. Indeed, it seemed that every button and blind spot was flashing red alert. In that electric atmosphere, lending each other an ear had ceased to be the pleasurable experience they'd known as best friends. Instead, it was often just short of unbearable. At barely forty years of age, these partners had already experienced their first loss of hearing.

Kiryn's major button had to do with always feeling blamed. In her mind, she constantly harangued herself for her "screwups." "It comes straight from my past," she told Donald in one of the retreat's many touching exercises. "Whenever anything went wrong in my family, it was blamed on yours truly. I was convinced I was a complete loser. Still, I'd always planned to make up for it by being a great mother." Any time her husband brought up an issue that had the slightest connection with responsibility, Kiryn was stung by a painful emotional mix of toxic guilt and toxic shame. This rendered her incapable of hearing Donald with accuracy. Very often she'd end up acting out, which invariably caused Donald to shut down. Kiryn concluded, "Maybe I was no Goody Two-Shoes, but I wasn't responsible for *all* the problems in my family, either."

Donald contributed to the failure of communication too. His weekend bounty was the discovery of his own listening challenges, as well as a glaring blind spot about anger. Donald had learned in his family-of-origin that the only safe way to express anger was indirectly—otherwise, he'd be the recipient of an intense guilt trip. Donald continued this pattern with his wife. "I guess I'm a dyed-in-the-wool passive-aggressive," he kidded. "The fact is I *do* blame Kiryn for a lot of what goes on with the kids. And I can get pretty self-righteous. But I've also learned that I indict myself too—all the time. I feel so damn guilty that I don't have more time with the kids that I practically stick my fingers in my ears when she tries to tell me the slightest thing that might be troubling them."

The Law of Deep Listening has everything to do with trust—building it, breaking it, and eventually, with or without facilitation, rebuilding it. Let's take a closer look at that sequence. In the intoxication stage of relationship, this special kind of listening is how we first learn to trust each other. Later, during the power struggle, buttons and blind spots start to crowd out real relating. Not knowing how to take responsibility for our emotions, we inevitably start manipulating, nagging, and otherwise acting out our unlovable feelings. As listeners, our first defense to those behaviors in a partner is to unwittingly tune each other out; trust then falls by the wayside. But lovers can learn to listen again, *deeply* listen, thereby rebuilding trust. In the example of Donald and Kiryn's altercation, the inability to accurately hear the other person's emotions—even though the speaker was fluent in the language of emotions—is what got them into trouble, and deeply listening to each other is what got them out.

Believe it or not, there are times when being emotionally literate and honest with a partner shows poor discernment on our part and can even be self-destructive. This is the case when our mate isn't willing or able to honor our heartfelt communications by deeply listening to them. Eduardo learned about the need for discernment the hard way. Ever since his sweetie, Celine, had taken an adult-ed course on emotional intelligence, she'd been urging him to get in touch with his true feelings and tell her all about them. One day, when Eduardo finally got up the gumption to admit to her that he was afraid of the dark, Celine yelped and called him a coward. Needless to say, Celine's EQ would need to be complemented with a little training in DL—that is, deep listening—before her guy would ever bare his soul again.

Mirabelle and Kent were both intent on listening well. As long as one used I-statements to express feelings, the other would listen. Unfortunately, Kent's decibels and bulging neck veins exceeded the limits of emotional management. Yet even when he scared the daylights out of her, Mirabelle dutifully tried to listen. It was a relief for her to learn that the correct communication formula alone doesn't constitute responsible expression; language and tone of voice work together to encourage safe, respectful emotional dialogue. Kent made good use of that new knowledge too, agreeing to examine the wiring of his extreme emotional charge—the force behind the rage he'd acted out on Mirabelle for years. He discovered that his belligerence was tied to his very young years, the by-product of mistreatment by a juvenile-delinquent older half-brother.

Here's the bottom line for Mirabelle and others like her: *As a rule, if you're on the receiving end and are frightened by any communication from your mate, deep listening isn't appropriate.* What's called for instead is a time-out, a primary tool used in anger management (a subject to be discussed in Chapter 6, "Peacemaking").

Nancy's was a different story. No matter how gentle and responsible her mate's words were, she simply wasn't able to tolerate Lenny's direct communication of anger via I-statements. Even in the presence of their couple coaches, she'd declare that he was attacking her. This inability to deeply listen to responsibly expressed anger was a serious symptom of unhealed childhood trauma: Nancy's mother suffered from a psychiatric disorder and had episodes of explosive rage. A courageous client, Nancy showcased high emotional integrity when she took responsibility for her traumatic button. She found a therapist specializing in adults raised by mentally ill parents and worked to desensitize herself to the issue. Though listening to anger remained difficult for her, Nancy was able to hear Lenny enough to stay emotionally in touch with him, and for this he was grateful.

An Invitation to Reflect on the Law of Deep Listening

As you approach the exercises in this chapter, remember that the presence or absence of New Couple chemistry profoundly affects a couple's experience with each law.

- Do you consider yourself a deep listener? How do you listen to your partner today compared to when you first met? How does the current depth of your listening affect your self-love? Your emotional intimacy?

- Are you aware of tuning out when your partner is speaking? If so, why do you do it? If it's in order to avoid issues or emotions, what is it you're avoiding? If it's in response to your partner's acting out, what form does his or her behavior take? When you tune out, are you yourself acting out your feelings? Do you ever use the silent treatment? How does your tuning out affect your self-love? Your emotional intimacy?

- Are you aware of times when your partner tunes you out? If so, is your partner tuning out to defend against your acting out?

- Are you able to inform your partner when the timing is not appropriate for you to deeply listen, and suggest a better time?

SELF-LOVE LOVES DEEP LISTENING

The last major benefit of deep listening is its tendency to elevate our self-love. In that regard it works wonders. Deep listening is the same process by which parents create high self-love in their children and therapists help their clients recover from deficient self-love (and a variety of other emotional ills). When parents are able to validate and encourage the expression of their children's full rainbow of feelings, they help to create the initial sense of self-worth. These little ones then grow up with the healthy conviction that they deserve all forms of safety and respect, and *without* the excessive need for external approval. They're convinced from the outset of the value of their own feelings, thoughts, and intuition—indeed, of their very value as human beings.

Deep listening is also how parents minimize the traumatic impact on their children of life's scrapes, falls, and tragedies—and the technique works well for couples too. Its success lies in the fact that when, as children, we're encouraged by emotionally integrated parents to tell the story of our pain, we can to a large degree let it go. The words "emotionally integrated" are key here, because parents—like love partners—are capable of listening to the emotions of others only to the extent that they've already accepted their own. We can assume, then, that if our parents couldn't listen to us, their parents couldn't listen to them.

Children who grow up with unlistening parents mature into adults who have an intense need to be heard. While when it comes to exploring trauma, a trusted psychotherapist is our best ear, partners can still listen far more fully to each other's emotional truth than most of us currently do. And in that process, we can make real headway with self-love.

In the beginning of a relationship, as we've noted, most of us listen beautifully to our partner; through loving attention, we draw out our lover's deepest feelings. It's no fault of our own that the rigors of the power struggle whittle away at our ability to be there for each other in this way. But whittle they do, so that eventually deep listening must be done remedially if the relationship is to survive. Easier said than done, though, since by that point our listening skills may have atrophied through lack of use.

Fortunately, the same skills of deep listening that come so naturally to new lovers can be learned as we drift apart. If those skills are used in combination with the skills and commitments outlined in the Law of Emotional Integrity, we can re-create the emotionally safe atmosphere that we started our relationship with. Deep listening also helps us deal with blind spots and buttons, resolve new conflict, rebuild trust, and (as noted above) shore up sagging self-love. With a little bit of luck, and possibly a trusted outside hand, deep listening can also help to dissolve the residue of early trauma.

An Invitation to Reflect on the Law of Deep Listening

- Who deeply listened to you when you were a child? How did this make you feel? How did it affect your self-love?
- Who did you want to listen who didn't? How did this make you feel? How did it affect your self-love?
- What feelings, issues, and subjects did those around you seem interested in listening to you talk about? What feelings, issues, and subjects did they not seem interested in? How did this make you feel? How did it affect your self-love?
- What impact did this early experience have on your ability to deeply listen to your partner today ? (For example, do you tune in to and out of the same feelings, issues, and subjects that these early role models did?)

GIVING THE GREATEST GIFT OF LOVE

Whereas one member of a couple might be more naturally gifted as a listener than the other, *both* can learn to listen emotionally and with competence. As with all the skills in this book, the willingness to try is paramount. And that willingness can be stimulated in a partner by our own modeling: perhaps the greatest inspiration for learning to really listen is having been on the receiving end—in other words, having ourselves been heard in this loving fashion.

Deep listening is a gift of attention, of staying present—emotionally, mentally, and when possible with our eyes—as our mate relates information that he or she considers important. It's this perception of importance that gives any message its emotional weight. And it's our self-discipline as listeners—restraining ourselves from interrupting, judging, advising, or intervening in any way—that makes the speaker feel not only emotionally "held" but also honored. Naturally, as Mirabelle and Kent learned, the communication itself must be responsible, aligned with the guidelines of emotional integrity. When the speaker uses I-statements as much as possible and avoids acting out, all the listener has to do is sit tight.

This used to be difficult for Tess. She seemed to get ants in her pants whenever Allie tried to air her feelings about the infighting at the women's clinic where she worked as a nurse practitioner. "At those times, I wasn't aware that what I was really doing was jumping away from my own feelings," she said. "I couldn't listen to Allie because I couldn't admit to myself how trapped and despairing I felt about my own job at the bank." In this case, deep listening collided with a blind spot. Until insight shone through, Tess "left" whenever her partner expressed feelings that she couldn't face in herself.

Deep listening isn't complicated. It doesn't ask you to interview or mirror your mate or to listen either actively or reflectively, as some other listening techniques do. Both partners just have to agree to be attentive while the other is talking. Of course, timing is always a consideration. If the moment isn't good, we need to say so, suggesting an alternate time when we'd be able to lend a loving ear (or preferably two).

Some of us, however, will find that even after practicing, we just can't deeply listen to our mate; we can't help but interrupt, perhaps, or we have trouble sitting still, being present, making eye contact, or otherwise staying focused. Since a problem of that nature is always an issue of buttons or blind spots, we can roll this issue over to the tenth New Law of Love and sign up for some transformational education.

Deep listening can happen anywhere: in the tent you pitched for the kids in the yard, in the car during your commute to work, or on a back-country trail; it can even happen over the phone in a pinch, if circumstances don't allow for face-to-face conversation. If we use this skill judiciously, we find that deep listening, like I-statements, can become part of the natural music of our couple's conversation. Though we don't interact via deep listening *all* the time, our use of this practice will have a cumulative effect on our relationship. Similar to the effect of journaling, meditation, or prayer on the individual, regular practice seasons a friendship. Over time, deep listening instills in any couple a profound mutual respect.

THE SESSION: IN SEARCH OF A LOVING EAR

The best way two people can get trained in the art of deep listening—not to mention handling common communication breakdowns—is through learning (and then incorporating into the relationship) an exercise called "the Session." This amazingly simple tool was born of great personal necessity for us. We were on the beaches of southern Thailand, one scant year into our marriage and six months into a yearlong trip around world. Though we were often in each other's exclusive company twenty-four hours a day, we found ourselves growing apart—one of us becoming slightly agitated, the other somewhat sullen, and both losing interest in sharing what was really going on.

How could this be, we wondered? Here we were, two trained listeners and supposed experts in providing emotional support, yet we were shutting down on each other on the biggest adventure of our lives. At first we thought that we needed couple counseling, but this was logistically impossible. Then it occurred to us to counsel each other, but this was therapeutically impossible. To our amazement, we found an alternative way to build a bridge back to each other.

What we felt we needed was sacred space—in other words, an opportunity to talk and be heard without commentary, feedback, or facilitation. The result was the Session, and it revived—indeed, transformed—the quality of our relating (not to mention saving our trip!). It doesn't involve therapy, counseling, or any mirroring or similar exercise requiring interpersonal finesse. Rather, the Session asks for two loving ears, an open heart, and hundred-percent undivided attention for as little as ten minutes per person. Since we discovered this miraculous exercise, we've not only taught it to countless couples, but ten years later we still do it ourselves three to five times a week. Here's how the Session works:

The two partners arrange a block of time for their Session, allowing a minimum of twenty minutes so that both partners get at least ten minutes of listening time. They can go longer if they like—in fact, twenty minutes per person is ideal—as long as both get equal time, *no exceptions.* Time-keeping is the Listener's responsibility.

The Session takes place in a private, quiet area. All disruptions and distractions are to be eliminated: telephone ringers, pagers, televisions, radios, and stereos are to be turned off; the answering machine is to be turned down; the doorbell is to be ignored; and if children are in the picture, they need to be safely looked after. This is intimate time and must be treated as precious. No alcohol is to be consumed prior to a Session, and no snacking, drinking, or smoking is allowed *during* a Session. The point is for partners to be as present as possible for each other.

The first Speaker—whoever *listened* first during the previous Session—talks about whatever he or she wishes, including the events of the day, feelings from the past, or issues involving the relationship. The only exception is *any topic about which the Speaker is angry at the Listener.* This topic must be saved for the Peace Process, detailed in Chapter 6, "Peacemaking." This is a crucial judgment call. Because the Session is a precious tool that can dramatically enhance trust and intimacy, it's worth using correctly.

Partners are to avoid blame and you-statements (e.g., "*You* don't like my cooking"). Instead, they use I-statements with specific feelings (e.g., "*I feel sad* that you didn't like the lasagna"). Positive feelings can be included too (e.g., "I loved how you surprised me at work today" or "I was so proud of how you managed your anger in the car"). If the Speaker runs out of things to say before his or her allotted time is up, both partners sit in silence making eye contact.

The Listener's job is simply to listen with eyes, heart, and full attention, *imagining that by listening to the beloved, he or she is giving a beautiful gift.* The Listener is not to respond or talk under any circumstances, except to ask the Speaker to repeat something that was inaudible.

When the Speaker's time is over, both partners switch roles. The second Speaker is not to use this turn to respond to the first person's words, however. That response is to be saved until the next Session.

Once both partners have had a turn, the Session is over. To provide a sense of completion, they may choose to thank each other and hug.

Brief Instructions for "the Session"

1. Set aside a minimum of twenty minutes and go to a private place where you won't be disturbed. Be as present as possible for each other during that time.

2. Divide the time equally, with the Listener keeping time.

3. Have the Speaker talk (using I-statements) about whatever is of concern to him or her, including issues involving the relationship (but *excluding* topics about which the Speaker is angry at the

Listener). If the Speaker runs out of things to say before his or her allotted time is up, sit in silence making eye contact.

4. The Listener attends fully to the Speaker, not responding unless it's necessary to ask the Speaker to repeat something inaudible.

5. When the Speaker's time is over, switch roles. Remember that the second Speaker can't use this turn to respond to the first person's words. That response should be saved until the next Session.

6. Once you've both had a turn, your Session is completed; thank each other and hug.

At first, some partners find speaking—and being listened to—for ten or fifteen minutes sans interruption a little awkward. In addition, some initially find that the format feels a little artificial or contrived. It's a good idea, then, to commit to at least three Sessions per week for one month. This is usually enough to get the kinks out of the system and allay any discomfort. Jed, a forest ranger, and Magdelene, his partner, a field biologist, learned the Session in response to some communication difficulties they were having.

Jed's report: "After we started doing Sessions, I realized that after I speak in *normal* conversation, I'm so preoccupied with what I'm going to say next that I barely hear Magdelene at all. I'm sure that tendency has caused a fight or two. The Session ties my tongue, which is a good thing: it forces me to settle in and relax. I can really *hear* her now."

Magdelene took the baton: "My first reaction normally is to leap into action and solve Jed's problems—and he can't stand when I do that. Sessions nip that whole thing in the bud. I've always wanted for us to be close, but I didn't know that this was the way—like a deep itch I never knew how to scratch. And it's so simple. The Session's made us better pals than ever."

Herb and Thelma's first experience with the Session was a bit more dramatic: "We were fresh from an argument," Herb admitted. "Thelma was still very unhappy with me. Maybe it wasn't the best time to try it." Thelma smiled apologetically. "You can say it, honey," she said—and then said it herself: "I jumped right down his throat. It wasn't fair to Herb—I mean, his hands were sort of tied. When it was his turn, he said he thought he deserved my dumping on him because he'd been pretty harsh right before. But I told him, 'It's right there in the instructions: no anger!'"

These days Herb and Thelma do one Session a week, religiously. Says Thelma, "Now Herb stops me if I get hot. He says, 'That's a peacemaking subject!'" And her husband is a true convert: "I think *every* couple should do Sessions. Why wait until you *have to* have a 'big talk'?" Herb asked. "It's like going to the gym. I might not always be in the mood, but I always feel so much better afterward."

Sessions do have the impressive ability to lighten the load for each partner; they also help us feel closer than ever. As the anonymous poem that introduces this chapter points out, when our lover "just listens," it's possible to get in touch with how we really feel. And that genuine emotion might just surprise us. In the guaranteed silence, jumbles of feelings (some of which we didn't even know we felt) often get sorted through; mini-insights, great ah-*ha*'s, even brainstorm solutions to thorny problems frequently make themselves known. In addition, the Session dissipates day-to-day free-floating stress. Finally, Sessions serve to remind us that, as lovemates, we're honored to gingerly and reverently hold the contents of each other's heart.

Even just a few experiences with the Session can be powerful. Each time we're the Speaker, we increase our levels of emotional awareness, emotional fluency, and emotional honesty—each of which augments self-love. With practice, we start to listen deeply to each other as a matter of course, both in and out of Session.

Once we've reached that level of greater comfort with the basic Session, we can choose to schedule "Special Sessions" for matters of particular concern or issues on which we have strongly differing opinions (as long as we don't feel at risk of acting out over those issues). Sessions might be focused on problems at work or with the kids, for example, or on future plans—even life dreams.

Special Sessions are exceptional in that the Listener has permission to respond to what the Speaker said when it's his or her turn to talk. They're exceptional in their level of accomplishment as well: when we provide each other with this kind of open space, perplexing problems often find easy resolution. (For excerpts from some Special Sessions, see Chapter 5,

"Equality.") The more Sessions of any kind we have under our belt, the more we'll notice a fresh feeling about each other, a deeper friendship. Indeed, Sessions can teach us how to be the finest emotional confidant either one of us has ever had.

DEEP LISTENING PAST AND THE TRADITIONAL COUPLE

The traditional couple was too often the lonely couple. In days gone by, deep listening, like all interpersonal and couple skills, was a foreign notion to most spouses. And since higher-order needs were equally exotic, the emotional alienation created by this listening vacuum wasn't even considered abnormal. Indeed, other than certain tender wives and still fewer husbands, traditional couples had little conception that a specific way to pay heed to each other existed. The possibility of deep listening's gifts—maintaining and rebuilding trust, making and keeping the peace, and enhancing self-worth—was even farther from their minds.

The myth has long prevailed that women, due primarily to their natural disposition and to their training as nurturers, are somehow more suited to communication in general—and listening in particular—than men. Certainly, maternity evokes a powerful sense of empathy that women can use with their mates as well as their children. Despite this maternal edge, when it came to feelings and issues about the relationship itself, more often than not *neither* traditional spouse felt listened to, much less empathized with.

For their part, men were often doubled over in toxic shame about their personal problems and feelings. They ended up telling their woes to the local barber or bartender, if anyone. Indeed, in our parents' generation, Willy Loman (Arthur Miller's tragic salesman) was the archetype of the lonely breadwinner. Women fared somewhat better in the expression of emotions. Since the culture didn't shame them so intensely for their feelings, they were freer to share them. Often they listened to each other, seeking support from their family-of-origin, hairdresser, or coffee klatch. With this separation along gender lines, the traditional arrangement deprived both sexes of a brilliant best friend—that is, the beloved other; and in many quarters it still does.

Naturally, these unfair gender patterns imprinted the next generation. As a result, father-son relationships were impoverished. Many boys couldn't tell their fathers how they felt because their fathers didn't know how to listen. And if they'd tried a few times and failed, they sure weren't going to risk another disappointment! Unwittingly, these fathers set their sons up, not only to repeat their own isolation but also to serve in their stead: often these youngsters were recruited by their mothers, who yearned for a male ear, to fill the role of confidant. Though unintentional, this command-performance closeness was burdensome and unhealthy for boys, who shouldn't have been in the mix when it came to maternal emotional needs. What loving son could refuse his mother—at least at first? But because many *wanted* to refuse, this all-too-common scenario caused boys to grow up with a distaste for feelings in general.

Roger would do anything to avoid the tears of his one and only. "I felt so sorry for my mother growing up," he remembered. "She had the blues really bad, and no one told me I shouldn't try to help her mop them up." But whereas this toxic guilt, a hangover from his relationship with his mother, killed Roger's enthusiasm for deeply listening to his wife, other men have paid a higher price for parental miscommunication: a simmering resentment of women in general.

Daughters of the traditional couple didn't do much better. Like their brothers, they didn't really expect their fathers to listen to them. This low expectation seriously undermined their confidence in the importance of their own feelings and opinions and sent them subtle but destructive messages about "normal" relationships with men. Girls grew up to accept strong, silent types and jokers (who—however affable—would distract instead of listen). Again like their brothers, they were often conscripted into service as their mother's—and sometimes their father's—chosen listener. Some were even unfree to make deep connections among their peers.

Sometimes parent-child listening was taken to the extreme. Certain misguided, nonlistening couples talked to their children instead of each other not only about family issues but also about their marriage. Triangulation, as this unhealthy family dynamic is called, tears kids apart. Though they might try to function as mediators, and sometimes even succeed to some extent, that's simply not their place, at any age.

As unaware of the principle of emotional integrity as they were of this New Law of Love, traditional couples frequently acted their feelings out rather than expressing them healthily. As we mentioned in the previous chapter, this made the expression of feelings traumatic to their children. Often individual partners came from families where anger wore the face of rage, fear the face of neurosis, or (as in Roger's case, above) sadness the face of depression. Given that background, even spouses who expressed the less-pleasant feelings to each other in a nonadversarial fashion found the mere presence of genuine emotion terribly scary. Staying shut down, tuned out, or perpetually busy—in short, doing everything in their power to avoid listening to each other—was thus a simple matter of self-preservation. Lola's father would shout at and sometimes hit her mother when he got mad. Until the cross-generational impact of this was pointed out to Lola, lending her big, strong hubby an ear even for minor work-related frustrations was out of the question.

When the exceptional couple of yesteryear was able to take pride in the success of their marriage, the secret was unfailingly the same: "We just knew how to listen to each other," these loved ones would say with the humility of sages imparting an ultimate Truth. Surely, in some ways, being loving has always meant being a good listener, just as a kind ear has always epitomized emotional support. Now we know that listening for—and actually fielding—a spouse's full range of feelings is the element responsible for listening's magic.

When couple psychology finally made its debut in the mid-sixties, the importance of an emotion-focused listening emerged. "He [or she] doesn't care about my feelings; she [or he] never listens to me" became the anthem for troubled relationships. Indeed, it seemed that—regardless of whether there was violence, alcoholism, or philandering—the demise of every marriage was attributed to a breakdown in emotional communication.

Even without complications such as violence or alcoholism, couples struggling with higher-level dialogue still had a hard time of it. Diagnosis was definitely not a cure; to many mates' great disappointment, knowing that they needed to open up their mouths and their ears didn't rescue their marriage. Some were still unwilling or unable to be aware of, talk about, or be honest regarding their feelings. Others still just couldn't listen. The pileups of the infamous power-struggle stage (many caused by unhealed childhood wounds, as we've seen) tended to preclude successful communication.

Former traditional couple Wilbur and Phyllis struggled in this sad state of affairs for years. Though each was blessed with prodigious inter-personal skills, they'd never tried those skills on each other in an attempt to connect. Wilbur wrote ad copy for television; Phyllis directed and taught drama at the local university. The listening in their crucible had become so scant, and real sharing subsequently so sparse, that by year twelve of their union, these two lived nearly parallel emotional lives. Though their jobs required a high level of emotional output, when they got home to each other they just turned off. Sometimes they clued each other in on the biggest stories at work, listening with genuine interest, showing great empathy, and defending the other staunchly. But when it came to each other, to issues at the heart of their relationship, either they shared the pleasant feelings or they shared none at all.

Phyllis and Wilbur's modus operandi wasn't developed intentionally, as a means to estrange themselves from each other. On the contrary, their intention was to give each other a break. Like many other traditional couples, this one was absolutely committed to "not being negative." And as Wilbur often whined with a loud sniffle and a wide smile, "No one lis-tens to me anyway."

So with lots of good intentions, each cordoned off from the other long personal litanies of disappointment, heartache, and frustration. The flip-side of that coin was the loss of countless opportunities to be close. It was their daughter who was ultimately instrumental in getting help for this tone-deaf marriage. Indeed, as so often happens, it took a crisis—a bicycle accident that nearly took their baby's life—to precipitate Phyllis and Wilbur's transition from a traditional to a truly New Couple.

"Before the accident," Phyllis began, "I hardly knew the man behind the jokes. But there was no cutting up in Anita's hospital room. Night after night we'd sit holding each other, crying together, our daughter unconscious amid a tangle of tubes and bandages. That's when we finally met, soul to soul—and I fell in love with my husband all over again."

"I'd never cried before as an adult," Wilbur admitted. "I didn't even know I had that many tears inside me. It wasn't just my fear about Anita. I was torn up about our marriage too. At first it was as if our relationship were lying there on that bed, unconscious. It was anyone's guess whether it'd ever get up again."

The hospital chaplain had encouraged them to open up. "He helped us with our first talk," Phyllis explained. "It was actually embarrassing. We just weren't used to being real with each other." Soon the clergyman prompted them to do Sessions on their own, which they did—every day throughout the two-and-a-half-month ordeal.

"And we still do them almost every other day," Wilbur said proudly. "Phyllis usually pushes it, but I'm always grateful when she does. The Session has revolutionized our marriage—pretty powerful for something that our daughter describes as 'cute.'" He thought for minute and then added, "I didn't learn anything like this in my communications courses at broadcasting school. You'd think it would be so simple to teach about emotions. But it's been the hardest—and most rewarding—thing I've ever done." Phyllis nodded her agreement and then added her perspective: "I've always been crazy about Wilbur's sense of humor. Little did I know that he used it to keep his feelings at bay and that it was actually hurting us." Unable to pass up an opportunity for humor even now, Wilbur said, "She made me promise that if I started being emotionally literate I'd stay funny too!"

Phyllis considered herself a hard nut finally cracked. "I hate to think it took Anita almost being killed, but that's the reality. Thank God I still have my daughter, and I got my husband back too. Wilbur used to brag about my soliloquies on stage, and I'd be so proud. His new compliment is that I'm 'all ears.' I consider this my greatest achievement!"

An Invitation to Reflect on the Law of Deep Listening as It Pertains to Your Parents

- Were your parents deep listeners? How did this affect their self-love? Their emotional intimacy? How did this make you feel?
- Were you aware of your parents tuning each other out? If so, why might they have done this? If it was in order to avoid issues or emotions, what was it they were avoiding? If they tuned out in response to the other's acting out, what form did this behavior take? When they tuned each other out, were they acting out their own feelings? Did they ever use the

silent treatment? How did tuning out affect their self-love?
Their emotional intimacy? How did this make you feel?

- How would your childhood have been different had your
parents subscribed to the Law of Deep Listening? How would
your own couple be different (or, if you're single, how would
past relationships have been different)?

DEEP LISTENING AND THE NEW COUPLE

The New Couple need never be the lonely couple. That's due in large part
to the benefits of deep listening. Myrna and Sheldon had forged a strong
union through eighteen years of listening to each other truly and deeply.
A crew foreman for a moving company, Sheldon was a recovering alcoholic who'd just celebrated twenty years of sobriety, and he was a dedicated Boy Scout leader. Myrna, his forty-six-year-old wife, managed an
independent bookstore and served on the boards of several nonprofits.

They'd mastered the art of emotional listening back in their early
days and still swore by their Sessions. Because the pair lived thirty miles
outside town, they took advantage of drive time to do a modified form of
the Session. But like all New Couples, these two knew that the work of
relationship—which makes possible the joy of relationship—never really
ends. They'd valiantly plowed through the bulk of their power-struggle
issues, and their day-to-day life was a picture of co-creativity. Still, there
was the odd intruder upon their serenity, and for the last five years his
name had been Domico. When it came to this young man—Sheldon's
former sponsoree in Alcoholics Anonymous—Myrna had a button, Sheldon
had a blind spot, and neither one was getting heard.

"I don't want to hear that name again today, if you don't mind," Myrna
asserted. "He's back on his feet and he's finally got a therapist. I thought
you said he resents it when you treat him like a—" "That's *enough!*" Sheldon
exclaimed with venom. "End of conversation." Myrna responded plain-
tively: "You never speak to Domico that way, even when he forgets your
appointments." The words nipped at Sheldon's ears like an arctic chill.
Though their Twelve-Step relationship had ended years before, Sheldon and
Domico remained close. The younger man was successful in his sobriety,
but a mild depression lingered. Sheldon did worry about him overtime.

He turned to his wife and came clean: "It's that damn guilt. I know I lie to myself. He's not my son—and even if he were, he's grown up. It's some other unfinished business. I'm just using my concern over Domico to avoid myself in some way." Clearly moved, Myrna now felt emotionally safe enough to acknowledge her own part in this dysfunctional dance: "I just feel so betrayed, like I can't trust you at all, when you obsess over that guy. It's the only thing we fight about anymore. You know, it's just like my father sticking me in the house with my half-sister. She got away with murder, and I was always expected to clean up."

Myrna and Sheldon: Continued

Sheldon called Myrna on his cell phone at lunchtime during a big move, ostensibly to check in. His wife was having a tough day at the store; in fact, she'd been crying. "I just have the old-and-uglies today," she explained. "I caught a glimpse of myself in the mirror and didn't recognize the dowdy woman who looked back at me."

"Oh, really," Sheldon said absentmindedly. "Sounds tough. Well, I gotta go." Myrna knew that her husband hated it when she bemoaned her looks. His mother, always finding something new wrong with her face, had bounced from one plastic surgeon to the next. This was Sheldon's button. An otherwise wonderful deep listener, on this specific subject he felt pressure "to do something," to rescue his wife from her emotional pain. But frustration and toxic guilt precluded him from staying focused on her words, much less present with her feelings. It was something they both had to look at.

Later, at home, he said, "I feel so helpless with you, just like I did with Mom. How's a guy, little or big, supposed to put the most important woman in his life out of misery?" he asked. "Age happens, for gosh sakes. I'm powerless too. It looks like it's my week for taking on others' problems, huh?" Together they had Special Sessions with themes: for her it was grieving for lost youth and rescuing self-love; for him it was a distorted sense of responsibility. These Sessions significantly cleared not only the air between them, but also Sheldon's ears on this one formerly deafening subject.

· · ·

Long *the* basic counseling skill, deep listening has more recently been pronounced *the* parenting skill. Today deep listening is primed to become *the* couple skill as well, for clearly the power of this fourth New Law of Love to transform any relationship—not least of which are our love unions—is phenomenal. When we commit to learn to listen to each other from the heart, we can rest assured that, no matter what happens outside, *we will be heard at home.* Our couple might then become the first place where we've ever experienced truly loving attention and respect, advancing both our self-love and emotional intimacy light years ahead. What could be a greater gift of love?

As couple skills go, deep listening is relatively straightforward. For certain of us, however, its acquisition may require more patience and discipline than for others. Some of us might even need additional instruction—or healing—before we can really get it down. Soon, though, we'll see the benefits of learning to allow for the more general expression of feelings in our relationship.

Started early and continued through the life of the relationship, deep listening reduces the chances that the din of the power struggle—amplified by all its blind spots, buttons, and issues—will deafen us both. When, as a New Couple, we both commit to ratchet our hearing up one notch, we're practicing prevention whether we realize it or not. Because of our sensitive hearing, innumerable gusts and flurries of stress will be imperceptibly, yet continuously, blown off course and away. We'll never even know the storms that might have occurred. In addition, deep listening protects us when small squalls do blow our way, ensuring that little experiences of not being heard don't grow into perceived massive betrayals.

As an easy couple tool, the Session stands in a league of one. A great training ground for learning the skill of deep listening, it also functions as a daily stress reducer par excellence. Couples continue to find the Session to be eminently worth the tiny expenditure of their time—twenty to thirty minutes. And the effort required for love's sake—biting our tongues, keeping our opinions to ourselves, and letting our lover source his or her own solutions (and feelings)—pays amazing dividends. In fact, deep listening is unbelievably economical: we can reduce stress, solve problems, avoid fights, and raise our self-love—all while vastly enhancing our overall ability to be emotionally intimate. We might even save money on therapy!

If we let the fourth New Law of Love help us stay tuned to the truth of our beloved's mind and heart, we'll soon see how the habit of lending an ear unreservedly, and really making the beloved's emotions feel at home with us, can seal our friendship for life.

The Key to Deep Listening

Learning the skill of listening to your partner straight from the heart—that is, listening for the words *and the feelings underneath* with compassion—is the key to the fourth New Law of Love.

This means holding . . .

- Sessions on a regular basis
- Special Sessions as needed

5. EQUALITY
the fifth new law of love

It must be a peace without victory . . . only a peace between equals can last.
WOODROW WILSON, address to the U.S. Senate,
January 22, 1917

If you think that the concept of equality in love partnerships is as warmed-over as a peace sign, you're right. As *concepts,* both have been kicked around at least since the sixties, when a number of bras and flags went up in flames. Today diversity is the watchword in Western society, and discrimination of any kind is still highly politically incorrect. As *realities,* however, neither equality nor peace between lovers is yet fully realized.

It's true that couples who openly embrace the kind of traditional marriage where gender dictates both the balance of power and the playing of roles are now the exception. It's also true that most people are shocked when, in this enlightened era, someone espouses the belief that men are superior to women (or that one skin tone is somehow better than another). And finally, it's true that most couples strongly defend the fact of equality in their own partnership. Yet despite all these truths, inequality *still persists* in almost every realm of connubial life. And since we need to be equals before we can fly a peace flag over our household, the Law of Equality has to be the fifth New Law of Love, preceding the Law of Peacemaking, the sixth.

There are a host of standard measures by which the power within a relationship is determined—measures such as age, gender, race, religion, ethnicity, financial status, income-generating potential, socioeconomic background, gifts, talents, physical health and abilities, and intellectual prowess. Though we've come a long way in our thinking about how these measures affect the roles and responsibilities of coupledom, who among us can say that we've reached an honest balance when it comes to the daunting list of specifics, including moneymaking, household management and repairs, errands, car maintenance, manual labor and physical security, lovemaking, parenting, childcare and education, family-of-origin relations, and caring for aging parents? Clearly, we have a long way to go.

Though the term may suggest it, the Law of Equality isn't specifically intended to raise the status of women to that of men in heterosexual relationships. It goes way beyond that. This law concerns itself with a standard of *fairness* in all love unions for *both sexes*. It asks us to take responsibility for how the power is distributed in our couple—in other words, who's got the clout—and to make sure we both consider the distribution fair. If, for example, we discover a glimmer of sexism along the way, it's up to us to take care of it.

Equality—which is integral to respect and love of self and other—also requires that we approach all conjugal roles and responsibilities without assumption or expectation. In other words, nothing is presumed; both partners have an equal voice, and *everything*—from finances to cooking to who picks up the children at school—is negotiable. The only exception is core agreements, which are nonnegotiable. (These will be discussed in Chapter 6, "Peacemaking," along with negotiation itself.)

In practice, the Law of Equality invites us to do the following:

1. *Honestly examine the major facets of shared life and acknowledge those in which the power is out of balance.* A couple might realize, for example, that a discrepancy in age has thrown off their balance of power.
2. *Explore how this "advantage" might translate to unfairness for one or both partners.* To continue our example, the younger partner might realize that he or she automatically defers to the decisions of the older.
3. *Get in touch with, and share, any feelings associated with this dynamic, negative* and *positive.* In our example, the younger partner might feel relief at not having a lot of responsibility, resentment at not being *trusted* with responsibility, and fear that the disempowerment is justified because of an additional fear of being incompetent. The older partner, who enjoys a certain amount of freedom in not having to negotiate, might also feel resentful of the burden and guilty for being domineering.

4. *Offer a good-faith promise (backed by specifics) to restore harmony and/or negotiate toward fairness.* Our couple above, having mutually agreed that things were unfair, might commit to start paying attention to how decisions evolve between them and to negotiate as needed. They might also make a date in a week's time to see how they're doing.

This process isn't appropriate in every situation of inequality, of course. We can work out many issues without turning them into questions of equality—the trading off of shopping for unloading and putting the groceries away, for example. Other issues are too complex to be handled by the Law of Equality alone. For example, when only one of us perceives an imbalance and we're not able to come to agreement, we need to apply the conflict-resolution skills presented in the next chapter.

As you can see, New Couples manage power through conversation— actually, a series of ongoing conversations. The topics of the equality discussion revolve around all the power issues mentioned earlier—differences in age, gender, moneymaking ability, intelligence, and so on—and any unfairness they cause in the relationship. Talks about all kinds of responsibility, but especially the touchy main issues (such as the day-to-day earning and management of money, the care and rearing of children, and good old housework), are essential to the fifth New Law of Love.

Some areas of responsibility are typically shared, while others are taken on by one or the other of us as a specialty. And that's fine: equality doesn't require *matching* responsibilities; it asks only that *nothing be assumed* and *everything be open to negotiation.* Some power imbalances need to be rectified; others—those that don't create any hard feelings—need simply to be acknowledged. What's key is how both partners *honestly feel* about any issue of power.

Obviously, our intention to honor the fifth New Law of Love needs to rest on a solid foundation of emotional integrity, especially when it comes to our ability to become aware of, and tell each other the truth about, a range of potentially incendiary issues and the feelings associated with them. This law also demands that we exercise our newly developing (or already developed!) skill of deep listening.

It's important to remember that, like the other nine New Laws of Love, equality is an ideal. It doesn't require a ten-out-of-ten performance, just a heartfelt commitment on the part of both lovemates.

EQUALITY'S GREATEST CHALLENGE:
THE TRANCE OF TRADITION

Unfortunately, filling this prescription for fairness can be tricky. We all come to relationships with various superiority and inferiority complexes, feeling sure of ourselves in some ways and unsure in others. We might know, for example, that we're better at sports, worth more on the job market, or less silver-tongued than our beloved. Still, as we've said, our hearts are generally in the right place, and the unfairness that crops up between us usually isn't deliberate. *Rather, inequality typically results from unspoken tolerance of unnegotiated assignments of responsibility based on traditional (read: gender) roles.* In fact, the strong hold that the notorious trance of tradition has on the Law of Equality is equaled only by its hold on the Law of Priority, specifically on the challenging process of individuation that priority involves. And yet the responsibility for inequality falls squarely on our own shoulders: when we function discontentedly in a capacity that we accepted without question, doing nothing to correct the situation, we're imposing inequality on *ourselves*. As has been so wisely remarked, "No one can take our power away; we've got to *give* it away."

Similarly, when we're in an ostensibly equal couple, no one can impose a role or duty upon us if we're not willing to accept it. Jeanette and Cal, both in retail working forty-plus-hour weeks, sincerely considered themselves completely modern and as equal as could be. Except for one small glitch: she did ninety percent of the housework.

"I definitely didn't recognize it as an issue of power," Jeanette confided to her best friend, "nor did I realize that it was my responsibility to make things right. I guess I was just resenting Cal in silence." When she finally approached her partner about this dissatisfaction, he was genuinely surprised. "I assumed you liked to be in control. You like everything just so." And it was true, though neither had properly diagnosed it: Jeanette did suffer from a mild case of compulsive overdoing; she was simply incapable of walking through a room without tidying it or picking something up.

That wasn't the core issue between them, however. The real dilemma was the outdated (but widely applied) gender software that had programmed her to do—and him not to do—cleaning chores around the house. Cal said, "I figured I'd married another superwoman like my mother. She juggled career, house, and all five of us kids—and I know how hard it was for her." He added thoughtfully, "It's pretty lousy—I mean, that I didn't see it when it came to you."

The reason that Cal didn't notice how duties were divvied up in his home, and that Jeanette took them on without negotiating, is that they were both locked in the trance of tradition. Part cultural, part psychological, this phenomenon begins to take hold of us when, as children, we're imprinted with traditional mores. We watch our parents function according to overt and unspoken rules, biases, and notions of status passed down through family, religion, and ethnic group. Often we're also directly or indirectly encouraged to keep these conventions up ourselves.

Like DNA, such internalized ideas contain very specific information—details about how we, as men, women, husbands, and wives, should behave in our relationships. These stereotypes generally lie dormant until the stress of the power struggle hits or we have children (two events that sometimes coincide, or collide). At those high-pressure times of life, we start unconsciously seeking what's known: before we realize it, we're betraying unnegotiated expectations about responsibility and power and are defaulting back into the spousal roles of those who raised us.

A couple of examples will show how stealthily the default sneaks up on us. Take Eugene, for example. The week he was promoted to regional manager of his company—a promotion that would eat into his free time—he developed the real, albeit hazy, expectation that his girlfriend, Dorothy, would assume all the responsibility for grocery shopping and preparing their dinners. And then there's Sue. A few years after she and Vincent moved in together, she started expecting Vincent to organize all their social engagements, in part because he was "the gregarious one," but also because her father had always done that task in his marriage with her mother. Although both these couples were able to correct their dynamics with simple awareness, others of us don't have it so easy. The lower our level of self-love, the more desperately we tend to revert to what's familiar—even if it hurts us.

IDENTIFYING EQUALITY BLIND SPOTS

When we find ourselves slipping on issues of equality, we know we've got equality blind spots. Blinding as the glaring sun, these rob us of the awareness of what's fair; they press buttons and set our couple up for trouble. And as Henrietta and Dexter discovered, the process of becoming aware of these blind spots is a lot like that of unearthing buried feelings.

Henrietta and Dexter didn't wait till the power struggle to discover their own embedded inequality chips. In fact, their struggle with financial equality—which, like housework, is a mega-issue for couples—debuted on their first date at a tony new downtown restaurant. So transfixed were these near-strangers with each other that they barely touched their food. When the bill arrived, Dexter made a deft and practiced lunge for his wallet. At first, Henrietta sat primly with her hands folded on the table. Then she grinned and, in her best imitation of Blanche Dubois in *A Streetcar Named Desire,* drawled, "I've always relied on the kindness of strangers."

After they shared a laugh, Henrietta confessed, "I guess you can take a girl out of the South, but you can't take the South out of a girl." Then she proved herself wrong by placing several twenty-dollar notes inside the restaurant folder. Dexter, clearly ill at ease, mumbled a thanks. Luckily, these two were talkers. The sexist blind spot they'd bumped into—namely, the unwritten rule that guys pay for their dates—proved grist for discussion until late into the night. And it started this relationship off with a bang.

STRIVING FOR EQUALITY IN PARENTING AND FINANCES

Unquestionably, cultural programming and early wounding pile a lot on our plates. Yet Dexter and Henrietta, in the above illustration, were only dealing with the first course. Had they decided to marry and have kids, they'd have found, like most equality-conscious couples, that their challenges were quadrupled. The problem isn't just the centripetal force of tradition (which, as we've said, hits us twice as hard when we become parents). It's also socioeconomics and the family-hostile structure of the workaday world.

Unless we're self-employed or independently wealthy, we may feel that the odds are stacked against us, no matter how deeply we care about transcending gender inequalities—not to mention creating a new, fair kind of family where both parents contribute equally to the financial picture and the raising of children. Those of us who committed to each other without heeding the fifth New Law of Love and sharing in crucial exploratory chats might, to our horror, suddenly find ourselves severely equality-challenged, facing the three modern-family monsters of finances, childrearing, and household management (not to mention a no-pun-intended laundry list of other related duties). Pragmatically, it's easier by far to collapse into traditional caregiver/breadwinner roles—and emotionally, to let the chips fall where they may.

Burt and Cara had a powwow before their first child was born and consciously decided to go with the traditional formula, except that he risked his lucrative job by insisting to his employer that he be allowed to consult from home. Although the arrangement worked well for Burt, the couple's decision ended up being unexpectedly distressing for his former-executive wife. She was torn between wanting the "housewife" role and wanting to resume her professional life.

This pull isn't uncommon. On the one hand, the vulnerability of nesting can cause us to cling tenaciously to custom—a tendency that's especially strong in people suffering (knowingly or unknowingly) from childhood emotional abuse, neglect, or abandonment trauma. On the other hand, as parenthood deepens and strengthens the trance of tradition—with all its latent expectations about roles and responsibilities—we find some of our contemporary personal values squarely in opposition to those of tradition.

Self-sufficient Cara, like so many of her peers today, had worked hard for her independence and place in the world. As a result, the shift of identity she opted for with parenthood proved so conflictual that it bordered on traumatic. On the one hand, she couldn't overcome the fear that she'd somehow betrayed herself. On the other, she profoundly enjoyed the coziness of being cared for by her husband as an at-home mom—so much so, in fact, that she worried she might never want to go back to the office.

Even when both partners earn enough individually so that either one could choose to stay home with the children—meaning that the couple could switch caregiver/breadwinner roles after the nursing period if they wanted to—men choose the home role infrequently. The question isn't whether having the mother at home and the father at work is good for the children, for certainly it's fine; rather, it's whether the decision for

him to stay duly employed and for her to stay at home has been negotiated. Is the choice based on true preferences or on the trance of tradition
(as embodied in equality blind spots)?

In planning for families, few of us sit down to have that "big talk"
together. It's the exceptional couple who, like Burt and Cara, examine how
the traditional arrangement might affect them—how it might, for example, cut off their chance to experience a novel family life in which the
father is at least as involved with the children as the mother is. While men
don't often take the opportunity to delve into total-involvement parenting
(and rarely even see it as an option), men who've really considered being a
New Dad report feelings from curiosity and excitement to foreboding.
Almost invariably, however, they also experience some level of discomfort
with the unmacho implications of not being out in the world like most
guys; many are downright afraid of being judged by colleagues, friends,
and family, and of the toxic shame the judgment might evoke.

Lori is right, of course, when she says that biology generally influ-
ences the decision. She and her husband, Lester, both want all their children to be breast-fed, and they also want to have one parent stay at home
(and can afford that choice). Given the overlap of these two decisions, it
makes logistical sense that she be the stay-at-home parent. Nevertheless,
not all mothers breast-feed. And many husbands bow to the pressure of
conventional wisdom (which in this case is really sexism), which says that
babies and young children are better cared for by women. Others believe
that by going through the pregnancy, mothers "earn" the right to stay
home. (These men clearly care about being fair.) Employment practices
also contribute to the decision of who stays home with the children. How
would men feel about the chance to bond early with their children if they
were automatically granted two or three months of maternity leave?

The unacceptable part of the customary division of labor is the fact
that too many partners opt for what's familiar without finding out what
they truly desire. With no opportunity to experiment and little chance to
negotiate, they're tugged by the trance of tradition into the roles their
parents knew. Again, we need to stress that this route isn't in and of itself
unfair. What makes it unfair is failing (as a result of blind spots) to negotiate the issue in advance. And this happens all the time! The upshot, in
many cases, is that one or both partners end up feeling victimized and
resentful. If the habit of ceding to unarticulated pressures regarding out-

moded, unnegotiated roles continues unchallenged over the years, it has the potential to damage a couple's chemistry—sometimes irreparably.

As luck would have it, Godfried and Priscilla were spared this fate, simply because they were aware enough and committed enough to hash the issue out. Though the pregnancy was unexpected, this couple was so thrilled with the future child that graced their tenth year of marriage that they neglected to be explicit with each other about how their roles and responsibilities would shake down once the baby was born. They discovered a conflict in their expectations not long before the due date and sought professional help in resolving it.

"I was champing at the bit, really ready to jump into teaching right when it happened," explained Godfried, who'd been planning a career change from insurance to education. "I just dumbly assumed that Priscilla would spend a couple months at home and then go back to work. I couldn't believe it when she announced to me that she wanted to quit her law firm and spend the first year and a half at home with our child."

He took off his glasses and rubbed his eyes. "It'll take several years for me to catch up to my current salary if I go into teaching," he said, "which means we'll both have to work full-time. She *knows* this. Now my choices are either put up with another year and a half at a job I can't stand, or deny my wife her special time with the baby. And what about *me?* Nobody asked me whether *I'd* like to spend a couple of months at home taking care of our child."

Then it was Priscilla's turn to speak: "I want to be fair to Godfried, but my mind's been set on this forever. My mother never got over her regret at having to go back to work directly after bearing me. I vowed I wouldn't repeat that mistake." She turned to her husband. "Didn't I already tell you that? Anyway, you've been talking about leaving that job for years. Why now?"

By confusing *announcements* with *agreements,* neglecting to disclose underlying assumptions, and failing to negotiate responsibilities, this couple put not only their friendship in jeopardy, but also the emotional stability of their family-to-be. It was in our office that Priscilla and Godfried figured out how they got into such a bind.

Priscilla's equality blind spot—an unexamined sense that she was entitled to stay at home—was linked to the pain she'd felt watching her mother suffer. What's more, since her mother had blamed her father for "forcing" her to work, Priscilla had internalized a fear that her husband would force her to return to work prematurely. The unconscious tape ran, "No one's going to keep me from being with my baby." After several counseling sessions, however, Priscilla saw that Godfried didn't deserve this mistrust.

Their conversational explorations were deeply healing. In fact, in retrospect, Priscilla noted, "It seemed that something hard inside me just melted away." She also got in touch with her anger at her senior partners at work—anger that she'd at least partially displaced onto Godfried— because they'd refused to entertain the idea of keeping her on half-time. This recognition made her love of law real to her again, and the idea of dropping out for a long period became moot.

The conversations helped Godfried as well; he relaxed considerably. Though it had previously been a blind spot, he now was in touch with the deep loss he'd felt at having a politician father with little role in raising him. When invited to ponder the option, Godfried realized that he was sincerely excited by the idea of being an at-home father.

With some coaching, the couple brushed up on their deep listening skills and succeeded in some adroit negotiations. Priscilla would stay home for nine months but start looking for a new job after six. Godfried, who'd worked out a new arrangement with his boss, would handle all his paperwork from the virtual home office that he'd set up for the occasion. "I can definitely live with that for a while," he said, "and at the same time, I'll look into some teaching jobs." Though they still needed to balance their books, the couple was confident. Indeed, Priscilla and Godfried soon replaced ominous silence with deep listening, near-brittleness with creativity and loving flexibility, and past and future resentments with a commitment to fairness for all.

KEEPING MARITAL POLITICS CLEAN

Clearly, equality is all about the *politics* and *power* of relationship. In the context of love, however, neither term need be a dirty word. When we acknowledge power issues up front, openly discussing "who's got what," we significantly diminish the likelihood that our wonderful, God-given strengths and advantages will devolve into tools of manipulation. We're able to transform what might have become dirty politics into the politics of peace and love.

Furthermore, a genuine effort to embrace the Law of Equality can have an awesome impact on preserving our all-important chemistry and elevating our self-love. By keeping sexual politics clean and striving in every case for a fair deal, we solidify trust. And sometimes we're pleasantly surprised: as Godfried and Priscilla so potently demonstrate, the very act of admitting to invisible imbalances—and any related dependencies—often leads to the negotiation of excellent agreements. Such an approach not only averts the buildup of a host of insecurities, resentments, and conflicts down the road, but also speeds us through the power-struggle phase and into the coveted phase of co-creativity. Additionally, if we choose to heal any dependencies that we consider unhealthy, we push ourselves into greater initiative and self-actualization, increasing our love and respect for ourselves and each other. Finally, when we embrace the Law of Equality, we enhance our chances of remaining true peers; we're inspired to create together a real democracy à deux, perhaps better than anything we've imagined.

An Invitation to Reflect on the Law of Equality

As you approach the exercises in this chapter, remember that the presence or absence of New Couple chemistry profoundly affects a couple's experience with each law.

- Reflect on the following areas in your couple: age, gender, race, religion, ethnicity, financial status, income-generating potential, family-of-origin socioeconomic background, physical health and ability, intellectual ability, and gifts and talents. In which areas is the power in or out of balance? How does the imbalance make you feel? How does it affect your self-love? Your emotional intimacy?

- Do imbalances result in unfairness in your couple? If so, what are they? How do they make you feel? How does unfairness affect your self-love? Your emotional intimacy?

- Do you have any expectations—open or covert—*of your partner* with regard to roles and responsibilities in any area of your life together (including moneymaking, household management and repairs, errands, car maintenance, manual labor and physical security, lovemaking, parenting, child-care and education, and family-of-origin relations)? If so, are these based on power or on interests and abilities? Have they been negotiated? Do you consider them fair? How do these expectations make you feel? How do they affect your self-love? Your emotional intimacy?

- Do you have any expectations—open or covert—*of yourself* with regard to roles and responsibilities in any area of your life together (see categories in previous question)? If so, are these based on power or on interests and abilities? Have these been negotiated? Do you consider them fair? How do these expectations make you feel? How do they affect your self-love? Your emotional intimacy?
- Are there areas in your relationship not open to negotiation? Why is that? How do these nonnegotiables make you feel? How do they affect your self-love? Your emotional intimacy?

EQUALITY PAST AND THE TRADITIONAL COUPLE

The original institution of marriage wasn't created for equals—and rarely was it fair. How could lovemates possibly see to the equitable distribution of power in their relationship when the power had already been parceled out—by society and religion? The picture within individual marriages wasn't much brighter. It was often *might* that made *right:* the partner who could outmuscle, outearn, outsmart, outspeak, or otherwise outmaneuver the other pulled the strings.

These paradigms notwithstanding, our own parents and grandparents would probably have said that they considered themselves equals—just different in terms of the roles they played. That's because they themselves bought into society's delegation of power. The stereotypical roles of breadwinner and housewife weren't negotiated; they were assumed. The effects of differentials such as age, money, employment status, and family background weren't discussed with an eye to reassuring and maintaining the dignity of the lower-status mate; they were simply accepted. And grievances related to these kinds of imbalances weren't routinely aired, let alone redressed; they were left to fester. The result? Even though most traditional spouses didn't have the luxury of questioning marital inequalities—and wouldn't have admitted to them anyway—they must have known, in their heart of hearts, that none of the above was particularly fair.

> *The subject of money won't muddy the pure waters of love. Rather, it will reflect the patterns of light and dark in those waters, that is, it will reflect our real relationships. Ironically, the more the power of money is recognized in marriage—and balanced—the freer love can be.*
> BETTY CARTER, *Love, Honor and Negotiate*

The waters of Eleanor and Tyler's love were far from such purity. After eight years of marriage, they still espoused buttoned-down roles for both husband and wife. Tyler was a fifty-one-year-old widower who'd lost his first wife to cancer. His eastern-seaboard family expected him to be a high achiever, and he was; in fact, the midsized manufacturing company he'd founded had just gone public. Eleanor hailed from a simple farm family in the Midwest. At thirty, she was bold, beautiful, and ever a handful for her husband. They'd gone to a psychiatrist on the recommendation of his cardiologist, who worried that marital stressors were exacerbating Tyler's heart problems. It was more than evident that neither one was thrilled to be sitting on the sofa.

"We don't really have any troubles at home," Tyler said by way of introduction. "My heart man saw me one day after we'd had a little spat. He's overly cautious." Eleanor raised her hand in protest. "No, dear," she countered, "let's let her help us." She then addressed the therapist: "His stress is my fault, Doctor. The truth is I'm remiss in my wifely duties." Tyler shifted uncomfortably in his seat as Eleanor divulged what she termed a "lack of passion" for her husband. She explained that it was her belief that, as a spouse, she was bound by duty to demonstrate her love every night. Her husband's faced reddened.

This was only the tip of this couple's iceberg. The fact that he was twenty years her senior had become increasingly problematic; this normally confident man was now not so sure of himself. The anxiety that his glamorous young wife would "stray" was a constant in his life. Her recent mention of a new trainer at the health spa had pushed the issue through the roof. Still, Tyler did try to even the score, using the only means at his disposal. "It's humiliating," Eleanor cried. "He's loaded, but he lords it over me. I have to beg for every penny. What else can I do but threaten him?"

The power struggle of Tyler and Eleanor's marriage had gained animosity over the gender-based job assignments they'd originally embraced; indeed, over time, these roles began to have serious consequences. Simultaneously, important differences—namely, those in family background, money, age, employment status, and looks—became sources from which they drew power and which they used against each other as weapons. Though neither wanted their marriage to disintegrate, their actions were proof that the money-power equation profoundly affects how partners communicate, negotiate, and end up feeling about each other. But because these traditional spouses were strangers to emotional honesty, deep listening, and the principles of the Law of Equality, they had no idea how to make things fair.

As Eleanor and Tyler met with their psychiatrist over the weeks and months, they began to understand the feelings and issues that underlay their difficulties. Eleanor came to realize that she felt disempowered by her dearth of marketable skills. This, in addition to the shame of her humble background—and the terror of possibly returning to poverty someday—created a button within easy reach of her husband. Like many women, she also suffered from a rabid inner critic, which not only blamed her for her husband's poor health but convinced her that it was her obligation to be always available for sex. All she had to balance against the power that was Tyler's (by virtue of age, wealth, and their own agreement to be traditional spouses) was her beauty, age, and feminine wiles.

Tyler, though superficially in the one-up position, fared just as poorly. The seniority conferred on him by his age backfired; he was plagued by toxic shame and serious insecurity because of the age difference. His own inner bully, with the help of cultural conditioning, precluded him from being vulnerable with his mate and healing these fears (which, lacking an outlet, were transformed into jealousy). He took refuge in passive aggression—specifically, controlling her with his money.

Fortunately, some holds were barred; though Tyler and Eleanor routinely acted out verbally, she'd never openly threatened to sleep with anyone else and he'd never threatened to leave her destitute. This left a door ajar so that they could understand and integrate the wisdom of the fifth New Law of Love. In the safety of counseling and a series of Special Sessions, these two learned to listen with open hearts. Slowly, they revealed the pain long concealed by sword rattling. "I know I baited you with money," Tyler admitted. "But I had no notion that it felt like a threat to your survival. I'd never want to make you afraid. I guess it was just my midlife nonsense," he concluded.

"I can't believe you took me seriously," Eleanor said, wiping away tears. "I'm not interested in men without substance. *You're* all I want— especially when I see this tender side of you." She smiled at her partner reassuringly. "Anyway, I exaggerated about the new trainer. But I never have to be at the spa when he's there—and I *won't* be anymore."

As for the sexual expectations, the couple had more work to do. Eleanor still saw lovemaking as part of her duty. "Well, I don't!" her husband countered. "Good Lord. No wonder you're never in the mood," he exclaimed. He self-consciously added, "If I felt obligated to perform for you on command, we'd both be in hot water!"

Eleanor and Tyler made a new commitment to each other: to do their best to stop acting out their difficult emotions through shaming and taunting. To support that commitment, they agreed to listen respectfully whenever the other pointed out shaming behaviors. In addition, since the deeply entrenched habit of shaming wouldn't likely die a quiet death, they agreed to use their peacemaking skills to deal with any angry feelings that surfaced; and if issues remained unresolved, they'd address those in a Special Session to be held within twenty-four hours.

Eleanor saw that in giving herself permission to question assumptions about her role as a wife, she'd allowed her life to open up in unexpected ways. She felt a new pride, for without realizing it, she'd quietly begun to reclaim her inner authority. In fact, as she commented later, "Stopping those mind games I was playing with Tyler gave me back my dignity. Now we can really be friends again."

Another boon for Eleanor: she rekindled an old interest in refurbishing antique furniture and registered for a upholstery course—a step that showed how her new commitment to be fair to herself blossomed into greater self-love. Tyler supported her return to school, realizing (with some contrition) that he hadn't exactly encouraged her in the past. Indeed, Eleanor's neglected creativity had been yet another casualty of their unquestioned role assignments.

For his part, Tyler felt much calmer when the burden of sole responsibility was lifted—which was good for his heart. And knowing that Eleanor was truly committed to him, and not just duty-bound, made it safe for him to open up to her emotionally. This boosted not only their respect for each other, but their life in bed as well.

This couple illustrates beautifully the process of demystifying power, status, and obligation in romantic love. As Eleanor said, "Power is just a consolation prize. All anyone really wants is love."

An Invitation to Reflect on the Law of Equality as It Pertains to Your Parents

- Reflect on the following areas in your parents' relationship: gender, finances, income-generating potential, socioeconomic status, physical differences, intellectual ability, gifts, and talents. In which areas was the power in or out of balance? How did this affect their self-love? Their emotional intimacy? How did this make you feel?

- Did imbalances result in unfairness in your parents' relationship? If so, what were the imbalances? How did unfairness affect their self-love? Their emotional intimacy? How did their situation make you feel?

- Did your parents have any expectations—open or covert—of each other with regard to roles and responsibilities (including moneymaking, household management and repairs, errands, car maintenance, manual labor and physical security, lovemaking, parenting, childcare and education, and family-of-origin relations)? If so, were these based on power or on interests and abilities? Were they negotiated? Did both partners consider them fair? How did these expectations affect their self-love? Their emotional intimacy? How did these expectations make you feel?

- Were there areas in your parents' relationship not open to negotiation? Why was that? How did these affect their self-love? Their emotional intimacy? How did these nonnegotiables make you feel?

- How would your childhood have been different had your parents subscribed to the Law of Equality? How would your own couple be different (or, if you're single, how would past relationships have been different)?

EQUALITY AND
THE NEW COUPLE

The New Couple has the courage to be fair—to themselves and each other. And when it comes to putting together the nuts and bolts of their partnership, they start from scratch. They see the folly and injustice of prefab role assignments and notions of status or superiority. Still, they grapple with the blind spots the Law of Equality warns about—blind spots regarding conjugal roles and responsibilities and differing abilities and advantages. They're not looking for a perfect score or trying to measure up to anyone else's standards; instead, rather simply, they're looking for what's fair—a quality that can be determined only from the individual vantage points of the partners themselves.

The straight path to equality is and always will be through openhearted conversation, brokered using the skills of emotional literacy, honesty, and management, along with deep listening. While we can talk about some issues early in the relationship—age and earning power, for example—others just come up when they do. The goal is to talk about them as early as possible and to be as honest as possible. It's best not to wait until the power struggle sets in, because by that time our talents and advantages (such as interpersonal gifts and inheritances) might have soured into liabilities, and unnegotiated responsibilities and expectations might already have gotten both partners' backs up.

What follows are examples of Special Sessions held by six couples. These Sessions, excerpted for brevity, share the common themes of insecurities about major differences and expectations of self or other based on family and cultural conditioning. (Remember that in Special Sessions, unlike regular Sessions, the Listener can respond to what the Speaker said when it's his or her turn to talk.)

Physical Size Differential

At six-foot-seven and 240 pounds, P.K. was a middle school coach by day and a bouncer by night—though the latter was just on weekends. He got to know Angelica, a child-care worker who'd just started to wait tables at the dance club where he worked, as a result of a brawl in which she was knocked to the tile floor. Like a gentle giant, P.K. pushed aside tables, helped the petite woman off the ground, and checked on her every ten minutes until her shift ended early in the morning. Within days, their romance was big news at work. Just prior to their betrothal, Angelica asked for a Special Session.

She started hesitantly: "I didn't want to tell you this—I was afraid it would hurt you—but I have to get it off my chest. I've never had a problem with being tiny; in fact, it's been fun. But back home, in my early twenties, I had a boyfriend built like you who was physically abusive. It took a lot to finally run away from him. The other women in my therapy group helped me see that I had a lot of victim stuff from being around violence as a little girl. I swore after that I'd never be with a big guy again. I know that you're different; you're my protector, and I love and trust you so much. God knows I'm the noisy one when we fight! And I love seeing you with the kids you coach. Anyway, I'm not asking you to do anything differently or be any different way. I just want you to know how I used to feel about big guys."

P.K. looked serious: "It's really hard for me to hear that anyone mistreated you—and that you put up with it. But at least you got help. Even though I'm really glad about the way things turned out for you, it ticks me off to think about any guy laying a hand on a woman—or anyone not his own size, for that matter. My father was a tough guy, but he never, ever raised a hand to my mother, my brother, or me. Probably because of him, it's just not where I go. It seems to me that I can keep things calm just being in a room with people. I told you I've only had to get physical a handful of times at work, and you were there for one of them.

"The girls' coach at school has been raving about a really intense self-defense program she's taking for adult women. They're trained to deliver a knockout blow to huge guys in padded suits—they're martial artists, in fact. It's the best thing I've ever heard of. I'd really appreciate it if you'd consider the course. I'd even pay for it. Maybe it would help you get over feeling small, and it would *surely* make me less nervous about you coming home from work just before dawn."

Financial Status and Two Closet Sexists

Corey had just been promoted to a managerial position at the aggressive superstore chain for which he'd worked for five years. Wei Ling, his wife, was a women's historian who managed a flower shop part-time; financially, this latter was almost purely a labor of love. To her husband's dismay, she seemed dedicated to becoming an eternal student as well. Still, in many ways this couple personified the progressive marriage. They had no problem splitting chores right down the middle, and there was no question for either of them as to her keeping her surname. Earlier in their relationship, Wei Ling and Corey had stepped out of their normal lives for ten months to cruise the South Pacific in an old sailboat they'd restored together over weekends.

Though their house was deeded to Wei Ling, part of her settlement from a previous marriage, it was Corey who handled the mortgage payments and related expenses. Eating out, holidays, and all extras also seemed to come down to him, though for some reason they both remained mute on the subject for the first seven years of their marriage. It wasn't until Wei Ling announced her intention to take out a loan for a second master's degree that Corey put his cards on the table. He scheduled a Special Session on the topic of their financial future—and past.

Corey began: "Babe, you know I really appreciate this great old house you've provided us, and I want to support you in your interests. But we've never really gotten clear about our roles in terms of finances. I don't want to stress you out, but I don't want to start holding the money issue against you, either. It's true that I should have mentioned it before, but I guess I was waiting for you to—which isn't fair. It's not that I don't like my job, but now you're talking about another degree, more debt, and no end in sight—and there seems to be an assumption that I'm going to continue to foot all the bills. What if *I* wanted to leave *my* job? I'd be trapped. I wonder if you ever plan to participate in our major expenses. A part of me—I guess it's old-fashioned—thinks that ultimately the financial buck stops with me, and I feel guilty and ungenerous in even bringing it up."

Wei Ling lowered her eyes: "You're right. I feel nervous and guilty too, talking about this. I try to push the question of our finances out of my mind when it comes up, or I make myself feel better by the thought that the house is mine. And I keep hoping you won't notice or mind that I'm not pulling my weight financially. I know I'm not being realistic— or fair to you. I guess it's partly my upbringing. Even though I call myself a feminist and believe that women should have not only equal rights but equal responsibilities, there's a part of me that just plain resents men. I'm not proud of how I feel, but it's like, *Well, they control the economy, so they should bear the brunt of the bills.* Pretty hypocritical, huh? I feel embarrassed that I don't make as much money as you do. I'm afraid that even if I tried, I couldn't come near your income. Staying a student is safe; that way I never have to find out what I'm capable of."

Corey's face was open and full of love when he responded: "That's all I wanted to hear. I don't want you to get a job you hate or to grovel. We'll work the details out. Still, I really needed for us to clear the air. You're truly amazing. Who'd have thought we'd both have such sneaky inner sexists, or that they'd be running our show?"

Gender and Cultural Prejudice

Palmer and Grace met in her Asia-Pacific country of Malaysia at the multinational corporation where they both worked. She was a local hire; he, a European on overseas contract. Besides their jobs, they shared a passion for scuba diving. They especially loved seeking out the mysterious whale shark. Palmer and Grace were both cognizant of the divide in their cultural and socioeconomic backgrounds and the jumble of feelings that divide evoked. Palmer had rebelled against the bigoted messages he'd heard at home growing up—messages about Grace's part of the world. And he worried about any vestiges of this conditioning that might influence him still.

He broached it in a Special Session: "I'm only too aware that I'm of colonial descent. It's lousy. I feel guilty and ashamed for the history of exploitation and domination of your culture. Some of my colleagues are actually racist and look for local wives who'll let them sort of run things. Still, sometimes when we're having an argument and you become silent, I feel an urge to take advantage of the situation and just take over. It scares me for us. I don't want to be a brute. I really appreciate your gentleness. You're very different from the women in my family."

Touched, Grace picked up her side of the dialogue: "Palmer, you're so honest. I'm really impressed. I know that I go quiet sometimes. I feel embarrassed not to be more assertive. You've seen how women in my family defer to men. I don't want to lapse into that behavior, but it's hard to shake. And to tell the truth, when you raise your voice, I'm finished.

"As for the colonial past—yes, I was filled with prejudices by my parents and grandparents too. They idealized your people, but there was also a lot of resentment. It's very confusing. I reacted to my parents by putting your culture down—even though, in my heart, that response didn't feel good. Then I realized, as I got older, that the only way I was going to make it out of my village was by learning English and going to college. One thing led to another, and soon I was working for a foreign company. I found myself right in the mouth of the tiger. Since I've fallen head over heels for you, I'm glad you opened up this can of worms."

Palmer took a deep breath before responding: "I know what you mean, especially about my raising my voice. I know that it's unacceptable when I let the decibels get up there. Everyone in my household hollered when I was growing up. I'm part deaf! I don't blame you for being angry about the political history. We're on the same page with this one. Thank God *we* get to choose differently. Incidentally, I'm proud of your talent for English. As you know, languages don't come easily to me."

Assumption of Gender-Based Special Knowledge (or Lack of Knowledge)

Hazel and Eli couldn't contain the joy they felt at the birth of their twin boys. A computer programmer, she'd been lucky to get an open-ended leave of absence from work. Meantime, Eli, a plumbing contractor, had added hours and now was working time and a half. Caring for two babies single-handedly while Eli was at work ten hours a day proved too heavy a workload for Hazel—and she let her husband know it. Even so, when it was Eli's turn to father, he'd hold Ogden the "wrong" way or forget to put talcum powder on Chester's bottom. Hazel just didn't seem able to cut him any slack; she was always on his case. Confused and frustrated, Eli requested a Special Session limited to the subject of co-parenting.

Eli jumped right in: "Hazel, hon, I know you feel overwhelmed by the boys. Your long days are rough. In fact, I don't know how you keep your patience with the babies, even with your mother and sister helping out. Honestly, I wouldn't want to change places with you if I could. Still, we're supposed to be partners in this. When I'm home at night, I'm as committed and available as any dad could be. I love those little guys, and I want to father them! But sometimes you act as though I can't do anything right. I've read all the books too, but you give me the impression I'm undoing everything you learned in your New Mum classes. I don't necessarily agree with you every time, either. I only bite my tongue because I don't want bad vibes around the babies. *That* I'm positive is bad for them. Anyway, thanks for hearing me out."

Hazel looked perplexed. Then she answered Eli: "Boy, am I that bad? I know that I don't seem able to control my anxiety about doing everything perfectly for Chester and Ogden. I watch myself hassling you and I know it's unfair. Who knows? I'm probably driving myself bonkers too! Yuck—I guess I'm turning into a control-freak mom. My mother sort of drummed it into my head that men don't have the maternal instinct. My father wasn't allowed to set foot in the nursery—but of course, unlike you, he didn't want to. I thought that was bizarre. I know that studies have proven some children are actually better off with their father functioning as primary parent. The conditioning is definitely in me, though— it's like I have a superiority complex when it comes to parenting. I owe it to all three of my men to get a handle on it."

Physical and Intellectual Prowess

Melisande, a professional jazz dancer, and Thurston, a university lecturer, recognized their tremendous compatibilities right away, but the shadow side needed to be spoken about. For her, it was a painful sense of intellectual inferiority. For him, it was a matter of feeling one down athletically.

Melisande went first: "I don't know if you've noticed it, but I feel blocked around you sometimes when we're having a discussion. I find myself clamming up, especially when the topic turns to literature or history. You're so brilliant. I'm the dancer, the right brain of the family, which is cool, but I feel intimidated by your intelligence. You can talk circles around me. I find myself grasping for what I know and being overly attached to being right. Sometimes I tune you out almost completely. I suppose I'm feeling ashamed that I can't keep up."

Now it was Thurston's turn to tell Melisande his feelings about her revelations: "I'm surprised, in a way. But I *have* noticed that you get testy or a bit vacant sometimes when I talk. I've just assumed that you were one more person I was boring to death with my diatribes. It's made me feel embarrassed. It's a relief to know what's really going on for you. I have great respect for your emotional sensitivity. I can get really stuck in my head."

Thurston had lots to share about his own insecurities. "I, for one, have the coordination of a hippo caught in quicksand. I'm in awe of your kinesthetic ability. When we go to a wedding or out to a club, it's tough on me. Dancing is my chance to play the fool. I'd gladly trade some of my gray matter for an ounce of your grace."

Melisande responded: "Thanks for saying so—but I'm shocked you feel that way. You seem so confident. Anyway, you're very coordinated and I'm proud to be in your arms on the dance floor. You're a dish, and that's that!"

Inherited Wealth and Gender Roles

Stan knew he was in trouble when he met Frederick, a twenty-nine-year-old scion from a wealthy family. In the first place, neither had ever experienced chemistry as intensely as they did with each other. And then there was Frederick's fortune—more than ten million dollars. As attractive as that wealth might seem to some, Stan—a successful thirty-two-year-old classical musician—had been around the block enough to know that such an imbalance in means had the potential to wreak havoc in their relationship. What neither had banked on was the emergence of vaguely traditional gender role-playing. They'd assumed that they'd be spared the stereotyped gender roles as an automatic—and positive—consequence of their sexual orientation.

Stan pulled the long straw and began: "I worry that you might wonder if I'm after your money. How could you not be suspicious of any friend or lover who doesn't have comparable wealth? The truth is I care about *you*—not your dough. I've been careful with my finances, and for your information I'm pretty well off. Anyway, I just had to get that out in the open. The big issue—and what I'm really nervous about—is this weird pattern we've gotten into. I keep reminding myself of my father, the way he acted with my mother; you know, overbearing, opinionated—like the proverbial macho-man with his submissive wife. We both know it's true. Sometimes you do seem pretty shy and retiring, and it brings the worst out in me. I don't get it—you're such a dynamo out in the world. It's strange that you let me prevail here at home. At any rate, I'm starting to feel guilty. I don't want to be obnoxious; it's not who I really am."

Though he'd listened beautifully, Frederick was eager to respond: "This is why I'm so crazy about you: you say what's on your mind! It's so refreshing. Now about the money: yes, it's one of the ugliest parts of my life—that inability to trust people, that ever-present fear of yet another agenda. One does get paranoid. And it's happened, of course, in the past—with both lovers and friends. It's mucked up my ability to discriminate between who's trustworthy and who isn't. Let's just say that in my case, it was the money that brought the worst out in everybody. *You* just try to get sympathy for being too rich! Finally, believe it or not, I found a support group for high-end trust-fund babies. You've gotta love it! Sometimes I think I owe it my sanity. And I could tell that you were financially responsible soon after we met. Still, this is a big issue for me too. Let's agree to discuss it anytime either of us needs to.

"As for the other problem, I don't know what's gotten into me. I'm horrified. I'm not the docile type. In my family, it was my father who kowtowed to my mother; he practically leapt to her every command. I couldn't stand it, so you can imagine how alarmed I feel acting the obedient wife with you."

Stan paused, then concluded: "Thank goodness you're aware of this awful traditional dance we're doing. It feels as if we're beginning to detangle it right now just by talking. Let's continue doing Sessions on this as well as the financial thing."

When we commit to the fifth New Law of Love—and face the potentially volatile subjects of power and politics head on—we're actually pioneering a new way: the way to fairness and true equality between partners. We're acknowledging that the traditional paradigm, with its anachronistic expectations and assumptions about conjugal roles and responsibilities, has been burned into the unconscious of lovers for too long (and is too potent) to be fully shed in a single generation. We're also demonstrating a wise awareness that, unless openly and lovingly discussed, the weighting of any kind of power to one side of our couple will ignite insecurities and resentments with long-term ill-effects.

Though it's better when we apprehend the thief at the front door and catch such imbalances and tendencies to act out passé roles up front, a pre-emptive strike isn't always possible. Tradition has us entranced, and inequality blind spots are found in even the most vigilant couples. A generous helping of forgiveness is recommended. We make huge headway, however, just by being sensitive to how imbalances and expectations affect us and our beloved. Our skills of emotional literacy, honesty, and management will serve us well as we sit down together for those little chats and big talks— not to mention Special Sessions—as will our ability to listen deeply. However, since equality and fairness tend to create complexity, new ways of interacting are often required. The negotiation skills and couple agreements presented in the next chapter are invaluable in building that new structure.

When we take responsibility for the power and roles in our union, we seal our friendship and keep our passion primed. In fact, rectifying imbalances and dependencies can be incredibly empowering. Certainly, that process nurtures our self-respect—and ultimately our self-love. What's more, it can also unlock our creative potential, helping clear the path for our individual life missions (if we're not both already on our way in this regard).

It takes guts to truly embrace a standard of fairness, but when we make equality a central plank of our platform, our New Couple is well on its way to success.

The Key to Equality

Insisting on fairness and respect for yourself and your partner is the key to the fifth New Law of Love.

This means . . .

- Honestly examining and sharing your feelings about differences, expectations and assumptions, and unnegotiated roles and responsibilities, along with any unfairness that results from these
- Committing to rectify unfairness to both partners' satisfaction

6. PEACEMAKING
the sixth new law of love

Peace is not God's gift to His creatures; peace is our gift to each other.
ELIE WIESEL, Nobel Lecture, the day after accepting the
Nobel Peace Prize, December 1986

If the technology of war seems out of control in the world, at least the technology of peace is well within reach—that is, within the privacy and sanctity of our couple. This sixth New Law of Love—the Law of Peacemaking—picks up where emotional integrity, deep listening, and equality left off. Peacemaking offers us the power tools we need to transform our relationship into an emotional safe zone. It handles our buttons and blind spots by asking us to create couple agreements and learn a set of skills designed to help us manage anger and resolve conflict.

As with all New Couple skills, we gain competence at making and keeping the peace gradually. We practice, falteringly at first, and then one fine day our hard work pays off: we notice that peacemaking has imperceptibly become integral to the fabric of our relationship—the natural way we react to each other in testy moments. With the Law of Peacemaking, it's not whether we get in trouble that matters, for it's assumed we will. What's important, rather, is *how we get out of trouble.*

Those who've enjoyed the bonding experience of a well-resolved fight might already be able to imagine the potency of the peacemaking process. Peacemaking has the ability not only to transform relational fissures into some of our greatest strengths as a couple, but also to fortify our relationship overall. Knowing in our hearts that we have the commitment and the tools to work through any disagreement, no matter what the issue, is a fantastic feeling, a rare reassurance for partners. And the effort required is quite minimal—a matter of seconds to manage anger, and about ten minutes to get over most tiffs—considering that this could well be the most important human technology we ever master.

The first component of this law, core agreements, represents our own personal conditions for a relationship—that is, our individual bottom line. Some core agreements are recommended by the Law of Peacemaking, and some we write ourselves. The second component, anger management, requires a skill and several additional agreements. These agreements, however, are part of a technique, and they're prewritten; the skill asks only that, when the time is right, we utter—rather emphatically—two tiny but potent words. The final part of peacemaking, conflict resolution, employs another technique, this one deceptively simple, which we can either verbalize or write to our mates. Sometimes it's necessary that we formulate additional negotiable agreements in order to arrive at what's truly fair for both of us; at other times it's necessary for us to make amends.

If it sounds like making and keeping the peace in a couple requires too many, even scads of agreements, it doesn't necessarily feel that way. First of all, the most important ones are so basic that they almost seem transparent. Second, the bulk of the agreements are negotiable even after they're in place. Last, the number we need is up to the two of us. The fact that agreements are needed is evidence of one of the primary lessons this chapter hopes to teach: to be successful, equal partnership has to be an ongoing negotiation. The alternatives are bleak: a win-lose teeter-totter, a hot or a cold war, a free-for-all of button-pushing and blind spots—all of which have the potential to destroy the relationship. And what we'll never know until we try is that some of the mutual wins we arrive at via negotiation may prove to be absolutely brilliant, making us better friends than ever.

Despite the reasonableness of such an approach, some of us may not be comfortable with the idea of a predesigned method to promote and maintain peace in an intimate relationship. As was explained in Chapter 3, a particularly traumatic childhood can strongly predispose some of us to "white-knuckle it." Riddled with buttons and blind spots, we end up conflict- and anger-avoidant, or (opting for an opposite approach) perhaps quietly or explosively "rageaholic," or even both at different times. Frequently, these opposite types marry. The tendency toward either type is especially strong in those who (whether they remember it or not) were subjected as kids to shaming or guilt for having or expressing feelings, or were subjected to psychological, verbal, or physical acting out of anger.

Those of us who avoid anger and conflict are often afraid that if we get near either one, we'll get hurt or turn into abusers ourselves. Those of us who can't control our rage often secretly fear that we'll fail if we try. Whichever type we are, we deserve compassion and patience, for clearly we've already been through enough. Eventually, though, we would all do well to face such fears—an endeavor that could transform our lives. But at the end of the day, it's up to each of us as individuals to choose life in a relationship with—or without—the technology of peace.

CREATING CORE AGREEMENTS: DRAWING LINES IN THE SAND

While most of us have relegated *unconditional love* to the domain of angels and bodhisattvas—and are perhaps reconciled to experiencing only a shimmering moment of such love from time to time—we have yet to give up on the idea of *unconditional relationship*. We claim that it's uptight and legalistic to set standards in our relationship; we see such standards as signs of bad faith or lack of trust in our mate. We worry that setting standards within the relationship puts unfair demands on our partner. We seem to think that a conditional relationship is antithetical to that lofty, all-but-unattainable goal of unconditional love. In other words, we believe that true love means grinning and bearing it, accepting the good with the bad, no matter how harmful that bad might be. Yet this perspective couldn't be further from the truth.

In fact, a successful relationship without real conditions is to us mortal couples as elusive as a perpetual state of unconditional love. Why so? Because, as the street wisdom goes, *where there are no rules, we tend to make up our own—individually*. Though the notion of *rules* is inappropriately harsh for love unions, it must be said that when no conditions are articulated within a couple, *assumptions* do abound. And it follows that when no conversations take place to deal with equality issues, for example, each partner may assume that the other will take responsibility. For one of us the resulting assumption might read, *When the doorbell rings, the person closest to the door answers it,* while the other partner's assumption might read, *The man always answers the door.* The confusion and conflict that result from unspoken assumptions bring out the worst in all of us—bully, victim, nag, Peter Pan, martyr, guilt-tripper, master manipulator.

If, on the other hand, we do set conditions in our relationship—and these are honored as agreements—our self-esteem flourishes. This in turn brings out the *best* in both of us. Indeed, though it may seem paradoxical, a few seriously self-loving conditions are the best way for us to open the floodgates to blissfully unconditional mutual regard.

Specifically, the Law of Peacemaking proposes that, *as individuals,* each of us identify those conditions that we know we can't live without in our union. These are called the *core conditions* for the relationship. Ideally, these conditions—which are entirely up to the individuals involved—are drafted in advance of a lifelong commitment.

Those of us who are single can have our core conditions ready for the moment when we meet that special person with whom we have New Couple chemistry. If it's a green light after we know each other well enough to talk about the conditions, the two of us can sit down and forge the bottom-line conditions we've both come up with independently into formal couple agreements. If, on the other hand, we're already in a couple, not to worry. It's never too late to get down to the "cores." Indeed, many partners have formulated such agreements after the fact with great ease and joy—and have even committed them to writing.

Donna and Drew, for example, had always assumed that they were both committed to monogamy. Still, after bearing firsthand witness to the ravaging effects of an affair on their best friends' marriage—a marriage in which the monogamy issue was supposedly "understood"—they decided to make their exclusive commitment to each other explicit. The core agreement had a decidedly soothing effect on both of them.

Nonnegotiable, core agreements, once committed to, serve as ultimatums; they're "walking" matters. (See Chapter 9, "Walking.") For that reason, they really do need to be consensual. Any couple who can't agree to the core conditions of their relationship should refer to Chapter 10, "Transformational Education." If doing what those pages suggest doesn't result in agreement, perhaps the relationship isn't worth saving. We always have to think carefully about the wisdom of committing to—or trying to preserve—a relationship where our essential needs aren't accepted and valued.

Though on the surface, core agreements may appear a little heavy, cold, clinical even—clearly, they do have teeth—they're actually an invaluable gift we can share. Like nothing else, such pacts between us lend strength, structure, stamina, and substance to our relationship. Over the life of our love, they'll come to function as the very I-beams of the trust we feel for each other.

BATTLING THE SEVEN OUTLAWS OF LOVE

Though your individual core conditions, and the agreements you forge from them as a couple, are yours alone to design, certain general conditions are recommended. These are intended to shackle the seven outlaws of love: infidelity, sexual acting out, violence, lying, addictions, extreme self-destructive behaviors, and criminality. Many individuals regard these outlaws as *obviously* unacceptable and therefore don't think it's necessary to formally agree to disallow them. Still, it's always preferable to be explicit about such matters. Countless partners have come to counseling after the fact only to declare, "Well, I knew my spouse wouldn't like it, but he [she] never said, 'Absolutely not.'"

Core conditions aren't based on a moral yardstick of any kind; that's ours alone to apply. Rather, they grow out of *what has proven to work*—to both create and sustain vibrant relationships. All the outlaws named above—including, for example, infidelity and violence—are like big gashes in the vessel of a relationship; they typically defy repair. They destroy trust and all hope of ever establishing our couple as an emotional safe zone. Additionally, they stymie the fulfillment of higher-order needs for self-love and emotional intimacy. With the help of core commitments, these outlaws can be barred from our relationship.

Though all seven outlaws are destructive, some are worse than, more common than, and more complicated than the others. We'll take a closer look at how commitments to monogamy and sexual exclusivity (not the same thing!) can restrain two of the worst offenders, and then turn our attention to ways to combat violence (whether manifested in word or deed).

Committing to Monogamy

Monogamy is a matter of personal choice, but it's something that most of us commit to in principle. The rationale for that commitment isn't based only on physical health; it also takes into account—and this is to our credit—emotional well-being. And although we might say that we just "couldn't handle" two sexual relationships (not to mention sharing our beloved with someone else in this most intimate way), we who insist on monogamy are also displaying a healthy regard for our own most human and, incidentally, gender-neutral fears: those of abandonment or rejection, and of being found to be inadequate or unlovable.

While for most people the mere idea of our mate in bed with someone else is disturbing or worse, the act itself is severely traumatic and destabilizing. Indeed, as the sixties taught us, even when both partners agree to an open relationship, that arrangement generally doesn't work. Almost invariably, once one partner acts upon the option, the other, if emotionally honest, takes it as a sign of his or her own "not-enoughness" (if not as an actual betrayal).

And there's more to the recommendation of monogamy as a core agreement than merely the physical and emotional integrity of our couple. Though less widely acknowledged, the ramifications of multiple partners on the energy of a relationship are equally important. Sexual energy flows between two people like electricity in a circuit. When a third party is introduced, he or she breaks the circuit, diluting—*squandering* even— our own precious sexual energy. Even between partners who are aware of no abandonment buttons or lack of self-love, the energy loss of sexually open relationships precludes emotional depth. There's just no way around it: the highest realms of sexual ecstasy can be experienced only by mates who are bonded on the deepest level of friendship and feeling—and who reserve themselves for each other exclusively.

Committing to Sexual Exclusivity

Beyond monogamy, the sixth New Law of Love also encourages us to make a core agreement with regard to sexual exclusivity—that is, an agreement to not interact (read: *act out*) with other people in a sexual manner. Sexual acting out has caused tremendous confusion and pain for many partners, since during our lifetime so many sexual taboos have been lifted—and the subject continues to be terra incognita for most of us.

A crucial refinement on the notion of monogamy, sexual exclusivity is much more far-reaching than a straightforward agreement to not sleep with another. In fact, it can proscribe a wide range of sexualized behaviors and interactions not only *with* others, but also *about* others with one's mate. These include, in the first category, flirting, staring, rubbernecking, and making sexual comments, compliments, and jokes; and in the second, comments to one's mate that demonstrate sexual interest in, excitement about, or titillation by another. Often both categories of behavior are rationalized as acceptable, on the grounds that the offenders "aren't actually *doing* anything." This is a serious misjudgment, however; for in the sanctity of the love union, these partners *are* doing something—not only sexually acting out and expressing their sexual energy outside the crucible of their relationship, but also eroding fragile trust.

Mary Ann never thought about the impact on her boyfriend of her words about a popular musician until late one night, after a concert. That's when Bruce made himself exceptionally vulnerable and informed her that her remark—she'd said that she wanted to "jump the lead singer's bones"—had cut him to the quick. Bruce also took the opportunity to expand their definition of sexual exclusivity right there on the spot: "I don't want to know if some guy turns you on—unless it's serious." Clearly, Bruce isn't being a prude or advocating that his girlfriend be emotionally dishonest. Rather, he's requesting that Mary Ann spare him gratuitous comments that are disrespectful and hurtful and that detract from his feeling cherished as her main squeeze. It's only loving.

Mary Ann and Bruce's story notwithstanding, at first glance a core agreement to refrain from "innocent sexual fun" may seem like a psychic chastity belt—a form of pandering to unreasonable insecurities (petty at best and paranoid at worst). The truth is almost all of us suffer when our beloved "plays"—or places sexual attention—elsewhere. Some of us—those plagued by classic toxic shame—are just quieter about it than others. We might subscribe to the popular belief that flirting is harmless, "no biggie," but then proceed to indict ourselves for feeling hurt over it. This is an example of the wholesale, self-destructive invalidation of our own feelings that the toxic emotions precipitate.

If we're on the receiving end of a breach in sexual exclusivity, we may feel that we have no recourse but to retaliate in kind. As Rafael and Meagan learned, this can create a mess of betrayals and counter-betrayals. By the age of thirty, Rafael had enjoyed a string of serially monogamous unions. He could never figure out why his romantic partners always seemed more insecure about their relationship than he did—until, that is, he met Meagan. For this twenty-eight-year-old delighted in the same innocent game he did; and in her own colorful relationship history, she'd always made sure she found herself playing "the distancer" to her lovers, who would suffer not so gladly as "the pursuers."

Though like most charmers, each was generally emotionally aware and honest, it was with odd confidence that these seasoned flirts reassured each other that jealousy lay outside their respective emotional repertoires. It seemed that they were just too cool to be jealous. Soon, however, the veneer—a protection against the experience of vulnerability and toxic shame—wore thin; and while witnessing the other's ways with other members of the opposite sex, both Meagan and Raphael experienced painfully discomfiting moments.

Instead of coming clean and revealing their real feelings to each other, the couple let the situation snowball. Unconsciously, they started to loosen their boundaries with others—especially those whom they thought their mate would perceive as a particular threat. The bottom was hit when Raphael attended a bachelor party in which a stripper "danced" on his lap. Meagan retaliated by scheduling a "girls' night out" and purchasing front-row seats at a Chippendales performance.

This was Meagan and Rafael's first opportunity to take a good long look in the mirror, and neither liked how the reflection felt. After stewing for a day or two, they scheduled a Session, and in the safety of that dialogue, their true emotions emerged haltingly. It was all there for both of them—insecurity, betrayal, and yes, even the dreaded and much-denied jealousy. Still, there was palpable relief as they went about creating emotional safety in their couple—by getting specific about their individual conditions and hammering out the following core agreement on sexual exclusivity: "In honor of the specialness of our sexual chemistry and out of our respect for each other as people, we agree to reserve all our sexual energy for one another; this includes touching, playing, flirting, and all other seductive behaviors with others."

While the effect the above kinds of acting out sexually isn't usually as traumatic as that of physical infidelity with another, it's important to realize that *any* form of sexual involvement with a third party (whether subtle or egregious)—even if that third party is a pornographic image—will likely feel like a betrayal to one's mate. At the very least, it will leak vital sexual energy from the crucible of the couple—if it doesn't break the circuit completely. In addition, it will gnaw away at emotional intimacy and self-love and usually push a variety of painful emotional buttons.

A core agreement for sexual exclusivity averts such recklessness and heartache and honors the specialness of the connection. Couples are encouraged to define for themselves—as soon as possible—what, beyond standard monogamy, they expect in terms of sexual exclusivity. This can be challenging, because many of us have been shamed for being sexually insecure, possessive, or jealous. We can take advantage of our best-friendship closeness to exercise emotional honesty as we communicate these difficult feelings to each other.

An Invitation to Reflect on the Law of Peacemaking

As you approach the exercises in this chapter, remember that the presence or absence of New Couple chemistry profoundly affects a couple's experience with each law.

- Do you have a formal agreement regarding monogamy in your couple? How does this agreement—or the lack of one—make you feel? How does this affect your self-love? Your emotional intimacy?

- How would you define sexual exclusivity for your couple? Be as specific as possible. How would an agreement regarding sexual exclusivity make you feel? How would it affect your self-love? Your emotional intimacy?

Emotional Exclusivity

Many of us feel uncomfortable or hurt when our partner maintains an intensely emotional relationship with someone of either gender outside our couple. (Of course, if this third party is a family member, this is an issue of individuation, as discussed in Chapter 2, "Priority.") Though not exactly sexual or romantic in nature, such a relationship can feel like a genuine betrayal of the emotional primacy we have the right to expect with our partner. These sticky dynamics are much more complex than sexual acting out, and we usually require some facilitation to determine whether we're detecting a truly codependent or otherwise inappropriate relationship, or whether it's our own low self-love that ails us. Usually it's a confounding combination of both. The resources listed in Chapter 10, "Transformational Education," are strongly recommended for such cases.

More at the Core

Core agreements that proscribe violence, dishonesty (including criminality), and addictions and compulsivity—essentially, all issues of priority—provide an equally stabilizing function in couples. Indeed, such agreements are the "good cops" in our emotional safe zone. Relationships in which outlaw behaviors are tolerated can be true hell on earth—a state none of us deserves to live in. Unfortunately, outlaws figure in the autopsies of many a once-hopeful relationship.

Partners who find such a list of core agreements to be more than they can insist on—or who sense a tendency to minimize or deny the existence of outlaws in their relationship—have a strong need for outside support. Chapter 10, "Transformational Education," offers considerable help in this area.

Couples are encouraged to create whatever additional core agreements they need. For some, these might cover areas vital to their sense of individual security—finances, for example, which they might choose to protect in the form of a standard prenuptial agreement. Other partners might craft cores to safeguard cherished personal values and life goals, such as a religious or spiritual orientation or a decision regarding having children. (This sort of core agreement has some overlap with essential compatibilities as defined in Chapter 1.) We recommend that couples who do want a family also both agree that physical discipline, meaning any nonloving touch, is unacceptable. Couples concerned about spiritual issues might want to agree on the children's religious or spiritual upbringing as well.

Expectations regarding caring for aging parents or other relatives for whom either partner is responsible, financially and otherwise, should also be explicitly covered in an agreement. Each one potentially critical, these topics are best addressed as early as possible, preferably before a couple commits to each other.

Finally, many couples find that the Ten New Laws of Love handle everything. And though the Law of Priority has already asked us to do the work of relationship using a new model, some partners make it easy on themselves by committing to all Ten New Laws of Love, in addition to the specific cores recommended in this chapter.

Recommended Core Agreements for the New Couple

Here is a suggested script for your couple's core agreements, to be modified as you wish:

Inspired by our deep respect and love for each other, and by the preciousness of our chemistry, emotional intimacy, and trust, we, [add your names], agree to commit to the following:

- *Monogamy and sexual exclusivity [as defined by your couple]*
- *Physical behaviors that are exclusively loving and protective*
- *The Ten New Laws of Love*

Your couple's additional core agreements then follow. For example:

- *A family of at least one child*
- *Parenting education at all developmental levels and outside support when necessary*

Couples with a history of pathological or compulsive lying, any form of addiction, extreme self-destructive behavior, criminality, or mental illness are encouraged to draft a core agreement committing to stop the behavior; in addition, ongoing recovery or treatment are crucial for both parties, offering structure as they attempt to rebuild trust.

An Invitation to Reflect on
the Law of Peacemaking

• What core agreements would you like to establish in your
  relationship? How would these make you feel? How would
  they affect your self-love? Your emotional intimacy?

ANGER MANAGEMENT: THE BEDROCK
OF OUR EMOTIONAL SAFE ZONE

Though unglamorous perhaps, effective anger management is the bedrock
upon which the peace and health of all relationships—including those of a
romantic nature—rest. Over time, unmanaged anger caused by buttons and
blind spots not only shuts our hearts to each other, but turns our household
into a place where angels—and everybody else—fear to tread. Chapter 3,
"Emotional Integrity," introduced the idea that all feelings—anger not least
among them—inevitably find release. And as we've seen, if we don't express
feelings responsibly using I-statements, we can't but act them out irrespon-
sibly either directly or indirectly. Our understanding of this distinction is
fundamental to our ability to both manage anger and resolve conflict.

Our commitment to anger management signifies a commitment to neither act out nor tolerate the acting out by our mate of any kind of anger.
This includes garden-variety anger, rage, resentment, frustration, impatience, irritation, and annoyance, and the contempt cluster of emotions—
namely, hatred, scorn, disdain, and contempt. This commitment comes into
play when emotional management isn't enough—that is, when one of us
acts out *despite our knowledge of the information and skills outlined in Chapter 3.*

Anger management asks that we recommit to the definition and
inadmissibility of all forms of acted-out anger. Additionally, it asks that
we both agree to use the anger-management tool known as the "time-
out," and if an incident needs further resolution (which it often does) to
hold a "time-in" as soon as possible to determine what course of conflict
resolution we should take. (More on this process later.)

Anger management isn't about stifling our anger, stuffing it with no
planned opportunity or means to work it through. It's about taking
dominion over our anger button, controlling the impulse to release an

explosion of bile or rage the moment that button is pushed. (And, as we've said, anger isn't the only kind of button.) Neither is anger management about promising never to act anger out again—that would be absurd. Rather, it's about doing our best. The study of anger is still a fledgling subject, so almost none of us have been taught (either at home or at school) methods for handling anger appropriately or healing its excesses. Instead, our entire culture has conditioned us through role-modeling to express it inappropriately.

What's more, as is by now abundantly clear, we're all sitting on veritable powder kegs of anger stored from a lifetime of large and small psychological insults and injuries. Given the destructive potential of these powder kegs, many of us will need to learn how to discharge this surplus safely and appropriately through catharsis, initially with the help of a trained professional. Then, with less raw anger to manage, we won't have to keep a finger in the dike to prevent catastrophe. (The "Peacemaking" section of Chapter 10 provides further suggestions along these lines.)

Still, it's essential that we agree not only on the unacceptability of mismanaged anger—and commit to use a procedure for those times when anger erupts—but also on a common definition, so that together we can name what threatens us. The naming of anger can be challenging, however, because acted-out anger occurs in a seemingly infinite variety of forms, be they passive-aggressive or aggressive-aggressive, verbal or physical. While it's not hard to recognize and label violence, the breaking of objects, and over-the-top verbal abuse as acting out, some of the subtler forms of the latter—such as sarcasm and teasing—can be trickier to nail, especially in the confusion of the moment.

Surely the worst problem is that, like sexual acting out, many forms of acted-out anger are socially acceptable; they're common currency in our homes, schools, and workplaces, and they show up to an alarming (and increasing) degree on radio, television, and the big screen—as entertainment, no less! All this family and cultural conditioning creates tremendous pressure on those of us who are trying to master the distinction between acting out anger and expressing it appropriately. As with sexual acting out, those of us touchy about tolerating the verbal acting out of anger shame ourselves for being too sensitive or unable to take a joke, roll with the punches, or be a good sport. We often end up minimizing or rationalizing the offensive behavior as acceptable—or denying it altogether.

Labeling Our Anger:
Positively Identifying
a Sometimes-Negative Emotion

Though the labeling of acted-out anger is difficult, we owe it to ourselves to master the skill, because it's the first step in managing anger. In fact, vagueness or a lack of consensus at this crucial first step sabotages the entire peacemaking process.

In her book *The Verbally Abusive Relationship*, communication expert Patricia Evans details fifteen categories of verbal abuse. Not surprisingly, most of them are couched as you-statements and bear the disrespectful tone of an abusive authority figure. A modified list, some categories of which were mentioned in Chapter 3, follows:

1. *Withholding:* Keeping to oneself in order to punish the other. Known as "the silent treatment" (or, in the United Kingdom, "putting {add name} in Coventry"), this type of nonverbal communication can be seen as a form of psychological abuse.

2. *Countering, contradicting, and interrupting:* Insulting a partner's intelligence while precluding his or her free verbal expression. "You've got it all wrong, again."

3. *Discounting:* Questioning or devaluing a partner's experience or perceptions. "Give me a break!"

4. *Joking:* Offering jokes, teasing, or sarcasm at the expense of a partner. Typical areas of vulnerability for this form of shaming include femininity or masculinity, sexual desirability, intellect, competency, and physical appearance.

5. *Blocking and diverting:* Changing the subject, making accusations and counter-accusations, and other tactics aimed at preventing discussion and avoiding divulgence of information. "Do we have to get into *that?*" "*My* spending? You've never saved a penny in your life." "Do you expect me to walk on eggshells around here?"

6. *Accusing and blaming:* Charging one's partner with inappropriate behavior (either falsely or not) or of breaking an agreement, if that charge is made to avoid responsibility for one's own anger or insecurity. "You were supposed to pick me up at work." "You're so controlling [or demanding or whatever]!"

7. *Judging and criticizing:* Making direct or indirect judgments or criticisms, whether through words, tone of voice, or nonverbal communication (such as a sneer, raised eyebrow, or mocking laugh). Includes character assassination and invalidation or negation of a partner's feelings.

8. *Trivializing and devaluing:* Saying or implying that what a partner does, thinks, or says is insignificant. "That's ridiculous." "You must be kidding."

9. *Undermining:* Attacking a partner's self-esteem by squelching his or her interest and enthusiasm or by making sabotaging, interrupting, and disrupting comments. "Big deal." "Nice meal? It's just food."

10. *Threatening:* Intentionally frightening the other by raising his or her worst anxieties. "I wouldn't do that if I were you." "There are a lot of people out there who'd appreciate me."

11. *Name-calling:* Using names disguised as endearments (such as "My Little Dummy") or names that a partner has objected to in the past.

12. *"Forgetting":* Claiming not to remember or "getting foggy" on vital details, a covertly manipulative form of lying. "I said *what?*" "When did you hear me say that?" "I don't remember that."

13. *Ordering and commanding:* Adopting an authoritative, dominating, and disrespectful tone and/or words. Can be psychologically violent, as in "Shut up!" "You're not leaving this house." "Turn that radio off *now*."

14. *Denial:* Lying about facts or invalidating the reality, experience, or memory of one's partner. (Not to be confused with ego-defense denial, in which the speaker believes the delusion.) "I never said that." "You're crazy."

15. *Interrogating:* Delivering a stream of questions in a hostile, intimidating, shaming, or imperious way; implying (as in the category of commanding and ordering) that one is in authority. "What time did you get home?" "Who drove you?" "How much did you have to drink?" "What were you wearing?"

An Invitation to Reflect on the Law of Peacemaking

- What's your typical style of acting out anger: passive-aggressive (including victim talk, patronization, sarcasm, teasing, denial, and withdrawal), aggressive-aggressive (including verbal abuse, coercion, threats, and throwing and breaking things), or both? How does acting out make you feel? How does it affect your self-love? Your emotional intimacy?

- Which types of verbal abuse, if any, do you engage in? How does delivering verbal abuse make you feel? How does it affect your self-love? Your emotional intimacy?

The Time-Out Tool

Once two partners have agreed on the definition of acted-out anger, they need to agree to use the anger-management tool. This tool entails three specific steps.

First, when one partner acts out anger, the other simply calls out, quite emphatically, "Time-out!" The first partner then stops talking. Period. Midsentence, midword, whatever. Since the ball is always in the court of the one on the receiving end of the anger, it's always his or her responsibility to put the tool into action—and it's always the responsibility of the other partner to cease and desist.

Lest there be any question on this point: everybody hates being timed-out. *Everybody.* It's extremely frustrating to be at the beginning or in the middle of a cathartic and seemingly justified release of pent-up frustration (or clever but scathing commentary), only to be stopped in our tracks by our mate. To the person timed-out, this rage-buster seems like a rude interruption—an adult-inappropriate, infantilizing gimmick better used by parents with out-of-control kids. That point is well taken. Indeed, most acting out between adults, regardless of our age, is a result of both partners regressing into youngsters—either a pair of neighborhood bullies, or a bully and his or her victim. So this unassuming technique is age-appropriate after all! Be that as it may, respecting a mate's time-out is one of the most emotionally mature acts of self-discipline that we'll ever muster or master. Along with deep listening, it's one of the greatest acts of love.

The second step is to choose, together, whether to stop discussing the conflictual topic, stop talking altogether, or leave each other's company. The decision will depend on the severity of the conflict and its potential for escalation. Partners who want to choose the last option but are in a car, in an airplane, or in some other situation that makes leaving impossible can simply refrain from talking. The rub comes if the partner who was interrupted is unwilling to honor the time-out, despite having agreed in principle ahead of time. When that happens it's the responsibility of the person who called the time-out to remove him- or herself from the presence of the other. It may seem unfair that, in addition to being "victimized" (by being acted out upon), that partner is obligated to leave a place he or she might want to be. Nonetheless, that partner needs to do whatever it takes to remain emotionally safe from further acting out.

The third step is a "time-in"—an agreed-upon coming-together to discuss how to proceed. This step takes place whenever both parties feel that it's safe to reconvene—that is, when they both trust that they're able to refrain from further acting out. This could be a few minutes after the initial incident, or up to (but not exceeding) twenty-four hours later. If the intervening cool-down period has been enough to dissipate tension, no further resolution is necessary. If, however, one partner is still experiencing residual anger—which, frankly, is most often the case—both partners will need to decide jointly which of the three conflict-resolution options would be most appropriate: the Peace Process, the written Peace Process, or a negotiable agreement (all discussed below).

CONFLICT RESOLUTION: CREATING A LASTING PEACE

Whereas the purpose of anger management is to minimize the possibility of hurting each other with our acted-out anger, the purpose of conflict resolution is to heal fractures and get back to trust and love, which are always waiting. For if emotions are like the weather, then love is like the sun: it's *always* out, even if clouds or the earth itself blocks our view. The so-called negative feelings, like bad weather, simply lead us to forget the fact of love's omnipresence.

Weather happens. And in couples, conflict happens. Who among us hasn't felt anger hit us like a hurricane, sadness fall like rain, fear blanket us like freezing snow, and depression—the numbing of all feelings—descend like the dark night. Who among us hasn't despaired that love would be forever lost?

The New Couple conflict-resolution tools—the Peace Process, in spoken and written forms, and negotiated agreements—are exceptionally powerful ways to bring your couple back to a state of love, trust, and peace, especially when used in tandem with the time-out.

The Peace Process

The Peace Process is a safe, effective method for resolving most interpersonal conflicts. The only time this tool *isn't* suitable is when we're addressing anger related to core conditions or agreements. (For more on resolving core issues, see Chapter 10, "Transformational Education.")

As we've already noted, the Peace Process works well as a conflict-resolution tool following a time-out (if during the time-*in* that follows, we determine together that it's the appropriate method of conflict resolution). But that's only a fraction of its usefulness. We can use the Peace Process *any* time either of us feels angry, upset, or in our heart "separate" from the other—as long as neither feels at risk for further acting out.

Does this mean that all heat and tension have to have totally subsided before we can use the Peace Process? No—but both partners must feel sufficiently in control of the initial anger in order to participate in the "Process" in good faith and to the letter. It doesn't even matter if we don't yet know exactly why we're upset or what feelings are involved. The Peace Process will help clarify these issues.

THE TRIANGLE TEST: ASSESSING
PEACE PROCESS READINESS

One simple way to find out if we're ready for a successful experience with the Peace Process is the Triangle Test, inspired by the work of Eric Berne, founder of Transactional Analysis. Assume that we each have three main parts or subpersonalities, each positioned at a corner of a triangle. At the top is "the Adult," at one bottom corner is "the Child," and at the other bottom corner is "the Critic." The Adult, our "preferred" self, is wise, rational, loving, emotionally literate, and honest. The Child is creative, spontaneous, and playful, but also codependent, rebellious, vulnerable, and easily guilt-tripped, shamed, frightened, and intimidated. The Critic is tyrannical, judgmental, perfectionistic, disrespectful, bullying, shaming, and guilt-tripping. *Whenever we communicate, one of these selves is "holding the mike."*

Only one of these three selves is emotionally mature enough to participate in the Peace Process, and that's the Adult. The other two are the selves that act out, the ones that got us into conflict in the first place. Before taking our turns in the Peace Process, we need to ask ourselves, "Who's got the mike? Where am I on the triangle?" (Although it can be tempting, we need to refrain from asking each *other* these questions, because to do so is to allow the Critic to talk!) Having the Adult at the mike doesn't necessarily mean that we're not angry, only that we're committed to expressing our anger in a healthy way—using I-statements.

The Peace Process tool itself is an adaptation of the Emotional Map and Duplication Technique introduced by relationship expert Barbara De Angelis in her book *How to Make Love All the Time*. It uses a special listing of emotions (and quasi-emotions) called the Path to Peace, which is based on the chart of emotions introduced in Chapter 3, "Emotional Integrity." The main difference between the two listings is that, unlike the chart of emotions, the Path to Peace excludes all unhealthy emotions (toxic guilt and shame as well as the contempt cluster of hatred, scorn, disdain, and contempt) that are never appropriate to use in the Peace Process. The Path to Peace also includes betrayal, understanding, and responsibility, which, although not technically emotions, are still necessary to express to our partner in order for us to arrive at real peace. We'll present the Path to Peace first, and then discuss how to use it in the Peace Process:

THE NEW COUPLE'S **PATH TO PEACE**

- *Empathy step:* Understanding, appreciation, gratitude, compassion, admiration, and love
- *Ownership step:* Healthy guilt, healthy shame, responsibility, and embarrassment
- *Fear step:* Fear, anxiety, worry, insecurity, and jealousy
- *Sadness step:* Sadness, grief, disappointment, hurt, and despair
- *Anger step:* Anger, betrayal, resentment, frustration, annoyance, irritation, and impatience

HOW TO USE THE **PATH TO PEACE** IN THE PEACE PROCESS

Sometimes only one of us is angry; in that case, only one of us needs to use the Path to Peace. Still, it might happen that something our mate says on his or her "way up the Path" will trigger us into new anger or resentment, in which case we simply ask for our own turn when he or she is finished. Specific issues and conflicts, however, usually involve two people;

in these cases, we alternate as many turns up the Path as necessary until we've both returned to a state of love and trust.

The Peace Process takes about ten minutes per "trip up" the Path. When we're ready to use this tool, we need to go (with this book in hand) to a quiet place by ourselves where we'll have no interruptions whatsoever. As we sit facing each other, the partner with the most heat goes first.

We can resolve only one issue per trip up the Path, and it must be a single, specific incident *in real time.* For example, we can "go up the Path" to resolve the *specific incident* of our mate making plans to meet friends for dinner on the upcoming weekend without consulting us first, but we *can't* use the Peace Process, or by extension, the Path to Peace, to resolve the *general issue* of our mate's seeming habit of not consulting us. The second issue isn't specific enough. And though it may be true that a pattern exists, generalizing—saying, "You *always* . . . " or "You *never* . . . "—almost *always* creates more discord. Generalizing involves a degree of measurement-taking that can't be absolutely accurate (and thus can't be absolutely fair). Furthermore, anger causes us to distort issues, again endangering fairness. For these reasons, single incidents in real time can be resolved far more successfully than general issues can using the Peace Process.

When we take our turns going up the Path to Peace, the one expressing anger is "the Speaker"; the other person is "the Listener." Beginning at the bottom of the Path on the anger step, the Speaker formulates a brief I-statement using any of the feelings listed there (see above). For example, "I feel frustrated that you forgot to help our son with his homework when I was traveling—and he failed his test." He or she then communicates that I-statement to the Listener. It's essential that these I-statements be brief—mere sound bites—because the Listener needs to be able to repeat them back verbatim. This repetition both assures the Speaker that the Listener is really listening and gives the Listener a chance to experience what it's like to be in the other's moccasins.

Neither the Speaker nor the Listener must ever abuse this precious peacemaking tool by acting out while using his or her way up the Path. In other words, both partners need to keep the Child and the Critic under wraps! It's essential, and only fair, that the Speaker use a respectful, nonintimidating, nonshaming—yes, Adult—tone of voice at a low decibel level. If this is impossible, the Speaker is still too angry to engage in the Peace Process properly. It's always the Listener's job to determine if this is the case and to terminate the Process by calling a time-out.

After the first I-statement is communicated by the Speaker, the Listener takes a deep breath and repeats back exactly what he or she just heard, using precisely the same words. These are the only words uttered by the Listener, with two possible exceptions: asking the Speaker to repeat the previous I-statement, and (if these statements are running too long to remember) reminding the Speaker to "Please use sound bites."

On the anger step, at the bottom of the Path to Peace, the Speaker is limited to a total of five I-statements. (Communicating anger is a delicate business, and we don't want to overwhelm the Listener.) On all the other steps, however, the Speaker can deliver as many I-statements as the heart dictates, as long as the minimum—one from each step—is met, *no exceptions.*

Feelings on certain steps are easily accessible, while those on others may take a bit of effort to contact. This is normal: as the Law of Emotional Integrity has taught us, we inevitably have emotional blind spots. And yet we have to make the effort to get in touch with even the difficult feelings. Trying to skip a step to avoid particular feelings doesn't work, because every level of emotional truth must be found—and communicated—in order for the Peace Process to work its magic. With a little patience, we can surprise ourselves with the richness of our own emotional landscape.

If the Listener simply can't control him- or herself and lapses into sighing, rolling the eyes, repeating the Speaker's statements in a sarcastic or mocking tone of voice, or showing impatience, the Speaker must terminate the Process by calling a time-out. These acting-out behaviors are a big-time abuse of the Peace Process.

Once we've completed the anger step of the Peace Process, we continue together up the Path to the sadness and fear steps (all of this taking only moments). Again, the Speaker can make as many I-statements as desired, and the Listener repeats back precisely what he or she hears.

At the ownership step, the Speaker (still using I-statements) has the opportunity to plunge into quintessential Adult territory—and the heart of peacemaking—by "owning" something. Ideally, this means acknowledging how he or she contributed to the initial conflict. For example, "I feel guilty that I gave you the silent treatment when I found out that you didn't help our son before his test." If the Speaker is unable to identify any such responsibility in a particular incident, it's enough to recall and communicate having committed a similar "crime." One example of such peripheral ownership is, "I'm guilty of having forgotten his parent-teacher conference last semester." As always, the Listener repeats verbatim what was said.

At the empathy step, the Speaker does the best he or she can to reveal some understanding or appreciation of the Listener with regard to the incident. For instance, "I understand that you were swamped with two parents' jobs while I was away," or "I really appreciate that you surprised them with a barbecue." The Speaker can be exhaustive in this effort; at this step, the more I-statements, the merrier.

If the Speaker can't find anything to say on either the ownership or the empathy steps, the anger step may well have been incomplete. In this case, the Speaker is to go back to the beginning of the Path and work his or her way up again.

A SAMPLE PEACE PROCESS INVOLVING TWO TRIPS UP THE PATH TO PEACE

A complete Peace Process follows necessitating two trips up the Path to Peace. The conflict that prompted the first trip occurred when Bob made some weekend dinner plans with friends without consulting Carol:

Anger Step (first communication)

SPEAKER (CAROL): I'm frustrated that you didn't ask me before you made plans with Ted and June for Saturday night!

LISTENER (BOB): *Repeats Speaker's words verbatim:* I'm frustrated that you didn't ask me before you made plans with Ted and June for Saturday night!

Anger Step (second communication)

SPEAKER (CAROL): I resent that you didn't first check in with me at work before committing to our friends.

LISTENER (BOB): *Repeats verbatim.*

Sadness Step (first communication)

SPEAKER (CAROL): I'm disappointed that it apparently didn't occur to you that I might want to spend the evening alone with you.
LISTENER (BOB): *Repeats verbatim.*

Sadness Step (second communication)

SPEAKER (CAROL): I'm hurt that you didn't take into consideration that we've been out with others every weekend for the last month.
LISTENER (BOB): *Repeats verbatim.*

Fear Step (first communication)

SPEAKER (CAROL): I worry that you'll do it again.
LISTENER (BOB): *Repeats verbatim.*

Fear Step (second communication)

SPEAKER (CAROL): I'm afraid that you were unable to say no to them.
LISTENER (BOB): *Repeats verbatim.*

Fear Step (third communication)

SPEAKER (CAROL): I'm anxious that you'll expect *me* to do the canceling if we decide not to go.
LISTENER (BOB): *Repeats verbatim.*

Ownership Step (first communication)

SPEAKER (CAROL): I take responsibility for not clearly telling you that I miss private weekend time with you.
LISTENER (BOB): *Repeats verbatim.*

Ownership Step (second communication)

SPEAKER (CAROL): I feel guilty that I signed you up for dinner with my parents last month before I consulted with you.

LISTENER (BOB): *Repeats verbatim.*

Ownership Step (third communication)

SPEAKER (CAROL): I'm ashamed that I yelled at you when you told me what you'd done.

LISTENER (BOB): *Repeats verbatim.*

Empathy Step (first communication)

SPEAKER (CAROL): I understand that Ted put you on the spot and pressured you when he invited us.

LISTENER (BOB): *Repeats verbatim.*

Empathy Step (second communication)

SPEAKER (CAROL): I feel compassion for your difficulty saying no to pushy people. I know you're working on it, and I have difficulty too.

LISTENER (BOB): *Repeats verbatim.*

Empathy Step (third communication)

SPEAKER (CAROL): I really appreciate your letting me go up the Path to Peace and listening so patiently.

LISTENER (BOB): *Repeats verbatim.*

Bob is feeling relieved about the initial incident at this point, but now he's angry about something Carol said while going up the Path. In order to work through that anger, he takes a turn up the Path as Speaker.

Anger Step (first communication)

SPEAKER (BOB): I'm angry that you said I'd expect you to call and cancel as though I expect you to do the dirty work.

LISTENER (CAROL): *Repeats Speaker's words verbatim:* I'm angry that you said I'd expect you to call and cancel as though I expect you to do the dirty work.

Anger Step (second communication)

SPEAKER (BOB): I'm frustrated because *I'm* the one who called the last two times we canceled outings.

LISTENER (CAROL): *Repeats verbatim.*

Sadness Step (first communication)

SPEAKER (BOB): I'm disappointed that you didn't acknowledge how hard I've been working on this issue.

LISTENER (CAROL): *Repeats verbatim.*

Fear Step (first communication)

SPEAKER (BOB): I worry that you think I just want to pass the buck.

LISTENER (CAROL): *Repeats verbatim.*

Ownership Step (first communication)

SPEAKER (BOB): I feel guilty that I blew it this time with Ted and June.

LISTENER (CAROL): *Repeats verbatim.*

Ownership Step (second communication)

SPEAKER (BOB): I'm embarrassed that I'm not more assertive.

LISTENER (CAROL): *Repeats verbatim.*

Empathy Step (first communication)

SPEAKER (BOB): I understand that I do have a long history of allowing you to get us out of messes like this and that you can't completely trust me yet.
LISTENER (CAROL): *Repeats verbatim.*

Empathy Step (second communication)

SPEAKER (BOB): I'm grateful that you want to be alone with me.
LISTENER (CAROL): *Repeats verbatim.*

Empathy Step (third communication)

SPEAKER (BOB): I love you and really enjoy going out on dates with you!
LISTENER (CAROL): *Repeats verbatim.*

IMPORTANT PEACE PROCESS POINTERS

Not surprisingly, most Peace Process issues revolve around various forms of acting out (especially of anger), the breaking of agreements, and the lack of needed agreements. (The type of agreement called for in Bob and Carol's case—called a *negotiable agreement*—will be covered in the next section.) The first three steps provide an opportunity to fully express our so-called negative feelings to our mate while maintaining our emotional safe zone. Since those negative feelings are going to come out one way or another— that old law of emotional physics again!—we use the Process to guarantee that our anger, sadness, and fear can be released without casualties.

The couple above did a good job of keeping their focus on a single issue and refraining from second-guessing, ascribing motives to, and psychoanalyzing each other's behavior on the anger and sadness steps. Instead of saying, "I'm angry that you're codependent with our friends," the first Speaker stuck to describing the behavior and her reaction to it: "I resent that you didn't first check in with me at work before committing to our friends." The Speaker waited on the motivational issue until the fear step, then expressed, *as a fear,* a guess about what might have been behind her partner's behavior: "I'm afraid that you were unable to say no to them." This was a wise move on her part, since it kept her from making assumptions about her mate—assumptions that not only would have been disrespectful, but might also have resulted in another collapse of trust.

The ownership step is based on a crucial (and for some, radical) assumption: that *without exception, every conflict takes two.* The corollary of that assumption is that each of us bears a degree of responsibility that must, in the name of justice and resolution, be "owned." As we noted earlier, the ownership expressed in the Peace Process can reflect either responsibility specific to the current conflict (as when the first Speaker said, "I take responsibility for not clearly telling you that I miss private weekend time with you") or similar culpability from the past (as when the first Speaker said, "I feel guilty that I signed you up for dinner with my parents last month before I consulted with you").

The everyone-is-guilty assumption doesn't imply that we both start every argument jointly, or that one of us doesn't hurt the other more in a particular argument—although such comparisons are fodder for another fight and are thus not recommended. Rather, it maintains that in the day-to-day conflicts that occur between two intimates, each so-called victim has colluded in the offense in some way (however well concealed). This collusion could be the simple act of not calling a time-out before feeling seriously transgressed, or it could be not insisting that an agreement be negotiated about an item of great importance.

This revolutionary premise underlying the ownership step also borrows from the universal principle of our shared humanity—the fact that all of us possess a variety of facets, including "shadow" sides, and that we're all capable, on some level, of acting out. It's that understanding that opens our hearts as we work our way through the ownership step. And with open hearts, we refuse to take a high-and-mighty, pot-calling-the-kettle-black position, even though we might blame our beloved for a particular problem.

We choose instead—and what a powerful choice!—to build an "empathic bridge" back to our beloved, letting him or her know that we've "been there and done that" too, or that we recognize we weren't exactly a saint in this instance either. The noblest element of the ownership step in particular (and the Peace Process in general)—and one of its greatest benefits—is that it moves partners through the need to be right (or to have been "wronged") and over and over again helps us transcend together what's literally a microcosmic representation of the dynamics of war.

Brief Instructions for the Peace Process

1. The Speaker starts at the bottom of the Path to Peace.
2. Focusing on a single incident in real time, the Speaker communicates at least one I-statement at the anger step but not more than five.
3. After each statement, the Listener repeats verbatim what the Speaker just said.
4. The Speaker continues up the Path, communicating at least one I-statement at each of the remaining steps.
5. The Listener continues to repeat each statement after it's spoken.
6. The Speaker uses sound bites throughout, for easy repeating, and never skips a step.

THE WRITTEN PEACE PROCESS

We always have the right to decide that the Peace Process isn't working when it seems that one or both of us simply can't get the mike into the hands of our Adult self. At these times, it's best to take another time-out on the subject and agree to give it another go when we both feel ready. If this still doesn't work to our mutual satisfaction—that is, we don't yet feel that we can completely trust each other on the issue in conflict—we may need some hands-on coaching (see the "Peacemaking" section in Chapter 10), but it would be better to first try the written Peace Process technique described below. If this flops too, our issue is probably "too heavy" for the Process, meaning that a major button, blind spot, or un-resolved trauma is most likely being triggered. (And, it's a good bet that this is happening for both of us at the same time.) Since it's a shared issue, the negotiable agreements covered in the next section may be able to restore sanity to our debate.

The written Peace Process is just like the spoken one, except—you guessed it—it's in writing. In the peace and privacy afforded by this exercise, we often discover more emotions on each step than we would have verbally. For that reason, it's okay to make up to *ten* I-statements on the anger step in this form of the Process. (However, all the other instructions given for the spoken Peace Process apply to the written version as well.) To get the greatest benefit, we need to read the letter aloud to our partner as soon after writing as we can, going slowly enough to allow him or her to repeat each I-statement verbatim. (Remember: if this is one of those double-trouble topics where we profoundly disconnect, then it's time for Chapter 10, "Transformational Education.")

Sometimes, after successfully resolving a difficult conflict by participating in either a written or verbal Peace Process, we can glean even greater insight by excavating the issue more deeply using a Special Session. As we've seen, these gems are better than open discussion, since they provide the structure we need to ensure that we both have our say. Again, though, a Special Session wouldn't be appropriate in cases where our anger isn't fully dissipated. Remember that the Listener reserves the right to time the Speaker out and terminate the Session if he or she detects any reignition of hostilities. Then it's either back to the Peace Process or on to Chapter 10.

Negotiable Agreements: Little Pacts for *Pax*

Once the core agreements are in place, never to be questioned again, the sixth New Law of Love proposes that couples adopt a second kind of agreement: negotiables. If at this point the New Couple is starting to look like the *Rule* Couple, let us reassure you that, by definition, this couldn't be. For agreements aren't rules, though some partners may argue this point. Whereas rules are imposed by an authority figure onto a subordinate, like a boss onto an employee, agreements are tools of fairness and democracy, created together, by and for peers. And if we can't hope for a successful relationship without core agreements, then we'll never be able to extricate ourselves from the power struggle without *negotiable* agreements.

It's a golden rule of peacemaking that the heart must be lightened before the head can be effectively engaged. In a state of unresolved anger, we're incapable of thinking clearly. Therefore, the drafting of negotiables (like any planning or problem-solving) must never be attempted before all our feelings have been completely resolved on both sides via the Peace Process. Skipping this exercise can result in an ineffectual or unsatisfactory agreement, and it risks forcing us to revisit the initial argument, necessitating yet another time-out. Therefore, we *must* follow the peacemaking protocol to the letter, first managing anger via a time-out and then melting hard feelings using the Peace Process. Only then, if the situation calls for it—that is, if we think we're likely to stumble over the same issue in the future—do we go on to create a negotiable agreement, the last step in the New Couple's way to making the peace.

To fashion a negotiable agreement, we begin by identifying our needs. This is best done as early in the relationship as possible. Some needs we're obviously already aware of, like not wanting people to smoke in the house; others will become clear as we spend more time with each other, like the desire for time on the shared computer. Once the needs have been identified, the next step is to communicate these needs to one another as directly and specifically as possible. Then, after discussion, we can create simple agreements.

For our first example, let's look at standards of tidiness, which are an issue for most couples. When we're single, we can be as obsessive as we want, labeling and dating everything in the freezer if that makes us happy, or we can indulge in slovenliness, collecting as many inches of dust as we please. But cohabitation means shared space. To make our home a haven, we may have no healthy choice but to put out what we consider fair and get the details into an agreement.

Orville realized that most of the acting out in his relationship with his girlfriend, Jean, occurred in the kitchen, owing to their vastly different conceptions of the word *clean*. Following several Peace Processes, which included two trips each up the Path to Peace to discharge all the tension that had built up between them on the subject, they made a couple agreement to remake the deal that had worked for them as roommates in a big house years before. It read, "To the very best of our ability, we agree to leave the kitchen the way we found it."

When Paul and Toni's three-year-old was going through a spate of nightmares, Paul was always the one to console her, despite the fact that both parents got up early for work. Paul took responsibility for his feelings—and relieved a lot of resentment—when he proposed, and Toni accepted, the following agreement: "We agree that whatever the problem, we'll alternate wake-up duty for Shireen."

Sometimes things don't go as smoothly as it did for these couples. In that case, we need to enter into negotiation. Not as fancy as it may sound, negotiation is a straightforward process in which one of us proposes, and then the other counter-proposes (and so on, back and forth), until we reach a scenario we both feel comfortable with. Before committing to the sixth New Law of Love, Katie and Ellen frequently fought over the presence of the television in the bedroom. Though it seemed to soothe Ellen, TV was one of Katie's biggest buttons—especially having it on in the background, which her parents had done constantly when she was growing up. Here's the heart of the negotiation that took place after they'd completed a written Peace Process and read their letters to each other:

KATIE (PROPOSING): I propose that we move the TV into the den.

ELLEN (COUNTER-PROPOSING): Well, couldn't we leave it in the bedroom but never watch it on weekends?

KATIE (COUNTER-PROPOSING): But the time it mainly bothers me is on work nights. How about we turn it off then?

ELLEN (COUNTER-PROPOSING): I don't think I can sleep without hearing the ten o'clock news. But I'd be okay switching it off right after that.

KATIE (COUNTER-PROPOSING): But I can't fall asleep peacefully with it on at all. I'd be willing to move my CD player into the bedroom and play beautiful music at bedtime to help us both sleep.

ELLEN (COUNTER-PROPOSING): Actually, that sounds sweet. Okay, we'll do that for three nights a week, if you wear your earplugs the other two. You *know* they work for you.

KATIE (AGREEING, BUT WITH PROVISION): It's a deal, but let's reevaluate in two weeks.

Becoming proficient at creating negotiable agreements draws on the full battery of our developing New Couple skills. Not only will we need the time-out and the Peace Process (in spoken or written form), but, as Ellen and Katie demonstrate, we'll need to avail ourselves of deep listening, emotional awareness, emotional fluency, and emotional honesty. On top of all that, we'll need as much self-knowledge—especially about our buttons and blind spots—as we can summon.

If this seems daunting, rest assured: the ability to identify needs and work to meet them is a natural extension of everything we've learned and practiced up until this point. And as we practice still more, we'll find that the more we're in touch with, and expressive about, our emotional reality, the more obvious our own needs will be; in fact, some can just be skimmed off the surface. There will be times, though, when we'll find it difficult to know our own boundaries, understand what's fair for us, set limits, or articulate what we need. At those times, we'll benefit from the insights shared in Chapter 7, "Self-Love," and in Chapter 10, "Transformational Education."

Of infinite variety, negotiable agreements cover every conflictual corner of our relationship not already handled by our "cores." As Ned and Alice discovered, negotiables can help bring balance to areas of inequality, including the sexist ruts we often get into regarding household chores. This couple had both given up expecting him to do anything but scorch their shirts when he had an iron in his hand, so she agreed to do all the ironing in exchange for his vacuuming the house.

Together we design as many—or as few—negotiable agreements as we want, on an as-needed basis *throughout the life of our love.* Some negotiables concern our couple directly—like where vacations will be spent, how money will be generated, whether in-laws will live in, which parenting style we'll adopt, even how much (if any) contact with former partners we'll feel comfortable with. Others are highly individualistic, like those respecting the desire for further education or the need for silence, private time, a special diet, or a smoke-free environment. Both couple-oriented and individualistic negotiables can involve some serious wheeling and dealing, and they may need to be reassessed and possibly renegotiated down the line.

No issue is too small to negotiate. What couples actually fight about— the socks left in the hall, the cap left off the toothpaste, loud music, the dishes—often cloak more difficult-to-discuss matters; still, we can easily handle commonplace issues with negotiable agreements.

Ironically, the beauty is often in the breaking. For when we break a negotiable agreement, we have to make amends (a process that, incidentally, involves another explicit agreement!).

Amends-Making:
When "I'm Sorry" Doesn't Cut It

Amends-making can be almost magical in its ability to put things right again between us. An integral part of the negotiable-agreement-making process, it involves the giving of a small "favor" or gesture thought up by the "offended" partner—anything from a foot massage to a bouquet of flowers to the handling of an irksome errand. The only requirement is that whatever we decide upon has to satisfy the recipient and be considered fair by the one making amends. In order to meet this requirement, we sometimes have to engage in a mini-negotiation.

Not so Bob and Carol, whose Peace Process was presented above. After working their ways up the Path to Peace, they succeeded in restoring trust by making the following negotiable agreement: "We agree to always confer with the other before making *any* plans that affect the two of us." Since they both thought such an agreement was necessary, it required almost no negotiation. Ironically, it was broken within a week—by Carol—and she was obligated to offer amends. In this case, taking over Bob's dishwashing duties for the day nicely filled the bill. Though such a gesture may appear strictly symbolic (and therefore flimsy), its power to melt away residual animosity shouldn't be underestimated. While a straight apology may be music to our ears, sometimes it feels dismissive, not to mention insincere. Amends, with their tangible offering of apology, run circles around "I'm sorry."

Whether or not amends (and negotiation to determine them) are involved, negotiable agreements are creative. Though they're much less strict than core agreements, they pack a punch. And because "cores" are really just announcements about what is and isn't acceptable in our relationship, they're generally easier to craft than "negotiables." As we've noted, the challenge of negotiable agreements lies in getting clear about exactly what we want as individuals. The challenge is especially great if we've been conditioned to subordinate—and hence have lost touch with—our own needs. If drafting such agreements tries the limits of our self-love, we can view the process of persevering to consensus as a brief assertiveness-training course. Fortunately, because negotiable agreements are subject to renegotiation, we don't have to create something on the first go-round that we need to live with forever. Furthermore, a breach of a negotiable agreement, unlike that of a core agreement, isn't a walking matter. If a certain negotiable agreement is broken repeatedly, however, and we're unable to renegotiate it to both partners' satisfaction, we may need to check out Chapter 10.

Brief Instructions for the Peacemaking Procedure

When anger is acted out in your couple, the partner who recognizes the anger first calls a time-out. Then both of you decide which of the following options is appropriate:
- Stop discussing the conflictual topic.
- Leave each other's company.

• Refrain from talking at all.

When you're both in Adult mode, as determined by the Triangle Test, you then take a time-*in* to jointly decide whether to resolve conflict via a Peace Process, a written Peace Process, or, if there's no remaining anger, a negotiable agreement. Finally, you move on to the conflict-resolution method chosen, doing one of the following (or all three in sequence):

• Work your way through the Peace Process. (If either of you is unable to remain in Adult mode and follow the format, try again later. If the tool fails again, proceed to the written Peace Process.)

• Draft and share a written Peace Process.

• Create a negotiable agreement.

An Invitation to Reflect on the Law of Peacemaking

• What negotiable agreements would you like in your relationship? How would these make you feel? How would they affect your self-love? Your emotional intimacy?

PEACEMAKING PAST AND THE TRADITIONAL COUPLE

The traditional couple must have heaved a giant sigh of relief when television recognized the entertainment value of reality and beamed Archie and Edith Bunker into their living room. For years, they'd been miserably trying to match the plastic personas of Ward and June Cleaver. The fact is traditional couples didn't have the benefit of what we might call peacemaking "technology." Instead, they were forced to struggle with buttons, blind spots, marital conflict, and the highly misunderstood emotion of anger catch-as-catch-can. More often than not, the cost to their love and trust was dear.

Not that there wasn't a lot of advice on these subjects. Indeed, conventional wisdom strongly urged lovemates to turn the other cheek, forgive and forget, let the issue go, or kiss (or have sex) and make up. Sweet, swift, and certainly well-intentioned as such counsel may have been, it just plain didn't work; in fact, by modern psychological standards, it was patently avoidant. For clearly, anger and conflict are complex. They don't go away with a peck on the cheek, be it figurative or otherwise.

Still, the unfortunate influence of such archaic solutions prevailed—and proved harmful to both couples and individual partners alike, as it still does today. Lacking education about buttons, blind spots, and unresolved emotional trauma, traditional spouses ended up condemning themselves for their own negative, albeit healthy, feelings, or for being what they diagnosed as unkind, uncaring, or unforgiving. What recourse, then, did our parents, grandparents, and great-grandparents have other than to turn all this frustration inward and double-lock it away, putting on a false front and waiting for the emotional explosion?

Most curious of all, perhaps, was the adage warning partners never to go to bed angry. Anger always needs to be fully acknowledged and healed in order to be "overcome," which often takes time. Being true to such advice would have required a couple to pull many an all-nighter. Additionally, if anger has been acted out, getting back to deep trust requires further work—namely, a real protocol to resolve both partners' feelings and the issue at hand, plus a plan to give anger proper and safe egress next time it threatens to erupt. (The sixth Law of Love suggests couples handle nocturnal anger episodes with a time-out; they are comforted with the knowledge that a time-in will follow as soon as possible the next day.)

Conventional marriage vows were perhaps intended to function as core agreements, and they did point partners in the right direction. But because they didn't tell people how to get or stay there, they were inordinately difficult to keep. Indeed, the words "love, honor, and obey" and "have and hold, in sickness and health, until death do us part" were not only tall orders, they were also terribly vague.

In the past, goodwill, patience, and willpower stood in for anger management to vastly varying degrees of success. And "talking problems over when everyone's calm" epitomized conventional conflict resolution. Given that couples knew no way to systematically clear all feelings, those who were able to be successful this way were remarkable. A few daring traditionals—generally those in extreme situations—went outside their couple to seek counsel from a clergy member or wise in-law—again, with a range of results.

Usually, however, with the trance of tradition in full force, and spousal inequality and sexism yet to be pronounced politically incorrect, even the concept of win-win was unknown. Historically, arguments and grim tolerance supplanted healthy negotiation, and announcements stood in for negotiable agreements. All in all, this left mates no choice but to take unfairness in stride. That's what Herbert and Gin did, for example. When Herbert accepted a job transfer five states away without bothering to ask her feelings about it, Gin didn't so much as flinch.

Despite many noble efforts, without the relationship-sustaining package that the Ten New Laws of Love provides, the traditional couple's ability to make real and lasting peace was often seriously hampered. An unprioritized marriage, neglected higher-order needs, few (if any) emotional or listening skills, and entrenched inequalities all conspired to lock many of them in a perpetual power struggle. This is why, for all their attempts to create harmony, our predecessors deserve our utmost regard and compassion.

All the Makings of a Traditional Tragedy

"How do you two normally negotiate big life decisions?" After the Sikh priest popped the key question, Singh and Polly just looked at each other blankly. The thirty-four-year-old importer and his thirty-five-year-old travel-agent wife had been married for nine rocky years. It had taken the threat of splitting up for them to schedule this first encounter with a counselor.

Despite an earlier decision not to have babies, they found themselves unexpectedly pregnant—and equally unexpectedly wishing to keep the child. The central conflict was over religious upbringing. They'd survived a couple of knock-down drag-out fights already—fights that had ended just short of violence. During the last one, Singh had screamed that he wanted a divorce, and Polly had thrown one of his family heirlooms out their second-story bedroom window. They had no negotiation or anger-management skills, and evidently no core agreements. Now they were expecting a child—and about to walk.

Though he considered himself a "modern mystic," Singh was insistent that his child be raised Sikh. The situation was complicated by pressure from his wealthy grandfather, who'd capitalized his business and was a powerful influence in Singh's life. For her part, Polly was a champion of mixed marriages and multiculturalism. Her love for her husband had inspired her to master a couple of curry dishes and learn to speak passable Punjabi, the language of the Sikhs. Now, however, the growing fetus in the young woman's belly was catalyzing what seemed to be old and confusing loyalties to her Protestant religion and causing Polly to draw a line: "It's not just my Christianity," she said. "I'd be a hypocrite not to admit that my faith lapsed long ago. I just can't believe how *intense* Pappa's being—*and* Singh!"

"Stop trying to make me feel guilty," her husband retorted. "I want to give my child some cultural identity in this American melting pot. Besides, I'm afraid that if we don't do what Pappa wants—poof!—he'll ask for his investment back, *my inheritance.*" Polly was chagrined: "I never felt comfortable with Pappa's degree of involvement," she said, looking at the clergyman as if for affirmation. "And now, with the baby coming, our very security depends on him."

Throughout their relationship, a string of major "negotiations" had been handled largely by default: her weekends away leading art tours, his loan of their house to a particularly wild old college buddy while they were on vacation one year. And then there was the parrot he'd bought her as a surprise housewarming gift. Though she'd been wanting a cat—and had told him so many times—Polly couldn't bring herself to disappoint him because he seemed so pleased. "I thought it wouldn't bother me so much," she told him later. "Now I can never have a cat—it'd be cruel to both of them."

Certainly, the most glaring hole in this couple's negotiations was the manner in which Singh's grandfather had initially gotten implicated in his enterprise. The young husband had come home from work one evening smiling ear to ear. "Our financial problems are over!" he announced to Polly. "And it's thanks to the generosity of Old Pappa." End of discussion.

In addition, because they had no negotiation skills, they'd both felt a lot of anger over various issues over the years. Lacking anger-management skills as well, they'd acted out that anger. Many of the resulting bruises still smarted. Still, Polly and Singh learned in this school of hard knocks that for things to work out, *they* needed to work them out; so they got pretty good at making peace. And now, genuinely wanting their relationship to succeed, they felt additionally inspired for the sake of their child. They committed to use the New Couple technology of peace.

Peace at the Eleventh Hour

First came the core agreement regarding the child's religious upbringing. This they wisely approached by holding daily, hour-long Special Sessions focusing on this issue. Early on, Polly realized that it wasn't so much an attachment to Christianity that caused her to contest a Sikh upbringing as a fear that her child would in some way be marginalized in the sometimes overly homogenized American culture. On the other hand, she didn't want to risk losing her in-laws' support.

For his part, Singh was able to admit that the overall effect of his grandfather's gesture wasn't strictly positive: "It messes with my autonomy," he said, "and it makes me wonder if I could be successful without Pappa's support." These insights facilitated the construction of a highly creative core agreement—namely, that the child would attend temple for Sikh training *and* be taught the stories of the Old and New Testaments at home by Polly. Once the grandfather passed on, they would see how they both felt about the issue.

Next, the couple learned about acted-out versus responsibly expressed emotions—especially anger. Having been so often on the receiving end, neither felt inclined to argue with the standard definitions of verbal abuse. This didn't preclude them, however, from experiencing a rush or two of embarrassment as each read down the list. They committed to using the time-out tool and participating in as many Peace Processes as necessary to keep the air cleared. "It's not just for us, after all," Singh remarked. "Imagine how cool it will be for our kid not to have to watch a bunch of crazy spats. He—sorry, or *she*—will probably be the first to be spared in generations, maybe ever!"

Polly, in particular, appreciated the negotiable agreements. Their first? To keep the parrot at Singh's office so that she could have a kitten at home. The second concerned a specific kind of acted-out anger—namely, the threat of divorce. The couple was relieved to agree never to throw that one around again. "It was terrorizing," Polly explained. "Now we either mean it—or we don't say it at all." But her husband had the last word: "Well, let's just say it was close. I seriously don't know how we ever got by for those nine years without all of this stuff—or how any other couple could."

An Invitation to Reflect on the Law of Peacemaking as It Pertains to Your Parents

- What core agreements might your parents have benefited from in their relationship? How would these have affected their self-love? Their emotional intimacy? How would the resulting changes in their relationship have made you feel?
- What were your parents' styles of acting out anger (passive-aggressive, aggressive-aggressive, or both)? How did their chosen style affect the health of their self-love? Their emotional intimacy? How did witnessing their acting out make you feel? From which parent did you learn your style of acting out, or was it from both?
- What types of verbal abuse, if any, occurred in your parents' relationship? How did this affect their self-love? Their emotional intimacy? How did it make you feel to witness it?
- How would your childhood have been different had your parents subscribed to the Law of Peacemaking? How would your own couple be different (or, if you're single, how would past relationships have been different)?

PEACEMAKING AND THE NEW COUPLE

New Couples put the peacemaking trio—core agreements, anger management, and conflict resolution (which includes negotiable agreements)— to work in their union before they have to start counting casualties. Callie, the twenty-seven-year-old co-owner of a beauty salon, and Seamus, a thirty-five-year-old psychiatric social worker, were a mere six blissful months into the intoxication stage of their relationship when they hit a roadblock and paid us a visit.

It was Callie who insisted. "Seamus's place is gorgeous," she said, opening the session. "He's got a million-dollar view of the river, but he refuses to give an inch. He hasn't spent the night at my house in ages." She paused to get her thoughts straight. "I know I have roommates, but they all think he's great. I don't get it."

"The problem is privacy," Seamus responded. "I know that your roommates are sweet and fun. But they're young, and they haven't yet developed the need for peace and quiet. If it isn't the music, it's the coming and going at all hours. The final straw was that time they barged into the bedroom with your birthday cake right after we'd made love." He looked at us with pleading eyes.

Though these city dwellers had both invested a good deal of time and money in transformational education as individuals, neither had ever been exposed to relationship training. Fortunately, they took to peacemaking technology like ducks to water. As Seamus said, "This seems so basic, yet I never learned any of it in graduate school." Callie added, "I'm really grateful to get this information early in our relationship. If my own parents had used time-outs, my whole childhood would have seemed like heaven on earth." Right there in our office, on their first visit, this fledgling New Couple committed without hesitation to using the time-out and the Peace Process in verbal and written form as necessary. They left armed with instructions not only for these, but also for the Session; they had a handout on the Ten New Laws of Love as well.

Callie couldn't wait to help Seamus manage his anger. On the way home in the car, she timed him out when he started to tease her about her driving. Though somewhat taken aback, he honored her request, making their first peacemaking exercise in the field a success. Once back at their respective homes, each further clarified their feelings via a written Peace Process, reading their letters to each other the next day in person. The revelations they shared in the chat that followed were truly amazing.

Callie went first: "I always thought that you were withholding from me by not coming over. The truth is I feel controlled by you. That's my big button. In my military family, I couldn't tie my shoes without my mother correcting me."

Seamus's discoveries were equally profound. "Your apartment is chaotic; that's the real problem. When I'm there, on some unconscious level it feels like my crazy household with eleven siblings all over again. I never had a moment of peace growing up. And being the firstborn, I felt eternally responsible. That's why I can't relax at your place."

As each listened deeply to the other's childhood stories, their hearts opened and a triumph seemed within easy reach. Callie cheerfully accepted a negotiable agreement stipulating that Seamus's visits would be limited to those times when her roommates were away—often two weekends a month.

But Seamus's mind was racing ahead: he was hot on the Ten New Laws of Love and excitedly suggested to Callie that they adopt them as their first core agreement. Her reaction disappointed him: "I really like the ideas about love and relationship in theory," she said hesitantly, "but I don't know. There's just something about committing to all the laws wholesale. It seems kind of rigid to me; I think I'd feel really boxed in." Still, for Seamus, there was no doubt: "Look, I've already been through the ringer with my ex. I'll never get that involved again without a game plan," he said, knowing that these words might invite a stalemate.

The couple decided to give it a month; then they'd talk again about whether to adopt the laws as a core agreement. Because they'd strengthened their relationship through their work together, this period of time together was particularly alive. They decided to get away together for a weekend at a resort upstate. On the drive back Sunday afternoon, Seamus suggested an impromptu stop at the house of his favorite uncle, a colorful man whom Callie had only heard about.

From the moment they stepped through the front door, the man fussed over Callie. Her discomfort increased as they toured the house, especially when Seamus trailed behind. When the two of them ended up alone in the guest room, the uncle asked Callie if she'd like to try the waterbed. Before she knew it, he'd pushed her down on it roughly and was standing over her laughing. Seamus had missed the entire incident.

Callie struggled off the bed and rushed up to Seamus in the adjacent room. "We're out of here," she said. "Don't ask why." She marched straight out to the car, got in, and locked the doors, waiting for him in shock and fury. When finally Seamus got behind the wheel, she relayed to him what had happened. He dismissed it lightly: "Oh, he has a reputation for being a tease," he said. "He hassled my last girlfriend too, but she didn't seem to mind."

Callie was beside herself: "How could you have brought me to such a place?" she screamed. "I don't care if he's family, he's a lecher!" Seamus countered weakly that her safety wasn't his responsibility. When she raised her voice in response, he abruptly timed her out. Callie was in no mood to keep a couple agreement, so their fight escalated until he dropped her, in tears, at her apartment. The one thing they were able to agree on was that they needed some time and space away from each other.

Two days later, Seamus and Callie met at our office. As Seamus talked about the incident, he recognized that he had a major blind spot and confessed it contritely: "When it comes to my own family, I guess I just go numb, especially around the chaos. And then all this loyalty stuff kicks in. It's reflexive," he confessed. "That's what I grew up with: no boundaries, a bunch of acting out, and everybody just nervously laughing to cover it up."

We took the opportunity to point out that the couple's conflict was actually an issue of individuating from his family, which falls under the Law of Priority, the second New Law of Love. Seamus caught on easily: "Oh, I see. I was more concerned about not disappointing my uncle by not dropping in than about keeping Callie emotionally—let's say it, *sexually*—safe."

The exchange fairly floored Callie. "So are you still interested in the Ten New Laws of Love?" she asked with a tinge of irony. "From what I understand, that would mean you'd have to set limits with your uncle." We stepped in to clarify: "Not exactly, Callie. Seamus wouldn't necessarily have to confront his uncle," we explained. "But he *would* have to prioritize your safety over his family loyalty."

It was Seamus's serve, and he knew it. This was where the rubber would hit the road if he were to accept the core agreement that he himself had suggested. "I know, I know," he said gravely. "This would force me to face and heal something I've been avoiding my entire life—my codependence with my family. And if I want to have a healthy relationship with you or anyone else, I have to go there." He smiled wanly at Callie. "And what about you?" he asked.

The seriousness of what Seamus was broaching didn't escape her. She was clearly impressed: "You're brave," she said. "And that you'd go to the wall for me like that—well, it's pretty thrilling." With that comment, Callie flashed Seamus what had to be her sexiest smile and then contin-

ued: "I guess I need some depth work myself. On my fear of being dominated," she added, as though a light had just gone on. "Even though they
seem so natural, so logical, a core agreement to commit to all Ten New
Laws of Love just felt like I was signing up for a rerun of the boot camp
where I grew up."

Just a few meetings later, their first—and comprehensive—core
agreement under their belts (along with some serious practice at peacemaking), this New Couple walked out of our office and into their relationship excited and well equipped. As Seamus said at the door, "I guess
we just laid the foundation of our emotional safe zone—and a whole lot
more. It doesn't matter now if we go wrong, because we know exactly
how to make it right again."

It's long been seen as perfectly normal for us to undertake permanent
partnerships without any formal, mutually agreed upon conditions or
established way to keep or restore the peace. As a result, over the span of
a single relationship, a couple is capable of acting out anger many more
times than they kiss and of collecting many more unresolved conflicts
than moments of joy. Unless acknowledged and healed, every single conflict and incident of acted-out anger will put a crack—some invisible,
some dramatic—in the trust of our couple and cause a dissipation of our
precious chemistry. While we can handle a certain percentage of these
anger episodes with a simple time-out, the other peacemaking skills are
also primary to the New Couple.

The truth is problems actually benefit couples. Over time, if we handle
them with even a modicum of skill, they take the fulfillment of our
higher-order needs for emotional intimacy and self-love to new heights.
Because every time we call a time-out on our mate—or honor this simple
anger-management technique when it's used on us—we're making sure
that neither one of us gets hurt. Every time we resolve an issue using the
Peace Process, we don't merely avoid a grudge (and potentially a lot
worse); we simultaneously compound our trust in ourselves and each
other. That's because this enlightened tool facilitates a thorough and safe
ventilation of the full range of our feelings, thereby bringing about healing for both of us individually and for the relationship itself.

Whether core or negotiable, every agreement we create stabilizes our
relationship. Each time we respect a negotiable agreement, we introduce

more sanity into our power struggle and assure a more rapid advance into co-creativity. Negotiables are powerful—even in the breaking. For there's nothing like the feeling when our partner acknowledges that he or she has blown it and offers to make amends. The experience of trust being mended through that process is almost palpable. (And incidentally, amends-making, and receiving, can both be a lot of fun!)

Since both cores and negotiables are designed by the couple alone (with the help of a few recommendations from this book), they represent an amalgam of our basic needs. This summary of needs can be priceless if our mission in life isn't already apparent. For the more in touch we are with what's basic to us as individuals, the more our big direction can come clear. In fact, our core and negotiable agreements form a tapestry, a beautiful creation unique to our couple alone.

The sixth New Law of Love invites us to consider adopting the technology of peace. Unlike the technology of war, it's free.

The Key to Peacemaking

Keeping the peace and maintaining an emotional safe zone in your couple is the key to the sixth New Law of Love.

This means . . .

- Clarifying your core conditions individually and creating core agreements
- Learning to manage your anger using the time-out tool
- Learning to resolve conflict using the Peace Process tool
- Learning the skill of creating negotiable agreements and making amends when those agreements are broken

7. SELF-LOVE
the seventh new law of love

Let each person in relationship worry about self—*what* self *is being, doing, and having; what* self *is wanting, asking, giving; what* self *is seeking, creating, experiencing, and all relationships would magnificently serve their purpose—and their participants!*

Let each person in relationship worry not about the other, but only, only, only about self.

This seems a strange teaching, for you have been told that in the highest form of relationship, one worries only *about the other. Yet I tell you this: your focus upon the other—your* obsession *with the other—is what causes relationships to fail.*

NEALE DONALD WALSCH, *Conversations with God, book I*

Self-love is a confusing topic for couples. The old thinking has long been that to enjoy a healthy relationship, we need to put aside the preoccupation with—and therefore love of—ourselves, and shift this focus onto another. The new thinking is that to love another, we need to be psychologically whole and love ourselves first. Especially in the former perspective, the love of self and the love of other were seen as somewhat mutually exclusive.

Though it obviously calls for a balance, the newer thinking is definitely closer to the mark. Self-love is now firmly established among the psychological community as a higher-order need that all adults must honor, whether we find ourselves in a relationship or not. And many "other-loving" behaviors, long conventionally held as the very models of how to treat a partner, are now being recognized as subtly self-sacrificial and codependent. But—and here's the rub—the love of, and by, another person is also essential for healthy adulthood.

Certainly, two *already* fully self-loving individuals would make an ideal couple. It's a long road to buddhahood, however. More often than not, our higher-order need for emotional intimacy compels us to form relationships long before we're "completed." Hence, either limping or striding, we all enter into romantic unions suffering in some way from a deficit of self-love.

Here's another twist to the self-love-in-relationship story: as we pointed out in Chapter 1, two people with New Couple chemistry often reveal almost identical emotional landscapes over time. It's a cosmic joke: only emotional equals attract. This means that regardless of how we might compare ourselves to our beloved in private, and how others might see us both on the surface, our levels of self-love probably match pretty closely.

The seventh New Law of Love welcomes all these coincidences and conundrums. For coupledom is a grand design, a secret system to help unfinished adults heal from the slings and arrows of our past. While most of us think we're forming unions strictly to have the experience of being loved and of loving another, in reality we're jumping on the fast track to love of self. For true love is a two-sided enterprise in which we build a healthy relationship with ourselves *and* with our beloved *at the same time*. In fact, these two projects are not only interdependent, they're synergistic.

This chapter teaches us how we can explicitly use our partnership not only to accelerate the raising of our self-love, but also to spare both partners significant turmoil. While the idea that it's never too late to have a happy childhood involves a bit of magical thinking, it really *is* never to late to elevate self-love. And one of the best forums in which to do that is the safety of a couple committed to this seventh New Law of Love. As we grow ourselves up and into self-love, it's more than possible that we'll find ourselves flying steadily alongside our mate.

To some of us, the term *self-love* might seem too strong, too much like self-centeredness, egocentricity. By contrast, *self-esteem* seems more socially acceptable, only halfway toward the outrageous idea of outright love of self. And while it's very fortunate that, both as term and as concept, self-esteem has finally caught on—especially with regard to young people—the idea of raising self-esteem in the context of intimate relationship doesn't quite nail the issue. The seventh New Law of Love prefers *self-love* to *self-esteem* (again, both as term and as concept) because it's much more direct, and we all have a long way to go to learn that there's nothing shameful about truly loving ourselves. In fact, all selfishness, greed, self-centeredness, egocentricity, egomania, and self-obsession—subsets of what psychologists call *narcissism*—are manifestations of the extreme opposite—that is, harrowingly low self-love.

SELF-LOVE: WHAT IT IS, WHAT IT'S NOT

Self-love is our deep personal conviction that, when the music stops, we're absolutely okay. Self-love enables us to take for granted that we're essentially lovable and worthwhile—in and of ourselves *and* regardless of whatever roles, titles, or successes we may (or may not) enjoy. High self-love leads us to trust our feelings and intuition *automatically*. Because it reinforces our sense of personal rights, it helps us say no, set limits, stick up for ourselves, and keep ourselves safe both physically and emotionally *as a natural response* to any kind of threat. In fact, the ability to use the time-out, an anger-management tool discussed in the previous chapter, demonstrates this component of high self-regard. Self-love lends us much more than the power to care for ourselves as individuals in every way we can conceive; it empowers us to *thrive*. It leads us to our mission in life and enables us to experience true emotional intimacy with another. Perhaps most important, this incompletely understood but essential brand of love endows us with dignity, giving us the ability, whatever the circumstances, to hold our heads high.

It's important to note that the self-love of this seventh New Law of Love is distinct from the narcissistic "love" that popular culture would have us buy into. The latter is conditional, dependent on external factors such as money, looks, credentials, and talent. While in our hearts we all know that conditional love is absurd, none of us seems impervious to the brainwashing. The crazy quest for this ersatz Grail is ever our goal—and that itself is a sign of tarnished self-love. If we can't hit homers like Mark McGwire, look and act like Gwyneth Paltrow, think like Stephen Hawking, or write a check like Bill Gates, on some level we have trouble believing that we're worth the oxygen we consume.

So as we busy ourselves chasing our tails, the props of conditional self-love always remain ephemeral. Even those born with (or, through hard work, able to acquire) such externals as wealth still live in terror of losing them—unless they love themselves solidly at the center. Despite our sincerest efforts to control conditional self-love, it continues to author our highest highs and most rock-bottom lows. It ebbs and flows with every failure and success, dims and brightens with each new perceived area of incompetence and mastery, rises and falls with our youth and age—and generally tosses us about through all the vicissitudes of life. Such is the agony and ecstasy of a false love of self.

Obviously, conditional self-love isn't at all like the real McCoy, which by definition is constant and therefore affords peace. By comparison, *un*conditional self-love would appear to be true bliss. And in fact it *is* bliss, when we can manage to achieve it; but it typically comes long and hard. We arrive in adulthood with our tanks very low. We're burdened by a host of buttons and blind spots, by toxic guilt and shame and their accompanying fear of abandonment. Unable to love and take care of ourselves completely, and to honor our own feelings, personal rights, and intuition absolutely, we attempt to compensate. We try to bolster our conditional self-love with a variety of impressive externals. Inevitably, we also end up, to varying degrees, seeking from others—be they mates, children, parents, other relatives, bosses, colleagues, or friends—the love and validation we can't give to ourselves.

An Invitation to Reflect on the Law of Self-Love

As you approach the exercises in this chapter, remember that the presence or absence of New Couple chemistry profoundly affects a couple's experience with each law.

- What are your conditions for loving yourself? How do these conditions make you feel? How do they affect your emotional intimacy?
- What are your strongest areas of self-love? (For example, do you automatically trust your feelings? What about your intuition? Do you stick up for yourself? Keep yourself physically and emotionally safe from those who might act out

in your presence? Do you have the ability to set limits and say
no? Are you devoted to developing your talents and passions?
Do you cherish your own dignity?) How does each strong and
weak area of self-love make you feel? How do these areas affect
your emotional intimacy?

WHY LOW SELF-LOVE?

It's no mystery that humanity's almost universally low self-love comes
primarily from the circumstances of nurture—in other words, from the
raising that parents do. We're born with high self-love, every one of us.
It's only our interaction with others (especially our earliest caregivers)
that impairs its proper development. Far from being an indictment of our
parents, though, this is a simple fact of the evolutionary process: as we
advance as a species, each generation becomes more educated and able to
refine what went before. This is as germane to parenting as it is to information science. Though our parents inherited many ideas on the subject
of childrearing, they had nowhere near the information, tools, emotional
support, or opportunities for healing that they needed in order to be what
child psychologists call "good-enough" parents. In fact, in their day, the
words *self-esteem* and *self-love* were rarely used.

Unfortunately, to everyone's loss, no one taught our early caregivers—or indeed, any of theirs before them—the ABC's of fostering self-
love in children. Our parents and other crucial early caregivers often had
little idea how to validate our feelings or deeply listen to our ideas and
concerns. Nor were they informed about the nature of emotional trauma,
not to mention instructed on how to help young ones recover when something traumatic did happen. In fact, we now know that many of the old-
fashioned techniques our own parents used to rear and discipline us were
themselves traumatic—and thus the source of much of the low self-love
that partners suffer today.

For instance, when a child is instructed repeatedly to be a "big boy"
and not cry, he becomes traumatically shamed about the expression of
sadness and grief; when children are spanked, especially by the very people
who represent safety and protection, the violence of the nonloving touch
is traumatic. If such acts are accompanied by words such as "This hurts

me more than it hurts you," they add a layer of toxic guilt, making the child feel responsible not only for his own beating, but also for hurting the parent.

Still, as we've said, everyone's guilty but no one's to blame: our parents were themselves victims of unenlightened childrearing practices and plagued by their own unresolved trauma and deficit of self-love. Despite their most steadfast and heartfelt efforts—their genuine desire to do well by us—they visited their trauma and low self-love upon us as well. All in all, evolutionary status and cultural conditioning had the last word: there was simply no way our parents could have been raised to enjoy unconditional self-love or could have raised us to have it.

Just as it's only in relationship with others that our self-love is stunted, so it's only in relationship with others that it can be restored. Naturally, as we grow up, friends, teachers, parents of friends, colleagues—even family members, including parents!—all substantially aid us in mending certain areas of low self-love. There will, however, always remain impaired areas that fail to develop properly. For while almost nothing can keep us from maturing physically, unmet needs arrest our development emotionally. Though as adults we look all grown up, our exterior rarely tells the truth about our interior. Those aspects of our emotional self that correspond to each unmet psychological need have been unable to mature.

IN DEFENSE OF INNER CHILDREN AND RUSSIAN DOLLS

This is where the oft-mocked wounded "inner child" enters. This term has been used and abused to death. Furthermore, it turns some people off with its implications of weakness and shame; others object to it because of its membership in the psychobabble family; still others claim that it's been used indiscriminately to excuse a lack of responsibility (and perhaps it has, though merely acknowledging emotional immaturity—or that young part—isn't the same as using either one to justify unacceptable behavior). Still, since the term captures the concept of emotional immaturity, nothing describes the phenomenon of our invisible and "unfinished" interior more accurately than "inner child." (If you prefer, however, "irrational self" works just as well.)

The point is this: by whatever name we know it, this inscrutable dimension of our humanity must not be theoretically dismissed; for, as all of us who have been in love know, it *does* exist—*and it has the power to sabotage even the most auspicious matches.* Furthermore, it's much fairer to ascribe difficult behaviors and attitudes to a *part* of us than to condemn ourselves—or our partners—as immature *in our entirety,* which is what many people who lack an inner-child understanding tend to do. Without a grasp—and appreciation—of the inner child, we struggle to develop compassion for ourselves and our mates and to raise our self-love.

As the years (and the hurts) pile up, so do the various aspects of our inner child, each frozen at a different age. Though that accumulation happens unconsciously, we end up like those wooden Russian dolls— each adult hiding inside of us many smaller versions of ourselves, incomplete and low in self-love. (Some of these inner-child versions are healthy, bearing qualities such as joyfulness, curiosity, spontaneity, playfulness, and openness. They aren't discussed here, however, because they pose no self-love problems for partners.)

Often in a state of semi-slumber, these inner-child selves are awaiting the arrival of nothing less than a new parent. This person need not be a literal, full-fledged mother or father figure, of course. To the child within us all, a real-life lover will do just as well to complete whatever our parents left undone when they raised us. The child hope is that this someone will at least be able to validate emotions, listen deeply, and show interest in our gifts—the basics of good-enough parenting. If there was even greater lack or trauma, the younger parts of us might even be seeking a mate who can provide for us at the level of lower-order needs—that is, food, shelter, and a basic sense of belonging or physical safety.

Some of our inner-child issues are all too familiar to us, while others remain alien. Our metaphorical child selves are capable of lying low for years on end—until, that is, they're triggered by a relationship. Then, sometimes to our great embarrassment, they make a surprise appearance. The determination of these inner selves must not be underestimated: one way or another, they busily push their little agendas. Still, it's never our partners' responsibility to finish this parenting job—even if, out of the kindness of their hearts, they genuinely want to. Anyway, they've already done a lot to help us raise our self-love merely by facilitating the emergence of our inner-child selves into the light of day. It's our responsibility—and ours alone—to pick up for ourselves where our parents left off.

TRANSFERENCE: EMOTIONAL HANGOVER FROM THE PAST, BLIND SPOT IN THE PRESENT

Transference, the stuffy-sounding but skittish phenomenon whereby we "transfer" the role of primary caregiver or sibling onto another, is inevitable in couples. Identifying and labeling this phenomenon was one of Sigmund Freud's greatest contributions to psychology, although he limited his work with transference to the relationship between therapist and client. But the truth is transference happens in all relationships all the time. And it's most profound in those relationships possessing a dimension of romance. In the intimacy of the sexual-emotional connection, our child self is reminded of the first bond of its lifetime—the one it had with its parents or parent surrogates. This memory link results in a radical case of mistaken identity.

And we further encourage that mistaken identity by unconsciously picking mates who remind us of the people who raised us or were around us when we were little. Though for many lovers this is hard to believe, it's a resounding truth of couple psychology—and a trick of chemistry: we're turned on by people who have the same qualities our parents did, both positive and negative. Granted, these qualities are typically very attractively disguised; in addition, they're generally supplemented by qualities that are improvements over those of our early caregivers—positive qualities our parents didn't appear to have.

It's not surprising, then, that in those moments when our partners exhibit negative traits that echo our past, we experience a kind of déjà vu. We might wonder when we've felt this unpleasant sensation before; or we might know exactly. At any rate, the catalyst provided by today's experience with our beloved affords us a platinum opportunity to sew up that old business and heal once and for all. In fact, without those irksome features of our mate to dramatically bring to the surface what's unfinished, we could go a lifetime suffering low-grade, chronic deficit self-love. That's why, as outrageous as it sounds, a part of us (wise, but beyond awareness) actually chooses lovers *because of* the specific kinds of headaches they'll bring—and the cure they'll force us to take.

Naturally, for the system to work optimally, our partner can't function solely as a catalyst. He or she also needs to act as our favorite catch-basin, in other words, to be committed to being there to also help us catch and heal the old problem and support us through the process of growing our self-love. It takes two people equally committed to this enterprise to get the process of transforming transferences off the ground. Exactly how a couple can do this is detailed below.

Transference and the Intoxication Stage

As unsexy as it may sound, all partners enter the first stage of relation-ship part adult, part well-disguised kid unconsciously seeking a good-enough mother and father. Naturally, at this early and ecstatic point, we're spared most signs of our lover's low self-love; for we are, after all (at least figuratively), under the influence. Chemistry has been discovered and is being celebrated, and though transference is definitely in play, it's mainly positive. That's because the unfolding mystery of a fresh relationship brings out the best in both partners; in fact, it leads each new paramour to perform many of the functions children need from their parents. For example, we typically hang on each other's every word, fuss over each other's every feeling, and exhibit our most loving and nur-turing adult behaviors.

At the two-month point in their relationship, Katharine and Marlon were beautifully serving each other's inner-child needs, though neither knew it. In fact, it was precisely because her father had had no time for her schoolwork that Katharine so delighted in her boyfriend's seem-ingly insatiable interest in her career. For his part, Marlon treasured Katharine's professional stability. His own single mother had never been able to hold down a job. As this couple shows, it's natural that everything be copacetic during the first stage of relationship. And the child part of us can't help but get lulled into believing the fantasy, the promise that was never made—namely, that this near-perfect parenting will continue forever.

Transference and the Power Struggle

To the chagrin of lovers since time began, transference is destined to go from positive to negative. Somewhere between two weeks and two years after our relationship starts—whatever the duration of our particular intoxication stage—the personas drop, we begin to get used to each other, and that wonderful deep listener and emotional confidant of not too long ago becomes a little less available. Indeed, our new flame might prove *really* "different"—that is, aloof or clingy, impatient or unreliable, critical, bossy, compulsive, or unbearable in some other unforeseen way. We might even step on some emotional landmines. There's no denying it: this most precious person now has "behaviors," buttons, and blind spots—all, incidentally, precisely correlated to areas of deficit self-love; and sadly, we two now have "issues." For as surely as night replaces day, beloved *will* become beloved enemy, at least at times. And the power-struggle stage of our relationship will have officially commenced.

Though the adult part of us expects some eventual change in the personality of our mate, the child experiences the onset of the second phase of relationship as an about-face and a betrayal. "Where's this person who was supposed to be here for me?" he or she laments. Additionally, when our partner's new behaviors unconsciously remind us of parental shortcomings or childhood traumas—*and there will always be occasions when they do*—things get much worse: *big* buttons get pushed, blind spots catalyzed, and painful areas of low self-love triggered. Indeed, frequently the emotional flashbacks can be so intense for us that our adult self loses ground, becoming subsumed by our inner child's emotional memory and distorted perception. Having emotionally confused the identity of today's partner with that of an early caretaker, we start acting out all sorts of feelings, including anger.

How does this work? On the exceptional occasion when Giles was unable to express himself clearly, Cynthia was positive that he was being obstinate and intentionally vague in order to frustrate her. While Giles's lack of clarity was sincere, Cynthia confused it with her father's befuddlement, which he often feigned to tease her. This is how, with no grownups minding the store, many of us become convinced that all the frustration, fear, or pain of a particular issue—possibly even our entire life—derives solely from our beloved.

The Eighty/Twenty Principle of Transference

As we've suggested, transference precipitates the power-struggle stage of relationship. This by-product of low self-love is likewise to blame for almost all the irrational, extreme, out-of-control—in short, childlike and bullying—behaviors that necessitate the use of anger-management technology.

As monumental as this crisis of mistaken identity is, affecting every single romantic partnership, the majority of us in love have never even heard about transference. As our relationships unravel, we unwittingly and indirectly blame each other for what happened to us as kids. In fact, very unscientifically, as much as eighty percent of the emotional juice of each couple conflict is leakage from the mysterious reservoirs of stored feelings from childhood. Only the remaining twenty percent actually pertains to the contemporary situation. This is called the eighty/twenty principle of transference.

Holly intensely disliked the blues. In fact, she became enraged every time her boyfriend, Russell, played this kind of music on their piano. Her seeming *over*reaction had always been a mystery to the couple—until they were introduced to this principle. It helped them identify the real issue behind Holly's blind spot: twenty percent of her anger *did* relate directly to Russell, for he frequently broke the agreement he'd made with her to play only at specified times. The other eighty percent, however, was unresolved anger at her older brother, who'd tormented Holly throughout her elementary-school years. The blues, his favorite music, supplied the soundtrack of the unhappiest moments of her childhood. In Holly's case, the button wasn't only transference; it was a symptom of old trauma as well. When these two go hand in hand, as they often do, we call it *traumatic transference*.

The Hard Underbelly of Transference: Parental Idealization

If transference really is couple enemy number one, why is it such a mystery to the general public? It's true that the concept that we "marry our parents" has been embraced in psychological circles for decades; and the spousal accusation "You're just like my mother [or father]" has been batted about for just as long. These words have been interpreted by most mates very loosely, however.

The first reason that transference remains largely unknown among the general public is that it's kept a very low profile (though its symptoms are highly visible). With relationship education virtually nonexistent until recently, most couples are simply uninformed. Just as the deleterious effects of cigarettes and monosaturated fats on our bodies weren't broadly known thirty years ago, the severe effects of transference on couple health have yet to be made part of today's popular consciousness. Generally, the only partners who truly understand what's going on in the power struggle—that is, that they're displacing onto each other negative feelings that would be more appropriately assigned to their family members—are the ones who find themselves in the office of a couple counselor versed in this theory.

The second reason that the truth of this phenomenon has yet to catch on is that transference functions like a blind spot. As Chapter 3, "Emotional Integrity," explains in detail, most of us skim the surface of our emotions like feather-light bugs on a lake; below churn dark, mysterious waters composed, in the main, of archaic feelings associated with our parents and siblings. This deeper emotional reality is difficult for many mates to contact, mainly because of a seriously underestimated, but monumentally important, childhood need—that is, the need to idealize our parents or early caregivers.

When we were tiny, these people weren't just bigger than we, they were bigger than life. And they *had* to be, for we were dependent on them for our very survival. That's why as very young children we felt the need to perceive them as perfect, in every way up to the task of raising us. Still, special though they were, they (like all nurturers) were only human; and if they were typical, they were grossly underinformed with regard to the finer points of parenting. As a result, they occasionally strayed from the mark and failed to meet some of our core emotional needs.

When such a fall from grace did occur—say, for example, our mother ignored us instead of empathizing with some upset, big or little—we had two choices: we could acknowledge our mother's failing (shattering the idealization that made sense of a scary world), or we could rationalize the failing away. Because the first option was simply unthinkable, choosing the second option was a matter of great psychological urgency.

Though feelings of disappointment, shock, anger, or fear did arise in response to our mother's behavior, we bypassed them, denying to ourselves intellectually that the lapse in appropriate care ever happened. Responding to the developmental need to keep thinking of our parents as heroes, we then blamed our disappointment (or other emotion) on our innocent little selves. As Alice Miller writes in *For Your Own Good,* "The child's dependence on his or her parents' love . . . makes it impossible in later years to recognize these traumatizations, which often remain hidden behind the early idealization of the parents for the rest of the child's life."

Regrettably, it takes very few instances of maintaining the parental idealization at our own expense to cause us a lot of trouble. These experiences are the genesis of our epidemic inability to completely love ourselves, the toxic guilt that distorts our sense of responsibility, the toxic shame that convinces us we're not lovable, and the fear of abandonment that results.

Small wonder, then, that most of us enter partnership more or less unindividuated and stuck in the mire of parental idealization. Other factors also collude to candy-coat our early histories. First, we often simply can't recall our early traumas, in part because the events that had the greatest impact on us occurred while we were in the cradle, crib, and preschool. Second, though some people do naturally have an accurate grasp of the early events of their lives (sometimes having worked hard to achieve it), many partners share a very understandable human propensity to screen out memories that are unpleasant. This is, incidentally, an involuntary defense against memories we couldn't assimilate as children.

But whether our early hard times are truly forgotten or are simply screened out, they remain a blind spot. Tucked away, they still have great power, convincing us that even huge reactions to small incidents in our couple are strictly the fault of our mate. Unless our early traumas and the idealization that disguises them can be "unpacked," they have the potential to trap us forever in the power struggle and impede the growth of our self-love.

The Voyage Out: Overcoming Transference

So how can we keep transference from eating our love alive? Better yet, how can we turn this massive blind spot into an opportunity to build trust and to raise both partners' self-love?

The first step is the identification of transferential issues in our couple. That step is relatively straightforward, but it's not always easy. *Any button, blind spot, or issue that requires the use of a time-out indicates transference.* The emotional charge behind these elements is a giveaway. A high percentage of couple conflicts that *don't* need anger-management technology also belong in this category—specifically, those we're unable to resolve to both partners' satisfaction using the Peace Process. The key question in identifying transference is always, "Have I ever felt this way before? If so, with whom, and when?"

Usually we have to step back a little to answer this question, as Manfred discovered. At first he didn't want to acknowledge that it was mainly transference that made him loathe to go to parties with Bette. "Even though she says no one else seems to notice, she's not herself at a party. She laughs too loud and smiles too much. I don't know what's going on with her, but it embarrasses me. I just want to disappear into the woodwork," he complained.

While it was true that Bette did talk a lot at get-togethers, especially with people she'd just met, the real problem was a resentment that Manfred had hidden from himself for years—a resentment not toward Bette but toward his older sister. Only after a few sessions of couple therapy was he able to recognize how he felt about his sibling. "She's always been really great to me," he began, "but my stepfather thought she walked on water. And now I see that I feel the same way at parties with Bette that I did with my sister and stepdad—just standing on the sidelines like I don't exist." He rubbed his chin. "It's hard to admit that I'm still so mad at her. It was years ago, and it wasn't really even her fault. It was my stepdad who was being unfair to me."

Manfred was willing to transcend the idealization of his older sister in order to find the real issue that had been triggered by Bette. Overcoming idealization didn't mean that he stopped loving (or liking) his sister or his stepfather. Rather, it meant that he got hold of a piece of his emotional truth that had been tucked away for many years. This enabled him to flesh out the picture of his family relations, avoid displacing feelings onto Bette, and have compassion for the little boy he once was.

Many of us, whether we realize it or not, go through our love relationships still trying to please, reject, avoid, or rebel against the idealized members of our families-of-origin. As we saw in Chapter 2, this failure to individuate—to become psychological peers with our family members—prevents us from prioritizing our couple. But the problem isn't irreversible. If we're able to spot transference, pin down the connection with the past, and then transform that connection through the process of individuation—in other words, if we can do what Manfred did—we can focus with new honesty and clarity on our current relationship. Though it often takes some digging and courage, "owning" transference is a watershed both for the individual and for the couple, since it's fundamental to our ability to individuate from our families-of-origin and to maintain our relationship as an emotional safe zone.

This wisdom notwithstanding, many of us prefer not to deal with the past. Why go there? we ask. The past is dead and gone. Let's live for today. This thinking is understandable, of course, but it's based on a faulty assumption: the past *isn't* dead and gone. The reason so many of us have trouble being and living in the present is that issues held over from the past preclude it. We simply can't raise our self-love or extricate ourselves from the power-struggle stage of our relationship without recognizing and healing the past when it shows up as transference between us.

This makes it vital that, like Manfred, we recapture the relevant old information. As is often the case when we try to remember dreams, at first there might be only a thread. But if we grab that thread like the tail of a tiger, we might be able to pull the whole scenario back into view. Lovemates can be excellent sounding boards for each other in this effort, but it takes time. Putting together a coherent picture of earlier relationships with the prime players in our childhood—a picture devoid of idealization, distortion, or fantasy—happens issue by difficult issue, not in a single fireside chat or even a single New Couple Session. But the effort is gratifying: when we succeed at even the first step in the process—remembering who "made us feel this way" in the first place—both partners generally feel a tremendous relief. Sometimes that step alone is enough to resolve the issue and lift our self-love a notch.

Occasionally, in attempting to trace back a particular feeling, some of us will have zero recall. In these instances, it's important to be willing to accept, at least in theory, that it's a transference the source of which we don't yet (and may never) know. Those of us who have no memory of sizable chunks of our childhood may be masking events that are too painful to remember. This kind of forgetting can indicate unresolved emotional trauma and the need for outside assistance. (See also Chapter 10, "Trans-formational Education.")

The next step in healing a transferential issue comes under the juris-diction of the Law of Emotional Integrity. It involves taking responsibil-ity for all the original emotions now unfairly reappearing in our love life. Often it's necessary that we actually work through these messy emotions. There are many ways to do this, *but it's never necessary to confront par-ents—or other primary caregivers—directly.* (Therefore, it makes no differ-ence whether they're living or deceased.)

How does taking responsibility for these old emotions work? First we hold a Special Session with our partner in which to safely talk about the incident or relationship that's being triggered by present circumstances, keeping the focus *off* our partner's twenty percent of the issue and *on* the earlier eighty percent. This sometimes is enough to interrupt the trans-ference. If more work is needed, another simple and often highly effective method for working through transference is to write a no-holds-barred letter to the person who first upset us expressing as many negative feel-ings as we possibly can. This, of course, we never send; in fact, once the letter is good and complete, we might even choose to destroy it. If we've been taught other forms of catharsis, such as pounding on or yelling into a pillow or provoking our own tears with sad music, these too can be helpful. In cases where such exercises fail to neutralize the transference and the accompanying emotional charge—be it anger, sadness, or fear—Chapter 10 may be of some help. (Any reader who's frightened by the above suggestions shouldn't attempt to try them but should instead go directly to the guidance in Chapter 10.)

When we identify transferential issues and undertake to resolve the early hurts at their roots, we're taking care of our eighty percent. Though the held-over feelings won't dissolve overnight, our commitment to fac-ing them sends a strong signal—namely, that we're assuming responsi-bility for reparenting the child within; no longer are we willing to let this part of us act out a potpourri of feelings or put forward dated agen-das that affect our lover negatively.

What's left now, of course, is the other twenty percent of the issue—that which *does* pertain to our current relationship. This can be dealt with using the Peace Process, sometimes with the help of negotiable agreements, as taught in Chapter 6. (But remember that until a given transferential issue is acknowledged and at least brought forward for resolution, the Peace Process won't work.) If we wish to debrief an issue even more thoroughly, we can schedule a Special Session as well.

Brief Instructions for Working Through Transference

First you need to recognize that you're "in transference." The tell-tale signs are

- Any button, blind spot, or issue that repeatedly requires a time-out
- Any button, blind spot, or issue that's too heavy for the Peace Process

Once you suspect transference, ask yourself these questions:

- Have I ever felt this way before?
- If so, with whom, and when?

To break the transference, do as many of the following as seem appropriate:

- Hold a Special Session with your partner to discuss the incident or relationship that's being triggered
- Write a letter packed with negative emotions that you never send to the person who first upset you
- Use other emotion-releasing techniques that you've been taught.
- Refer to Chapter 10 for additional guidance

Katharine and Marlon Revisited

Two and a half years into their relationship, Katharine and Marlon, whom we met earlier in this chapter, continued to make new discoveries about themselves and each other. Whereas during their intoxication stage the transference they experienced was strictly positive, it became a source of strife during their power struggle. Indeed, Katharine lost her certainty of Marlon's love. The thirty-one-year-old city planner explained: "Marlon had a crisis at work and had to stay late for days on end. He'd return home exhausted. That's when our great career discussions started to peter out. Before I knew it," she admitted, "I was snapping at him."

During the Session she subsequently requested, Marlon surprised Katharine with his strong declaration of commitment to her. Additionally, it became evident that the transference issue had literally flipped on its head: her child self had been soothed by her partner's initial interest in her professional life; now that same self felt neglected and double-crossed. Marlon entered the conversation: "I could tell there was much more to Katharine's feelings than frustration over my long hours. How could she question my commitment to her?" he asked. "It just didn't fit."

Katharine looked at Marlon with pride. "Can you believe it?" she said. "He actually helped me identify my transference. At first, I couldn't stand it. I thought, *How dare he try to pawn this off on me?* Then I saw the grain of truth: Daddy used to make me feel like that when I was little." And the issue was doubly upsetting for Katharine: she'd considered the matter worked through ten years earlier with her college counselor. "I was afraid I was turning into a veritable parent-basher. But obviously," she concluded, "if Marlon is needing to time me out, it must not yet be over with Dad."

For Marlon, a thirty-four-year-old real-estate broker, the crunch came when his partner expressed an interest in changing careers. "The day Katharine announced that she wanted to take several months off to attend a fashion design course before changing jobs, I got irate," he said. "In fact, I'm ashamed to admit it, but I called her a flake—and really hurt her feelings." When Katharine pointed out that she'd already been with her company for nearly a decade, the transference bells rang in Marlon's head. It was his mother's unreliability that came immediately to mind, and the suffering it had caused them both. "How could I blame her?" he asked. "My father walked out. She raised me all alone. But the bottom line is, I was only a little kid. I suppose I've never quite gotten over not knowing when the electric company was going to put our lights out."

For Marlon and Katharine, these insights alone were enough to defuse their couple conflict. But because they were committed to raising their self-love and minimizing any future scenes relating to these buttons, they followed up individually to work through the notorious eighty percent. She needed to address unhealed feelings caused by her father's emotional neglect, while he needed to delve into fears relating to material well-being.

An Invitation to Reflect on
the Law of Self-Love

- What are the traumatic incidents or periods of your childhood (minor or severe) that you've been able to identify? What buttons, blind spots, or tendencies to act out your emotions have resulted over the years? How do these make you feel? How do they affect your emotional intimacy?
- How have these early traumatic experiences shown up in your power struggle? Who is it (parents, siblings, etc.) that you transfer onto your mate? How does unhealed transference make you feel? How does it affect your emotional intimacy?
- How do your relationships today with family-of-origin members compare to those with other adults? Do you behave with all as an equal or do you respond to some with more caution (treating them as authorities, for example, seeking to impress or get approval from them, or fearing their admonition or rejection)? Do you behave with some as though they're responsibilities, subtly feeling sorry for them, burdened by them, charged with their emotional comfort, or irritated or impatient with them? How do these relationships make you feel? How do they affect your emotional intimacy?
- If you're in minimal or no relationship with members of your family-of-origin, do you consider yourself individuated from them? In other words, are you working to resolve any strong negative emotions related to them? Are you transferring them onto your partner (or boss, colleagues, clients, siblings, friends, or strangers)? How does this make you feel? How does this affect your emotional intimacy?

SELF-LOVE PAST AND
THE TRADITIONAL COUPLE

To the traditional couple, the concept of self-love would have been virtually alien. The marriage ideal has long been conceptualized as something much bigger and grander than the focus on one's solo self. And surely

today's ideal of self-love—which concentrates on validating our own feelings and intuition, and pursuing personal dreams—would look worse the
further back we went into the less-enlightened past. In fact, it would
become indistinguishable from base selfishness.

Tradition's moralistic putting down of self wasn't the only thing that
squelched healthy notions of self-love in the past. The long-standing
dearth of knowledge about the psychology of self and romance also
played a part. A mere century ago, in fact, childhood experiences were
seen as largely irrelevant to adulthood, not to mention couplehood. How
we "turned out" both as individuals and as spouses was seen as mainly a
matter of character.

Even today, among our own parents' generation—people for whom
self-esteem is still a new idea—self-love might seem too bold a goal.
Indeed, the majority of them have yet to be even *introduced* to their young
emotional selves. Our parents, and the couples that came before them,
had no inkling about idealization and transference, no concept of how
these deadly dynamics entrapped them in the power struggle of their
own relationships. Indeed, like many couples today, although they may
have expected rough waters might hit eventually, they knew nothing of
any of the developmental stages of relationship; in fact, they didn't realize
that there *were* stages! And if someone had raised the notion of the
"resolved" power struggle, known as co-creativity, it would have been
dismissed as a fairy tale. Like communities of old anticipating the Black
Death before antibiotics, many among those who raised us—and those
who raised them—could do nothing but anticipate the souring of love's
sweetness as "what happens." Most tragic, perhaps, was what they were
left to privately conclude: that they'd failed, either as spouses or in their
selection of a mate.

While certain forms of selflessness undoubtedly had a civilizing effect
on marriage, selflessness has long outgrown its usefulness. Under no circumstances is it healthy, or even workable in a relationship, to depriori-
tize our mental or physical well-being or dishonor our emotions or
dreams. The negation of self in relationship is always codependent and
always self-destructive.

Forty-something, married for seventeen years, Donny and Melinda
had no intention of ever divorcing. But the fumes of their power struggle
were affecting their three daughters—especially the twelve-year-old, who

was acting out with her teachers. The school counselor met with the couple and suggested that they speak with a marriage specialist. The first couple session was awkward, for these traditional spouses preferred to keep the details of their marriage private. But, to their credit, they followed up, because they suspected that the school counselor was right: that Dottie's behavior was in part a symptom of their own unresolved anger.

"My wife criticizes me with every breath she takes," the normally reserved Donny exclaimed in their second session, the pain of condemnation flickering over his face. Melinda, a stay-at-home mother, defended herself weakly: "Am I so awful for wanting you to know how I feel?" She turned to the counselor: "I know he needs time on his own," she said. "Am I just being needy and selfish?"

Donny, a commercial airline pilot, really did want to please his wife—which was part of the problem. Pleasing others at his own expense was something he'd learned well under the often severe tutelage of his father. In fact, displeasing Dad wasn't really an option. It seemed that everything Donny did, from forgetting to mow the lawn to missing an A in science, incurred his father's verbal wrath (and sometimes more).

Like all unaddressed traumatic childhood experiences, Donny's showed up in his marriage. Forty years after the fact, Donny's father's loud voice still rang in his ears, precluding him from properly hearing that of his wife. Melinda had only to tell him she'd prefer two lumps of sugar to the one he'd given her for Donny to feel overwhelmingly put down. Little did he know that ever since they'd moved into the power struggle from the intoxication stage, Donny's young self had been perennially on call. Just as with his father, in his marriage he could barely relax, so worried was he about his wife's every need. When the burden got too heavy, Donny would turn glum and withdraw darkly from Melinda, leaving her anguished and confused. Resentment was something he'd never dared show his father, but Melinda was far less scary.

Not that, under pressure, Melinda was always so delicate. Whereas her normal habit was to tiptoe around Donny, fearing a mood, she did occasionally get frazzled. Most recently, she'd slipped and referred to her husband's "midriff bulge" at a party. That comment had pushed his biggest Dad-button—but of course he'd never let on.

In counseling, Donny easily saw the connection between his inability to stick up for himself when Melinda acted out and the experiences of his childhood. Unfortunately, though, he had no recollection of the era in which he might have idealized his father. "I was the son," Donny explained plainly. "I know I bore the brunt of it; that's why I left home as soon as I could."

Because high achievement had always helped Donny build his conditional self-love and keep his experience of toxic shame at bay, he wasn't aware of his emotional currents. At first he wasn't eager to examine his buttons or buy into the eighty/twenty principle, and when it came to early family dynamics, he became downright intransigent. "It stunk then, and it stinks now," he nearly barked. "Why dig it all up? If only Melinda would keep her remarks to herself," he concluded, "we'd be back on course—and our daughter would straighten out."

His wife sat bolt upright. "If you think your dad didn't affect you, why are you so concerned about 'scarring' the girls?" she challenged him. "*You've* got scars and hurts, Donny," she continued, "and thank goodness you're not taking them out on our daughters. But you *are* taking them out on me, and that affects us all!" Donny looked pensive. "I don't want to be like my dad," he responded quietly. "I thought that it was enough not to pressure our kids—but I guess they deserve *happy* parents too."

When it came to her own family-of-origin, Melinda had a harder time facing the facts than she had inspiring her husband to do so. Her loyalty was deep-rooted, and admittedly her story wasn't as obvious as his. In fact, far from being the scapegoat Donny had been, of all five siblings Melinda had been her father's favorite. "I have nothing to report," she began. "My parents adored each other—and were very proud of me." The only wrinkle, apparently, was her younger sister. Melinda's grudge against her was still fresh. "She was the baby—and so selfish," the woman stated flatly. "She tried to make us all miserable. If it hadn't been for her moods, everything would have been perfect growing up."

Melinda's childhood story was yet unread. The description of her parents was monochromatic, and that of her sister all darkness—a giant blind spot. Like her husband, Melinda at first considered it unnecessary to delve into the past. "That's ancient history," she complained. "Why can't we leave our poor parents alone? They did the best they could." Still, Melinda exhibited classic features of low self-love: she didn't believe that she was entitled to have any feelings but cheerful ones, and she apologized not only for her own emotions and behaviors but for Donny's as well. When her husband acted out by shutting her out, instead of sticking up for herself she blamed herself and spiraled into toxic guilt. Her child self was convinced that she was unworthy of her husband's love.

It took several sessions for Melinda to remember when she'd felt this way before. Donny helped. "I don't know why you're so loyal," he objected at session five. "Your father really expected a lot of you. Remember when you didn't get first place in your sixth-grade piano recital? He forbade everyone to speak to you at dinner that night. And poor Pammy—all he did was *yell* at her." This stung, for although she knew it was true, her husband's words made Melinda feel the reality of her father's hardness for the first time. Still, her rejoinder was defensive: "That's because he believed in excellence. I wouldn't have the good life I have today if he hadn't instilled in me that I deserve it!"

But Donny was on a roll. "If you ask me," he persevered, "your sister rebelled against his impossible standards and got creamed for it. *And,*" he said with extra emphasis, "I think your sister and mother were jealous that you got the lion's share of his attention." Melinda was amazed. Never had her husband advocated for her in any way. "Why are you suddenly on *my* side?" she asked. Donny shook his head fondly. "I've *always* been on your side," he said. "I just haven't dared say so. You've always seemed so protective of your family—your dad especially—that I've been afraid you'd bite my head off if I pointed out flaws!"

Loyalty to our family-of-origin isn't in and of itself unhealthy. But if, like Melinda, we have symptoms of low self-love and find ourselves power-struggling, we're most likely stuck in an idealization of our early caregivers that has us transferring denied negative feelings for them onto our beloved.

Melinda took action on behalf of her marriage and registered for a workshop focusing on father-daughter healing. There she recognized that eighty percent of her juice with Donny did in fact come from unfinished issues with her father and sister. "I cried a lot," she said afterward, "but it felt good, like a deep cleansing." She went on, "I was always afraid that I'd have to tell my parents off to their faces, but it turns out that's not necessary at all. I can clear old junk without ever worrying their gray heads." An unexpected gift was how her heart opened to Pammy. "I never idealized my sister," she said. "I scapegoated her. Now that I *see* that, well, I really need to call her."

Meanwhile, in one-on-one work, Donny tackled *his* eighty percent. He wrote several angry letters to his long-deceased father, an activity that he at first thought "pointless." This process uncovered a lot of grief, however—grief that took him unawares. "In many ways, my father never died," he said. "But he can't hurt me now."

Thanks to all the effort that both partners put into their inner work, fresh air finally began circulating in Donny and Melinda's relationship. Donny realized that his wife's demands on him paled next to those of his father. "I've definitely been dumping on her—and on the girls too," he admitted. "Who'd have known that my funks sent her back to Pammy?" And his wife now understood that a mere glance or word could bring Donny's father back to life. The couple's transference work represented the ultimate act of fairness to each other and (because of its positive impact on their self-love) to themselves as well. As Melinda said, "I'm sure that on some level, wherever they are, our parents are cheering for us."

An Invitation to Reflect on the Law of Self-Love as It Pertains to Your Parents

- What were your parents' conditions for loving themselves? How did these conditions affect their emotional intimacy? How did these conditions make you feel?

- What were your parents' strongest areas of self-love? (For example, did they automatically trust their feelings? Their intuition? Did they stick up for themselves? Did they keep themselves physically and emotionally safe from those who might act out in their presence? Were they able to set limits and say no? Were they devoted to developing their talents and passions? Did they cherish their own dignity?) How did your parents' ability to love themselves affect their emotional intimacy? How did that effect on intimacy make you feel?

- How did your parents' relationships with their family-of-origin members compare to those with other adults? Did they behave with all as equals, or did they handle some more carefully—perhaps as authority figures or as responsibilities?

How did these relationships affect their emotional intimacy? How did they make you feel?

- How would your childhood have been different had your parents subscribed to the Law of Self-Love? How would your own couple be different (or, if you're single, how would past relationships have been different)?

SELF-LOVE AND THE NEW COUPLE

As we've seen, transference stymied many a traditional relationship. It's a wily beast even in the hands of a self-aware New Couple.

Raleigh and Dolores: Part I

When they met two years ago, Raleigh and Dolores were no strangers to the psychology of self-esteem. "Back in the seventies I followed a guru around India. Then in the eighties, I processed till I dropped," Raleigh bragged, referring to the many human-potential-movement workshops he'd attended. Dolores, his wife of eight months, also had a history of self-discovery. "I have journals stuffed with everything I've learned about myself—buttons, blind spots, and all," she said. Her great self-knowledge was due to an intensive course of depth psychotherapy she'd been through years before. Raleigh was a forty-six-year-old field biologist; Dolores, a thirty-four-year-old landscape architect. With these essential compatibilities, and a strong draft of New Couple chemistry, Dolores and Raleigh seemed born to be together.

Raleigh's biggest issues revolved around a proclivity to neglect himself: unable to prioritize his needs, he often ate poorly and generally ignored his body's signals. He also drove himself intensely in his work. "I know I push myself hard, but if *I* don't, who will?" Though he poked fun at himself, bitterness tinged his words. Raleigh's mother, largely at odds with her role as housewife, had been overwhelmed by her life—her successful stockbroker husband, her massive house, and the endless entertaining expected of her. Mostly, though, she couldn't handle the four boys who emerged from her womb in as many years. As the youngest, Raleigh got very little of his mother's care or attention. Much of the delicate job of caring for the baby of the family fell to an occasional au pair girl and his older brothers—hardly models of sensitivity.

"My earliest memories are of my brothers, not my parents," Raleigh told Dolores shortly after they met. "I was the lost child amid the chaos of my family," he recollected, revealing his familiarity with psychological terminology. "The guys were all larger, louder, and smarter than me. My father was always at the office or on a business trip. My mother? Sure," he continued, "she'd put in a cameo appearance now and then, or show up at the last minute when my brothers got too rough. Mostly, though, I remember only the scent of her perfume." Saved by his wits and sheer self-reliance, he learned early that the best way to get his needs met was not to have any.

Still, today Raleigh considers his self-care issue basically handled: "Look, I've shed a tear or two and pounded my share of pillows. Everything's cool now with my parents, and I'm carrying out my mission in life. What else is there?" he asked rhetorically.

Dolores had been married once before, for eight years during her twenties. "I'll be the first to admit that I got married for all the wrong reasons," she told Raleigh during one of their initial heart-to-hearts. "I had mega-abandonment issues. I just *had* to be married; it was that simple. I knew in my gut that Milton was all wrong, but I was bound and determined."

At first, this desperation made no sense to her. "My parents and I were so close when I was a kid, they absolutely suffocated me. You'd think I'd be allergic to marriage." During the two powerful years of therapy that followed her divorce, however, the shadow side of this parental "closeness" came into focus. Her parents had entered the power struggle just after Dolores, their only child, was born. "Mom and Dad told me point-blank that they'd decided to stay together for my sake. I soon became aware that there was this terrible difference between how they treated me and how they were with each other. It was unbearable." Her voice dropped. "One of my earliest memories is of trying to make them smile at each other. The way they would compete for my attention—it was like my own private *Sophie's Choice*."

Raleigh listened attentively as Dolores continued: "It was the reasoning of a child, of course, but I figured that if they were so unhappy, it must have been because of something I'd done wrong. Deep inside, I knew the awful truth: I was defective." She paused. "Now I realize that parents are supposed to help children love themselves, not vice versa. Not that anyone had ever told my folks this either. So while I was smothered by their needs," she continued, "*my* emotional needs were being abandoned. To the lonely child I still was, marriage had always seemed the perfect stuffing for the big hole inside." With a great sigh, Dolores concluded, "I just thank God it's all in the past."

Thus, with a rock-solid grip on their own psychological stories, did these two come together. Still, relationships always bring up our deepest self-love wounds. And, in spite of all the work they'd done on themselves alone, Dolores and Raleigh were headed straight into the power struggle.

A triathlete and marathoner, Dolores took immaculate care of her body: she ate carefully, rested adequately, and worked out daily. This contrasted sharply with Raleigh, who'd been struggling for years to motivate himself simply to jog on a regular basis. Despite his good intentions, his exercise routine typically dwindled to two weeks on, one month off. Then would come a point when Raleigh couldn't tolerate any further self-recrimination. He'd resolve to recommit, and the ordeal would begin anew.

When they were first married, Raleigh felt confident that Dolores would be an inspiration. And so she was—for exactly five weeks. Then he cut back on his running and soon stopped altogether. "I'm not sure exactly what's up," he confided to a buddy, choosing his words with care. "I feel sort of competitive with Dolores, then frustrated, then almost envious. I just want to give up. This feels a hundred times worse than before we were together. Now I *really* have reason to beat myself up."

The friend suggested that Raleigh schedule a Session so that he could let Dolores in on his dilemma. The next day, after work, Raleigh and Dolores sat facing each other in their living room. Dolores seemed to have trouble restraining herself from speaking as Raleigh bared his soul. Finally she interrupted him: "I don't *get* it. I try to help you. Now I feel guilty that I don't share your problem—like I'm supposed to stop working out to make you feel better."

They tried a spoken Peace Process next, but got stuck each time. A visit to us was next. We listened to each of their stories, worked briefly with the contemporary issue, and then asked them both to close their eyes. "See if you can bring up all those hard feelings, the ones when you're right in the thick of it," we suggested. A few moments passed. "Now turn up the volume. Can you remember ever feeling this way before in your life? The younger you were, the better." In thirty seconds Raleigh fairly exploded: "Just my entire childhood! My brothers beat me *at everything*. Finally I just got sick of it and quit trying."

This minor epiphany, as he later called it, opened up a new world for Raleigh: "I've always known that my parents were as absentee as they come," he said, his voice strained, "but who's ever heard of transference due to jock brothers?" It took him a moment to add, "It's clear that I was fooling myself in thinking that I was no longer affected by my family relationships. Because here it is again—I don't take care of myself, just like they didn't take care of me."

Raleigh could now see how the despair caused by his brothers' crude "care" still lived inside him and had been triggered by Dolores. He looked at his beloved. "You forced the issue," he said gratefully. "With my overwork and bad food habits, I probably would have ended up with a heart attack by the time I was fifty."

As frequently occurs, an old area of low self-love—inability to commit to a healthy regimen of self-care, in this case—was exacerbated when Raleigh fell in love. Though he never blamed Dolores for his exercise lapses, the transference was a complete blind spot. Raleigh went on to work with us one-on-one to undo some of that early conditioning. "I've gotten two of my three brothers more or less off my back," he proudly declared. "In another few months I hope to be jogging along faithfully, with or without Dolores."

During Raleigh's breakthrough session, Dolores was pleased about his discovery. But when we asked her, she denied that the feelings the incident brought up were linked to anything in the past. In her mind, the matter was put to bed.

Raleigh and Dolores: Part II

Months after their couple meeting, Raleigh left for a stint of fieldwork tracking cougars for an environmental-impact report. He returned a week later with a terrible case of poison oak. His life became increasingly miserable as more and more painful blisters appeared. Dolores promptly asked for several days off to care for her husband. Soon, however, she found him an impossibly rebellious patient. He refused to wear gloves and scratched himself till he bled, spreading the infection. Furthermore, despite her imploring, he insisted on attacking the mountain of data he'd collected in the cougar project. Every time he sat at his computer, Raleigh loudly cursed his rash and moaned in pain. On the third day, Dolores lost it: "Can't you get yourself together?" she hollered. "Will I have to babysit you forever?"

As soon as Raleigh was well enough, they were back in our office. The issue wasn't just Dolores's frustration over nursing him through his bout of poison oak; it turned out that she was impatient with Raleigh quite often. His general morning sluggishness really got to her, for example. However, when we inquired a second time about whether she'd ever felt this way before, Dolores was emphatic. "Look," she said, "I've been through this before and come out the other end. I've even forgiven my parents," she added, "and it wasn't easy."

Her partner, who remembered the childhood story she'd told him so many months before, wasn't satisfied with this report and encouraged her to look at the transference. Though reluctant to rehash old business, she finally agreed that he had a point. "Maybe you *do* remind me of my parents' neediness," she said at last, "especially with this poison oak. I felt that it was my job to keep you from falling apart—just the way I did with Mom and Dad." She was clearly exasperated. "I can't *believe* this is all coming up again."

Still, Dolores was quick on the uptake. She saw that her reluctance to acknowledge her eighty percent—indeed, any unfinished early business at all—was like the notorious marathoner's "wall" with which she was so familiar. "It's somewhere around the three-quarter mark," she explained, "and just before I get there, I always think I'll die, I'll never make it. Then it comes, and goes, and I get a second wind and coast to the finish line."

Dolores enrolled in the Hoffman Process (a weeklong self-love intensive) to address the latest shard of hurt from her childhood. Before she went, though, the couple tidied up their twenty percent. They completed two Peace Processes, and covered more ground in several Special Sessions. Finally, they hammered out a negotiable agreement stipulating that Dolores wasn't to offer physical fitness tips to Raleigh, nor was he to ask. The agreement helped them avoid the Critic-Child dynamic that had unconsciously hurtled both of them back into their pasts.

For our own couple, self-love has proven the most challenging and redemptive of all the New Laws of Love. Though we've been basking for years now in the co-creativity stage of our relationship, there are still times when we encounter old (and sometimes even new) areas of unresolved emotional trauma—issues that make themselves known to us through those telltale buttons and blind spots. Even having cracked colossal idealizations, shed seemingly fossilized family roles, and worked through maddening transferences, there are still times when each of us seems to mutate into the worst caricature of the other's parents and siblings. (And yes, we still count on transformational education when we can't bust our own ghosts!) The results for both of us have been personal empowerment and the strengthening and sweetening of our emotional intimacy beyond anything we could have imagined.

If there's any wisdom to the seemingly crazy propensity of human beings to jump into relationships long before we've worked the kinks out of our character and gotten good and mature, the seventh New Law of Love reveals it. Self-love is a healing system that's been kept secret from couples for far too long. It can turn individuals into not only their own greatest friend and advocate, but *the person they really want to be*. Commitment to this law can also literally save relationships: imagine the biggest issues transformed into opportunities, conflicts into experiences of compassion.

While it's important not to set the bar too high, the intention to apply this law represents a heroic journey for modern couples. For such an endeavor always involves a foray into the unknown or forgotten, a metaphorical return home, in order to set right what's been left amiss. Using our transferences to grow ourselves up—and become true adults vis-à-vis every member of our family—enables us to polish the jagged edges of our individual pasts and clear the way for our future together.

Along with peacemaking, emotional integrity, and deep listening, self-love serves as a cornerstone of our emotional safe zone. The beauty of owning our transferences—a process necessary to self-love—is that we get to the absolute source of our upsets rather than taking them out on each other. This ownership drains much of the negative emotional drama from our relationship by radically reducing acting out and acting in. Emotional intimacy can't help but blossom in the honesty of that environment. The foundation of growing self-love then supports us to develop talents, discover buried dreams, and achieve our mission in life. With transference vaporizing and the power struggle retreating, we can be model emotional intimates, primed for our next great adventure—and doing our bit to coax modern love out of the Dark Ages.

The Key to Self-Love

Committing to raise your self-love by learning to do the following is the key to the seventh New Law of Love:

- Accept and validate your own emotions, ideas, intuition, and talents
- Stick up for yourself
- Recognize and heal transferences within the relationship

8. MISSION IN LIFE
the eighth new law of love

There is more in a human life than our theories of it allow. Sooner or later something seems to call us onto a particular path. You may remember this "something" as a signal moment in childhood when an urge out of nowhere, a fascination, a peculiar turn of events struck like an annunciation: This is what I must do, this is what I've got to have. This is who I am.

JAMES HILLMAN, *The Soul's Code*

Would that we each had the blessing of a "signal" childhood moment, announcing definitively the nature of our life's true calling. To the great frustration of many of us, however, both single and in couples, this isn't how it unfolds. Our ultimate place in the world often remains a mystery through our school days and on into adulthood—sometimes even well into our parenting years. Still, veiled or revealed, mission in life is a higher-order need: it's integral to our ability to love ourselves and, by extension—this is the revolutionary part—to keep our New Couple chemistry vibrant. If we don't devote our working hours to what satisfies our soul, we die on the vine.

That's why a commitment to discover and fulfill our own mission in life—*and to support our partner in the same*—has to be one of the Ten New Laws of Love. As we find out who we really are as individuals, all our relationships grow and flourish. The benefits of that process accrue not just to ourselves and to the world, but to our beloved as well. And if we're foundering in life, unsure of our mission, there are few places as well suited to helping us find our big direction as the creative crucible—

and emotional safe zone—of our most intimate relationship. Mission in life (along with, for some of us, the joy of our growing children) is the essence, the melody, the very heart of our final phase of relationship, co-creativity.

Mission is what gives meaning to our lives. More than a good job or even a prestigious career, it's our ultimate fantasy work, as only we can define it—our "job from heaven." Always unique, this mission—this *calling,* if you will—tends to grow into ever truer versions of itself as it incorporates the unique palette of aptitudes that we were born with. When we commit to work that not only challenges and satisfies us but also helps, however modestly, to turn our world around, we feed our self-love; and perhaps nothing is more deeply fulfilling.

Those of us who don't yet feel called are at risk of feeling inadequate with regard to our mission in life, fretting over our lack of purpose just as someone who'd never heard the voice or seen the face of God might worry that she or he was spiritually lacking. Yet it's important that we be patient with ourselves. If we lack Mozart's luck—he's one who saw his future as a young child—the discovery and fulfillment of our life's mission could well span our lifetime. And yet however off the mark each little job we undertake may look or feel, hindsight invariably teaches us that everything we've ever done has served as a stepping-stone. Furthermore, as we enhance our self-love, new gifts and talents have a tendency to emerge. We are, after all, works in progress, and we owe it to ourselves to enjoy the journey's twists, U-turns, and occasional detours.

Whatever our dream arenas, the Law of Mission in Life is an invitation that challenges each couple to commit two sets of talent in a tangible way to the good of the world. This doesn't mean sacrificing a nice home, creature comforts, and fun for humanity's sake. In the first place, because true work doesn't represent a zero-sum option, it needn't compete with our material objectives. Furthermore, as anyone who's manifesting his or her personal vision will attest, doing what we were put on earth to do *is* fun; if we're not enjoying our work, we haven't yet found our mission.

A genuine mission in life is always a worthy goal, a great central organizing theme, not only for a single human life but (much more to our point in this book) for couples as well. It's so central to the evolving definition of *human being* that Abraham Maslow, father of humanistic psychology, claimed that all of us have not only the right, but also the need, to pursue a mission. In fact, the Maslovian concept of "self-actualization"—of doing our best and highest work—crowns his famous "hierarchy of needs."

In his mega-successful job/mission-hunter's bible *What Color Is Your Parachute?* Richard Bolles tells us how to find our mission in life (a term he popularized). Thanks to him and his many successors, it's no longer too deep—or too self-aggrandizing—to ask "Is there something special that I'm meant to contribute to this world?" And who could ever forget anthropologist and myth-master Joseph Campbell on public television lovingly entreating us to "follow our bliss"? The implication was that if we human beings didn't all let that which we love be that which we do, he couldn't predict what this world would come to.

Philosopher-inventor R. Buckminster Fuller's comments on the subject were tantamount to a quantum leap for mission in life. He stated categorically that *every child is a genius,* then squarely placed responsibility for discovering and bringing to fruition these seeds of brilliance on the shoulders of parents, educators, and caregivers. Like Campbell, Fuller linked mission to the survival of our species. *We* link it to the survival of the modern couple.

Harvard University's Howard Gardner has done revealing research in this area, adding depth to the every-child-is-a-genius notion. He proposes that there are seven ways of being "smart"—verbal, mathematical, musical, spatial, kinesthetic, interpersonal, and intrapersonal—and that *everyone* possesses at least one (if not a combination of several) of these intelligences. This, of course, has dashed the traditional view that children are either gifted or not. According to Gardner's findings, they're *all* gifted. If a child's talent isn't obvious, we simply aren't doing enough to excavate it. Schools, as many of us know only too well, reward mainly math and verbal smarts. All other forms of genius are generally overlooked or even punished. (Were you that chatterbox in class—a young interpersonal genius? Was your beloved that daydreaming intrapersonalist—a poet-philosopher-visionary in the making? Even though you may have gotten in trouble then, you two can make beautiful music together now.)

An Invitation to Reflect on the Law of Mission in Life

As you approach the exercises in this chapter, remember that the presence or absence of New Couple chemistry always profoundly affects a couple's experience with each law.

- Where are you in your life in terms of discovering your mission?
- How does this make you feel? How does it affect your self-love? Your emotional intimacy?

THE IDEAL OF IDLENESS

For some of us, the concept of pursuing a purpose might seem too high-brow or stressful. Maybe we see the ideal life as retiring at forty off a lottery ticket. Those who've researched the subject of happiness beg to differ; in fact, they're weighing in with the life-purpose pioneers cited above. Chief among them, Professor Mihaly Csikszentmihalyi, author of *Flow: The Psychology of Optimal Experience,* informs even the most inveterate leisure lizards among us that doing nothing, or doing uninspired work—even with lots of money—will *eventually* make us miserable.

Until he tried the life of leisure, Donovan would have debated this contention. "I used to believe that Great Spirit designed me to kick back on the beaches of Maui. But after three months of soaking up the rays, I almost went crazy." Eight years later, six of them spent working with the elderly as a recreational therapist, he concedes that to be truly happy, we need to use our own unique gray matter, the sum total of our personal riches.

Professor Csikszentmihalyi also asserts that because we're all multi-talented, capable of a variety of endeavors, the more pistons we fire in a day's work, the happier and more mentally healthy we'll be. This too supports the view that finding our mission in life—and doing it—is where we're headed as human beings and what it takes to make us happy.

What's good for the lone individual in our era is also crucial for us as romantic partners. For if we ignore the question of why we as individuals were put on planet earth, our souls sicken, and that sickness inevitably infects all our relationships.

MISSION VULNERABLE:
BIG-PICTURE CHALLENGES

Earth-shattering and thrilling as a calling ought to be to each one of us, the mission-in-life imperative has scarcely penetrated society's conventional wisdom. Despite the growing awareness of our need to rekindle the spirit in work, personal mission has yet to become an ideal of education. Indeed, without giving due consideration to natural talents and passions, we continue to counsel our young people to go for "good jobs," meaning those that promise the highest incomes. The more traditional among us might deem the notion of meaningful work not just impractical but downright radical. Given this cultural vacuum—this failure to embrace the higher-order need of mission in life as essential to the well-being of individuals—we can hardly expect mission to be honored as crucial to the health of couples. Even many relationship experts overlook the primacy of dual missions.

Socioeconomics: The System That Stifles

With society so slow on the uptake, mission in life, like self-love and emotional intimacy, is clearly very vulnerable: it's generally either ignored entirely or crushed by the pressures of life. As we pointed out in Chapter 5, socioeconomic factors are often stacked against those of us who choose parenthood, making it exceedingly difficult to be fair in the assignment of roles and responsibilities. The rigidity of the workaday world also negatively affects our ability to be fair to each other—and ourselves—when it come to following our bliss. Some of us, like our client Alfred, fear that we can't afford to do work that really turns us on. His semi-chronic fatigue, tied in part to a six-figure job that left him limp, ultimately taught him that he couldn't afford *not* to.

For those of us who have the nerve to head down the road toward our mission and then decide we want children, the choices get even more complicated. If one or both of our missions entail financial risks, which many do during the early research phase, the very security of our new family can be jeopardized. Wisely, few couples play these odds. Instead, some solve the dilemma by putting one or both missions on hold. While this is pragmatic and appropriate in the short term, it poses risk of another kind: that with one leg up, we'll fall off the horse. We may find ourselves locked into dual breadwinner ruts for more than two decades, until the kids are out of college. By the time we feel free to put purpose over practicality, our passions look like pipe dreams.

The belief that we can't fight the system often overwhelms us. For that reason, it's one of the greatest challenges to mission in life. But we *can* fight it. Hal and Jane found a way to achieve everything they wanted in life, including mission. Both in their mid-thirties, they were passionate to adopt twins *and* switch to more fulfilling lines of work. They sagely held off on doubling the size of their family for ten full years, until they were well established with their work. Though making room for mission required creative financing—and a loan from Jane's mother— today they're more than pleased with their planning.

Intimate Saboteurs: Partners Off the Path

No wonder nothing short of a New Law of Love, enshrining two missions in life as part of our couple's vision, would suffice to guarantee that our Big Assignments not go down the drain. For it's perversely true that our very dependency on each other for support automatically magnifies our power to sabotage each other. Indeed, the second biggest challenge to mission in life, after socioeconomics, lurks in the intimacy of our romantic union. If tuning into, and then heeding, our vocational calling can be daunting to us as individuals, imagine trying to accomplish it if our one and only isn't on the bandwagon. When a partner doesn't believe in mission in life as a concept—that is, as a higher-order (and therefore nonoptional) adult need—and doesn't actively support the process of its discovery and fulfillment, then the job of our dreams can end up a nightmare—or worse, nonexistent. In either case, our relationship will inevitably suffer.

Maria narrowly escaped having her mission derailed by a less-than-enthusiastic partner. This unassuming housewife was subjected to spousal needling when, at fifty-five, she dared crop her hair and start attending poetry readings. On the day Maria shared her idea of opening a café to host literary gatherings in their small town, she met a brick wall in the form of Lewis, her husband. If this vision-quester hadn't had the self-love—and the chutzpah—to push for this piece of her bigger purpose, the popular Café Goddess would still be but a figment of Maria's imagination, and she'd still feel victimized by Lewis. Instead, her man is a convert to (and a fixture at) her hot spot. She especially loves it when he makes unannounced guest appearances with his twelve-string guitar.

An Invitation to Reflect on the Law of Mission in Life

- Do you support your partner's mission in life? How does this make you feel? How does your support (or lack thereof) of your partner's mission affect your self-love? Your emotional intimacy?
- Do you feel supported by your partner in your mission in life? How does this make you feel? How does your partner's support (or lack thereof) of your mission affect your self-love? Your emotional intimacy?

Internal Saboteurs: Beliefs That Kill

Unquestionably, partners often hurl monkey wrenches into each other's master plans—with varying degrees of success. Yet spite rarely lies behind our attempts to refute the logic and potential for joy promised by mission in life. Rather, these attempts are due to often outrageously self-limiting beliefs, either conscious or unconscious, that are fueled by low self-love and the trance of tradition. Lewis, for instance, didn't believe that his wife (or he, for that matter) could make money doing something she loved.

There's no shortage of mission-killing myths, and most are commonly accepted. Take these three:

- There can be only one mission per marriage.
- Both partners can't have great jobs if they also have kids.
- People can't make enough money doing something they love to support a family.

What these all have in common is fear, an emotion that can attach itself to anything challenging. For perhaps a majority of us, the fear of being unable to provide adequately for our children has hardened into the almost unassailable belief that we must choose between family and at least one of our missions. We see the difficulty of maintaining two missions and decide it's impossible, easily garnering abundant evidence for our sad conclusion. Like Gray and Flora, we come to believe that we have no choice but to put in workaholic hours, even at a job we intensely dislike, just to foot the bills. It took eight years of being bushed and bitter—and a breakdown in their couple—before these parents of three gave themselves permission to think about the possibility of work that thrilled.

If these reigning beliefs aren't enough to discourage us all forever, there are plenty more to annihilate ambitions for our next lifetime too. Other skeptical songs we might be tempted to sing include "It's pure pie in the sky," "Marriage alone is enough (for personal fulfillment)," "You can't win for losing (especially if you tried once and got burned)," "Money and status fulfill," "My mission is to be a good wife and mother," "My purpose is to be a provider," "Exciting work is selfish," and "The seat of my pants is on the seat of my chair." Hummed sotto voce under all of these is the anthem of low self-love: "I don't deserve to have a mission in life." Not only is each of the above a lie, but they're also lethal to love (as is *any* conviction that precludes *both* of us from finding out and then living out who we really are). Thanks to such traditional tapes, millions of us—including many who see themselves as modern and emancipated—can't begin to imagine the richness of life that's possible as a dual-mission pair.

The eighth New Law of Love helped the following partners debunk two mission-unfriendly myths that, until crisis struck, neither one knew ran them. Reginald, a data-entry supervisor, had been living with his fiancée, Joliet, a clerk at a convenience store, for five years when the fire that had been smoldering in him since high school finally caught and flamed: "I can't stand my work anymore," he announced to her one night. "I want to go to law school! I can finish my BA at night and be enrolled by fall."

Joliet's mind raced ahead to married life with a student: the stress, the law boards, the bottom-level income—again. Deep within her rocked the memory of her own shameful and worrisome childhood just above the poverty line. "After all the work to get where you are, why now?" she pleaded. Then resentment about the financial burden of

Reginald's child from a previous marriage crept up her neck. "Haven't I put up with enough? When are we going to have *our* day in the sun?"

Reginald was confused. Maybe a career change *wouldn't* be such a good idea, he thought. Joliet had been a good sport about Autumn, and he wanted to be fair to her in return. Joliet's fears about his mission had sent him into the trance of tradition—specifically, the brutal belief that since "marriage means compromise," he had to give up his dream.

The decision he faced was also an issue of self-love. He could choose to be creative (working toward the job he really wanted), or he could succumb to codependence with his partner (assuaging her worries by sticking with the status quo). This latter option—subordination of self in order to placate a partner—spells disaster for many a mission.

As for Joliet, early financial insecurities had led her to set her sights sorrowfully low. Personal dreams and ambitions were for other people, according to Joliet. In fact, her belief was that the biggest accomplishment she could expect out of life was "to get married and get by."

Fortunately, Reginald couldn't keep down his healthy yen for something more in life. Furthermore, he had the wisdom to know that without Joliet's support, his mission was destined to rise and fall like a Roman candle. Though his career dilemma caused a wobble in their relationship, he came out of his daze and persuaded his fiancée to negotiate. At the same time, he demonstrated deep love and respect for Joliet by prodding her to reflect on her own fantasy job. Four years later, Reginald is finishing law school. Joliet is still behind the counter at the little store, but now as a means to finance art classes. This is the first real step in her newly acknowledged mission—to illustrate children's books.

Unlike the last couple, others of us look like mission mavens, perhaps even the ultimate modern couple. Under the glossy surface, however, we may simply have been seduced by another insidious—and age-old—myth: namely, that money, power, and status fulfill. For years Alfie and Georgia genuinely thought they were "purposeful" in their white-collar jobs. But in truth, both were trapped in high-stress careers that paid well and satisfied little. In fact, the politics alone were eating them both alive. "They say that the one who dies with the most toys wins," Alfie commented with irony in our office. "Well, we're dying—inside." When Georgia spoke, it was with even less humor: "Our emotional intimacy is in the red too." These two were aching for a mission makeover. "We have some serious navel contemplation ahead of us," Alfie said. "But whatever we do next, we're committed to really going for the gold—not just the money."

An Invitation to Reflect on the Law of Mission in Life

- What are your limiting beliefs with regard to mission in life and partnership?
- Do your limiting beliefs match the mission-killing myths mentioned in the discussion above? How do they make you feel? How do these limiting beliefs affect your self-love? Your emotional intimacy?

MISSION IN LIFE PAST AND THE TRADITIONAL COUPLE

We're sorry to say, though we can do so with relative certitude, that the majority of Homo sapiens who have died since the inception of the species have died with their bliss unattained. Though the idea of vocational calling wasn't wholly unfamiliar to our parents' generation, neither was it a mainstream concept. Until very recently, every child was definitely *not* seen as a genius; and every person, mated or otherwise, was *not* expected to give his or her gifts for the betterment of our planet (beyond contributing to its population). World literature provided a solitary, striking exception: it exalted the human thrust toward purpose in life as *the existential search for the authentic self.* That literary view obviously didn't result in a major fad, however.

To be sure, there have always been a few people drawn in a special way to their work—people who have felt a calling to the arts, medicine, science, teaching, law, politics, the religious life, or other professions— and they've generally been highly respected. From the Confuciuses, Madame Curies, and Dr. Kings of the world down to a revered local rabbi, the vocationally enlightened have always been considered a cut above the rest of us mere mortals.

Though the "exceptional" have sometimes revealed their inspiration, it's often remained private. What we outsiders have seen is prodigious

talent (generally) and an apparently exceptional drive, sometimes abetted
by a special kind of privilege—wealth or beauty or connections, perhaps.
In the absence of some clear formula, however, we've been left to wonder
what separated such people from your average Jack and Jill. But today, to
our great advantage, all this has been demystified. Barbara Sher, a pioneer
in the field of life-work identification, calls what makes or breaks our
mission "the right circumstances," and she insists that these are available
to us all.

If mission wasn't part of the average couple's reality in days past—let
alone a traditional couple *value*—how could our mated forebears possibly
have created "the right circumstances" in which to incubate their life
dreams? If, by chance, one partner of the traditional team *did* feel a tug in
the direction of self-discovery, he or she would most likely have been
yanked back into line—into mediocrity—by the *wrong* circumstances,
especially the prevailing myths regarding mission in life.

The Dominant Traditional Myth: Householding as Mission

As we saw earlier, there are many myths still active today that deny the
need for and validity of personal mission. Out of these many myths, none
has endured longer, or had a greater effect, than the traditional myth that
householding constitutes a couple's main mission. The pressure of centuries of supposedly biology-based gender inequalities forced fathers of
yesterday to take on the out-of-home job, though that work typically had
little to do with his passions or gifts. Mothers' aptitudes and aspirations
likewise received little attention, unless they fell within the maternal role
of raising the children and supporting the husband.

This dominant traditional myth was almost indelibly etched in the
fabric of the society our forebears knew, because the roles it dictated were
built into the structure of Western economy. High-ranking corporate and
government posts (including the presidency of the United States), which
represented societal ideals, were typically husband-*and-wife* responsibilities; in these posts, wives functioned as adjuncts to their husbands. While
some of the men working these jobs were definitely carrying out their
mission in life, others weren't. And their wives almost *certainly* weren't—
unless, of course, their specific supportive functions were the truest

application of their inherent genius. In the absence of such a match, traditional helpmate roles precluded women from finding themselves.

In conjunction with the dedicated-worker-and-family-leader male role and the good-wife female role, the procreative purpose was paramount for traditional adults. Thus our parents and grandparents were also plugged into the roles of male provider and female nurturer. Society so valued these roles that everything was subordinated to the needs of the children, including (if they had any) both partners' dreams. Dads exchanged heart for dollars in the most lucrative jobs they could find, locking their genuine interests out in the garage or in their daydreams, or abandoning them completely. Day after day, the life-force of our fathers (and their fathers) was depleted by practicalities, deeply meaningful work never known. Many of these men ended up in middle or old age regretful about past choices and panicked about their mortality. The real tragedy? Unlike women's traditional mission, which included the many gratifications of mothering, men's mission wasn't even about fathering. Instead of enjoying the pleasure of close relationships with their children, our fathers were made to focus on bankrolling our mothers and us.

Whether they wore blue or white collars, traditional fathers risked mild to severe symptoms when continually oppressed in the daily grind of ungratifying work. The lucky ones suffered the rather average rat-race anxieties, along with a sense of purposelessness or isolation. Others suffered nervous breakdowns, substance and behavioral addictions, and heart conditions. Such awful but common side effects, rooted in deficit self-love, tore at the fabric of the traditional couple. Society and the next generation lost too. Dissatisfied breadwinners not only failed to make the contribution that was dormant within them, but (perhaps worse) also role-modeled disaffection to their boys, in many cases raising yet another crop of working stiffs. And though we speak of it in the past tense here, the male family-for-mission tradeoff is still pervasive today.

As for mothers, Western and Eastern civilizations have long mythologized childrearing as the adult female's natural and principal vocation. For several decades, however, this traditional premise has been disputed around the world. Indeed, educated and uneducated stay-at-home mothers alike often complain of a sense of purposelessness not unlike the cog-in-the-wheel discontent expressed by their traditional male counterparts. The "mad" and depressed housewife is so common as to have become clichéd. And problems of purposelessness only escalate once the children are grown: the empty-nest syndrome is another unhappy consequence of the attempt to elevate motherhood alone into a mission in life.

Clearly, raising children isn't enough for women today. (Indeed, studies have long indicated that those with the highest self-esteem enjoy both family *and* career.) Nor is it enough to work at "any old thing" strictly to earn the highest wage possible (often minimum wage), as men do. In fact, many mothers who work for the paycheck only thoroughly resent the fact that they can't be at home. While not having the *choice* to be at-home moms causes much of this bitterness, what's most devastating is that *the work itself is joyless.*

Overcoming the Dominant Traditional Myth

Unquestionably, the myth of the happy householder has, in terms of passions undiscovered, been tragic for the spirit of scores of traditional partners—and continues to be so today. Still, the parenting-versus-mission dilemma was—and is—paradoxical because, after all, raising children is the ultimate grow-ourselves-up experience. Not only can it make us wise, but it can also throw open within us doors of compassion that we might not otherwise have known existed. And because higher purpose always has to do with the betterment of humanity, householding (which centers on the betterment of our own youngsters) has the potential to dramatically aid us in the discovery of that purpose. Kenneth's situation is a good example of this. Kenneth was a corporate honcho who, after the birth of his fifth child, was inspired to get his teaching credential; he quit the oil industry and now devotes the leadership—and loving-father—gifts he's developed to kids in his local elementary school.

Rosemonde, twenty-four, is another demythified traditional. Raised to be a good wife and mother, she was that—and much more. Though modesty precluded such a self-assessment, this woman was profoundly spiritual. When she wasn't caring for her three children, husband, in-laws, and parents, she volunteered as personal assistant to her minister. In her wildest dreams, kept secret even from her husband, she craved to help others find their connection to God—and actually to be ordained. But her wistful conclusion that "a wife and mother is all I'll ever be" clung to Rosemonde like a self-fulfilling prophecy. Fear clouded this would-be cleric's ability to recognize her own vocation—fear of discovering her own true identity, of competing, of failure, of being unavailable to her loved ones.

Her husband, Bret, was also able to pull himself out of the past. Although he earned a good living as foreman at his uncle's lumberyard, since childhood he'd dreamed of being a land surveyor. The mere thought of retraining, with the risks involved in giving up his job, overwhelmed him with anxiety. "We have three kids to put through private school and college," he told himself. These *could* have been his final words on the subject, as they often are for couples unfamiliar with the eighth New Law of Love. Fortunately, however, when Rosemonde and Bret were taught about every human's—and partner's—higher-order need for a mission in life, they quickly caught the wisdom and logic of prioritizing their personal visions. "We deserve it," Rosemonde asserted, "and our children need positive role-modeling."

Rarely have we seen the deleterious effects of a neglected mission in life surface so poignantly as among the mates of professionals, military employees, and diplomatic officials stationed abroad. These expatriate wives seem to have it all: luxury cars, country club memberships, exotic travel opportunities, unlimited world-class shopping, and lavish homes— all courtesy of their husband's plush overseas contract. Virtually all have live-in maids; some even have drivers. The traditional wife's dream come true—or so the myth would have us believe.

Droves of these "lucky" women have ended up in our office, depressed, angry, and lost. Typically, their depression has confused them and baffled their spouse ("What's there not to like?"). Their anger has generally been directed at their husbands ("The children and I hardly ever see him anymore"). Creative, intelligent, and multitalented, most such women we've spoken with have insisted that they're content to be wives and mothers.

Vocationally, these intrepid globetrotters have represented a broad spectrum of awareness. Some have strongly identified with a traditional role; a handful have interrupted work that manifested their mission (or training that prepared them for it) to "trail" their husbands. The majority, however, have been simply unaware of the higher-order need for mission in life and have never seriously considered developing their own gifts or dreams.

Beth, a forty-five-year-old homemaker, came to us with what she diagnosed as a bad case of culture shock, though she'd already been overseas for two-and-a-half years—well beyond the average duration of this malady. Her husband, Lars, loved his exotic post: his salary was almost double what it had been at headquarters, and he enjoyed the travel throughout Asia that made up seventy percent of his work. Occasionally, Beth and the kids would join him at a five-star resort for a weekend, but for the most part he traveled alone or with colleagues.

Since childhood Beth had dreamed of an academic career, but she'd never gone to college. Before their posting abroad, she'd worked at a part-time job in sales that paid handsome commissions. Now she wasn't working outside the home. "I'd still love to get my BA," she said, "but my husband doesn't think it would be a good idea for me to go back to school now. We're saving to put the kids through college, you know. Anyway, Lars has enough to worry about without adding me to his list." Though she took her husband's side, loss was written in her eyes. "Everyone is so used to having me at home. I'm a really good cook, you know," she added. Still, Beth was perplexed by her eldest son's behavior. "Jason got so angry the other day, he screamed at me to 'get a life.' It seems he's the only one in the family who doesn't want to be my career."

Beth mentioned one day, with little-girlish pride, that she'd taken one college course—an evening class in literature, her field of interest—and had received an A-plus. She said she'd always been—and would continue to be—curious how her life might have unfolded had she completed a degree, although she insisted that it didn't matter. Rundown and despairing, at one point she actually blamed herself for being "a used spare part." We suggested couple counseling. She said that her problem had nothing to do with him—and he agreed.

Despite the marital roadblock, Beth was undeterred in coming every week to work on her low self-love, which inevitably led back to the constricting myth of the rich, happy housewife. She came to see that what she'd originally mistaken for culture shock was actually what we call *premission existential angst*—her intuition communicating the truth of her deeper self. When angst of this sort arises, it's a powerful signal that shouldn't be misinterpreted or ignored. And yet clearly hearing our intuition is a function of high self-love. Only after months of work to elevate her self-love was Beth ready to face head-on the pain of her sidelined aspirations—and to apply the wisdom of the eighth New Law of Love.

This brave work was interrupted when her husband's company announced the family's immediate transfer to Saudi Arabia. To our delight, we received a note from Beth some months later. This housewife was now a student in a correspondence course, working toward her BA; although Lars wanted to pay, Beth was financing it herself by working part-time as a secretary. Her postscript: "I know he's upset with himself for discouraging me, or he'd never have offered to help."

Sometimes traditional spouses disparage their other half's urge toward meaningful work as self-indulgent or dismiss it as "just a phase" or perhaps a midlife crisis. John's case was classic. At fifty-five, when his kids left home, he turned morose. His bowling buddies helped him figure out what was wrong: he'd had enough of the nine-to-five grind. His true desire was to move to the mountains and join a ski patrol. He knew that his wife would flip, but he mentioned the idea over dinner one night anyway. Sure enough, at first Gillian interpreted both John's descent into the dumps and his plan to recover from it as "pure selfishness." His subsequent withdrawal from her disturbed her enough that she eventually felt motivated to examine her own underlying button. "I never thought I had the right to do what I loved, and I guess I wanted company," she confessed. "He's right: we're finally free, and I intend to start dreaming myself."

An Invitation to Reflect on the Law of Mission in Life as It Pertains to Your Parents

- What were your parents' limiting beliefs with regard to mission in life and partnership? Do any of these match the beliefs mentioned above? How did limiting beliefs affect your parents' self-love? Their emotional intimacy? How did the situation make you feel?
- Did your parents support each other's mission in life? How did their support (or lack of it) affect their self-love? Their emotional intimacy? How did it make you feel?
- How would your childhood have been different had your parents subscribed to the Law of Mission in Life? How would your own couple be different (or, if you're single, how would past relationships have been different)?

MISSION IN LIFE AND THE NEW COUPLE

As women have fewer children and live longer lives, their loving creativity is rising like an irresistible tide of desire to express and find their purpose in the world. . . . The drive is eventually as powerful as the drive to reproduce. It is the supra-sexual drive to evolve ourselves. . . . The cocreative couple forms the basic family unit of the cocreative society, that is neither matriarchy nor patriarchy, but partnership . . .
BARBARA MARX HUBBARD, *Conscious Evolution*

So what's the mutually self-actualizing couple like? Who might be exemplars of this New Couple ideal? The pharaonic couples of ancient Egypt, positioned shoulder to shoulder, heads held high, seem to represent the dual-mission dyad, at least in effigy. Rather than looking in opposite directions as "distanced" couples do, or losing themselves in each other's eyes as "enmeshed" couples do, renderings of the early Nile monarchs look straight ahead at a seemingly unified goal somewhere on the horizon. A beautiful and inspiring archetype.

But how can we make *two* dreams come true at the same time, without sacrificing the integrity of our relationship or the family? How can we avoid competing against each other, feeling threatened by our partner's obligations and successes, and stranding our children in daycare? How, in short, can we keep our families together and our wits about us with two major construction projects going up simultaneously? Well, it's not easy: *manifesting two missions in life can be the most complicated enterprise of our partnership.* Probably nothing short of a time- and emotional-management miracle on both our parts will actually do.

Nevertheless, a profusion of innovative employment and childcare practices, such as flex time, job sharing, family care, and virtual and home offices, prove that solutions to the socioeconomic obstacles to mission exist. As financial expert and visionary Robert Kiyosaki teaches, the issue is never really about money, it's about creativity—and only low self-love could convince us otherwise. All couples have a potentially infinite supply of creativity, and it's just as well, because *any* combination of two missions challenges both members of the New Couple to pull off an ingenious and dexterous balancing act. Still, it *can* and—for the sake of our love and our kids—*must* be done.

Increasing numbers of can-do couples, with and without children, provide ample living proof that it's possible. Despite the odds, these New Couples have successfully managed to hitch themselves, side by side, to their stars. And more often than not, they're pulling it off without privileged background or prodigious talent. Instead, they're daring to create *within their relationship* the right circumstances in which each partner can incubate his *and* her dreams—and make them happen.

Certainly, the Ten New Laws of Love create ideal circumstances to launch two missions. These laws help guarantee that we don't stop loving each other, put the health of the relationship on hold, or forget that accomplishing our individual missions is part of that health in the first place. The Ten New Laws of Love support us in maintaining our best-friendship status, so that (unlike rivals) we can act as each other's most trusted advisor and confidant. If there's a tendency toward workaholism, they remind us to check and balance each other.

The eighth New Law of Love helps modern mates cultivate an awareness of conventional vocation-annihilating beliefs and a determination not to be run by them. For example, New Couples don't buy into the idea that socioeconomics have them beat at the starting gate. Nor do they surrender to the other common lies: that they must choose true work *or* true love *or* children; that they have no talent and deserve no professional fulfillment; that there's room in a family for only one career; that making money doing what one loves is oxymoronic; or that "having it all" is too much for two people to juggle.

What's more, when those among us committed to this eighth New Law of Love find ourselves temporarily encumbered—as many of us do—by impossibility thinking, we're open to getting some help. The same is true when we simply don't know what on earth we're meant to do. Thank goodness, today there are many new methods to help us move through such confusion and madness.

The Dream Session

Discovering the right vocation is as momentous as finding a soulmate; and while both processes require that we follow the dictates of our heart, the identification and implementation of mission typically takes more work. As we've seen, it's an unfolding, creative process that's often rocky. Even after we think we're headed in the right direction, one or the other (or both) of us may feel stuck on the "what," "what next," or "how to" or, for whatever reason, may feel discouraged. These are critical junctures, and the support we provide each other can make the difference between success and failure. Though support can take many forms, the Dream Session is the most effective and loving way we know of to assist each other in building our dreams and working out the emotional kinks our mission might present.

Dream Sessions are just like Special Sessions except that they focus on the broad topic of our evolving purpose in life. Since Sessions are never interactive, each Speaker needs to keep him- or herself on track. The following questions help direct the broad brushstrokes of discovering and refining our mission:

- What am I doing when I'm most "in flow"?
- What am I doing when I'm feeling optimally joyful or most like my true, empowered self?
- What activities engross me so much that I lose track of time?
- If I had a magic wand, what (down to the detail) would my average workday look like? Where would I be? Would I be alone or with others? Who would these others be?
- How would I spend my life if I didn't have to worry about making money?
- Whose life do I envy? (No matter how out of reach or glamorous the careers of those we idealize—or idolize—might seem, they can serve as divining rods for our own bliss and for the ultimate harmony of our couple.)

Dream Sessions can be very energizing. We may do dozens over the life of our relationship, as the sands of our dual missions shift, each Session revealing further insight into our missions and how to manifest them. If we already know (or are engaged in a stage of) our life-work but find ourselves confused about logistics, Dream Sessions can help us determine what research we need to conduct, what issues we need to explore, and what action-plans we need to devise. This multipronged strategy can help us break through our confusion.

If this law presents any roadblocks that Dream Sessions (and the follow-up activity that they inspire) can't budge, perhaps the additional mission-in-life resources featured in Chapter 10, "Transformational Education," will provide the needed muscle.

Mission: Launched

Often our mission-in-life issues come disguised as something else. "I just need an attitude adjustment," Derek moaned during his first solo session. "Gretchen knows that something's wrong, but I just can't tell her that I hate going to work." This thirty-two-year-old tax accountant felt that he'd never be able to repay his wife, who'd supported them both as a chiropractic assistant while he was in school. The moment his accountancy practice opened—it was two years ago now—she quit, and she still talked about how much she loved not "needing" to work. Derek didn't know that he couldn't be "fixed," couldn't be made to feel comfortable in a job that simply didn't turn him on. And yet he believed that his marriage depended on this impossible adjustment.

Gretchen came to a solo session too—purely for Derek, she said. "I'd just like advice on how to help him through this bad patch," she explained. Soon, however, her patience wore thin. "I really don't get it," she snapped. "He's got a beautiful office, two assistants, and his partner is his best friend from business school. He won't talk about it, but I can tell that he's dissatisfied with work." As for her own ambitions, Gretchen claimed to have none: "I'm not the career-woman type myself." Though solidly middle class, Gretchen's parents had always been very tense about money. Somewhere inside, it relieved her to know that her husband could amply take care of them both.

Still, Gretchen spent twenty hours a week volunteering, both teaching inner-city kids how to dance and serving on a board for African-American art programs. It had never occurred to her that she might possibly get paid for doing what she loved: teaching and promoting dance. Nor was she aware of her envy of Derek's professional status. "No, really," she insisted. "I'm happy for him. He deserves it—he's worked so hard."

During their first couple session, Derek took little time to reveal the depth of his misery at work. Obviously uncomfortable, Gretchen finally bared her fears: "I can't give up dance," she cried. "I won't go back to that horrid chiropractic office."

Derek saw it first, and for him the moment was bittersweet. His wife had what he lacked: a passion. This despite the years of training and tens of thousands of dollars invested in his career. For her part, Gretchen had needed to hear Derek complain about his career to realize that she in fact desired one for herself—including all its prestigious trappings. This dream had long been buried. Gretchen's family had taught her that "making it" meant marrying a professional. She'd put in her hours, and now that Derek had arrived, so had she. Underneath these conclusions skulked the half-baked beliefs that "marriage alone fulfills" and "you can't make money doing what you love."

With her husband's support, Gretchen started working toward a master's degree in fine arts. Because her years volunteering on boards compensated for her lack of professional experience, she was able to find a part-time position as assistant to the director of a movement-therapy institute—and get paid for doing what she loved.

Eventually, Derek recognized that the mission-blocking issue for him was actually one of individuation. The real pressure to stay in his job came from his father, not his wife. "He makes such a display of pride about his son 'the professional,'" Derek said, "that I couldn't admit even to myself how unhappy I was." He'd continued his father-pleasing behavior out of toxic guilt—an inappropriate feeling of responsibility—for so long that it had nearly snuffed out any sense of what excited him. Now that his wife was focusing on her own career, which promised an eventual second full-time paycheck, Derek felt some relief. In Dream Sessions, Gretchen was able to help him explore his true direction.

Though Derek still hadn't identified his exact calling when we last saw him, he'd reconnected with a childhood fascination with Africa. Gretchen had stumbled upon an international agency that brings financial experts to developing countries to help organize cottage industries. It was looking as if he might be able to make his first trip to his great-great-grandparents' homeland as part of an economic assistance project. If that doesn't pan out, however, we know that Gretchen won't let him give up the search.

For Gretchen and Derek, identifying the problem was harder than solving it. Once their "diagnosis" was made—namely, ailing mission— they took the ball and ran with it on their own. Our work with them revealed only the beginning of their shining path. For though this might involve disorienting adjustments in income, self-image, expectations of family-of-origin, and in their relationship, it ultimately leads to true fulfillment and co-creativity.

You *Can* Win for Losing

For some of us, the ideal of mission in life burned brightly long before the life-purpose pioneers hit the scene. In our greener, idealistic days, we rushed out, hats full of stars, to change the world. But somehow we're the ones who ended up changed. Perhaps the world didn't seem quite ready for us. After taking a few hard knocks for our efforts, maybe we decided to be "realistic," opting out of what could have been truly worthy work. The negativity, self-reproach, and even self-destructiveness we now feel, having tried (and failed) to make a mark, can be fierce. And that negativity is contagious. People find it hard enough to jump through the hoops of their own mission without the heavy presence of a mate who feels burned. As the following couple *almost* found out, one dashed dreamer can easily sink a whole couple.

"Emilio's revisionist grasp of political philosophy is original and brilliant," was the comment his college professor wrote on a recommendation intended for a top midwestern university. "I expect to see him at the United Nations someday," it concluded. But Emilio never went on to graduate school. With his bachelor's degree in international relations in hand, he went straight to work for a left-wing political caucus. Within a year, however, he left, disgusted by his director's "hypocrisy."

Undaunted, Emilio soon founded an alternative newspaper. Its stance was so radical that it failed to attract advertisers and lost money every month. Just when the paper was about to fold, his girlfriend, Maddie, who was also the paper's managing editor, found herself pregnant with twins. The prospect of a surprise family obligated Emilio to get a "real" job—one that he *really* didn't like.

When we met them, it had been years since this would-be ambassador gave up the fight and settled down. Emilio was a union laborer on a construction crew. Maddie worked part-time as a copywriter in an ad agency. Though she'd been offered full-time creative positions several times, and privately craved the promotion, she dared not bring it up with her partner. Her potential clients would include multinational corporations that manufacture in developing countries, a detail that she knew would cause Emilio to see red. She knew that, as champion of the under-dog, he would see Maddie's promotion as selling out. "It's not worth the hassle," she said resignedly in her first solo session.

Despite his initial skepticism, Emilio's own therapy proved remark-ably powerful. He was amazed at the revolution in his own self-perception, and at how quickly it occurred. "I've been deluding myself," he realized during his first one-on-one session. "I thought I'd converted from ideal-ism to realism—but it was sour grapes, straight up!" Eventually, as this brilliant man's heart opened to himself, he was able to reframe all his denial, bitterness, and limited thinking as symptoms of past hurts.

For if Emilio was hard to deal with, his equally intelligent but domi-neering and sarcastic father had been impossible. And their painful rela-tionship had left Emilio with a veritable switchboard of buttons—and extreme views to go with them. "I always thought it was my foolish six-ties idealism that killed my dreams," he said. "Actually, though, it was my rage at Dad. I got into it with every father figure I could find."

Meantime, Maddie grew angry. She realized that although she'd always supported Emilio in the pursuit of his mission, he'd been nothing but an albatross around hers. Not that she'd noticed at first. After all, her interests had never stirred up much excitement in her family-of-origin either, a phenomenon typical of middle children. Fresh from his break-through, Emilio was able to be honest. "Mea culpa," he declared. "I guess I thought, 'If I'm stuck, we'll *both* be stuck.'" Armed with renewed faith, all the skills of peacemaking, and a mutual commitment to be true to their own and each other's vision, they began a new era.

A Treasure Trove Unearthed

Helping uncover the brilliant truth about each other can be an awesome event for a New Couple. When we meet, at least one of us might still be raw material, a block of marble yet to be hewn. Not unlike Michelangelo, when we're able to see in our lover the angel yet to be carved from the stone, we can help set it free.

William, an internationally known entrepreneur, was an expert at making money. Over the years he'd lost his shirt many times, only to begin again from scratch, remaking his fortune each time. The experience of crisis both humbled and energized him—and William loved it. A dozen years into his career, still clamoring for ever more wealth, he took a workshop expecting to improve his moneymaking capabilities. He discovered something even more gratifying instead—something that capitalized on other, as yet unharnessed talents: he found that he was good at helping heal others of what he called "poverty consciousness." He said that teaching others how to discover their life's purpose and create wealth for themselves fulfilled a "burning urge."

When he married, William well understood the importance of the Law of Equality. His wife, Bo, was already a successful fashion consultant with a national firm, and he knew that in fairness he had to make room for both careers. He also knew that, although Bo might hobble on forever semi-satisfied with her job, her work didn't excite her. Intuiting that his love's obscured mission would eventually pose a threat to their relationship, William vowed not to rest until that mission was revealed and realized. Bo was so inspired by both his clarity of vision and his enthusiasm for his work that she followed in his tracks. In three short years, they emancipated her "inner entrepreneur." He couldn't be prouder. "Hey," he admits, "she's better at business than I am! And not only the people-oriented stuff. Numbers, markets, financing—it all seems effortless to her." On Bo's future drawing board: a financial empowerment adult-ed curriculum for women.

Many husbands in young, single-career couples today put pressure on their wives to "do something." "She needs to stay busy; she'll get bored at home," they might say. These guys are half right: while certainly "staying busy" isn't the point, and on its own doesn't dignify anyone, no partner can neglect mission without detrimental consequences.

It takes a lot of emotional maturity to dedicate ourselves not only to our own dreams but also to those of our partner. As William and Bo so grandly teach us, we can help each other identify who we really are and support each other in never giving up. *Together* we can go down the golden road of mission in life with far more economy, potency, and fun than we can *alone*. This is the essence of the synergistic potential of the New Couple and the eighth New Law of Love.

Mission: Abetted

To our utmost surprise, following our bliss as individuals led us to each other—and almost immediately to a shared mission. Though we were fortunate to have been introduced to the concept of mission in life before we met, the struggle to find its truest expression took years; in fact, it continues today. During our initial wrestling with this issue, as individuals before we knew each other, unfinished family-of-origin emotional business contributed to our confusion. The decision to attend graduate school, where we met, was the mission-in-life turning point for each of us: we took major career and financial risks in committing ourselves to a new direction based on what gave us the most joy.

How did we reach that turning point? At precisely the same time in our lives, we had both entered a period of crisis that went beyond career to identity—what we recognize today as pre-mission existential angst, since echoed by Beth and many other clients. Though Seana had always recognized her gift for communication, she was never satisfied with her "success." After years as an editor, copywriter, and marketing executive, she decided that the thing she most wanted to sell people on was their own unlimited potential. Maurice, like his partner-to-be, had long been aware of his passion for interpersonal communication of the deepest kind, and he felt a strange incompleteness with his work as a musician. He finally realized that his greatest joy, and true mission, lay in work that involved both healing and teaching.

During our first months together, our dreams and ambitions revealed themselves to be uncannily alike. Hiking the California foothills, we spun out visions of traveling in Asia and plying our psychological skills in the international arena (though how we'd manage all this we didn't know). At the time, with graduate-school loans mounting, we could scarcely afford our own wedding. How could we have predicted the financial windfall that would come our way six months after we'd exchanged vows? Funded by that windfall, we traveled the world as we'd dreamed— twelve countries in as many months. How could we have foreseen the mysterious forces at work when, in Kathmandu, we encountered a Southeast Asian businessman who eventually paved the way for us to establish a private practice in Singapore—also part of our dream? Goethe's famous quote came ringingly true for us: "Whatever you can do, or dream you can, begin it. Boldness has genius, power and magic in it. Begin it now." We would amend it, however: *Begin it now, and nurture it as a couple.*

Twelve years later, our mission in life is to work as a couple to help other couples and single people create solid platinum partnerships that support the manifestation of their grandest dreams. We do this via our organization, NewCouple, Int'l., which promotes our writings, speaking, and NewCouple seminars. This book, seven years in gestation, is our firstborn, and one of many expressions of our mission in life. It wasn't until we dared to commit ourselves to the health of our couple—and kept fine-tuning the directions we got from our hearts—that we were able to begin actualizing our life-work. People often ask how we can tolerate so much time together. So far, it still brings us joy.

Having It All

Undoubtedly, laying the groundwork for a gratifying life together takes commitment, coordination, and an investment of time and (for most of us) education. Leaping before we look might be exciting, and sometimes even necessary, but it can create untold complications and stress, especially if we have kids. Still, our children deserve to grow up in the glow of two fulfilled parents, each of whom has quality time to spend with them. They need us both to "get a life"—in the words of our client Beth's son—for their own health as well as for ours. Obviously, the earlier in a relationship we make two missions a top priority, the better. And if we can wait to bring children into the equation until when we're *both* good and ready, better still—and certainly *easier*.

Not that it isn't possible to embark upon the life-work path after kids are present. Dimitri and Kayla were the parents of four children, two still in diapers, when they launched what they laughingly call their Grand Ten-Year Plan. And before that they spent months of research and many long nights of discussion, debate, and dreaming out loud. When these two finally pull off their dual missions, it will be the logistical coup of the century.

When this couple first attempted to formally identify what it was they wanted out of life, they realized that they already had half of their goal: four little ones—aged six months to four years—whom Kayla cared for 150 percent of the time. What they hadn't figured out yet was the career side of things. Previously a staff physiotherapist at a local hospital (and a licensed massage therapist), Kayla missed her patients; the politics and paperwork, however, she was glad to have left behind. She longed for her own private clinic where she could institute humanistic employment policies and have her babes at her heels, yet this seemed far too ambitious an undertaking. "I'll leave that one to the Bionic Woman," she muttered to herself.

Dimitri, for his part, was unhappily employed as vice principal of an elementary school. Medicine had been his first love at university, and he'd done well in his tough premed curriculum. Unfortunately, the medical schools that had accepted him were beyond his widowed mother's means. He lacked vocational guidance and didn't realize at that young age what the years would teach him: no better investment exists than training for a soul-inspired career. Daunted by the prospect of sky-high student loans, and not knowing how to think creatively about life-work planning, Dimitri rejected his "job from heaven" outright. Teaching, he concluded, would be a more pragmatic choice, so he went for his credential instead.

The teaching profession liked this would-be doctor. Before he knew it, unusual opportunities in his school district, compounded by the financial pressures of his expanding family, had conspired to promote him to the post of administrator—and chief disciplinarian! Like Kayla, he didn't like the politics of the workplace, and penalizing little ones wasn't his idea of fun. Dimitri wanted out—but how?

Five years into their shared life, both members of this love match ended up frustrated and without a hint as to how to improve their lot. They found themselves short-fused with the children and at loggerheads with each other.

Finding a way out of such a bind always demands highly creative problem-solving. But before mates can put their heads together, they must first put their hearts together. It was in couple counseling that the myth that babies bring couples together first got turned on its head for this otherwise savvy pair. It was in our office that Kayla and Dimitri came to the painful realization that since they'd become parents, their emotional intimacy had been ground to a nub. Counseling helped them untie, strand by strand, their tangled skein of years of unresolved conflict, unrestored trust. Over months of counseling they worked together to build emotional integrity, and with that progress came the power to identify and communicate needs and to negotiate to have those needs met. For the first time in their relationship, these two crafted an emotional safe zone in which to explore their missions in life.

Within that safe zone, both Kayla's and Dimitri's visions came into focus naturally. Dimitri's astonishing relief from severe migraines that plagued him his entire life under the care of an acupuncturist inspired him to study this powerful treatment—a bold first step toward his true life-work. As for Kayla, her clinic would certainly have foundered had her husband not fanned the flames of this big—but not impossible—dream. The plan was that once he'd completed his program, they'd found what would evolve into a multidisciplinary healthcare center. This decision consolidated their hopes and underscored their commitment to each other. As they moved toward their exciting nouveau mom-and-pop arrangement, Kayla and Dimitri became true partners in co-creativity.

Many people would have been deterred by the process that was to come. The "hows" of organization and planning that confronted the couple once they'd determined the "whats" of their missions were daunting indeed, as were the risks. But Kayla and Dimitri were familiar with (and understood the importance of) the various sorts of support they could get from outside their couple, and they availed themselves of these. Their Day-Timers, for starters: including three-, five-, and ten-year plans—and the multitude of "baby steps" in between—these became their bibles. Kayla's sister was a big help too. A part-time student, she traded room and board for assisting with childcare. Quarterly couple "tune-ups" with their therapist helped ensure that their intimacy didn't slip under the strain of their ambitious lifestyle. And when an osteopath Dimitri met at a healthcare marketing seminar expressed an interest in joining the practice, they welcomed her capital contribution to the venture.

From a financial point of view, this period demanded creativity and flexibility; a sense of humor didn't hurt. Dimitri's external program ran nights and weekends, allowing him to keep his salaried position for two years. Kayla took on massage clients during the day to save up for Dimitri's third year, when his internship would require that he quit the school job. Simultaneously, she began a series of evening adult-ed courses for first-time small-business owners. Ever resourceful and purposeful, she also made use of the Internet and the local university's business library to research regional trends and determine a prime location for their center.

Last year Dimitri *did* quit, and Kayla started earning a salary training interns at her old hospital on a three-quarter-time basis. It wasn't their most prosperous year, but they survived, nourished by their dreams. And now this year, Dimitri is a licensed acupuncturist. With the children old enough for daycare and school, the family is planning to move into a three-story Victorian—a move financed by the sale of their current home. The shared practice will occupy the first floor, and the family will live on the two upper floors. The kids can't wait. There's a neighborhood park nearly next door, they've been promised a puppy, and they'll be able to see their parents more than ever before.

Where there are two wills, hearts joined in love, and lots of support, there's always a way. Naturally, Kayla and Dimitri will be ironing out the logistical kinks in their co-created dreams for a long time. But they don't see that as bad news. Like many New Couples, they're taking full advantage of couple counseling, support groups, and vocational guidance. What's more, by following their bliss, they're actually helping others with similar hopes. How so? They're powering the trend toward home offices, flexible work schedules, creative childcare, and entrepreneurial schemes for partners—all great solutions for couples with children. Together, they're able to stay focused on their purpose despite the inevitable ups and downs—*even without any guarantee that their clinic will ever get off the ground.* This New Couple knows that the choice is simple: it's either risk the success and fulfillment of their missions in life, or accept the certainty of not trying. Fed by their emotional intimacy and energized by visions that thrill them, Dimitri and Kayla are handling the risks just fine. And their kids have never been happier, thriving in an environment where parents love both each other *and* what they do.

Whereas in our parents' and grandparents' days, this eighth New Law of Love may have appeared extraterrestrial, its time is finally here and now. A healthy unwillingness to overlook talents, miss opportunities, and dissipate love in uncreative busywork is rising like a groundswell under the feet of partners everywhere. Clearly, we're ready to commit to real work that not only inspires, but also makes a difference—improving both home and world. As for home, the impact of two missions per family on the institution of marriage promises to be as awesome as that of state-of-the-art parenting on the next generations of children. As for the world, it will be transformed. As religious leader and philosopher Matthew Fox says, the real crisis in our day is one of work, especially what we're willing to do for money—and the effect our decisions have on our environment, our social systems, our economy, and our children. When we partners support each other in doing what serves each of us best—and therefore helps everyone else—our world will be well on its way to a more hope-filled future.

The impulse toward a mission in life is a watershed for every individual and a hallmark of the co-creativity stage of relationship—something to be celebrated by every couple. Though we yearn for unique identity, few of us have been taught how to find our dreams or how to manifest them, step by step, once found. Nor have we been coached in how to remain resilient and focused in the face of setbacks, confusion, and the *error* part of trial-and-error. But it's the *intention* to commit to a noble direction that counts, and our tomorrows, like all long-range projects, must be seeded today.

Discovering and fleshing out the dual missions within *your* couple will be a lifelong journey. It's never too early—or too late—to discover your mission in life, whether individually or jointly. And if mission falls dormant in either or both of you at any point in your shared life, you can commit to bring it to blossom again—*together!*

The Key to Mission in Life

Committing to discovering and fulfilling your purpose in life is the key to the eighth New Law of Love.

This means . . .

- Doing work that you're passionate about and that contributes to the greater good
- Supporting your partner in efforts to do the same

9 . WALKING
the ninth new law of love

. . . But let there be spaces in your togetherness,
And let the winds of the heavens dance between you.

Love one another, but make not a bond of love:
Let it rather be a moving sea between the shores of your souls.
Fill each other's cup but drink not from one cup.
Give one another of your bread but eat not from the same loaf.
Sing and dance together and be joyous, but let each one of you
    be alone,
Even as the strings of a lute are alone though they quiver with
    the same music.
Give your hearts, but not into each other's keeping.
For only the hand of Life can contain your hearts.
And stand together yet not too near together:
For the pillars of the temple stand apart,
And the oak tree and the cypress grow not in each other's
    shadow.

KAHLIL GIBRAN, *The Prophet*

Granted, most of us know by now that to stay with someone until death does us part is potentially hazardous to our health; that the undying devotion celebrated in Top Forty songs, romance novels, and television soaps is the stuff of fantasy; that the super-responsible hero husband who rescues the sweet but dependent wife is a tired traditional myth; and that, on a more pragmatic note, to commit to our beloved in such a way that we open-endedly relinquish financial responsibility for our own person is a recipe for ruin. We're only too aware that in this crazy world, *anything* can happen—and each one of us needs to be able to generate our own decent income.

Certainly, when we fall in love, we're in a state of intoxication, pure and simple, and our good judgment, even our basic notions of self-care, may temporarily go down the drain. Inarguably, such spells of lovesickness, of thinking he's our knight, she's our baby, are wonderful, sometimes even divine. And the long era when guys paid all the bills had its practical, sensible place in history. The Law of Walking accepts all that as a given. What it's concerned with is exposing the age-old elephants in the living room—the unhealthy emotional and financial dependencies that allow lower-order, survival-based needs to run our relationships. The ninth New Law of Love—*the willingness and ability to walk, should it cease to be self-loving for us to remain*—is designed to prevent such dependencies, to keep us from maintaining a relationship for all the wrong reasons, and to promote healthy interdependence. Our litmus test for this interdependence is whether or not we're able to create and stand by the core agreements discussed in Chapter 6.

Remember that all people have both higher-order needs (for self-love, emotional intimacy, and mission in life) and lower-order needs. This latter category has two subsets: physical needs (for food, shelter, and bodily safety) and emotional needs (for a sense of belonging to both parents and "tribe"). Over the years, the lower-order needs spawned couple traditions that in our era are no longer either beneficial or pragmatic. Though lower-order needs have theoretically all been met for many of us in this so-called advanced culture, we haven't completely rid ourselves of the psychological sense that they're still unfulfilled. Our popular culture doesn't help: it continues to fan the flames of our dependencies, presenting as entertainment the old dramas of marital helplessness, guilt trips, and duty-bondage. These dependencies crowd the cinema screens, knock at therapists' doors, and continue in many and varied ways to contaminate the purity of couple love. And frankly, the more hurt we are, the more we buy into what they're selling.

Regardless of the material splendor that might surround us, emotionally we're bumped back into survival mode every time transference comes up with anyone. The real villain, as always, is low self-love. It convinces us that (1) we're incapable of taking care of ourselves materially and will end up destitute if we try, (2) we'll be abandoned or rejected if we assert our true selves, or (3) we'll be punished with some awful combination of both. As these fears crystallize into unconscious blocks and self-fulfilling prophecies, we partners end up either living out our worst nightmare, or (more commonly) living in paralytic fear that our prophecies will come about.

If lack of self-love weren't at issue, we'd be in touch with our natural genius and lovability from the start; we'd have no problem figuring out how to adequately provide for ourselves—materially *and* emotionally. But it *is* at issue; and because of it, our lower-order needs have devolved in our romantic relationships into now-obsolete emotional and economic dependencies that activate patterns of self-destructiveness in both women and men. Given the power of those dependencies to ruin lives and love, the ninth New Law of Love draws a line in the sand: *we can't really say yes until we're able to say no.*

WALKING: A POSITION OF THE HEART

How, then, is prescribing being willing and able to walk different from prescribing separation or divorce? Paradoxical as it may seem, the Law of Walking functions more as a safeguard for the healthy longevity of our relationship than as a license to leave it. For leaving and *being willing and able to leave* are as different as passion fruit and oysters. Willingness and ability to walk is a state of mind, a position of the heart—and the ultimate act of self-love. While we never use this law to threaten, manipulate, or punish our beloved, *meaning it* is its power. Like the martial artist who's never been in a fight, if we're ready to act in defense of our healthy needs, most likely we'll never need to.

Jewel meant it. She didn't fancy Bennie's flair for the dramatic. After his second blowup in a shopping mall, she moved into the guest room and informed Bennie that if he didn't get help managing his anger, she'd move back in with her former roommate, a friend from work. Her plans to go were already in place; she'd spoken with her friend and knew that she'd be welcome at her apartment. That was five years ago, and Bennie still thanks her. "If Jewel hadn't thrown down the gauntlet—and I hadn't learned to fight fair," Bennie later remarked, "I'd have ended up like my father, embarrassing and scaring the people I love. All my previous girlfriends had let me get away with it."

The ninth New Law of Love asks us to commit to developing the level of self-love that Jewel enjoys—to get to the point where we're able, from time to time, to honestly reassess our relationship. This means being able to comfortably ask ourselves, *Is this relationship still good for me? Do its challenges contribute to my self-actualization, or do they inhibit me? Am I inspired to grow and is my sense of self expanding, or do I feel compromised and limited? Does this relationship support who I really am and who I want to become?*

What Walking Isn't: The Nonsolution of Leaving

Certainly, as we all know only too well, leaving is an already overused solution, with one in two American marriages ending in divorce. But we can't stress it enough: *we're not talking about leaving.* We're talking about the *willingness and ability* to leave. The fact is a good number of us in that fifty-percent-divorce camp don't *walk* out of our relationships anyway—we *run.* And most of us give up without getting good help. In other words, we're not coming from a position of *willingness and ability* in the first place.

Bolting is frequently the result of not having been willing and able to take care of ourselves from the very beginning. We may, for example, have failed to set boundaries or define and communicate our needs—sometimes even the most basic needs, such as our need for sexual exclusivity or our need not to be put down. Indeed, we may have lacked the requisite self-love to be able to create *any* conditions for relationship whatsoever (even in our imagination), let alone core agreements. Without those boundaries and conditions to communicate and defend our self-respecting bottom line, our only defense alternative when we're under siege is to pull out the big guns. But "I don't love you anymore" is an awful way to tell our mate that our needs aren't being met. And it's a shocking way to learn the news.

In some ways, divorce might seem to be the modern solution to our marital problems—an affirmation that we can stand alone and don't need to rely on the couple—but of course it's not. Even those of us who ultimately bolt don't usually arrive at the decision quickly or easily. And the process itself is excruciating; in fact, it can bring up almost as much fear and grief than the prospect of death itself. What's more, as everyone knows, broken marriages create chaos for our whole society, not to mention for our kids. No, divorce isn't a *solution*. It's simply the only recourse most of us are aware of when we don't know how to figure out, and then directly communicate, what we really need in order to stay in trust and in love with another person—especially when material or psychological dependencies get in the way.

Daphne could never bring herself to tell Eban how much his incessant teasing and "constructive criticism" hurt and shamed her. Instead, she prided herself on being a good sport. From her clothes to her hair to the way she drove, her husband had an opinion—or a joke—about everything. "He's only trying to be helpful," Daphne would say. "Anyway, he's really funny." For two years this pattern continued, until one day Daphne accepted an invitation to lunch with a "super-sweet" guy in the office. The two never made it back to work that afternoon, nor did Daphne make it back to Eban. "I guess I never really loved him in the first place," she commented later. "It was just a big mistake."

For Eban, however, the loss and shock of Daphne's about-face was devastating. It forced him to take a long look at the "wittiness" he'd inherited from his mother's side of the family. "I've always been proud of my sense of humor. I didn't know that it was abusive to Daphne," he said, perplexed. "But come to think of it, it really bugged me when Mom used to do that to Dad—especially when he'd just shrug it off. I loved the guy, but it was kind of pathetic."

Regrettably, Daphne had never been taught how to recognize acted-out anger or take care of herself in the face of it. Until she hit bottom, it had been easy to rationalize Eban's behavior; after all, compared to her mother's rages, it was mild. But the real problem in her relationship with Eban was that, like countless others before her, she'd succumbed to the pressure of her family and peers to "find somebody"; this had led Daphne to hop into, and then out of, what sociologists today call a "trial marriage," before she knew herself or her own healthy limits.

Here's the irony: though it was Daphne who left in the end, she was afraid to tell Eban to quit harassing her lest *he* run off. It was dependence, not love, that kept her lips sealed. In the end, recognizing that she preferred sweetness over criticism, and having the courage to act on this preference—that is, to walk out—was Daphne's best shot at loving herself. And she's learned in the process. Her new relationship is based on love, not dependence. To ensure that it stays that way, she's embracing the Law of Emotional Integrity and this ninth New Law of Love (as well as the other eight!). Her beau knows that any form of acted-out anger is not okay, and that compulsive teasing is a walking matter for Daphne.

Others of us aren't as fortunate as Daphne. Lacking insight as to why our first marriage foundered, some second-timers plunge into an identical mess; others take a reactionary swing, bonding with what they hope is an opposite type of person. The song, however, is the same—and the dance toward separation begins anew. Thus, in addition to outrageous divorce rates, we have equally discouraging success rates on second marriages.

This is *not* to say that divorce is never appropriate. As every good physician can confirm, sometimes it's necessary to amputate. But divorce is tragic when, with foresight, it could have been avoided—in other words, when it's the result of failing, at the beginning of our relationship, to examine potential areas of emotional or financial dependence (areas that might inhibit us from knowing our needs and seeking to have them met) and then set basic conditions for our relationship.

What Walking Isn't: The Nonsolution of Staying

We hate the pain of divorce. Still, longevity in and of itself *is not a virtue.* It's equally tragic when we stay with someone despite severe dysfunction—until our relationship kills us or death really does break us apart. That sort of hanging on by the fingernails poisons our whole family and can do a worse number on the kids than divorce itself. Like those who separate due to unaddressed dependencies, we hangers-on also often refuse to avail ourselves of even the gentlest outside help. Our problem is that, seized by survival fears from the get-go, we're unwilling and unable to leave, and this keeps us from having a healthy bottom line. No one taught us the age-old wisdom that the best way to hold onto something is to be *willing and able* to let it go; that when we face the fears involved in surrendering something dear to us—even the love of our life—those fears don't have to turn into self-fulfilling prophecies.

DEPENDENCIES:
WHEN WE WON'T ROCK THE BOAT

Whether it's our style to cut and run or to insist that what has no life breathes still, the underlying problem is always the same: our fear of rocking the boat. And yet the only reason a few waves are so scary is that we're dependent on our partner, whether emotionally, financially, or both. Often we just feel safer leaving things somewhat vague, for when we honestly communicate our terms, our core conditions, we expose the parameters of our relationship. *This alone can seem to threaten its existence.*

So what could make our financial or emotional dependencies so strong that we're afraid to put out what we need? The cause, as you may have guessed, is invariably trauma—specifically, unhealed abandonment or survival trauma. And as we said in Chapter 3, emotional trauma bumps us down into our lower-order needs. In the case of emotional dependencies, we might be terrified that we'll be abandoned by our mate (our symbolic parent, thanks to transference) or that a failed marriage will cause us to be rejected by other people—namely, our tribe. If our problem is material dependency, the terror is that we won't have what we need to make it as physical beings. Either way, on some level it feels as if *we can't survive without this other person.* Dependent on the relationship, we're therefore desperate for it not to end; so we withhold from each other precisely the information we both need in order to nourish our chemistry and keep our relationship healthy and well.

But Don't We Know Better?

Like all the previous trauma discussions in this book, these revelations seem to fly in the face of our contemporary image of ourselves. And it's true: most of us *are* generally pretty savvy on the subject of personal power and autonomy, both monetary and psychological. These are goals we aspire to, at least in theory. After all, don't we already know a lot about dependencies? Didn't the feminist revolution dramatically bring home to us the disastrous impact, especially on women, of delegating responsibility for our material well-being to another? And as for emotional dependencies, didn't the recovery movement indelibly name not only chemical addictions for us, but also the "people addiction" of codependence (the kind of emotional dependency in which we're preoccupied with another as a way to avoid ourselves)? Robin Norwood let loose a can of worms—and clearly struck a nerve—when, more than a decade ago, she wrote her bestseller on this relationship scourge, entitled *Women Who Love Too Much*.

Natalie, who struggled in her recovery from codependence, was caught in the revolving door of walking: no sooner was she out than she was in again. It would be precisely two weeks after recommitting to work on their relationship that her husband, Russ, would start to get irritable. He'd then dismiss all their New Couple agreements—including the agreement to use peacemaking tools—and begin scaring the kids with his temper all over again. Natalie would pack bags for herself and the kids and move to a hotel just in time for Russ to declare anew his intention to stick with the program.

Just as some of us were feeling that Norwood's book, and our own experience, had confirmed that women were the clingy, suffocating ones, the *real* codependents, a profusion of later titles—including *Against the Wall: Men's Reality in a Codependent Culture,* by John Hough and Marshall Hardy—taught us about the male version of this gender-neutral emotional illness. We saw how men's codependence played out at work, in men unconsciously driven to win the approval of male colleagues and superiors—stand-ins for their dads. Leon, for example, would do absolutely anything for his boss. And whenever the older man praised him for a job well done, it was as though Leon were ten years old again, only this time his father was at the ballpark cheering his grand slam.

Further reading taught us that men were acting out codependently at home as well, sometimes taking "too much care" of their girlfriends and wives. On the home front, they exhibited not only the standard codependent placating behavior, but also the far more complex (and perhaps more typically male) "allergy to intimacy" that shows up as shutting down, distancing, or bolting. Men develop these maneuvers when little boys as a response to being emotionally "smothered" or made to caretake a parent, usually a mother, in obvious or subtle ways. What most of us don't realize is that these parental triggers are actually forms of abandonment: parents who smother or demand caretaking are needy, not nourishing; they're not "there" emotionally for their kids.

Boys who live with that sort of abandonment grow into men who keep thick walls around themselves or withdraw reflexively when confronted with even healthy emotional expression. They've got quick reflexes around any behavior in a partner that remotely resembles neediness. And yet they're needy themselves: like all of us suffering from early abandonment, these cool guys are emotionally dependent. The only difference is that because they're twice shy, they hide—that is, shut down, distance, or bolt—preemptively, lest they get burned again.

Clyde fell into the category of distancer, although when we mentioned that his behavior might relate to emotional dependence, he thought we were kidding. "Who me, dependent?" he asked incredulously during his first session with his fiancée, Rhona. "How can I be emotionally dependent when I need my space so badly that it's a constant source of static between us?"

All healthy adults routinely need time alone, yet if we were emotionally suffocated by our caregivers as children, we can't help but transfer the problem onto our mate—which makes our need for breathing room feel gargantuan. While we'll eventually have to work through the transference and the underlying trauma, we *still* need our space, and we must honor that need. This is where Clyde's dependence revealed itself: even though his need might have been excessive, he didn't make it known at the *beginning* of the relationship. His dependence was hidden in the action he *didn't* take—namely, not letting Rhona know that his need for private time wasn't optional. Clyde was careful not to rock the boat, and he ended up with a big, unruly issue as a result.

Like many distancers, Clyde might say that he didn't realize time to himself would be such an intense need until he was well into the relationship, or that he'd never been taught to negotiate. Alternatively, his justification might be that he *had* brought it up, but his girlfriend had been so hurt (or angry) with this perceived rejection that pushing for solitude simply wasn't worth it. Distancers can't tolerate reactions of hurt or anger in others, because their young selves feel threatened that they'll lead their partner to leave *them*. If not for that fear, such men (and more and more women in this category) would stay the course and simply insist that their partner negotiate so that privacy needs get met.

This terribly common couple dilemma veils distancers' dependence on their partners. It not only falsely stereotypes them as more independent, but also scapegoats their mates—traditionally women—as the *only* emotionally dependent ones. The reality, however, is that *both* suffer from emotional dependencies; in fact, as we noted earlier, they're dependent *to precisely the same degree.*

The key to peace for Clyde and Rhona were the peacemaking tools that ultimately led to the raising of each partner's self-love. Clyde did his part by acknowledging his transference and healing the troubled history with his mother. (Rhona's work looked much the same.)

An Invitation to Reflect on the Law of Walking

As you approach the exercises in this chapter, remember that the presence or absence of New Couple chemistry profoundly affects a couple's experience with each law.

- In what ways are you emotionally dependent on your partner? How does this affect your self-love? Your emotional intimacy?
- What childhood circumstances could have contributed to your emotional dependencies?

If, on the other hand, our dependencies run toward matters material, you can bet that the issue is nearly the same. The only difference is that now the child part of us feels threatened about its *physical* well-being; in other words, the lower-order survival needs for eating, being sheltered, or staying safe are kicking in. Again, early trauma is to blame—in this case, survival trauma. Whether that trauma was literal (such as losing our house through repossession or fire) or abstract (such as perceiving and absorbing our parents' Depression-era anxieties), it has powerful long-term effects on our ability to create or stand by self-loving conditions for relationship.

Thanks to gender conditioning, one of the ways men typically deal with their survival fears is by becoming frenetic wage-earners. Some women also choose that "male" route, becoming super-achievers and creating security for themselves. More typically, though, women fall under the spell of the trance of tradition by becoming financial dependents. Thirty years into the women's movement, the monkey is still on our back: the fact of "women who earn too little" is still an ongoing crisis. Indeed, every day countless women enter romantic unions in a relative financial fog, while others, often with dependent children, find themselves penniless due to divorce or desertion.

These "survivors" are especially vulnerable to the traditional good-wife-and-mother myth—which can victimize them yet again. That myth persuades them not to take out financial insurance against the success of their relationship—in other words, not to provide themselves (or their children) with the backup of their own marketable skills.

Sara, a bright, fiery woman, consciously decided not to go to college because it was, and had always been, her plan to get married, preferably to an older man. As the good-wife-and-mother myth would have it, there would be no risks involved. Sara's beloved, Isaac, beautifully fit the bill: a high-earning and loving man ten years her senior, he'd long looked forward to playing the traditional role of provider. What a setup for both of them! Sara would learn the hard way that having a financially solvent husband doesn't mean that "Daddy's home" (as the old song goes) to provide for all earthly necessities; Isaac would find out that being sole breadwinner doesn't guarantee hero status. Only three years into their relationship, the winds of fortune shifted and Isaac lost his job. With two babies in tow, the couple were forced to move into her parents' home. Sara now resents having to work as a receptionist, and Isaac wishes he'd married somebody who could "pull her own weight."

As we've said, and Sara and Isaac so sadly demonstrate, none of us escaped as children the early scenarios that lead adults to feel bereft of resources, inadequate, or uncherished—and subsequently dependent in various ways. Understanding the roots of this kind of human frailty helps partners develop compassion about dependencies, whether our own or each other's. If, for example, our partner was shamed while learning to read, she might end up disliking school, avoiding higher education, and concluding that she could never support herself. Then, like Sara, she might unconsciously react by seeking out a wealthy man to lean on. Or if our mate was esteemed by his parents only when he performed well in school and sports, he might choose Isaac's course, fearing that he couldn't attract a woman except as provider.

When Sara and Isaac finally felt safe enough to tell each other about these bits of their histories, a new empathy emerged for their current predicaments, which they now understand as symptoms of their pasts. Whatever the source of our partners' dependencies, we must never mislabel them as weakness. Instead, they must be known for what they are: unhealed childhood dents in our self-confidence that end up as craters in our self-love.

An Invitation to Reflect on the Law of Walking

- Are you financially dependent on your partner? If so, is this truly a temporary situation? How does financial dependency affect your self-love? Your emotional intimacy?
- What childhood circumstances could have contributed to your financial dependencies?

Damaged Discernment

The first step toward developing compassion for ourselves about our dependencies is *recognizing* those dependencies—not an easy task. It takes a tremendous amount of self-love and, yes, guts to face the fact that we're dependent on a relationship—especially if it's hurting us. Denial, rationalization, and minimization are emotional dependence's favorite disguises. They raise our threshold for pain and numb us to the unacceptability of our situation. The more intense our abandonment trauma, the stickier these psychic glues, and the more confused we'll be. Indeed, emotional dependence damages our discernment. We end up unable to determine what we want or need, incapable of recognizing when we should say no, insist on fairness, get help, or walk.

Extreme circumstances have an advantage, odd as that may seem. When our relationships are glaringly unhealthy, the situation black and white, the pain usually becomes more quickly undeniable. Substance abuse, infidelity, and violence leave little room for positive interpretation. That's why the Law of Peacemaking presents these transgressions as the center of the New Couple's core agreements.

Naomi was introduced to the power of core agreements by their absence. Orphaned as a child and raised in foster homes, she so feared that Ella would leave her that she tolerated her lover's yearlong affair with her best friend. Eventually, however, Naomi did get up the pluck to tell Ella exactly how she felt, describing the anger, the hurt, and the shame. To her shock, her courageous communication was met with a drink—in her face. Still, Naomi hung in. It wasn't until the lives of her own kids from a former marriage were risked by her partner's drunk driving that Naomi herself sobered up. Naturally, Naomi had to grieve her relationship with Ella, but by facing her dependencies, she gave her self-love a giant boost. As for her next relationship, her core conditions have been created in advance: she's insisting on a relationship built on sexual exclusivity, nonviolence, and a commitment to remaining substance-free.

Unfortunately, the most destructive emotional dependencies are subtle. Problems are usually quietly and systematically denied—often for an astonishingly long time. Angelica stayed with her emotionally unavailable husband ("Oh, you know how men are") until, after twenty years of marriage, he declared the relationship dead and left *her*. Not surprisingly, she came out of the shakedown feeling liberated. Three years later, she's a new person. "I realize now that I was there in body only. Knowing that, I'm actually grateful to him for leaving."

Transcending Depending

All this knowledge about the universality of dependencies notwithstanding, *insight isn't healing* (as Sigmund Freud first observed), though we wish it were. Beneath all our dependencies hides that mildly to severely traumatized inner child, quaking in fear that everything will be taken away again, or that we'll be abandoned. Until the trauma is healed for that inner child, our dependencies will continue to bruise us. But as we saw in earlier chapters, the healing of early trauma takes not only emotional integrity and the willingness to work through transferences; it also demands time and a heartfelt commitment from both of us.

Say we make that commitment to deal with our dependencies and embark on the road to true interdependence, undertaking to heal our emotional and survival fears. How exactly do we proceed? Well, while nothing will happen overnight, this book has everything partners need to make a powerful start. The good news is that when as a couple we embrace the other nine New Laws of Love, our healing begins, and we're automatically on our way to healthy autonomy.

Picking a partner based on chemistry keeps us from focusing on attributes, such as wealth and status, that could foster dependencies. Priority helps us identify the behaviors that allow us to avoid our feelings, while emotional integrity teaches us how to express and manage those feelings. Deep listening keeps the air clear between us and tunes up our trust, while equality averts buildups of injustice, gross and tiny. Peace-making gives us agreements so that we can get specific about our bottom lines, and self-love first shows us the nature of that which still scares us from the past and then helps us dissolve such hurts. Mission in life makes sure that we do something that matters, which builds our confidence to provide for ourselves in a joyful (but still material) way. And whatever dependencies we can't make healing headway with using *these* laws, we tackle with transformational education.

An Invitation to Reflect on the Law of Walking

- In what ways are you and your partner interdependent? How does this affect your self-love? Your emotional intimacy?

WALKING PAST AND THE TRADITIONAL COUPLE

Literature often captivates us with extreme remedies to miserable marriages. Certainly Tolstoy's Anna Karenina opted to "walk" after a fashion: she dived under a train. The vivid memories some of us have of our parents, however, aren't so entertaining. Some of us grew up under the cloud of a long-suffering marriage that never got a proper burial, a marriage that withered because our parents wouldn't or couldn't stand by what they wanted in life or love. Others of us grew up in homes that were broken because these same needs were expressed only when it was far too late.

In the early days, willingness and ability to walk—and the emotional and financial autonomy that combination represents—would have been antithetical to the purpose of marriage itself, which was largely to institutionalize the meeting of lower-order needs. Pressured by social convention, most traditional couples married for the express purpose of willingness and ability to survive—and be survived. And for this to work, it was necessary for our forebears to commit to a union for life. Though rigid, this arrangement enjoyed its place in the evolution of male-female relationships and obviously achieved its ends.

Later, in Western society, men and women started to marry for love. At first the love match was considered revolutionary. Those who dared attempt it were the first-wave New Couples. These latter-day traditionals were free to choose from their hearts. It could be said that the romantic traditional couple was granted a new freedom: to fall both in—and out—of love. And if precious love ever got lost, the partners didn't "have to" stay.

Some left and some didn't. What determined the choice? Their range of reasons for separation or staying was as wide as the sea. Whether they left their marriages or not, though, the crucial questions are these: Were they willing and able to walk *while they were together?* Did those who stayed recognize their own needs and have boundaries and conditions (at least in their minds) for staying in their relationships? Would these traditional spouses have been capable of taking self-loving action were these boundaries transgressed?

We all know that the sad answer to these questions, more often than not, would have been no. Though romantic traditionals married for love, "Know thyself" and "To thine own self be true" were hardly the catchwords of the day. And the early institution of marriage still locked our even recent ancestors into roles related to survival—that is, to the lower-order needs for food, shelter, safety, and belonging. The higher-order needs for self-love, emotional intimacy, and mission in life were still only a twinkle in society's eye; in fact, such personal objectives would very likely have been viewed as fanciful, if not self-indulgent.

Furthermore, even those needs that were acknowledged weren't translated into agreements. Beyond the *big* agreement—that couples stay together for life—there was no structure to protect a wide spectrum of individual values and goals, from monogamy and nonviolence to the pursuit of individual dreams. Lacking such explicit core agreements, husbands in the past might have ended up wondering if their wives had always been true; wives perhaps finished their lives stifling remorse over creative gifts unopened.

Eventually, the survival imperative softened. Women started working, alimony allowed a financial freedom of sorts, and divorce came into vogue. Naturally, the drive to procreate was in no way lessened, however, so children had to be taken into account. Though the traditional shackles of marriage had been loosened, couples were often loathe to break up (even when divorce might have been the healthiest option) because to do so would violate the integrity of the family. "Staying together for the kids" justified the preservation of countless embattled and lifeless marriages, just as having children was some couples' tragic answer to chemistry gone dry. An unquestioned societal and religious norm, the child-rationalized union often had the power to preclude either partner from being willing or able to walk—from being able, sometimes, even to *think* about it—regardless of the circumstances. Violence, incest, and substance addictions, and the devastating impact of such abuses, weren't good enough excuses to walk *even for those same kids*.

Claudius and Gena's devotion to their children was unparalleled: when their son and daughter hit school age, this ambitious couple attended every parent meeting, sporting event, and extracurricular activity scheduled. Children were important to their worklife too: Gena ran a daycare center out of their home, and had since their own kids were small. Their son still participated with the younger children after he got home from school.

One afternoon, Claudius came home unexpectedly during the day and had a chance to observe his wife's daycare in action. He was shocked by the punishments she had designed for the "naughty" boys; they weren't cruel, but they were sexually inappropriate. Claudius was especially concerned about their own son's participation in the group. More disturbing to him was his son's recent question: "Does Mommy let you touch her *down there* too?" Claudius broached the subject with his wife that night. Gena got extremely upset—crying, blaming herself, and threatening divorce. "Hysterics" being the one thing this spouse couldn't take, he never brought it up with her again. "I just don't get it," Claudius said in counseling. "All the kids and their parents adore her. She *couldn't* be doing anything wrong. At any rate, I'd never deprive our children of their mother."

Clearly, the idea that staying together for the kids serves their emotional needs can be a grave miscalculation (even when well intentioned). But many traditional parents, like many parents today, simply couldn't conceive that *kids suffer far more in unhappily married homes than in conscientiously separated homes*. Other parents used protection of the kids as a rationalization for perpetuating a withered union. Marriages preserved for children masked not only brassbound adherence to traditional family and gender norms, but also (more to the point of our discussion of walking) deep-seated personal dependencies, whether economic, emotional, or both.

"She loves me only for my money" and "I'm just a convenience" aren't just tragicomic musings by martyred spouses: they're the result of sexist family responsibilities that have existed since anyone can remember. Still, because men generally earned the main income in traditional homes, they did have a certain edge—they were in possession of their own economic resources. Therefore, if their marriage was on the rocks, they (unlike their economically dependent wives) were ostensibly free to walk. And unquestionably, some did jump ship. Those who did so legally and through all the proper channels "paid through the nose" in alimony and child support. The deserters, on the other hand, taking advantage of the lax laws of the day, left dependent wives and children to fend for themselves. The fact remains that neither the irresponsible ones, nor those who ended up writing checks to their exes for decades, were willing and able to walk when it counted—from the *start* of the relationship.

How about the men who hung in there—those whose chemistry was killed in the power struggle but stayed in the marriage nevertheless, playing the dutiful husband? More obviously unwilling or unable to walk, these partners were victims of the mythological roles of male-provider and family-leader. In addition to their fears of the opinions of the outside world—fears, for example, of being seen as failing as a family man, being branded irresponsible, or otherwise being cast out from the tribe—these traditional breadwinners had to contend with their own often ruthless "inner sexists": they judged themselves by the balance of their bank account and their ability to provide security. If the "little woman" was valued as nurturer and sex object, then the "man of the house" got his strokes by "taking care of things," serving as a "production object"—and by simply being needed.

Indeed, when our traditional fathers were divested of their I've-got-everything-under-control, family-financier status, it could spell trauma for them. Their need to be needed was as desperate as the clamoring of the so-called needy ones at home. And that need typified husbands' emotional dependency on their wives, not to mention the John Wayne unmentionable—namely, their *own* fear of abandonment. If anything shattered the myth, traditional dads could turn depressed or self-destructive.

Following the stock market crash of '87, Saul was forced into early retirement. If it had to happen at all, the timing seemed perfect. His wife's cousin had just asked her to be his full-time bookkeeper at a salary commensurate to what Saul had earned. For this retiree, though, the new situation wasn't relaxing or exciting or even tolerable. In fact, no one could bring him out of his funk, nor was he willing to explore any new interests. Saul refused even to play golf, saying that "lumps on logs don't belong on the green."

Six months into this crisis, his wife, Sabrina, succeeded in coaxing him in to see us for "a little talk." But talk he wouldn't. It wasn't until Sabrina left the guys alone that the demons her husband was nursing emerged. Sure, he admitted, he'd gotten a bum deal at work. "But the worst thing is I don't respect myself," he said. "And I don't see how my wife can either. *You two* can't give a man a paycheck. I don't know what I'm doing here." As fate had it, Saul soon found another job. And then, with the courage of Gary Cooper in *High Noon,* he set about to smoke out and banish that inner bully who'd convinced him that a man's self-worth is a matter of economics.

Traditional wives, on the other hand, were economic dependents; they didn't "work." In their cherished roles as homemakers, they made their husbands and children their mission. Although these women enjoyed certain economic benefits, this work was unsalaried and, for the most part, uninsured. In other words, if they lost their "job"—through divorce or their spouse's death—their income stood to take a nosedive.

Given that financial constraint, the traditional wife found herself free to walk only under risky or singular circumstances. As a rule, unless she personally owned sufficient stocks, bonds, property, or cash on which to live out her years and raise and educate her kids, a walking wife risked a dramatic decline in material well-being. If she was unskilled or uneducated, alimony might be all she'd have to live on—a tenuous living at best, since her ex could be uncooperative or broke, or he could skip town. Even professional training and a university degree offered the divorcée no guarantees. The job market moved on, after all; ageism was alive and well. Perhaps a newly divorced woman could get training or go back to school. But who would provide and care for the children of a student mother—and for how many years? The economic risks alone kept the traditional wife from being *able* to walk, willing or not.

But economic dependencies weren't the only thing that trapped the traditional wife in marriage. Willingness was a rare commodity too. Even the wealthiest fell victim to the standard rash of emotional dependencies:

fear of abandonment, fear of being alone, fear of who they'd be if stripped of the mythic good-wife-and-mother status—all these weighed heavily upon them.

Learned Helplessness

At the outer limits was the ultimate inability to walk: "learned helplessness." This severe form of emotional dependency robs us of our capacity to take action on our own behalf, even in the face of danger. Because it's revealed progressively in adult relationships, the helplessness does appear to be learned; the fact is, however, this terrible emotional ill is the result of traumatic abandonment in childhood—abandonment that's later retriggered. Learned helplessness explains why wives allow themselves to be disrespected, degraded, even battered. Though the traditional wife didn't have the benefit of this psychological classification—and, in addition to the brutality at home, was frequently judged by the outside world to be morally weak—the learned helplessness syndrome is still very much with us today.

In fact, today a mild form is often found in traditional wives who start out with careers. Although financially able to walk, these women are emotionally unwilling—if not unable—to do so. As was mentioned in Chapter 5, the power struggle triggers the trance of tradition, pregnancy exacerbates that trance, and the symbolic creation of a "new family" evokes the inner child, replete with her inability for self-care. Self-love starts dropping to the cellar at that point, and personal needs are subjugated to those of the husband and family, sometimes with no bottom line in sight. In that process, formerly independent traditionals lose their autonomy and identity at home; and sometimes they lose confidence in their ability to make a living as well, as Anna (below) did.

Cinderella Awakens

Anna, a dynamic thirty-year-old former sales executive, had worked at an international shipping firm for five years before she married. As befit her profession, she was powerfully persuasive and could talk almost anyone into anything. Unfortunately, *anyone* ended up including herself. Theo, her husband of three years, was a successful private investigator capable of supporting them both in grand style; and being a traditional himself, he preferred his wife at home. Burned out on her lucrative but stressful job, Anna gave it up gladly—and substantially raised her standard of living at the same time. In counseling sessions, she'd often express pride in the many luxuries her husband's job allowed them, and in the prestige and intrigue of his work. Although Anna would never call herself a traditional wife, she seemed to delight in playing mistress of the house and devoted herself passionately to the couple's two-year-old twin boys.

Anna came to see us after a close male friend, afraid she was headed for heartache, divulged to her that Theo had a reputation as a womanizer. Anna was aware that her husband was out late most nights, of course, but she'd attributed this (as had Theo himself) to the unusual nature of his work. However, after a string of late-night telephone hang-ups, and absences at ever stranger hours, Anna finally confronted Theo. He denied any wrongdoing and dismissed the issue, his way of handling *anything* unpleasant.

At the beginning of her therapy, whenever Anna came close to admitting the plausibility of the rumors, she'd roll her eyes in exasperation. "I don't know," she'd sigh and then quickly change the subject. It began to seem as if this natural salesperson had sold herself a bum bill of goods. And though she was an ace at selling, she couldn't quite convince herself that she was worth sticking up for.

Formerly professional and solvent, Anna might seem a far cry from the dependent wife of yesteryear. Nevertheless, she wasn't initially willing or able to walk away from a relationship that was clearly destructive. Like many other "helpless" wives, she denied in her head what she knew in her heart. On the surface, her dependency appeared to be largely economic: Anna loved her life of leisure and all its status. Her fondness for the creature comforts earned her the harsh epithet of gold-digger by some less well-heeled acquaintances. While it was true that if Theo had lacked funds she probably wouldn't have married him in the first place, beneath this material dependency lay a strong emotional hook that had its roots in childhood trauma.

Anna's father provided everything an upper-middle-class daughter could want. Still, he was on the road a lot. In fact, her mother was convinced that he had another family elsewhere. Once the knot was tied with Theo, Anna did what so many of us do: without being aware of it, she tried to turn her partner into the nurturing father for whom she'd always yearned. Later, when her carriage turned into a pumpkin and Theo's untrustworthiness was revealed, she simply lied to herself. The intensity of her need—which, as we know, parallels the degree of early abandonment trauma—effectively blinded Anna to what was right in front of her: a man equally unskilled at self-loving who humiliated her, emotionally abandoned her, and unwittingly exploited her dependencies.

As Anna's therapy deepened, she developed the courage to face Cinderella in the mirror and tell her the bad news: midnight has struck; the ball is over. Though it took well over a year, she not only grieved the lifestyle and her fantasy of being cared for, but also eventually faced the original pain of her own father's neglect.

As Anna grew more empowered, she became less frightened of the consequences of confronting Theo for a second time. Finally, she summoned all her courage and did it. As partners so commonly do in such cases, he admitted that he'd been with other women, but he claimed to have cleaned up his act. Anna's reaction showed that her self-respect was well on the mend: first she asked him to move out; then she set her boundaries—she wouldn't be willing to see Theo until, through counseling, he'd gotten at the root of his capacity to lead a double life. "Or else what would keep him from doing it again?" she pointed out. After that, she told him, she'd consider attending couple counseling to determine if there was any potential for restoring trust. For her own healing, Anna decided to continue individual work and commit to a weekly women-who-love-too-much support group. Her part-time job doing public relations for a local firm added an essential practical dimension to her plan.

In his course of one-on-one therapy, Theo gratefully came to understand why his own mother tolerated his father's outrageous sexual acting out and mismanagement of anger: like his own wife, she'd suffered from emotional and financial dependencies, though far more extreme. These resulted from her escape as an infant with her family from Nazi-infiltrated Europe, and from innumerable other difficulties throughout her childhood. Regardless of the irresponsibility of his acting-out behaviors, his father had brought a paycheck home every month without fail. For the first time, Theo also clearly saw the influence that the man's dubious role-modeling had had on him: not only did he himself grow up to be a reliable provider, but he was also able to justify deceiving someone he supposedly loved.

An Invitation to Reflect on the Law of Walking as It Pertains to Your Parents

- In what ways were your parents interdependent? How did this affect their self-love? Their emotional intimacy? How did this make you feel?
- Was your mother financially dependent on your father, or vice versa? How did this affect their self-love? Their emotional intimacy? How did this make you feel?
- In what ways were your parents emotionally dependent on each other? How did this affect their self-love? Their emotional intimacy? How did this make you feel?
- What childhood circumstances could have contributed to your parents' emotional or financial dependencies?
- How would your childhood have been different had your parents subscribed to the Law of Walking? How would your own couple be different (or, if you're single, how would past relationships have been different)?

WALKING AND THE NEW COUPLE

To have a passionate marriage you've got to stand on your own two feet.
DAVID SCHNARCH, *The Passionate Marriage*

The ideal couple state is true interdependence. In that state, each of us is a financially viable, emotionally autonomous entity, and that grounding allows us to enjoy true emotional intimacy with our beloved. When as individuals we have both the *internal* stance of being *willing* to walk and the *external* stance of being *able* to walk—in other words, when we *have* enough and *are* enough *unto ourselves*—we're free to be as supportive and generous as our hearts desire, without fear of being drained of our energy, goodwill, or resources. As though by alchemical reaction, our peak-performance New Couple state produces an environment of abundance in which both of us can relax and thrive.

That's a beautiful ideal for us all to strive for. Meantime, as we've said, down here on earth we're all wrestling with tiresome dependencies and various and sundry areas of low self-love. As with power imbalances and unfairness, just acknowledging our dependencies is half the battle won, and we have the New Couple model to take us the rest of the way. Still, it's only reasonable to expect our life together to present us with times during which we absolutely have to depend on each other. As part of our search for mission in life, for example, we might ask our partner to support us while we go back to school. And when we're challenged by circumstances—the loss of a job, the death of a parent, the birth of a child—we depend on our partner emotionally, often feeling that we couldn't scrape by without our beloved other. Although superficially these periods might mimic lapses into dependence, they are, in fact, the essence of *inter*dependence. As such, they prove precious in crystallizing everlasting bonds of the heart.

What the ninth New Law of Love asks of us is that, at the end of the day, we balance our "leaning styles" (in other words, that we alternate between dependence and supportiveness as circumstances dictate—but never in ways that are gender-determined), that we *work toward* the realization of emotional and economic symmetry, and that we trust each other's commitment to the ideal of interdependence. This heady stuff of the new exchange sounds good, but wishing won't make it so. Interdependence requires all the New Laws of Love. The sixth, the Law of Peace-making, with its powerful agreements, often gets a heavy workout, as Katrina and Seth so valiantly demonstrate.

Precious Metal: A Secure Start

When Katrina first came to see us, she said she'd been "riding a roller-coaster through heaven and hell." At twenty-four, she was slightly cynical and "single with a vengeance." The freedoms of serial monogamy suited her just fine, thank you, she asserted, and marriage wasn't on her agenda. At least it hadn't been until she met Seth.

Now six months into their love affair, Katrina was convinced that he was her soulmate "because he was all wrong: too old, not enough money, too cute, and still attached to his family." But, she had to admit, they had stellar chemistry and a whole host of essential compatibilities. There was only one serious problem: Seth was an occasional, but diehard, "metal-head." Once every month or so he'd put on his black T-shirt and jeans, kiss Katrina good-bye, and set off for a night of "slam-dancing." This scene was worlds apart from the academic environment in which they'd met—the MBA program at a prestigious East Coast university.

The first couple of times Seth departed for a "head-banger's ball," his girlfriend shrugged it off as one of his personal eccentricities. She'd never attended one and had no interest. "To tell the truth," Katrina said, "the idea of thousands of spiked male heads and studded black boots careening into one another in a deafening music hall seems downright violent." Although she couldn't quite understand the appeal, Katrina had accommo-dated stranger idiosyncrasies in other boyfriends. Nonetheless, as their rela-tionship deepened, Seth's attendance at these concerts started bothering her. She found herself dropping snide remarks about his music; then, as her anxiety mounted, she made indirect pleas for him to sit the next show out.

By the time Katrina came to us for a session, she'd suffered several full-blown panic attacks. The first she'd ever experienced, they'd all occurred leading up to or during the nights Seth spent at his concerts. When he got home from one such event, after her initial relief at seeing him she couldn't control her rage, sobbing and trembling as she yelled at him. Seth, who felt about Katrina as she did about him, was desperately confused. He feared for the emotional stability of his new paramour.

The therapy that she embarked on after that episode soon revealed that multiple unresolved traumas from her childhood were being trig-gered by Seth's concert-going. The chaos in which Seth would so gladly lose himself at a metal concert unconsciously reminded Katrina of the violent chaos of her own childhood—a classic case of traumatic transfer-ence. It was actually the deep love for—and, ironically, the safety she felt with—Seth that opened the young woman up to a kind of emotional vulnerability she hadn't experienced since she was a child.

"I don't know whether his metal habit is self-destructive or not," she told us in exasperation, "but I do know that I have no right to tell him what to do. But having said that, I still can't take it." She'd tried everything to keep calm, even going out of state to visit a close friend over one of those notorious weekends. The visit helped, but it was an impractical solution. At home, her symptoms only became more severe: eventually just spotting a heavy-metal bumper sticker would unglue her for the rest of the day.

For Seth, heavy-metal music had always provided a great outlet for his rebellious streak. It was actually self-preserving, a response to his needy family, members of whom still relied on him for their primary emotional support. Although the rigors and structure of graduate school and the straitlaced profession that he was preparing for all but canceled out his countercultural relief, he benefited from letting himself be swallowed up by the free-for-all of a metal concert every so often. As their relationship progressed, Seth's increasingly serious commitment to Katrina mixed with these constraints to forge a suffocating alloy that nearly replicated his childhood (and indeed his ongoing) experience with his family. Even though he was of aware of Katrina's worsening condition, his own traumatic transference was making him feel more and more despondent. His attendance at the concerts increased.

Finally Katrina made the decision to take care of herself. She told us that it was the hardest thing she'd ever done: "I was breaking my own heart. But I simply knew I couldn't subject myself to another cycle of anxiety attacks." In order for the breakup to be a clean interaction—not just a threat—she knew that the relationship had to be truly over in her own mind. To ensure that finality, she let herself begin to grieve before she even spoke to Seth.

When they finally hashed the issue out, Katrina told him that while she appreciated what the concert experience meant to him—and she sincerely did—her own life was becoming unmanageable. To remain in a relationship with him while he continued his steady diet of metal would be to ignore her own needs. Indeed, she said, it would be masochistic. Nonetheless, Katrina refused to make Seth choose. She felt that this would be a form of emotional blackmail. Through her tears, Katrina simply announced her intention to leave the relationship. She saw no other solution. In the end, she knew that her own emotional health came first.

Seth called Katrina seven days later and asked to see her. He told her he'd come to realize that in his heart she was much more important to him than his heavy-metal concerts. After several intensely emotionally honest—and therefore intensely intimate—conversations, they came up with a set of core agreements about concert-going, including one to enter couple counseling to deal with the fallout.

Seth was angry, at times enraged, over the loss of his wild life—or so he thought. Counseling taught him and Katrina, however, that his "sacrifice" was triggering far more significant resentments he'd harbored toward his mother since childhood. In point of fact, his mother had "loved him too much"; because of his father's emotional unavailability, she'd allowed herself to become completely emotionally dependent on Seth. She was so sweet and loving that he could never bring himself to "reject" her and rebel; nor could he risk expressing his anger at her directly. The difference between past and present was that Seth now felt he had a choice in the matter. Unlike his mother, who'd exerted great control over and pressure on him (and on whom he'd been truly dependent), Katrina exerted no pressure at all. He could choose to come back to her as an act of free will.

In time, Seth not only addressed the transference onto Katrina of his mother, but he also started to comprehend the self-destructive aspects of his concert mania, especially its general excesses and the physical threat involved in slam-dancing. We pointed out the potential in their couple for a *shared* Dionysian experience once emotional safety had been restored and some healing had taken place. It was only a few months before this was corroborated: Seth and Katrina began to experience lovemaking that both partners described as "close to cosmic." Within a year, Katrina had largely neutralized her trauma and Seth had become rather blasé about metal. When a triple bill of his favorite bands came into town, they went together, at Katrina's suggestion. After an hour, they walked out.

The beauty of Seth and Katrina's story lies in her ability to set a healthy, self-loving limit without judging, manipulating, or otherwise trying to coerce Seth into giving up something that had great significance for him. She was emotionally willing and able to *walk;* paradoxically, this meant that she could, in health, *stay* if Seth could support her in creating emotional safety for herself. Seth and Katrina illustrate that the principles of the Law of Walking are best established before a commitment is made, and never to be used as a weapon to force our partner to do our bidding. Katrina and Seth learned that we must be confident not only in our own capacity to take care of ourselves, but also in our beloved's ability to do the same. When we each have the resources—including core agreements specifying the essential bottom lines—to leave the relationship, and we put those resources on the table long before they're needed, our partnership can start out on a super-solid footing.

New Roles, No Rules

If only each sex knew the truth about real mobility, the incredible advantages to us as partners when we're willing and able—each of us—to walk.

What do those advantages look like for the new woman? The "freedom to stay"—to remain in the union because she *wants* to, not because she *needs* to—gives her a bottom line, which builds the healthy self-reliance she so yearns for. Never again will she have to spend a lifetime trapped in an unhappy marriage with no money to get out. On her way to freedom, she'll find herself empowered and able to develop the so-called masculine attributes of initiative, goal-setting, and assertiveness (if she doesn't already have them). She'll be proud of herself in a way her mother most likely never was.

Sharada said that she'd never in her life imagined that she'd be able to pay for her own automobile someday. "I just took it for granted that my husband would handle the big-ticket items. Once I had the money, I thought, Why not? I can pick whatever I want. Instead of a modest subcompact, I bought myself a convertible. I feel like a new woman!" When Amelia finally read her fiancé the riot act about threatening her, and he saw that she meant what she'd said about walking, he shaped right up (even agreeing to enter counseling). Standing up for herself gave her entrée into a whole new world of self-respect.

Advantages accrue to the new man as well. The "freedom to stay" *only if he wants to* releases him from the tyranny of his assumed role as economic provider. Formerly dominated by responsibility, he now can say no: never again will he have to linger duty-bound and guilt-tripped in a loveless union. His need to be needed, which concealed a shadow dependence on women, now can heal, because he knows that his partner can survive without him but chooses to stay with him purely out of love.

Gareth admitted that he was at first "secretly worried that my wife would leave me" when she finished college with a degree in computer science. Now they have their own software consulting firm, "and I get to be around my growing children—a luxury I'd never expected." The truly interdependent partnership is a highly creative place where the new man can safely exercise his new emotional honesty and be supported in developing the so-called feminine attributes of trust, openness, nurturance, and receptivity (if he doesn't already have them). The new husband won't require his wife's subservience or economic dependence in order to respect himself or feel capable and secure. His inflated ego and her deflated one, painful for both, can come to equilibrium. In this New Couple, real self-love can soar and finally free both to know their own power and live their dreams. For everyone, this individual liberation can be exhilarating.

Willingness and ability to walk isn't a threat, nor is it a thing New Couples *do*. It's a state of being that's both psychological and material. The ninth New Law of Love asks that we measure the parameters of our dependencies and explore their potential bases—be they fear of loneliness or rejection, fear of not being able to protect ourselves or cope on our own, fear of growing old alone, fear of having no value unless we're part of a couple, or fear that we can't support ourselves materially. The ultimate preventative medicine against divorce, this New Law of Love is like all potent cures—it packs a punch. It says to our partner that our self-love is so solid that we won't accept the unacceptable, and it cements our own intention to stand by our needs via the agreements we create.

When we embrace the Law of Walking, we prove our burning desire for each other and signal our unwillingness to (wittingly or unwittingly) preserve our relationship in allegiance to archaic rules or myths, or out of desperation. With our commitment to strive for real autonomy and interdependence, we avoid taking unnecessary risks with our emotional and material welfare—and our love. Our willingness and ability to walk enhances our self-love and teaches us how to really trust ourselves and our favorite other. *Love will not be lost in the process.*

The Key to Walking

Striving for interdependence and individual autonomy in your couple—that is, being willing and able to walk in order to stay together in healthy union—is the key to the Ninth New Law of Love.

This means exploring and committing to resolve . . .

• Financial dependencies
• Emotional dependencies

10. TRANSFORMATIONAL EDUCATION

the tenth new law of love

The tenth New Law of Love functions as a jump-start at those times when we find ourselves stalled on any of the earlier nine laws. Commitment to the Law of Transformational Education means that whenever we realize we're unable to apply one or more of the other laws or master certain of the skills and processes described in this book, we agree to do something about it—namely, get our self—or ourselves—to an expert. Unlike the Law of Chemistry, over which we really have no power—we either have it with each other, or we don't—this final law points up all the ways we do have power over laws two through nine. It's about everything we *can* learn and heal.

Transformational education is different from the regular, didactic kind of education, in that it's experiential and it both instructs the head and moves the heart. It helps us not only grasp concepts, gain insights, and acquire skills, but also heal on a deep emotional level (and hence grow and mature). Some types of transformational education can even offer a quantum leap in self-love, which is something every partner craves. Indeed, since such education has the potential to renew—even re-create—us as partners and as persons, it *is* nothing less than transformational.

Our hope is that this book is itself an agent of transformational education—that a close reading will not only teach but also catalyze a growth process in you and your couple. The other forms of this special kind of education introduced in this chapter are counseling and psychotherapy (couple, individual, and group); support groups, including Twelve-Step recovery programs; and workshops, intensives, and retreats. Websites and phone numbers for various educational options are cited at the end of this chapter.

The beauty of this potent New Law of Love lies in the fact that it not only ensures that every potential roadblock to the success of your relationship gets properly cleared, but it also helps avert conflicts over the issue of getting help itself. And believe us, we're only too aware of the potential for that!

First of all, "shrinks" and "getting shrunk" have received a bad rap and dreadful stereotyping for decades. Hollywood hasn't helped at all: movies typically portray therapists as pathetic, unappealing, unethical, neurotic, or stark, raving mad. And as is the case with any profession, the reputation is partially deserved. Obviously, therapists are only human—in fact, those worth their salt will say that they're in the field as much to develop themselves as to help others. Great ones are out there, however—lots of them—and they're worth hunting down.

Exceptions that do justice to the profession also exist on film. The movies *Ordinary People, The Prince of Tides,* and *Good Will Hunting,* for example, present complex and compelling portraits of dedicated (if overly involved) practitioners for whom psychotherapy is a mission in life. And each one succeeds in conveying the life-changing potential and magic of the encounter between therapist and client.

Unfortunately, though, these films also reflect contemporary society's rigid taboo against counseling, the public misconception that there has to be something desperately wrong with us to justify getting help, that help is appropriate only as a frantic last-ditch effort before crisis or breakdown. As this book full of garden-variety individual and couple counseling cases demonstrates, this is patently untrue. Still, depending on our family, culture, education, geographic location, and level of self-love, many of us do feel extremely reluctant to consult with a psychologically trained third party for any reason whatsoever.

The societal stigma alone is toxically shaming; it would have us believe that "submitting" to an hour in front of this type of helping professional proves, beyond a shadow of a doubt, that we've failed or are weak, self-indulgent, unresourceful, or "too Californian"—and, perhaps worst of all, at risk for being rejected by our partner or tribe (or both). In this age of personal trainers, financial consultants, and webmasters—when the average corporation spends megabucks on personal development for its employees under the guise of management and leadership training—it doesn't make sense that tuning up our psyches and relationships is last on our list. But that's certainly where society has placed it. That's why committing to the Law of Transformational Education is as revolutionary as it is profound. Such a commitment demonstrates our absolute dedication, as partners, to keeping our love and trust alive—whatever it takes.

Though the first nine New Laws of Love cover everything we need for a successful relationship, applying those laws might not always be easy. Every couple experiences certain laws as more challenging than others. Even those of us who are able to embrace all the laws intellectually may encounter obstacles applying some of them. We highlighted points in previous chapters where couples typically stumble and require outside help, and we offered many anecdotes showing couples who had recourse to counseling or personal-development courses. In cases such as those presented, outside help can be a relationship-saver.

Because this law has the potential to move us through any blocks we might encounter while working on the other nine, it offers the surest hope for the actual fulfillment of our higher-order needs—to honestly love ourselves, to discover and realize our mission in life, and to experience true lifelong emotional intimacy with another human being. It functions as our bridge across the sometimes ferocious rapids of true love. Indeed, thanks to transformational education, we dare say that the Ten New Laws of Love are a fail-safe system.

WHAT'S OUT THERE AND HOW TO SHOP

Of the three main categories of transformational education available to us—counseling and psychotherapy, group work, and workshops—counseling is usually our first recourse when we hit a snag in applying the New Laws of Love. (The terms *counseling* and *psychotherapy* have been used interchangeably throughout this book.)

Counseling

Counselors come in many different stripes; their backgrounds vary widely, as do their focuses. *Psychologists* have a Ph.D. (doctorate of philosophy in psychology) or a Psy.D. (doctorate of psychology); *psychiatrists* have an MD (doctorate of medicine with a specialization in psychiatry); *psychotherapists* and *counselors* have an MA or an MS (master of arts or science degree in counseling or clinical psychology); *clinical social workers* have an MA or an MS (master of arts or science degree in clinical social work); and *couple coaches,* who are relatively new on the scene, might have one of any variety of degrees.

We recommend that you choose a specialist who possesses at least a master's degree in counseling, clinical psychology, or clinical social work (or who is an intern in such a master's degree program) and is appropriately licensed. (The licensing issue can be confusing, because different states and countries have different licensure requirements and different names for practitioners of all levels.)

While each individual practitioner will define his or her work slightly differently, psychotherapists and psychologists (who often call themselves psychotherapists as well) generally specialize in depth work and are more likely to work with childhood issues. Still, some counselors do this too, and some psychologists and psychotherapists don't.

The first step in identifying a professional from whom to seek help is soliciting recommendations from trusted associates—perhaps the family doctor or other healthcare worker (such as an acupuncturist, nurse practitioner, massage therapist), a clergyperson, or a friend. Whether an individual or couple therapist, the practitioner selected must feel warm and empathetic and must inspire trust. Chemistry matters here, as it does in intimate relationships, although real rapport will take time to develop. As always, intuition should be relied on.

COUPLE COUNSELING AND COACHING

I had a friend who said she would always choose to have some therapy in a relationship. She said, "I'll never be in another unsupervised relationship again." . . . It was a tribute to the supervision of a guide, a healing companion for our psychological selves.

SARK, *Succulent Wild Woman*

The term *couple counseling* and the newer label *couple coaching* are generally interchangeable, although coaching tends to emphasize skill development over examining childhood stories to gain intellectual insight and doing emotional ("process") work. Today, couple work is typically conducted by a single practitioner working one-on-two with the couple. (Teams of couple co-therapists do exist, however; and for the balance they afford, they offer certain advantages. They can be hard to find, though, and married ones, like the authors, are even more rare.)

Any help sought from a professional must be compatible with the Ten New Laws of Love. In order to support these laws, a couple counselor or coach must specialize in working with the transference that exists between partners. Additionally, he or she (or they) needs to be competent in the specific aspect of the law that's posing the problem. A good place to begin the search is with couple counselors trained by relationship expert and author Harville Hendrix, whose approach complements the one in this book.

It's appropriate to ask a few questions over the phone before booking an appointment. Questions can determine, for example, whether the therapist specializes in working with couple transference. If the answer is yes, additional questions can focus on the specific law and then the particular issue that's causing difficulty. If the practitioner has expertise in this specific area as well (and isn't off-putting over the phone), it's worth booking an initial interview to find out whether there's a "fit" between all three (or four) parties.

Murray Bowen, one of the fathers of so-called family therapy, asserts that practitioners can take clients only as far as they themselves have gone in their own growth and healing. It's true that it can be extremely helpful to work with someone who's "been there," who's actually walking the talk and has been a client in couple counseling. Although it's not professional for therapists to reveal personal details, that issue is worth asking about in general terms. Many excellent therapists prefer to remain as anonymous as possible, however, which is a valid ethical stance. Whether they answer the question or not, their response will likely convey a sense of who they are as people and what sort of fit would result.

Since trust is the foundation of a viable client-therapist relationship, it's imperative that the couple therapist chosen be someone with whom both partners feel gut-level comfort and whom they sense they can eventually trust. Sometimes counseling can edge people out of their "comfort zone." Those "labor pains" shouldn't be mistaken for a poor fit, however. Still, no one should feel obligated to make a counseling relationship work that lacks connection or chemistry; it's the therapist's job to serve clients, not the clients' job to keep him or her from feeling rejected. Therefore, the therapist chosen must meet all of the above criteria.

INDIVIDUAL COUNSELING AND LIFE COACHING

For some partners, application of these laws might involve individual counseling as either an adjunct to couple work or on its own. In order to be compatible with the Ten New Laws of Love, individual counseling (like couple counseling) must combine intellectual insight (reviewing one's psychological story) with emotional process work. Additionally, the therapist's clinical orientation must focus on individuation from family-of-origin or inner-child work; recovery from codependence, toxic guilt, and toxic shame; transference between therapist and client; and recovery from childhood emotional trauma, including all forms of abuse and neglect.

Specializations appropriate to the laws include EMDR (eye movement desensitization reprocessing, a gentle but highly effective psychotherapeutic technique for resolving emotional trauma), breathwork (including holotropic breathing and rebirthing), primal therapy, Gestalt therapy, psychosynthesis, and psychotherapeutically oriented bodywork. Although they are not required for getting unstuck on any Law of Love, all of these are excellent modalities for augmenting emotional awareness and release. Because the power and intensity of the above techniques shouldn't be underestimated, they're recommended only in the hands of practitioners who are trained psychotherapists (though some truly gifted—yet technically untrained—healers provide exception).

The healer-heal-thyself maxim is as applicable to individual counselors as it is to those who work with couples, as is the need for chemistry and trust. Therefore, the earlier guidelines for selecting an acceptable couple specialist are all relevant, including the step of asking the practitioner if he or she has undergone counseling. As before, questions focused on issues of concern can help determine whether client and prospective practitioner are on the same page.

Individual consultation that addresses career or vocational aspirations is also compatible with several of the New Laws of Love. The career-vocational guidance field has changed significantly in recent years. A new crop of vocational counselors—now usually called *life coaches* or just *coaches* (but sometimes also *personal, career, job,* or *dream coaches*)—have raised this kind of counseling to the level of art. Instead of looking just for what people do well—or trying to corral them into areas where jobs are available—they assess the seven areas of intelligence and make use of discussion, visualization, and intuition rather than standardized aptitude tests. These coaches need not meet the professional criteria for psychotherapists, but it's important that they feel warm, empathetic, and responsible, that they inspire trust, and that they come highly recommended.

Group Work

The second type of transformational education that can be applied in conjunction with a commitment to the New Laws of Love is group work.

The two principal types of groups are therapy groups and support groups. While the former are generally facilitated by trained professionals, both are capable of delivering a profoundly healing experience.

THERAPY GROUPS

Many kinds of therapy groups exist, including ones for couples. These can be very helpful, but unfortunately couple therapy groups tend to spring up erratically and can be hard to locate. The same criteria outlined above for choosing a couple therapist (including experience with transference work) apply to therapy groups. In order to ensure complete emotional safety, it's essential that these groups be led by a credentialed therapist with training in running groups.

Group therapy for individuals can also be highly therapeutic, especially when it's topic-focused, addressing such issues as eating disorders, childhood abuse, anger management, and incest. Bereavement or grief groups can provide wonderful support following the death of a loved one. The criteria for individual groups would match those stated above for individual therapy.

Another group option is a program known as both Co-Counseling and Re-evaluation Counseling. Actually a short class, this low-cost, grassroots alternative to psychotherapy has a large international following. It trains participants in emotional-release work (catharsis) so that after completing several months of classes, they can pair up with other graduates and counsel each other free of charge. The techniques are simple, powerful, and revolutionary, as are the many books by its originator, Harvey Jackins.

SUPPORT GROUPS

The second category of transformational education includes all types of support groups. Designed to provide emotional support on an ever-growing variety of issues, these are typically—though not always—leaderless and either low-fee or free of charge. Most popular are the Twelve-Step programs for recovery from any number of addictions or compulsive behaviors: Alcoholics Anonymous (AA), Narcotics Anonymous (NA), Workaholics Anonymous (WA), Sex and Love Addicts Anonymous (SLAA), Overeaters Anonymous (OA), Debtors Anonymous (DA), and Gamblers Anonymous (GA).

Other Twelve-Step groups provide support for codependents (CODA), family members of alcoholics (Al-Anon), family members of drug addicts (Nar-Anon), adult children of alcoholics (ACA/ACOA), adult children of mentally ill parents (ACMIP), incest survivors (SIA), and those with other special issues. (Many of the groups listed above offer women-only, men-only, gay, lesbian, and/or bisexual orientations as well.) "Men's" and "women's" groups, groups for singles or divorcé(e)s, and groups focusing on issues such as general emotional support, life-mission or life-purpose identification, life-transition, accountability, or fertility exist in abundance and can benefit a couple in applying specific laws.

Workshops, Intensives, Special Courses, and Retreats

The final category of workshops, intensives, special courses, and retreats, though underutilized, often offers the most awesome results of all the modern varieties of transformational education. Some, though not all, of these options are pricey; nevertheless, because they promise (and generally deliver) a substantial amount of growth and healing—even remarkable breakthroughs—in a short period of time, they end up being cost-effective.

Though the majority of workshops are designed for individuals, couple-oriented options do exist. These include NewCouple seminars, Harville Hendrix's Getting All the Love You Want couple workshops, Marriage Encounter and Engagement Encounter workshops, and couple retreats, intimacy weekends, and relationship trainings produced by other organizations. The best referral sources are relationship experts, therapists, churches, synagogues, and word of mouth.

Among the intensives and workshops designed for individuals, those most compatible with the Ten New Laws of Love are those that focus on the inner child, relationships with parents, and healing the emotions. All are most effective when attended as an adjunct to individual or couple therapy. Among the vast number of options, the quality can vary from superb to questionable. Therefore, the recommendation of professionals or trusted friends is essential. (A word of caution: As the name implies, intensives are just that, and they can leave participants with an impressive "workshop high" that, like the intoxication stage of relationship, soon passes. Still, the high-quality intensives provide many permanent results.)

The weeklong Hoffman Quadrinity Process, operating since 1967, has an excellent international reputation. For many participants, it's equivalent to months of psychotherapy and results in a quantum leap in self-love. Whether people attend as a couple or separately, we recommend they go under the supervision of an individual or couple counselor, preferably one familiar with the Process. Another highly reputed intensive is offered by John Bradshaw's organization. Trainings that facilitate participants in becoming their most authentic self, such as Lee Glickstein's Speaking Circles, can also be highly compatible with the aims of this book, as can life-purpose, assertiveness, financial-empowerment, and personal-empowerment courses (such as Model Mugging, which integrates self-defense).

An Invitation to Reflect on the Law of Transformational Education

As you approach the exercises in this chapter, remember that the presence or absence of New Couple chemistry profoundly affects a couple's experience with each law.

- Have you ever availed yourself or your couple of any form of transformational education? If so, how do you feel about it now? How did it affect your self-love? Your emotional intimacy?
- What beliefs do you hold that could be obstacles in embracing transformational education?

TRANSFORMATIONAL EDUCATION LAW BY LAW

In this section, we'll look at each of the Ten New Laws of Love, identifying issues on which couples typically get stuck and highlighting styles of transformational education that are especially suitable for each. (The listing is intended to be suggestive rather than exhaustive.)

Chemistry

The most serious problem associated with the first New Law of Love is the waning of our best-friendship or sexual chemistry (or both). This book is designed to keep this from happening and to correct it if it's already begun. If we've experienced New Couple chemistry at some point in our relationship, a decline is always a symptom pointing somewhere in the nine other laws. For that reason, the first step in addressing a chemistry problem is to review the laws and determine which are out of balance. Then we can seek the appropriate transformational education.

If we've never experienced sexual chemistry with *anyone*—including a partner to whom we're highly attracted and with whom we enjoy best-friendship chemistry—we might be experiencing a symptom of some kind of unresolved issue (possibly even trauma) in our history. However remote or unlikely such an early scenario may seem to us, individual psychotherapy is appropriate. When addressing sexual issues, the gender of the therapist is extremely important; we need to trust our instincts as to whether we'd feel most comfortable with a man or a woman.

Priority

The main reason we're unable to prioritize an intimate relationship is co-dependence with people outside our couple—usually members of the family-of-origin or close friends. Codependence with family members—that is, anachronistic attachment to an earlier role as son, daughter, brother, sister, niece, nephew, cousin, grandchild, and so on—is actually a crisis of psychological individuation, the inability to stand among adults as a peer.

Many forms of transformational education help us heal codependence and resolve individuation issues. The Twelve-Step group called Codependents Anonymous (CODA) is the treatment of choice for codependence. It's most powerful when attended in tandem with individual psychotherapy with a codependence expert. Though we're often not aware of it, early emotional abandonment can underlie both codependence and our inability to individuate. Hence EMDR work with a qualified therapist can accelerate healing. Assertiveness training—and other self-empowerment courses, such as Model Mugging/Impact Self-Defense—and men's and women's groups and co-counseling are all highly indicated in the recovery from codependence. Finally, the workshops, intensives, special courses, and retreats listed above are also excellent.

Transformational education is also appropriate for the kind of co-dependence that occurs *within* couples. This codependence, or loving too much, can be seen when we're overly preoccupied with our partner and the attention is nonreciprocal, or when we're in a relationship with a mate who's verbally, psychologically, or physically abusive or who suffers from an addiction, compulsion, or mental illness but declines treatment. In both instances, the relationship can't be mutually prioritized. This between-mates type of codependence can be addressed using the same kinds of help listed above for codependence with persons outside the couple.

Substance addictions and compulsive behaviors—including the eating disorders of anorexia nervosa, bulimia, and compulsive overeating, as well as alcoholism, drug addiction, workaholism, and gambling—also keep us from being able to prioritize our couple, and they always need outside help. In extreme cases, hospitalization or a period in a rehabilitation center is necessary. Anonymous groups exist for almost every conceivable process and substance addiction, and they continue to be the most effective treatment for maintaining sobriety.

Whereas individual and couple therapy can often be effective at recognizing an addiction or compulsion, we can't expect such therapy to resolve any *other* problem until the addiction (including codependence) is being addressed and treated. Nor, of course, can we work effectively on any of the Ten New Laws of Love if an addictive problem ails us and we're not in recovery for it.

Emotional Integrity

The most common challenges associated with the third New Law of Love include emotional illiteracy, which is the inability to get in touch with our feelings and articulate them using I-statements; emotional dishonesty, which is the inability to acknowledge our true feelings to our mate, as well as any buttons, blind spots, and issues that affect either partner; and emotional mismanagement, which is the inability to express negative feelings responsibly. All three categories of transformational education positively affect our ability to take responsibility for our emotions. Especially effective are individual and couple counseling, Co-Counseling, breathwork, and special courses such as the Hoffman Process and Speaking Circles. For help with emotional awareness in particular, breathwork, primal therapy, and Gestalt therapy can all facilitate breakthroughs.

For issues related to emotional trauma, evidenced in our buttons, blind spots, phobias, excessive anxiety or panic, sexual jealousy, rage, and "neurotic" or "control freak" behaviors, individual psychotherapy with EMDR or an appropriate therapist-led group are a good first recourse. Unresolved grief from death of a loved one can be best dealt with in a grief or bereavement group (often offered through churches, hospitals, or hospices) and individual psychotherapy with a grief specialist. Grief over other major losses, including the death of a pet or the loss of material goods due to crime or disaster, can be managed in individual psychotherapy or specialized group therapy. Because major life trauma, such as the death of a child or the inability to conceive, is a major cause of divorce and emotional estrangement between partners, expert individual psychotherapy can be critical to the relationship.

Deep Listening

If we're unable to develop the skill of generally listening from the heart or listening well in Sessions, we can make great inroads in individual counseling and couple coaching. Speaking Circles also specialize in teaching individuals how to deeply listen; thus attendance at intensives or participation in ongoing groups with this focus can produce breakthroughs. Additionally, men's, women's, and emotional support groups that provide excellent opportunities to both deeply listen and be deeply listened to without comment or interruption can help bring this skill into our couple.

Equality

If we find ourselves in a relationship characterized by entrenched gender-based inequalities, couple and individual counseling can help balance things out, as can group therapy for couples and gender-specific support groups. Mates who are on the lower end of the power differential (and dissatisfied with this status) might also benefit from Codependents Anonymous, Co-Counseling, personal-empowerment courses, assertiveness training, and emotional healing intensives such as the Hoffman Process.

Peacemaking

If we need to master the skills of anger management and/or conflict resolution, tremendous help is available. If we're unable to initiate a time-
out, couple coaching and individual psychotherapy with a focus on
codependence, general trauma, or abandonment trauma would be a good
starting point. (Therapists who are unfamiliar with the time-out can be
shown the instructions from this book.) Codependents Anonymous, Co-
Counseling, personal-empowerment courses, assertiveness training, and
emotional healing intensives are all recommended as well.

If we're unable to honor a time-out or use the Peace Process due to
out-of-control anger, or if we recognize that we're sitting on a lot of rage,
then breathwork, primal and Gestalt therapies, and individual psy-
chotherapies with a focus on impulse control through the therapeutic
catharsis and containment of anger are all indicated. Healing intensives
such as the Hoffman Process, Re-evaluation Counseling classes, and other
catharsis-based therapy groups can also facilitate working through a surplus of anger safely.

If we need extra help mastering the Peace Process, this procedure,
which is outlined in Chapter 6, can be taken to a couple coach or counselor for help with practice—or we can attend a NewCouple seminar.
Because a failed Peace Process is often the result of transference, whatever professional we choose to work with must be skilled in addressing
that phenomenon. If we have difficulties with negotiation or negotiable agreement–making, couple coaching is again advised. We can
take the relevant sections of Chapter 6 to share with our practitioner if
need be.

If we're single and unsure of our core conditions for a future relationship, individual counseling is the best bet. If we're in a couple but
have difficulty creating or articulating core agreements—including
those defining sexual and emotional exclusivity—both couple and individual counseling can be helpful. If we fear that we can't stand by our
core agreements, individual psychotherapy with a codependence expert,
EMDR work for possible abandonment trauma, assertiveness training,
self-empowerment courses, men's and women's groups, Codependents
Anonymous, and healing intensives are all suggested.

Self-Love

If we're aware of deficit self-love—that is, we recognize our inability to trust our feelings and intuition, honor our talents, stick up for or care for ourselves, deidealize or individuate from family members, or work through the transference that comes up in our relationships—we can benefit from all forms of transformational education. The most powerful intervention for low self-love is the Hoffman Process, especially as an adjunct to individual psychotherapy; psychotherapy by itself is also helpful, as are the other healing intensives. Since low self-love can be the result of emotional trauma and growing up with addiction, abuse, and mental illness, Twelve-Step, therapy, and support groups addressing these problems can be invaluable. If as a couple we need facilitated practice identifying transferences, couple counseling is the place to learn. If we're unable to identify or recall the childhood relationship at the root of a transference or neutralize the associated feelings, these issues can all be addressed in individual and couple therapy and the Hoffman Process.

Mission in Life

If we're confused about our true life's work and unsure where our greatest gifts and talents lie, we can be inestimably helped by a coach—whether job, life, personal, or dream variety. Life-mission, life-purpose, life-transition, and accountability support groups, as well as Speaking Circles, can open us up to our true calling, as can workshops concentrating on financial empowerment and mission in life. The Hoffman Process can be of particular merit too, especially if we specify identifying our mission as a workshop goal. If we suspect that low self-love is contributing to our confusion, the self-love suggestions above are also appropriate.

Walking

If we're unable or unwilling to consider leaving a relationship where our essential needs are unmet, we're suffering from emotional dependencies (which may include codependence with persons outside our couple), financial dependencies, or both. If the dependencies are emotional, the same transformational education options mentioned in the codependence discussion (see "Priority," above) are appropriate. If the dependencies are financial, we can make great headway by attending courses designed for financial and personal empowerment, as well as for development of mission or purpose in life. Coaches can also be excellent resources to help get us up and running with our own money.

TRANSFORMATIONAL EDUCATION PAST AND THE TRADITIONAL COUPLE

Transformational education for couples has almost no history. Indeed, since our parents and grandparents were children, the dynamics of healthy relationship and the understanding of what it means to be human have been almost completely reconceptualized. While our parents and grandparents had some personal-development options, these were designed mainly for individuals. People of their generations could read books written to guide and inspire people in partnerships; but as for real hands-on education—such as couple intensives, relationship trainings, support groups for lovers, even couple counseling and coaching—these options have been available only in the last three decades, and they're just now becoming acceptable and widely accessible.

Truth be told, the various technologies for individual and couple development have been straitjacketed since their inception. The earliest form, psychotherapy, had its roots in the treatment of mental illness. Whether traditionals participated in therapy as individuals or as a couple, consultation with a third party meant that they were at least weak, if not crazy; we all have visions of the electroconvulsive therapy of days past, and of lobotomies, and of madmen and hysterical women in restraints. Until a quarter-century ago, when "talking to someone" started to become chic among the urbane and university-educated, all therapy was seen as a shameful and stigmatized last straw.

When the rare twosome did avail themselves of marriage counseling, circumstances were dire indeed—perhaps an attempted suicide by one partner, or what used to be known as a nervous breakdown. Back then, with the couple not yet understood as a system in which both members contributed to the problem, symptom reduction was the name of the game. Therefore, couple treatment often consisted of contingency planning for one partner's extreme dysfunction; and whatever the problem, the nonfunctional partner was often treated with medication, electroshock treatment, or both. Deficits of self-love were rarely addressed in terms of transference and early childhood wounding. Countless precious opportunities to bring partners together in true union were completely overlooked.

More recently, couples started marriage counseling due to "lesser" problems, such as affairs, addictions, and family violence. As the systems therapy approach became more widely accepted and applied, therapists and clients alike began acknowledging the role of *each* partner in creating dysfunction. Much couple work still foundered, however, due to intractability of the presenting issues, a poor fit with the therapist, lack of mutual commitment to the healing process, or too lengthy a delay before consultation and treatment. Furthermore, these early couple clients were limited by the shortcomings of a young field; much of the cutting-edge information we have today simply wasn't available.

An Invitation to Reflect on the Law of Transformational Education as It Pertains to Your Parents

- Did your parents ever avail themselves or their couple of any form of transformational education? If so, how did it affect their self-love? Their emotional intimacy? How did this make you feel?
- What beliefs did your parents hold (or might they have held) that would have been obstacles to embracing transformational education?
- How would your childhood have been different had your parents subscribed to the Law of Transformational Education? How would your own couple be different (or, if you're single, how would past relationships have been different)?

Transformational education is the ultimate New Law of Love. Our commitment to it as a couple means that we each agree to call a snag a snag, however large it may loom. It's our pledge that if we need assistance in learning any of the skills or processes required by the first nine laws, we'll do the research and get that assistance. In fact, we'll go right to the cutting edge and take full advantage of the most sophisticated, heartfelt, and amazing educational and healing opportunities that exist. What's more, we'll keep trying new opportunities until we've broken through. The tenth New Law of Love represents our promise to stop at nothing to make our relationship as successful as it can possibly be. And because New Couples vow to resolve all issues to the satisfaction of both partners, it also symbolizes friendship at its finest—a definite win-win.

When we embrace the Law of Transformational Education, we're not only communicating loudly and clearly just how important we are to each other, we're also participating in a revolution of the heart: strengthened by the belief that everything good *is* possible, we're helping make higher education and deep healing for couples an everyday reality. Perhaps someday soon, beloveds everywhere will be enjoying the first age of enlightened romantic relationship. In terms of all the New Laws of Love, the tenth could provide no grander finale.

LOCATING RESOURCES MENTIONED IN THIS CHAPTER

The following list of resources in the area of transformational education is by no means exhaustive. For more information, search the Internet or ask for referrals from your church, synagogue, temple, hospital, physician, alternative healthcare practitioner, or friends.

- NewCouple, Int'l.: (415) 332-8881; www.newcouple.com. Our organization offers NewCouple Seminars designed to accelerate participants' mastery of the concepts, skills, and processes described in this book in a safe, supportive environment. We also feature lectures and video and audio tapes based on the Ten New Laws of Love.
- Institute for Imago Relationship Therapy (Harville Hendrix's Couple Workshops): (800) 729-1121; www.imagotherapy.com
- Jewish Marriage Experience: (800) 569-2587
- Marriage Encounter: (800) 795-5683; www.wwm.org

- The Hoffman Institute (USA): (800) 506-5253;
  www.hoffmaninstitute.org
- The Hoffman Centre (Australia): 61-3-9826-2133; www.quadrinity.com
- The Hoffman Centre (UK): 44-181-333-2222; www.quadrinity.com
- Re-evaluation Counseling: (206) 284-0311; www.rc.org
- The Primal Therapy Institute (Arthur Janov's Primal Center):
  (310) 392-2003; www.primaltherapy.com
- John Bradshaw's Workshops (Center for Creative Growth):
  (510) 527-1200; www.creativegrowth.com
- Speaking Circles International: (800) 610-0169;
  www.speakingcircles.com
- Model Mugging / Impact Self-Defense: (800) 345-KICK;
  www.bamm.org

The Twelve-Step programs listed below are widely available. In addition to the phone numbers and websites here, you can find such programs locally by referring to a phone book, therapist, hospital, or church. An excellent general recovery resource website is www.recovery.alano.org.

- Alcoholics Anonymous (AA) (National Council on Alcoholism):
  (800) NCA-CALL; www.aa.org
- Rational Recovery (Nonspiritual AA): (800) 303-2873
- Codependents Anonymous (CODA): (602) 277-7991;
  www.codependents.org
- Adult Children of Alcoholics (ACA/ACoA): (310) 534-1815
- Al-Anon (for family members and friends of alcoholics):
  (800) 344-2666
- Workaholics Anonymous (WA): (510) 273-9253
- Narcotics Anonymous (NA): (800) 896-8896; www.wsoinc.com
- Nar-Anon (for family members and friends of drug users):
  (310) 547-5800; www.naronny.org
- Overeaters Anonymous (OA): (505) 891-2664;
  www.overeatersanonymous.org
- National Eating Disorders Organization (dealing with compulsive
  overeating, anorexia nervosa, and bulimia): (918) 481-4044;
  www.laureate.com

- Recovering Couples Anonymous (RCA): (314) 397-0867;
  www.recovering-couples.org
- Sex and Love Addicts Anonymous (SLAA): (781) 255-8825;
  www.slaafws.org
- Survivors of Incest Anonymous (SIA): (410) 282-3400;
  www.siawso.org
- Debtors Anonymous (DA): (781) 453-2743;
  www.debtorsanonymous.org
- Gamblers Anonymous (GA): (213) 386-8789;
  www.gamblersanonymous.org

The Key to Transformational Education

Being willing to do whatever learning and healing is necessary if you're stuck on any aspect of the first nine New Laws of Love is the key to the tenth New Law of Love.

glossary:
the new language of love

The following terms found throughout the book are essential to understanding the Ten New Laws of Love. The specific laws they relate to are listed in parentheses after each definition.

Acting In. The result of an unwillingness or inability to express feelings directly, acting in involves turning our negative feelings self-abusively against ourselves. Acting in, which is a response to feelings of toxic guilt and toxic shame, is typically experienced as "beating ourselves up." It often leads to codependence, compulsions, and addictions, our unconscious attempts to dull the pain of self-abuse. *(emotional integrity and peacemaking)*

Acting Out. The unhealthy expression of feelings, especially anger and fear. Examples of acted-out anger include sarcasm, bullying, and punishing silence; examples of acted-out fear include controlling behaviors, false joy and kindness, and general overcaution, such as triple-checking of locks and appliances. *(emotional integrity and peacemaking)*

The Adult. One of our three main subpersonalities, the Adult is our "preferred" self—wise, rational, loving, emotionally literate, and honest. The Adult is featured on the Triangle Test. *(peacemaking)*

Aggressive-Aggressive Behavior. The more overt and direct form of acted-out anger, aggressive-aggressive behavior includes verbal abuse, coercion, threats, throwing and breaking things, and violence. *(emotional integrity and peacemaking)*

Agreements. New Couple peacemaking tools, agreements are of two types: core and negotiable. *(peacemaking)*

Amends. A part of the negotiable agreement–making process, amends represent favors or gestures offered to our partner when we break a negotiable agreement. *(peacemaking)*

Anger Management. A commitment to neither act out ourselves nor tolerate the acting out of anger by our partner and a commitment to use the time-out anger-management tool are at the heart of anger management. *(peacemaking)*

Attributes. Attributes are personal characteristics, such as looks, status, money, and education, that in traditional marriages sometimes superseded sexual and best-friendship chemistries. Because attribute-based selections are predicated on lower-order needs, they alone aren't adequate criteria for partner selection. *(chemistry)*

Best-Friendship Chemistry. A uniquely energizing connection of two partners' personalities that includes the quality of emotional trustworthiness, best-friendship chemistry (along with sexual chemistry) forms the basis of New Couple chemistry. *(chemistry)*

Blind Spots. Evidenced by lack of awareness of specific emotions or issues (or lack of insight about what underlies specific issues), blind spots are often caused by emotional trauma in childhood and result in denial and transference in adulthood. *(emotional integrity, equality, deep listening, peacemaking, self-love, walking)*

Buttons. Like blind spots, buttons—emotionally charged issues that trigger emotional mismanagement, especially the acting out of anger and fear—are often caused by emotional trauma in childhood. *(emotional integrity, equality, deep listening, peacemaking, self-love, walking)*

Catharsis. The therapeutic release of any intense emotion, catharsis can, for example, take the form of laughter and tears (for joy), crying (for sadness), yelling and hard physical exertion (for anger), and shaking, trembling, and yawning (for fear).

Chemistry. The first New Law of Love, chemistry asks that we insist on a partner with whom we share sexual passion, best friendship (including the quality of emotional trustworthiness), and any compatibilities that are essential to us.

The Child. One of our three main subpersonalities, the Child is creative, spontaneous, playful, and vulnerable; it can also be codependent, rebellious, irrational, and easily guilt-tripped, shamed, frightened, and intimidated. The Child is featured on the Triangle Test and is functionally the same as the inner child described in the discussion of emotional integrity. *(emotional integrity, peacemaking, self-love)*

Childhood Emotional Trauma. A shocking, frightening, shameful, or painful event, incident, or ongoing early condition, childhood emotional trauma typically gets buried in the unconscious and then reappears as buttons, blind spots, issues, and transferences when we're adults. Unresolved emotional trauma is the greatest challenge to successfully applying the Ten New Laws of Love. *(emotional integrity and all other laws)*

Co-creativity. The final stage of relationship, co-creativity is characterized by interdependence, emotional intimacy, rising self-love, and activated dual missions in life. The traditional couple didn't typically arrive at co-creativity, because the transformational education necessary to resolve the power struggle wasn't available. *(Introduction and all laws)*

Codependence. The unhealthy preoccupation with another person, codependence often leads us to place others' needs before our own or to seek others' acceptance before we accept ourselves. Like all compulsive behaviors, codependence is an attempt to avoid our own pain. *(Introduction, priority, emotional integrity, self-love, walking)*

Conditional Self-Love. A false kind of self-love, conditional self-love is based on external factors, such as money, looks, credentials, or talent, while genuine self-love is based on our ability to love ourselves regardless of external factors. *(self-love)*

Contempt Cluster of Emotions. The result of anger and rage not healthily expressed and thus turned toxic over time, the contempt cluster of emotions includes contempt, hatred, scorn, and disdain. Along with toxic guilt and toxic shame, these unhealthy emotions are highly corrosive to New Couple chemistry. *(emotional integrity)*

Core Agreements. New Couple tools and part of the peacemaking technology, core agreements are a couple's nonnegotiable agreements based on each individual partner's core conditions. *The New Couple* recommends core agreements relating to nonviolence, monogamy with sexual exclusivity, honesty, all forms of sobriety, and noncriminality, as well as a commitment to the Ten New Laws of Love. Other core agreements can be designed based on partners' additional core conditions. *(peacemaking)*

Core Conditions. Part of the peacemaking technology, core conditions represent individual partners' nonnegotiable conditions for relationship and are the basis for core agreements. *The New Couple* recommends core conditions relating to nonviolence, monogamy with sexual exclusivity, honesty, all forms of sobriety, and noncriminality, as well as a commitment to the Ten New Laws of Love. Other core conditions are determined on an individual basis. *(peacemaking)*

The Critic. One of our three main subpersonalities, the Critic is our inner bully—tyrannical, terrorizing, judgmental, irrational, perfectionistic, disrespectful, shaming, and guilt-tripping. The Critic is featured on the Triangle Test. *(peacemaking)*

Deep Listening. The fourth New Law of Love and a New Couple skill, deep listening is the ability to listen to our partner straight from the heart—that is, to listen not only for the words but also for the feelings underneath, and to do so with compassion. This law also advocates holding Sessions on a regular basis and Special Sessions as needed.

Eighty/Twenty Principle of Transference. This principle reflects the fact that roughly eighty percent of the emotional charge involved in major couple conflicts derives from transference—that is, unresolved hurts from early caregivers and siblings—while roughly twenty percent derives from the contemporary situation with our partner. *(self-love)*

Emotional Honesty. The willingness to acknowledge, to ourselves and our partner, our true feelings and blind spots about feelings and issues that affect either one of us. *(emotional integrity, equality, peacemaking, and self-love)*

Emotional Integrity. The third New Law of Love, emotional integrity asks that we establish an emotional safe zone by examining and healing emotional blind spots, buttons, and issues that cause either partner strife. To do so we need to learn the skills that enable us to take full responsibility for our emotions; specifically, we learn to become emotionally literate (that is, aware and fluent), emotionally honest, and capable of managing all feelings (including extreme ones).

Emotional Literacy. A New Couple skill, emotional literacy involves both emotional awareness (the ability to differentiate feelings from thoughts and to know what we're feeling at any given moment) and emotional fluency (the ability to speak the language of emotions using I-statements). *(emotional integrity and all other laws)*

Emotional Management. A New Couple skill, emotional management is the ability to deal with negative feelings by expressing them responsibly via I-statements or, if extreme, by undertaking to heal them. *(emotional integrity and peacemaking)*

Emotional Numbness. An emotional blind spot resulting in our inability to feel emotion in the moment, numbness is typically a consequence of unresolved childhood trauma. *(emotional integrity)*

Emotional Safe Zone. An emotional safe zone is a relationship environment in which we feel no fear of being emotionally invalidated, lied to, or intentionally hurt. Emotional safe zones free us to be our most emotionally honest, expressive, and authentic selves. *(chemistry, emotional integrity, peacemaking, and self-love)*

Emotional Trustworthiness. Integral to best-friendship chemistry, emotional trustworthiness is the personal quality that makes our partner feel emotionally safe to and with us. At its most active, it's expressed as a type of support that validates our emotions, thoughts, intuition, and personal rights. Emotional trustworthiness is basic to our higher-order need for emotional intimacy and allows for the creation of an emotional safe zone within a couple. *(chemistry, emotional integrity, peacemaking, and self-love)*

Equality. The fifth New Law of Love, equality asks us to respect ourselves and our partner by insisting on fairness in our relationship. This means honestly examining and sharing feelings about differences, expectations and assumptions, and unnegotiated roles and responsibilities. Equality also means rectifying all unfairness to both partners' satisfaction.

Essential Compatibilities. Forms of compatibility that individual partners consider essential in a prospective partner, essential compatibilities include passions, dreams, and shared goals for life (such as whether or not to have children); spiritual, religious, or intellectual orientations; political or cultural worldviews; creative or artistic affinities; and complementary recreational, avocational, and lifestyle choices. *(chemistry)*

Healthy Guilt. Based on a bona fide violation of another, healthy guilt produces healthy results, including discouraging repetition of the transgression and teaching trustworthiness. *(emotional integrity)*

Healthy Shame. Based on a reasonable self-protective concern for the high regard of others, healthy shame produces healthy results, such as keeping us from behaving in ways that would result in social rejection (which few of us have the self-love to tolerate). *(emotional integrity)*

Individuation. Integral to prioritizing our relationship, individuation is the process of becoming a psychological adult vis-à-vis parents and other early caregivers, siblings, and extended family members. We can determine our level of individuation by the degree to which we assert our own authority with family members. If we're driven by the need for their approval or by the fear of disappointing, hurting, angering, or being rejected by them, we haven't yet completed the individuation process. *(priority)*

Intoxication Stage. The ephemeral first stage of relationship, which lasts roughly two weeks to two years, is known as intoxication. Though the passage out of intoxication is inevitable, popular mythology would have us believe that it means we've fallen out of love or have chosen the "wrong person." *(Introduction, chemistry)*

I-Statements. Facilitating the direct and healthy expression of emotion using the "I feel" format (such as "I feel angry that you interrupted me"), I-statements are key to emotional fluency and emotional management. *(emotional integrity)*

Mission in Life. The eighth New Law of Love, mission in life asks that we commit to discovering and fulfilling our purpose in life—in other words, that we find work that we're passionate about and that contributes to the greater good. This law also asks that we support our partner in doing the same.

Negotiable Agreements. Part of the peacemaking technology, negotiable agreements are a New Couple conflict-resolution tool. They're designed to address issues not covered by core agreements. *(peacemaking)*

The New Couple. Any couple that actively and mutually embraces the higher-order needs for self-love, mission in life, and emotional intimacy is a New Couple. *(Introduction and all laws)*

New Couple Chemistry. Best-friendship *and* sexual chemistries together make up New Couple chemistry. *(chemistry)*

Parental Idealization. An early childhood need to see our parents as perfect and completely competent caregivers, parental idealization often carries over into adulthood. Parental idealization is the biggest challenge to resolving transference, because overcoming it usually involves moving through fear and grief. Arrested parental idealization is the result of unresolved childhood emotional trauma and exacerbates transference with our partner. *(self-love)*

Passive-Aggressive Behavior. The indirect and covert form of acted-out anger, passive-aggressive behavior includes victim talk, patronization, sarcasm, teasing, denial, withdrawal, "forgetting," and sabotage. *(emotional integrity and peacemaking)*

The Path to Peace. Part of the Peace Process tool, the Path to Peace is a modification of the chart of emotions found in Chapter 3, "Emotional Integrity." *(peacemaking)*

Peacemaking. The sixth New Law of Love, peacemaking asks that we maintain an emotional safe zone in our couple by clarifying individual core conditions and creating core agreements, by learning to use the time-out, the Love Ladder, and negotiable agreements, and by making amends when such agreements are broken.

The Peace Process. Part of the peacemaking technology, the Peace Process, which entails a trip up the Path to Peace, is a New Couple conflict-resolution tool. *(peacemaking)*

Power Struggle. The second stage of relationship, the power struggle is characterized by the appearance of buttons, blind spots, and transference. This stage is resolved by a commitment to the Ten New Laws of Love. The traditional couple didn't typically move through this stage, because the necessary transformational education wasn't available. *(Introduction and all laws)*

Priority. The second New Law of Love, priority asks that we prioritize the relationship to keep chemistry alive. This means committing to the work of relationship (by adhering to the Ten New Laws of Love or a similar system) and the process of individuation, as well as managing all addictions (including codependence), compulsions, and psychological problems.

Process Addiction. Unlike substance addiction, which involves the consumption of an addictive substance, process addiction is the inability to stop certain behaviors, such as work, sexual activity (or preoccupation), and gambling, despite harm to one or more of the core areas of our lives—namely, health, livelihood, and primary relationships. *(priority)*

Russian Doll Theory. The concept that each of us hides within us a series of wounded inner-child selves, each one relating to a different age at which a primary need went unmet. *(self-love)*

Self-Love. The seventh New Law of Love, self-love asks that we commit to raising our self-love by learning to accept and validate our own emotions, ideas, intuition, and talents, by learning to stick up for ourselves, and by recognizing and healing transferences in our couple. Self-love is also a higher-order need. In that function, it's distinguished from conditional self-love in that it is independent of external factors.

The Session. A New Couple tool, the Session trains us to listen deeply and serves to preserve chemistry and deepen emotional intimacy. *(deep listening)*

Settling. Settling means committing to a partner with whom we don't enjoy all of the following: sexual chemistry, best-friendship chemistry, and whatever essential compatibilities are crucial for us. *(chemistry)*

Sexual Acting Out. Any kind of sexualized behavior involving persons other than our partner, sexual acting out includes flirting, staring, rubbernecking, and making sexual comments, compliments, and jokes; it also includes sexualized physical contact and comments to our partner that show sexual interest in or titillation by another. *(peacemaking)*

Sexual Chemistry. A uniquely passionate sexual connection with another person, sexual chemistry (along with best-friendship chemistry) forms the basis of New Couple chemistry. *(chemistry)*

Sexual Exclusivity. A standard of sexual behavior proscribing sexual acting out, sexual exclusivity is defined on a couple-by-couple basis. *The New Couple* recommends monogamy with sexual exclusivity as a core condition and core agreement. *(peacemaking)*

Shame Seizure. The sudden, overwhelming experience of toxic shame is known as a shame seizure. *(emotional integrity)*

Special Session. A kind of Session focused on a specific issue, the Special Session allows the Listener to address the content during his or her turn. *(deep listening, equality, peacemaking, self-love)*

Stages of Relationship. There are three natural developmental stages (or phases) of adult love relationship. The first stage of relationship is intoxication, followed by the power struggle, and finally co-creativity. Lack of knowledge about the stages of relationship has resulted in the idealization of the intoxication stage, the misunderstanding of the power-struggle stage, and the failure of partners to reach the co-creativity stage.

Substance Addiction. Substance addiction is the inability to stop or manage the use of consumable substances such as alcohol, drugs, or food, despite harm to one or more of the core areas of our lives—namely, health, livelihood, and primary relationships. *(priority)*

Time-Out. Part of the peacemaking technology, the time-out is the primary New Couple anger-management tool. *(peacemaking)*

Toxic Guilt. An unhealthy emotion, toxic guilt results when we unfairly accuse ourselves of being responsible for the emotional well-being of another. Along with toxic shame, it's a key characteristic of codependence. *(emotional integrity)*

Toxic Shame. An unhealthy emotion, toxic shame results from the erroneous belief that we're inherently inadequate and unlovable; this leads to an unreasonable fear of being exposed as such to others. Along with toxic guilt, toxic shame is a key characteristic of codependence. *(emotional integrity)*

Traditional. A traditional is any person who is unconsciously locked in outdated ways of relating to a partner (in contrast to a traditionalist, who consciously and deliberately adheres to ways of the past).

Traditional Couple. Any couple that doesn't actively and mutually embrace the higher-order needs for self-love, emotional intimacy, and mission in life is a traditional couple. *(Introduction and all laws)*

Transference. A case of mistaken identity, transference results when we unconsciously confuse our partner with those with whom we grew up. This leads us to emotionally "transfer" the role of primary caregiver or sibling onto our partner. Any button, blind spot, or issue that requires use of the time-out tool indicates transference (and probably involves unresolved trauma as well). Resolving transference requires that we seek to identify and work through our feelings about the original relationship that hurt us, a process that enhances our self-love. *(self-love)*

Transformational Education. The tenth New Law of Love, transformational education asks that we be willing to do whatever learning and healing is necessary if we get stuck on any aspect of the first nine New Laws of Love.

Traumatic Transference. Associated with our most highly charged buttons and difficult-to-acknowledge blind spots, traumatic transference is a specific kind of transference based on a traumatic incident, dynamic, or relationship with an early caregiver or sibling. *(self-love)*

Triangle Test. Part of the peacemaking technology, the Triangle Test helps us determine whether or not we're ready for a successful Peace Process. It features our three subpersonalities: the Adult, the Child, and the Critic. *(peacemaking)*

Unhealthy Emotions. Toxic guilt, toxic shame, contempt, hatred, scorn, and disdain are the unhealthy emotions. Usually the result of childhood emotional trauma, they're symptoms of low self-love. These emotions are among the greatest challenges to emotional integrity and applying the Ten New Laws of Love.

Walking. The ninth New Law of Love, walking asks that we strive for interdependence and individual autonomy—that is, that we become willing and able to walk (so that we can choose to stay together healthily). This law involves exploring and committing to resolve financial and emotional dependencies, a process that raises our self-love.

The Work of Relationship. The application of the Ten New Laws of Love or a similar system constitutes the work of relationship. For New Couples, the work of relationship involves learning the relationship skills of emotional literacy, deep listening, anger management, conflict resolution, and negotiation; it also involves undertaking the process of individuation and resolving transferences. *(Introduction and priority)*

Written Peace Process. Part of the peacemaking technology and a New Couple conflict-resolution tool, the written Peace Process is usually used when the verbal Peace Process has failed. *(peacemaking)*

references and reading
recommendations

Adams, Kenneth M. *Silently Seduced: When Parents Make Their Children Partners—Understanding Covert Incest.* Deerfield Beach, FL: Health Communications, 1991.

Assagioli, Roberto. *Psychosynthesis.* New York: Penguin, 1976.

Bass, Ellen, and Laura Davis. *The Courage to Heal: A Guide for Women Survivors of Child Sexual Abuse.* New York: Harper & Row, 1988.

Beattie, Melody. *Codependent No More: How to Stop Controlling Others and Start Caring for Yourself.* New York: Harper & Row, 1987.

Berne, Eric. *Games People Play.* New York: Grove Press, 1964.

Black, Claudia. *It Will Never Happen to Me.* New York: Ballantine Books, 1991.

Bolles, Richard. *How to Find Your Mission in Life.* Berkeley, CA: Ten Speed Press, 1991.

Bolles, Richard. *What Color Is Your Parachute?* Berkeley, CA: Ten Speed Press, 1970.

Bowen, Murray. *Family Therapy in Clinical Practice.* Northvale, NJ: Jason Aronson, 1978.

Bradshaw, John. *Bradshaw on the Family: A Revolutionary Way of Self-Discovery.* Deerfield Beach, FL: Health Communications, 1988.

Bradshaw, John. *Healing the Shame That Binds You.* Deerfield Beach, FL: Health Communications, 1988.

Branden, Nathaniel. *The Psychology of Self-Esteem.* New York: Bantam, 1971.

Campbell, Joseph. *The Hero with a Thousand Faces.* Princeton/Bollingen Series in World Mythology, vol. 17. Princeton, NJ: Princeton University Press, 1949.

Campbell, Susan M. *A Couple's Journey: Intimacy As a Path to Wholeness.* San Luis Obispo, CA: Impact Publishers, 1980.

Carnes, Patrick. *Out of the Shadows: Understanding Sexual Addiction.* Minneapolis, MN: CompCare, 1983.

Carter, Betty. *Love, Honor, and Negotiate.* New York: Simon & Schuster, 1996. Quote in Chapter 5 taken from p. 85.

Chaudhuri, Haridas. *The Evolution of Integral Consciousness.* Wheaton, IL: Theosophical Publishing House, 1977.

Craig, Gloria Vernon. *Collected Poems, 1995–2000.* Stockton, NJ: Sandbrook Publishing Company, 2000. Poem taken from p. 7.

Csikszentmihalyi, Mihaly. *Flow: The Psychology of Optimal Experience.* New York: HarperCollins, 1991.

De Angelis, Barbara. *How to Make Love All the Time: The Ultimate Guide to Bringing Love into Your Life and Making It Work as Never Before.* New York: Rawson Associates, 1987. See especially pp. 94–126.

Eisler, Riane. *The Chalice and the Blade: Our History, Our Future.* New York: Harper & Row, 1987.

Erikson, Erik. *Childhood and Society,* 2nd ed. New York: Norton, 1963.

Evans, Patricia. *The Verbally Abusive Relationship: How to Recognize It and How to Respond.* Holbrook, MA: Bob Adams, 1992. See especially pp. 73–97.

Fox, Matthew. *Creation Spirituality: Liberating Gifts for the Peoples of the Earth.* San Francisco: HarperSanFrancisco, 1991.

Freud, Sigmund. "Beyond the Pleasure Principle" (1920). In *The Standard Edition of the Complete Psychological Works of Sigmund Freud,* vol. 18. New York: Norton, 1959.

Freud, Sigmund. "The Dynamics of Transference" (1912). In *The Standard Edition of the Complete Psychological Works of Sigmund Freud,* vol. 12. New York: Norton, 1959.

Freud, Sigmund. "Remembering, Repeating, and Working Through" (1914). In *The Standard Edition of the Complete Psychological Works of Sigmund Freud,* vol. 12. New York: Norton, 1959.

Fuller, R. Buckminster. *Critical Path.* New York: St. Martin's Press, 1981.

Gardner, Howard. *Frames of Mind: The Theory of Multiple Intelligences.* New York: Basic Books, 1993.

Gibran, Kahlil. *The Prophet.* New York: Knopf, 1923. Quote in Chapter 9 is from pp. 16–17.

Gill, Merton. *The Analysis of Transference,* vol. 1. International Universities Press, 1982.

Glickstein, Lee. *Be Heard Now! How to Tap into Your Inner Speaker and Communicate with Ease.* New York: Broadway Books, 1998.

Goleman, Daniel. *Emotional Intelligence: Why It Can Matter More Than IQ.* New York: Bantam, 1995.

Gordon, Thomas. *What Every Parent Should Know.* Chicago: National Committee for the Prevention of Child Abuse, 1975.

Gray, John. *What You Can Feel, You Can Heal: A Guide to Enriching Relationships.* Mill Valley, CA: Heart Publishing Co., 1994.

Harris, Thomas A. *I'm OK, You're OK.* New York: Avon Books, 1973.

Hendrix, Harville. *Getting All the Love You Want: A Guide for Couples.* New York: HarperCollins, 1988.

Heyn, Dalma. *Marriage Shock: The Transformation of Women into Wives.* New York: Villard, 1997.

Hillman, James. *The Soul's Code: In Search of Character and Calling.* New York: Random House, 1996. Quote in Chapter 8 taken from p. 3.

Hoffman, Bob. *No One Is to Blame.* Oakland, CA: Recycling Books, 1988.

Hough, John, and Marshall Hardy. *Against the Wall: Men's Reality in a Codependent Culture.* Center City, MN: Hazeldon, 1991.

Hubbard, Barbara Marx. *Conscious Evolution: Awakening the Power of Our Social Potential.* Novato, CA: New World Library, 1998. Quote in Chapter 8 taken from pp. 207–208.

Jackins, Harvey. *The Human Side of Human Beings: The Theory of Re-evaluation Counseling.* Seattle: Rational Island Publishers, 1978.

Janov, Arthur. *The Primal Scream, Primal Therapy: The Cure for Neurosis.* New York: Putnam, 1970.

Kafka, Franz. *The Great Wall of China: Stories and Reflections.* New York: Schocken Books, 1946. Quote in Chapter 2 taken from p. 307.

Kahn, Michael. *Between Therapist and Client: The New Relationship.* New York: Freeman, 1991.

Kiyosaki, Robert. *If You Want to Be Rich and Happy, Don't Go to School.* San Diego: Excellerated Learning, 1992.

Kohut, Heinz. *How Does Analysis Cure?* Chicago: Univ. of Chicago Press, 1984.

Komor, Christian. *The Power of Being: For People Who Do Too Much.* Grand Rapids, MI: Renegade House, 1991.

Lee, John. *I Don't Want to Be Alone: For Men and Women Who Want to Heal Addictive Relationships.* Deerfield Park, FL: Health Communications, 1990.

Lee, John. *Recovery: Plain and Simple.* Deerfield Park, FL: Health Communications, 1990.

Lew, Mike, and Ellen Bass. *Victims No Longer: A Guide for Men Recovering from Sexual Child Abuse.* New York: HarperCollins, 1990.

Love, Patricia. *The Emotional Incest Syndrome: What to Do When a Parent's Love Rules Your Life.* New York: Bantam Books, 1990.

Maslow, Abraham. *Toward a Psychology of Being.* New York: Van Nostrand, 1968.

Mellody, Pia. *Facing Codependence: What It Is, Where It Comes From, How It Sabotages Our Lives.* San Francisco: Harper & Row, 1989.

Mellody, Pia. *Facing Love Addiction: Giving Yourself the Power to Change the Way You Love.* San Francisco: HarperSanFrancisco, 1992.

Miller, Alice. *The Drama of the Gifted Child: The Search for the True Self.* New York: Basic Books, 1981.

Miller, Alice. *For Your Own Good: Hidden Cruelty in Child-Rearing and the Roots of Violence.* New York: Farrar, Straus, & Giroux, 1983. Quote in Chapter 7 taken from p. 4.

Norwood, Robin. *Women Who Love Too Much: When You Keep Wishing and Hoping He'll Change.* New York: Tarcher, 1985.

Paul, Jordan, and Margaret Paul. *Do I Have to Give Up Me to Be Loved by You?* Minneapolis, MN: CompCare Publishers, 1983.

Perls, Fritz. *Gestalt Therapy Verbatim.* Moab, UT: Real People Press, 1969.

Radice, Betty (editor). *The Letters of Abelard and Heloise.* New York: Penguin Books, 1977.

Rogers, Carl. *On Becoming a Person.* Boston: Houghton Mifflin, 1961.

Roth, Geneen. *When Food Is Love: Exploring the Relationship Between Eating and Intimacy.* New York: Plume, 1992.

Rumi, Jelaluddin. *Unseen Rain: Quatrains of Rumi.* Edited by John Moyne and Coleman Banks. Putney, VT: Threshold Books, 1986. Quotes in Chapter 1 taken from pp. 6 and 19.

Sark. *Succulent Wild Woman: Dancing with Your Wonder-Full Self.* New York: Simon & Schuster, 1997. Quote in Chapter 10 taken from pp. 94–95.

Satir, Virginia. *Peoplemaking.* Palo Alto, CA: Science & Behavior Books, 1972.

Schnarch, David. *The Passionate Marriage: Love, Sex, and Intimacy in Emotionally Committed Relationships.* New York: Norton, 1997.

Shaef, Anne Wilson. *Escape from Intimacy: Untangling the "Love" Addictions—Sex, Romance, Relationships.* San Francisco: HarperSanFrancisco, 1990.

Shakespeare, William. *Romeo and Juliet.* New York: Penguin Books, 1960. Quote in Chapter 2 taken from p. 62.

Shapiro, Francine. *Eye Movement Desensitization and Reprocessing: Basic Principles, Protocols, and Procedures.* New York: Guilford Press, 1995.

Sher, Barbara. *I Could Do Anything If I Only Knew What It Was: How to Discover What You Really Want and How to Get It.* New York: Delacourte Press, 1994.

Sher, Barbara, and Annie Gottlieb. *Wishcraft: How to Get What You Really Want.* New York: Ballantine Books, 1986.

Skinner, Robyn, and John Cleese. *Families and How to Survive Them.* London: Cox and Wyman, 1983.

Small, Jacquelyn. *Awakening in Time.* New York: Bantam, 1991.

Steinem, Gloria. *Revolution Within: A Book of Self-Esteem.* New York: Little, Brown, 1993.

Stettbacher, J. Konrad. *Making Sense of Suffering: The Healing Confrontation with Your Own Past.* New York: Meridian/Penguin, 1993.

Walsch, Neale Donald. *Conversations with God, book I.* New York: Putnam, 1996. Quote in Chapter 3 taken from p. 3; quote in Chapter 7 taken from p. 124.

Whitfield, Charles. *Healing the Child Within: Discovery and Recovery for Adult Children of Dysfunctional Families.* Deerfield Beach, FL: Health Communications, 1987.

Whitfield, Charles. *Memory and Abuse: Remembering and Healing the Effects of Trauma.* Deerfield Beach, FL: Health Communications, 1995.

Woititz, Janet. *Adult Children of Alcoholics.* Deerfield Beach, FL: Health Communications, 1983.

index